COUNSELING AND LIFE-SPAN DEVELOPMENT

COUNSELING AND LIFE-SPAN DEVELOPMENT

R. MURRAY THOMAS

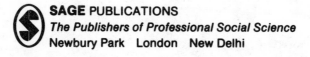

SAGE PUBLICATIONS
The Publishers of Professional Social Science
Newbury Park   London   New Delhi

For information address:

SAGE Publications, Inc.
2111 West Hillcrest Drive
Newbury Park, California 91320

SAGE Publications Ltd.
28 Banner Street
London EC1Y 8QE
England

SAGE Publications India Pvt. Ltd.
M-32 Market
Greater Kailash I
New Delhi 110 048 India

Printed in the United States of America

LIBRARY OF CONGRESS CATALOGING-IN-PUBLICATION DATA

Thomas, R. Murray (Robert Murray), 1921–
    Counseling and life-span development / by R. Murray Thomas.
      p. cm.
    Bibliography: p.
    Includes indexes.
    ISBN 0-8039-3613-3. — ISBN 0-8039-3614-1 (pbk.)
    1. Counseling. 2. Developmental psychology. I. Title.
BF637.C6T493 1989   89-34766
158'.3—dc20   CIP

FIRST PRINTING, 1990

Contents

Acknowledgments

The permission granted by the following publishers and authors to quote material from their publications is gratefully acknowledged.

National Academy Press for permission to quote pasages from Osterweis, Solomon, and Green *Bereavement: Reactions, Consequences, and Care,* copyright by the National Academy of Sciences.

Plenum Publishing Corporation and Professors R. M. Malina and A. F. Roche for permission to adapt data from pages 11-12 of Malina and Roche *Manual of Physical Status and Performance in Childhood,* Volume 2, 1983, copyright by Plenum Publishing Corporation.

Praeger Publishers for selected passages from D. B. Kandel, "Family and Peer Processes in Adolescent Drug Use," in *Handbook of Longitudinal Research: v. 2, Teenage and Adult Cohorts,* S. A. Mednick, M. Harway, & K. M. Finello, eds. (Praeger Publishers, New York, 1984), copyright ©1984 by Praeger Publishers. Reprinted with permission.

Springer-Verlag and Professor Timothy A. Salthouse for permission to quote passages from pages 69-70 of Salthouse *Adult Cognition: An Experimental Psychology of Human Aging,* copyright 1982 by Springer-Verlag.

Year Book Medical Publishers to reproduce by permission adapted height and weight tables from George H. Lowrey, M.D., *Growth and Development of Children,* 7th edition, copyright 1978 by Year Book Medical Publishers.

Preface

Although many good books about life-span development are available today, none that I have seen is designed precisely to answer those questions about life stages that are most important to professionals whose role is to help people solve their personal/social difficulties. My purpose in writing this book has been to offer such a volume.

The central question guiding this effort has been: "What information about stages of the life span can help counselors make wise decisions about their clients?" Or, cast another way, "What sorts of age-related normative data can improve the efficiency of counseling?" To answer such questions, I first identified key decisions that are typically made in the process of counseling, with the focus particularly on major types of problems that bring clients to counseling. Then, for each decision, I sought to determine which kinds of age-related information could enhance the counseling process. As a result, the entire contents of the book link life-span concepts and facts directly to the daily concerns of counselors.

To inform readers at the outset of what to expect in this volume, I shall begin by explaining what the book *is* and what it *is not* in relation to (1) the label "counselor", (2) the selection of which human-development theories to discuss, (3) the connection between human-development theories and approaches to counseling, and (4) the basis for choosing which empirical findings to include.

THE LABEL "COUNSELOR"

The term *counselor* in this book is assigned a generic meaning, applied to anyone who seeks to help others with personal/social problems. Therefore, it refers to such a diversity of professionals as counseling psychologists, psychiatrists, clinical psychologists, school psychologists, psychiatric social workers, school counselors, vocational counselors, social workers, pastoral counselors, teachers, and others in the helping professions. My hope is that such professionals, as well as interested parents and lay persons, might find something of profit in these pages.

THE SELECTION OF
HUMAN-DEVELOPMENT THEORIES

Periodically throughout the book I refer to particular human-development theories (such as behaviorism or psychoanalytic theory) and to particular theorists (such as Piaget or Erikson). The purpose in doing so is to identify the source of certain concepts about human development that are useful in understanding people's physical and mental status at different points in the life span, particularly as such status may affect counseling decisions. Thus, specific development theories are mentioned only incidentally, since the purpose of the book is not to survey, analyze, and compare human-development theories per se. Consequently, no comparative analysis of development theories is found in these pages. That task has been pursued elsewhere in considerable detail (R. M. Thomas, 1985b; R. M. Thomas, 1988; R. M. Thomas, 1989). When readers find particular theories of development missing from this volume, it is because I considered it unnecessary to describe those theories in order to make clear issues bearing on counseling.

HUMAN-DEVELOPMENT BASES
OF COUNSELING APPROACHES

As its title implies, this volume is founded on the assumption that wise decisions in counseling people at different stages of the life span derive, at least partly, from an understanding of significant developmental characteristics associated with those stages. Or, stated another way, each counseling approach is based on beliefs about the nature of development—about people's motives, aptitudes, perceptions, experiential backgrounds, privileges, responsibilities, and problems during successive life periods. Throughout the book, reference is often made to these connections between conceptions of development and methods of counseling. Chapter 3, which offers a brief survey of representative counseling approaches, considers such matters directly. In other chapters, attention to those issues appears in relationship to a particular life stage or in connection with problems frequently suffered by clients at that time of life.

However, the purpose of the book is not to provide a systematic comparison of different counseling approaches in relation to the human-development assumptions on which they are founded. Such a comparative analysis can be found in another source (R. M. Thomas, 1985a).

THE CHOICE OF EMPIRICAL EVIDENCE

The great bulk of material in this book is comprised of empirical evidence about the nature of people at different periods of life, about personal/social difficulties they face that call for counseling, and about techniques used for helping them to cope with those difficulties. The evidence has been derived from diverse sources, but chiefly from experimental research, field studies, surveys, and reports of clinical experience. My choice of the kinds of data to include was guided by the question: "Which sorts of available normative information might be most helpful to counselors in their working with a newly met client of a given age who presents a particular type of problem."

In pursuit of the above purposes, I organized the chapters in two major parts, plus a brief postscript.

Part 1, consisting of three chapters, serves as a foundation for the rest of the book. The first two chapters of Part 1 introduce key lifespan concepts that relate to the counseling process. Chapter 3 furnishes a review of common approaches to counseling.

The six chapters of Part 2 offer information about six successive periods of the life span. The age periods begin with prenatal development, infancy, and early childhood (Chapter 4) and end with the final years of life (Chapter 9). The first half of every chapter in Part 2 is comprised of a description of personal traits and social environments typical for people at that time of life. The second half offers a more detailed description of normative information about selected problems that clients often bring to counselors during that segment of the life span. Because of space limitations, it was necessary for me to make a choice of which illustrative problems to inspect in detail, recognizing all the while that other problems might have served the illustrative purpose quite as well. The criteria I applied for making the choice of each type are presented within the individual chapters. As a preview of the kinds of issues featured in those chapters, here is a list of the 18 topics treated:

Infancy and Early Childhood
    Child Abuse and Child Neglect
    Handicapping Conditions in Early Childhood
Later Childhood
    Unsatisfactory School Performance—Dyslexia
    Disturbed, Nontraditional Family Constellations
    Developmental Lag—Enuresis
Adolescence
    Educational Counseling and Guidance
    Accepting One's Physical Self—Anorexia and Bulimia
    Sexual Relationships—Teenage Pregnancy
    Juvenile Crime—Illegal Drugs
Early Adulthood
    Conjugal Relationships—Marriage and Divorce
    Career Planning
    Financial Planning
Middle Age
    Weight Control
    Bereavement and Acute Grief
    Reproductive Changes—Menopause
    Career Decisions
Old Age
    Depression, Loneliness, and Lack of Incentive to Live
    Lack of Intellectual Capacity to Manage One's Own Affairs

At the end of the book, Chapter 10 serves as a postscript entitled "The Search for More Answers." It identifies ways in which counselors can locate additional life-span information that may aid them in treating clients.

PART 1

Backgrounds of
Development and Counseling

1

The Use of Age-Related Normative Information

The usefulness of a life-span approach to counseling decisions can be suggested by the following seven problems brought to counselors by concerned clients:

—Mr. and Mrs. Williams, both in their late twenties, are speculating about whether it would be wise for them to have children. Their doubts arise from their recognizing that Mrs. Williams' mother had been diagnosed as schizophrenic when the mother was in her late teens, and, thereafter, the mother had led a wayward life. This resulted in the mother's becoming pregnant by a stranger with whom she had a single sexual encounter. The infant girl born of this encounter was subsequently raised by an aunt and uncle because the schizophrenic mother had been judged by the courts to be incapable of caring for a child. That daughter, now grown up and married, is Mrs. Williams. She and her husband seek genetic counseling to help them decide whether a child they might bear would be normal, in view of the fact that Mrs. Williams' mother was psychotic and her father's identity was unknown.

—Ms. Francesca Lorton, age 32, is the divorced mother of two children, Rhonda (age 2) and Mark (age 4). In the divorce settlement, Francesca and her husband were awarded joint custody over the children. The husband, Barry Lorton, has the children nearly every weekend, while Francesca has them during the week. Francesca comes to a counselor with the complaint that Barry "spoils the children on the weekends by giving them toys, taking them to amusement centers, letting them stay up late at night, and allowing them to eat whatever sweets they like." In contrast, during the week, Francesca maintains a routine of early bedtimes and a diet she describes as "balanced and healthful." Oftentimes, when she finds it appropriate to discipline the children or deny their wishes, four-year-old Mark tells his mother that he hates her and wants to go live, with his father. Francesca asks the counselor what she should do.

—A third-grade boy, Juan Garcia, has been described by his teacher as "hyperactive." He can't sit still for more than a minute, always chattering, wiggling, or walking around the classroom, distracting the others from their work. He seems bright, but he doesn't focus on his studies long enough to learn much. One of his biggest troubles is in learning to read. The teacher, with the consent of the boy's parents, sends Juan to the school psychologist to find out what might be done about Juan's problem.

—Thirteen-year-old Linda's listless, bleary-eyed appearance on several occasions has caused her parents to suspect that the girl has been using illicit drugs. When a teacher discovers Linda and three of her girlfriends smoking marijuana in a school lavatory, the junior-high-school principal reports the four girls to the police and to their parents. The juvenile court orders Linda and her companions to undergo drug rehabilitation treatment at a community counseling center.

—Sol Cohen, a 25-year old with a bachelor's degree in sociology, has been wandering from one job to another since finishing college. He has been a clerk in a clothing store, a counterman in a fast-food restaurant, a used-car salesman, and a helper in a window-screen repair store. Sol's family convinces him that he should go about selecting a life's work in a more systematic fashion, so he visits a counselor for professional help in career planning.

—Mrs. H. W. Kim, age 54, has been despondent ever since her husband died two months ago. Her distress was recently exacerbated by the injury of her 30-year-old daughter in an auto accident. To help her recover from her despair, Mrs. Kim's brother has sent her to his minister for pastoral counseling.

—At age 83, Martin Lefkovitz lives alone in a home that he has owned for many years. Although he used to pursue hobbies and interests outside the home, over the past decade he has increasingly dropped these activities and simply sat around the house. His health has deteriorated so that when his son or daughter visits, he spends much of the time complaining about his pains and about how useless he feels. He is increasingly forgetful, so bills go unpaid. His son and daughter finally succeed in convincing him to move out of the house and into a retirement facility. However, at the retirement center, he simply sits in his room doing nothing. The son and daughter ask the counselor at the retirement facility to meet with their father and see whether anything can be done to make his life more satisfying.

These seven cases have been presented as ones "typical" of different stages in the life span. In other words, to some extent, the types of problems that clients suffer are related to the segment of the life span in which they currently find themselves. This correlation between age and kinds of counseling problems is a result of the changes in people's personal traits and their social environments that occur with the passing decades. I am proposing that counselors who recognize the nature of such changes in traits and social settings are better prepared to aid their clients than are counselors who do not. The contents of this chapter are intended to introduce the application of that proposal.

SIMILARITIES AND DIFFERENCES AMONG CLIENTS

A typical assumption that counselors hold is that every client is unique. Therefore, when a new client appears, it becomes the counselor's task to understand this unique person and, on the basis of such understanding, to decide what treatment may best enhance the individual's welfare. Yet, while every client is unique, it is also true that, in many ways, each one is similar to certain others. It is the counselor's prior knowledge of these similarities that helps to guide decisions about how best to work with each new counselee.

Statements about the similarities among people are called *normative descriptions* or *normative data*, since these statements tell what is "normal"—in the sense of *usual* or *typical*—for such a group of people. The contents of Chapters 4 through 9 of this book are comprised almost entirely of normative descriptions, and, because the book is about life-span development, the normative data all relate to age levels or age stages of the life span from conception to death.

Although age is a significant variable, age alone is not nearly so significant for counseling purposes as is the interaction of age with certain other variables. These others include types of client problems, gender, and cultural background. The variable *types of problems* is important because some difficulties that clients suffer occur more frequently at one stage of life than at another. Furthermore, gender is often related to social/psychological difficulties that people encounter at different age levels. In addition, the expectations held within a culture regarding proper behavior for different age periods are frequently involved in the problems that clients bring to the counselor's office. (The term *culture* in this context refers to a group of people's shared goals, values, and patterns of living that differentiate members of that group from members of other groups. The basis for groups' cultural differences can be religious, ethnic, regional, language-related, class-related, or the like.) Therefore, the data in Chapters 4 through 9 do not center on age alone. Instead, the information frequently concerns age as it interacts with these three additional factors—types of counseling problems, gender, and selected cultural conditions (particularly ethnic status).

The contents of Chapters 4 through 9 are regarded as useful at key decision points in the counseling process, beginning with the counselor's initial encounter with a new client and closing with the termination of the counseling sessions. The question to be answered for each of these decision points is: "What information about people of this client's age and counseling problem, and about the client's gender and cultural condition, can help me arrive at wise decisions?"

The purpose of this opening chapter is to set a foundation on which the descriptions in the following chapters can be built. Such a foundation involves clarifying what is intended by the term *normative information* and by the phrase *useful kinds of normative data.*

THE NATURE OF NORMATIVE INFORMATION

As used throughout this book, normative information is defined as *a statement about the degree to which a defined group of people are alike.* Or, viewed another way, normative information is a description of *how people of a specified type or group are distributed along some dimension or scale.*

Examples of *types* or *groups* are: 12-year olds, elderly people, brunettes, women, carpenters, Puerto Ricans, cat owners, alcoholics, midgets, divorcees, tennis players, millionaires, philatelists, monogamists, podiatrists, drug abusers, and thousands more.

As counseling psychologists, we are not interested merely in a reiteration of the characteristic that defines the group. In other words, we are not interested in hearing that philatelists collect stamps, that divorcees are women whose marriages have been dissolved, or that drug abusers are people who ingest substances that damage their health. Instead, we are interested in learning what other characteristics are correlated with the status of being a philatelist, a divorcee, or a drug abuser. For example, we might find it useful to learn what personality traits philatelists tend to have in common that differentiate them from such a group as weight lifters or nightclub comedians. We might profit from learning what percentage of divorcees left their husbands because of wife abuse and what percentage left because they were attracted to another lover. We might also be better equipped to counsel drug abusers if we knew how they were introduced to drug use, at what age, and for what apparent reasons they have continued to use drugs. We may find it helpful as well to learn what family-life conditions and personality traits may differentiate drug abusers from non-drug abusers. In effect, the normative data that we seek concern the extent of correlation between (1) membership in a particular group and (2) factors that are significant for making counseling decisions.

USEFUL KINDS OF NORMATIVE DATA

The usefulness of normative information depends on (1) how closely it bears on the decisions made during the counseling process, (2) the precision of the data, and (3) the representativeness of the information.

Significant Counseling Decision Points

As suggested earlier, the function of normative information is to give the counselor a head start in working with a client. With suitable normative data in mind—or readily available—a counselor facing a new client need not start off completely ignorant of how to proceed. Instead, the data furnish some initial expectations or probabilities which then can be confirmed, revised, or rejected on the basis of the counselor's focused inquiries about this particular individual. The clues that guide the therapist to recall or consult pertinent normative information are such easily recognized characteristics of the client as age, gender, height and weight, facial features, cultural characteristics (language, dress style, mannerisms), educational level, and occupation. A further readily apparent characteristic is the type of problem that has brought the client for counseling. As already noted, among this array of factors, the four which become the chief concern throughout this book are age, gender, selected cultural traits, and type of counseling problem. I have chosen these four because they are the ones about which there is a host of normative information and because all four kinds can be of considerable aid in counseling.

As mentioned above, the question of prime concern to a psychologist is: "How are these four observable characteristics correlated with information that can help me make decisions during the counseling process?" And as the following discussion illustrates, the kind of normative data (correlations) that will be helpful at a given moment depends on which sort of decision the counselor is facing at the time. To demonstrate this observation, I am proposing seven key decision points typically encountered in the conduct of counseling. The decision points are presented under three phases of the counseling process: (1) identifying the nature of the client's problem, (2) adopting suitable counseling techniques, and (3) terminating the case. Each decision point is identified by a label and by a question defining the issue that the psychologist is seeking to settle. Then, following a description of the nature of the decision that is faced, I offer illustrations of normative information that can improve the efficiency of the counseling task at that particular juncture.

IDENTIFYING THE NATURE OF THE CLIENT'S PROBLEM

At the opening of the first encounter with the client, the counselor's understanding of the apparent problem may be enhanced by normative information about the frequency of such a problem, about conditions typically correlated with that kind of problem, and about how societal expectations are often involved with a client's difficulties.

Problem Incidence

What is the ostensible problem that brings the client to counseling, and how common is this problem within the client's age-group, gender group, and cultural group?

The term *ostensible problem* or *presenting problem* refers to the kind of explanation elicited when the counselor first asks the client, "How can I help you?" or "What seems to be the trouble?" The answer may be "I can't sleep" or "I feel depressed all the time" or "I want to drop out of school" or "My marriage is breaking up."

If the client has not come voluntarily but, instead, has been brought by someone else, the presenting problem is the reason given to the counselor for bringing the client for treatment. In this event, the person referring the client for counseling is often the one who states the problem. A parent may bring a boy for bed-wetting, a teacher may refer a high-school girl for continually cursing her classmates, the courts may send a young man who habitually uses illicit drugs, and a wife may send her husband, whom she describes as an alcoholic.

An inspection of psychological, psychiatric, and social-work textbooks and journals demonstrates that large quantities of normative information have been collected about such matters. In other words, much of the research in these fields is reported under types of personal/social disorders as well as under types of counseling theories or types of therapy. As a consequence, a client's referral problem can often guide the counselor to normative data that will be helpful in deciding how to handle the case. This is a principal reason that therapists profit from knowing the professional labels under which different types of personal/social problems are typically listed in textbooks, journal articles, and statistical abstracts. A counselor well acquainted with the labeled categories is equipped to translate a client's complaint into the terminology under which pertinent normative information is usually reported. To illustrate, normative information about the client complaints in the left-hand column below is usually found under such terms as those displayed in the right-hand column:

The Complaint	*Typical Labels*
"My sister died two months ago, and I just can't get over it. I'm still distraught."	Death, Bereavement, Grief
"We want to have a baby, but my husband's family has a history of schizophrenia, and we're worried that our child might be born schizophrenic."	Genetic Conditions, Psychoses, Schizophrenia
"I have to force myself to leave the house, and, when I'm away from home, I'm always uneasy."	Phobias, Agoraphobia, Obsessions, Anxiety
"I'm really not happy with my job. It was okay at first, but now there's no challenge. I sure wouldn't want to stay in that job all my life."	Career Planning, Vocational Guidance
"I know that smoking isn't good for my health, and my smoking is obviously a bad example for our kids, but I can't stop."	Addiction, Drug Addiction, Smoking Habit

"I care for my husband and children, yet I'm
drawn so strongly to be with her and to have
her affection that I just don't know what to do.

Sexuality,
Homosexuality,
Lesbianism

"The court sent him here because this is the
third time he's been arrested and put in a
juvenile detention facility."

Juvenile Crime,
Juvenile Delinquency,
Correctional
Counseling

Locating data about the client's type of problem may assist the
counselor by indicating how frequently such a problem is found
within the client's age-group and gender group and, perhaps, within
the counselee's cultural category (ethnic group, nationality, religious
denomination). For instance, clients often arrive in the counselor's
office for help with a drug or alcohol problem. The following statistics
illustrate the way in which normative information about such matters can help a counselor recognize how frequently such a difficulty
might arise within the client's age-group, gender group, or cultural
group. The data also suggest what trends have occurred over the
years.

Studies of drug use by American youths ages 18-26 in the mid-1980s
revealed that by their mid-twenties, 75-80% of young adults had tried
an illicit drug, including 50-55% who had tried some drug other than—
or usually in addition to—marijuana. Among high-school seniors,
these figures were 61% and 40%. Among the same age groups, 90% had
drunk alcohol at some time during their life, while over 65% had
imbibed within the past month and over one-third had engaged in
heavy drinking on at least one occasion during the past two weeks.
The trends in use of both marijuana and alcohol over the 1975-1985
decade showed a rise in incidence to a peak in 1979, then a steady
decline in use until 1984, when the decline leveled off. The decrease in
use of marijuana and alcohol was accompanied over the 1979-1985
period by an increase in the use of cocaine, with 17% of high-school
seniors having experimented with cocaine and 66% believing there
was no great risk in trying cocaine once or twice (Johnston, O'Malley,
& Bachman, 1986, pp. 13-20, 59).

In regard to sex differences, males were more likely to use most illicit
drugs. Daily use of marijuana among high-school seniors in 1985 was
6.9% for males and 2.8% for females. Among all young adults, the
percents were 7.4 for males and 3.4 for females, and among college
students, 4.9 for males and 1.6 for females. "The only exceptions to the
rule that males are more frequently users of illicit drugs than females

occur for *stimulant* use in high school and *tranquilizer* use among young adults post high school: in both cases females are slightly higher. ...Clearly this nation's high-school students and other young adults...show a level of involvement with illicit drugs which is greater than can be found in any other industrialized nation of the world" (Johnston, O'Malley, & Bachman, 1986, pp. 17, 20).

How, then, can a knowledge of such normative data aid a counselor in working with a new client who appears for help?

Using the foregoing statistics as our example, if the client is an American youth, it is highly probable that he or she has had personal experience with illicit drugs and alcohol. Hence, whatever the ostensible problem may be that has brought in the client for counseling, it is likely that drugs or alcohol could be involved in the case, in some way, so it would seem desirable during the counseling sessions to investigate such possible involvement, particularly if the client is a male. A second assumption suggested by the statistics is that the counselee's peer culture is one in which the use of illicit drugs and alcohol is not only acceptable but also quite likely encouraged. Such a peer environment can pose social-adjustment problems both for youths who are easily influenced by their peers and for those who choose to resist peer proposals that they use substances which they themselves regard as damaging to health and self-control.

In effect, knowledge of the incidence of attitudes, behaviors, and personal-adjustment problems for different age, gender, and cultural categories can suggest an agenda of issues that therapists can profitably explore during the process of counseling a client who fits those categories.

Correlated Problems

Among people of the client's age, gender, and cultural type, what other problems and conditions are often linked to, or underlie, the client's apparent problem?

Counselors can derive important help from normative information that describes the frequency with which the client's presented problem is related to symptoms, causal conditions, and predictions about the client's future.

Typical Symptom Clusters. The term *symptom* in this context is intended to suggest that the client's stated problem may be just one of a cluster of indicators of something more basic that is wrong in the person's life and that needs remediation. The analogy of measles can illustrate this point. When a girl is brought to a physician because of a rash of red spots on her skin, the physician inspects her to discover what other conditions are present. The physician observes the patterning of the rash, takes the girl's temperature, and inspects her tongue. He or she asks whether the girl has ever had measles and inquires about whether she has been around anyone with measles. If the temperature is high, the tongue is coated, the rash is of a particular type, the girl has not had measles before, and some of her classmates have recently had measles, then the physician concludes that the girl is suffering from measles. The physician can draw this conclusion because normative information based on many medical cases of the past informs him or her that a high correlation exists among such a combination of symptoms in cases of measles. Since the cluster of symptoms form the measles syndrome, the physician is not likely to consider the girl's original complaint—the rash—to have been caused by a food allergy, poison ivy, or a reaction to some medication, such as penicillin. In this example, the skin rash was only the *ostensible* or *apparent* or *presenting problem*. It was not the *basic* or *real* problem. The real or underlying problem—in the sense of what needed remediation—was the streptococcus germs that produced the rash and the related symptoms.

In like manner, counseling psychologists, psychiatrists, and social workers can profit from a knowledge of normative data about what conditions are frequently correlated with the apparent problem that has produced the counseling encounter. For instance, consider bereavement symptoms in children. A survey of research studies of children's reactions to the death of a parent or sibling has shown that such children typically appear sad, angry, and fearful. They often are withdrawn, dependent, regressive, and restless. Frequently they have trouble concentrating, and hence they suffer learning difficulties (Osterweis, Solomon, & Green, 1984, pp. 104-111).

> Children under age five are likely to respond with eating, sleeping, and bowel and bladder disturbances; those under age two may show loss of speech or diffuse distress. School-age children may become phobic or hypochondriacal, withdrawn, or excessively care-giving. Displays of aggression may be observed in place of sadness, especially in boys who have difficulty in expressing longing. Adolescents may respond more like adults, but they may also be reluctant about expressing their

emotions because of fear that they will appear different or abnormal (p. 111).

Knowing that these characteristics are often correlated with bereavement in the young can be useful to the counselor in at least three ways. First, they inform the therapist of kinds of reactions that can be expected among youthful clients who have lost a relative or friend through death. Second, characteristics can serve as indicators of the depth and length of the child's distress—the more pronounced and long-lasting the characteristics, the more disturbing the event has likely been for the client. Third, the amelioration or disappearance of such symptoms can suggest that the counseling goal is being achieved—that the client is adjusting constructively to the death.

Causal Variables. However informative a knowledge of correlated symptoms may be, it does not aid the therapist in identifying factors that have caused the client's problem. Therefore, counselors can profit also from normative information about correlated variables that can be interpreted as contributing to the counselee's difficulties. Efforts to change these variables may help solve the problem. It should be clear, however, that the task of estimating what has caused the disorder is a tricky business because causal factors are usually quite complex, making it difficult to tease out the amount of influence, or even the direction of influence, of the various factors. The confounding nature of complexity and direction can be illustrated by the following research results regarding the relative influence of parents and peers on the use of drugs by adolescents (Kandel, 1982).

In the early 1970s, Kandel collected completed drug-use questionnaires from 8,206 randomly selected New York State high-school students and from 5,574 of their parents. Questionnaires obtained from students on two occasions, six months apart, provided information not only about those individuals' drug habits but also about drug use among their closest friends. Analyses of the results led Kandel to conclude that the adolescents' parents and friends both influenced whether or not youths used marijuana and other illicit substances, but that friends had a far more potent effect than parents. Furthermore, "the highest rates of adolescent marijuana use occurred when both parent and peer reinforced each other's influence on the adolescent" (p. 30).

In the process of identifying the way in which complex causal variables determined drug use among students, Kandel observed that "Depressive mood, normlessness, the feeling of being all alone in the world, and self-esteem are related to the use of drugs, and particularly the use of drugs other than marijuana" (p. 30). In addition, correlations computed on a range of student characteristics indicated that "With the exception of certain demographic characteristics (such as age, sex, and race), on no other activity or attitude" in which friends were similar [such as level of educational aspirations, political orientation, participation in minor delinquency] was the similarity "as great as on illegal drug use. Similarity is lowest on psychological factors, selected attitudes, and reported quality of relationships with parents" (p. 31).

However, in trying to discover the direction in which causal factors operated in adolescent drug-use situations, Kandel faced the chicken-or-the-egg puzzle: "Do adolescents seek out drug users after they themselves have become involved with drugs, or do they start using drugs because they come to associate with other drug-using friends? The longitudinal analysis clearly indicates that prior association with drug-using friends predicts subsequent initiation into drugs. There definitely is a process of socialization in which adolescents influence each other over time and in which association leads to similarity. [However,] there is also a process of selection (assortative pairing) in which prior similarity precedes association, so that individuals who share some prior attitudes, values, and behaviors come to associate with each other" (p. 31). The statistical method devised for estimating the relative influence of such assortative pairing and socialization showed "that each contributes about equally to similarity observed at one point in time" (pp. 31-32).

The puzzle faced by Kandel in clarifying the amount and direction of causal influences on behavior is one faced in a host of investigations of the causes behind the problems that bring people for counseling. Sophisticated analytical techniques are required as well as caution in interpreting normative descriptions, if unwarranted conclusions about causality are to be avoided.

In seeking to explain why people grow up as they do, specialists in the field of human development often cite three sources of influence—heredity, environment, and developmental history. In other words, specialists assume that a person's condition at any point in the life span is the product of interactions among genetic endowment, current physical and social forces, and the individual's developmental history up to the present moment.

Genetic Endowment. The hereditary component derives from the combination of genes contributed by the father and mother at the time of biological conception. Genes are arranged along chromosomes, rather like beads on a string. The mother and father each contribute 23 chromosomes to make up the normal 46 that are located in the nucleus of every cell of the human body. The function of genes is to dictate the way in which basic characteristics of the growing human will develop. Genes not only design the essential form of the characteristics—such as skin color, brain structure, bone shape and size, and much more—but they also set the sequence in which the different human characteristics will arise and mature. For example, a genetic time clock basically determines when the child will be able to walk and when puberty will open the stage of adolescence.

Certain combinations of genes furnish a sound foundation for an individual's future development by fashioning characteristics that can enable the person to successfully perform the tasks faced at each stage of the life span. Other combinations produce a less propitious foundation for coping with the tasks of growth. Such undesirable combinations can result in mental retardation, in a disfiguring birth-mark on the face, in a weak heart, in extremely small stature, in hemophilia (an inability of a broken blood vessel to stop bleeding), in Parkinson's disease in later life, and more.

Problems related to genetic endowment usually arrive in counselors' offices on four occasions:

1. When a couple who are contemplating conceiving a child come for advice about how likely it is that the child will be born with normal or better characteristics, in view of the genetic history of the couple's own hereditary strains.
2. When someone who wishes to adopt an infant seeks advice about how likely it is that the infant is normally endowed, a judgment based on what can be surmised about the genetic characteristics of the child's biological parents.
3. When parents whose child displays a genetically based disorder seek guidance about how best to manage their attitudes toward the child and about how best to treat the child.
4. When an adolescent or adult who suffers a genetically based handicap comes voluntarily or is sent to learn how to cope with the condition.

In each of these cases, the counselor's knowledge of normative data regarding genetically seated traits among similar people helps furnish a foundation for the counselor's approach, which may include providing information, offering understanding and reassurance, suggesting cautions, giving advice, and the like.

Environmental Forces. The term *environmental influences* refers to all the physical and social elements in the individual's surroundings that affect how that person develops. Such influences cover a great array of factors—diet, climate, physical accidents, bacteria, parents' methods of child rearing, numbers and types of siblings in the family, the models of behavior portrayed in mass-communication media (magazines, films, television, videotapes), the kinds of teachers and classmates met in school, religious experiences, and far more.

Biologists, psychologists, and sociologists typically view human development as being the result of the interaction between a person's genetic inheritance and the particular environments experienced by the individual. A perennial debate in the field of human development centers on the question: "How much are a person's traits and talents governed by genetic endowment, and how much are they governed by forces in the person's surroundings?" The answer to this question depends on which aspects of development are being considered. The pace of a child's growth in height is apparently governed chiefly by genetic design and only very slightly by such factors as nutrition and exercise. In contrast, the way in which an adolescent interacts socially with peers is apparently governed chiefly by the social behavior of people whom the adolescent has observed and imitated over the past decade. Thus, it is important for counselors to estimate the degree to which a characteristic of a client has been determined by genetic forces as compared to environmental influences. Normative studies can furnish guidance in arriving at this estimate. In effect, knowledge of the way that nature interacts with nurture to produce a given trait or behavior pattern helps the counselor to judge the likelihood that alterations in the counselee's environment might solve the person's problem, or, in contrast, the likelihood that the counselee will need to learn modes of coping with a trait or condition which is not likely to be amenable to environmental changes. For example, a child whose poor academic performance results from genetically based mental retardation requires a different treatment program than one whose academic failure has been caused by long periods of truancy or by emotional distress induced by abusive parents.

The question of *how much* heredity, as compared to environment, contributes to a given characteristic is important. But equally significant is the question of *in what manner* or *how* nature interacts with nurture to bring about that characteristic. One way the *how* question can be phrased is: "How directly has heredity influenced the development of a characteristic?" In this case, we are envisioning a direct-ness scale that extends from *very direct influence* on one end to *very indirect influence* on the other. At the very direct end is the case of a child suffering from phenylketonuria. This mental defect results from hereditary metabolic dysfunctions that are not significantly im-proved by changes in the child's environment. The affected child will remain mentally defective.

At a less direct point on the scale is the case of hereditary blind-ness. A blind child raised in an environment designed for children with normal sight will typically display symptoms of retarded mental growth. Although sight cannot be restored, changes can be made in the environment to compensate for the handicap. A blind child can be given audio-records of books and can be taught to read by the braille method. These measures enable mental development to pro-ceed far more normally.

At the very indirect end of the scale are cases of social stereotyping. We recognize that genetic endowment has much influence in deter-mining a child's skin color, height, weight, facial features, acuity of hearing, and so forth. People within a given culture often associate certain intellectual or personality traits with such physical character-istics. In other words, people often hold social stereotypes which are not well grounded in fact. If a young girl's facial features and move-ments are usually viewed in her society as typical of endearing, clever girls, then people will often treat this child as though she were sweet and bright. Since the way in which people treat a child affects the way in which he or she comes to perceive himself or herself, his or her self-concept—his or her feeling of adequacy—is at least partly the result of social stereotypes associated with inherited physical traits. Thus, if the child perceives himself or herself as clever rather than dull, he or she may be motivated to display higher levels of mental development than if he or she believed himself or herself to be dull. Heredity, in this instance, has affected the child's develop-ment in a very indirect manner.

A large quantity of normative research has been reported on the relationship between environmental conditions and people's psycho-social problems. A counselor who knows the results of studies relevant to a current case is aided in estimating the sorts of issues to be in-vestigated and the types of solutions that may be suitable for that case.

Developmental History. The belief that a person's developmental his-tory influences current and future development is founded on the observation that at any juncture of the life span, the way a person has grown until that moment strongly affects the way in which he or she can develop in the future. At age 3, a child who moves into a new language environment—from Mexico City to Chicago—will more readily adopt "typical American" speech (free of a foreign accent) than will most 30- or 50-year olds who make the same move. Usually the older person's developmental history renders the acquisition of American speech patterns more difficult than such acquisition is for the young child. As another example, a teenage girl who was sexually assaulted by males in her family when she was age 5 through 10 brings to adolescence a burden of memories that affects her potential for future development.

Consequently, it is often useful for a counselor to learn about pertinent aspects of a client's developmental history—influential experiences from the past—which help cast light on that person's present condition. However, it is important to recognize that a particular incident or series of past experiences can affect different people in different ways. For one child, the behavior of an abusive alcoholic father can contribute to long-lasting despair and depression, whereas the behavior of the same father may stimulate another child in that same family to become a self-sufficient high-achiever. Therefore, it is not the past event itself that is important today. Instead, it is the residue of that event as it currently exists in the client's personality. The memory of the incident, not the incident itself, is the significant factor. Hence, a counselor's learning about events in the client's developmental history should not lead to an immediate conclusion about the present significance of those incidents. Instead, knowledge of past events can only suggest possibilities regarding (1) how the residue from earlier experiences may affect the client's present adjustment and (2) what implications that residue may hold for the counseling approach that will be most effective in such cases. Normative information about similar clients in the past can help a counselor to estimate what might be expected from the present counselee's developmental history.

Predictions About the Client's Future. Normative studies can also furnish expectations about what may happen to the client in the future (1) if the client continues in his or her current pattern of life or (2) if certain changes occur in this pattern.

Data useful in predicting likely outcomes of a current mode of behavior or of changed behavior are illustrated by the following two examples. The first bears on cases of counselees who claim that after using drugs or alcohol their ability to drive a car is not affected by the amount of the substance they have taken.

A study of driving skill has shown that a sample of male drivers, ages 21 to 45, who were under the influence of various amounts of alcohol, marijuana, secobarbital (a common sleeping pill), a diazepam (the world's most frequently prescribed psychotropic drug) did not safely perform 17 driving tasks in a laboratory auto-traffic simulator. The marijuana doses were judged to be from moderate to strong by the subjects in the studies, and the alcohol effects ranged from well below legal levels to slightly above. The secobarbital and diazepam were in therapeutic doses. Each of the four drugs impaired the perceptual-motor skills of the drivers (Smiley, Moskowitz, & Ziedman, 1985, p. 19).

The second example relates to the current child-raising practices of parents who have either come for counseling themselves or are concerned about the behavior of their child. The question at hand is: "What effect will strong parent-centered control of a young child have on the child's personality later in life, as contrasted to parents' using greater child-centered guidance?"

In a longitudinal study of 135 randomly selected Finnish children from age 8 until they reached age 20, Pulkkinen compared characteristics of 20-year olds with the same subjects' traits and their parents' child-raising practices at ages 8 and 14. At age 20, the youths' attitudes and life-styles were analyzed in terms of two bipolar dimensions. The first dimension was labeled *Reveler versus Loner*, with revelers oriented toward peer values and involved in problem behavior (such as drinking), while loners were more oriented toward parental values and social norms. The second dimension was labeled *Striver versus Loser*, with strivers being optimistic and responsible and losers being alienated. In relating the lifestyles of 20-year olds to earlier child-rearing and environmental conditions in the youths' lives, Pulkkinen concluded that both child-rearing practices and environmental factors had contributed to those lifestyles, but that "Child rearing was correlated with children's behavior more consistently than environmental conditions, although various aspects of life were interrelated in a complex way as revealed by case studies. Weak self-control, as exemplified by the ways of life of Revelers and Losers, was related to selfish (parent-centered) treatment of children, and the strong self-control of Strivers and Loners to child-centered guidance. The life conditions of Revelers were unsteady and conflicting, and those of Losers were being financially poor and lacking encouraging models for life. The conditions of Strivers and Loners were more favorable, which was reflected in the emotional atmosphere at home" (Pulkkinen, 1982, p. 102).

Societal Expectations and Pressures

How may attitudes that are held by society (with "society" meaning social groups important in a client's life) toward people of the client's age, gender, and cultural type influence such an individual's problem? Furthermore, how free is the client to choose what ambitions, lifestyles, and methods of personal/social adjustment he or she will adopt?

Throughout this book, the term *culture* is intended to mean the pattern of attitudes, values, and modes of social interaction to which a group of people subscribes. The group that shares these characteristics is referred to as a *society*. Most of the child-rearing, educational, law-enforcement, and social-pressure efforts in a society are aimed at teaching people to adopt the group's cultural commitments. The process through which people learn to abide by these commitments is usually called *acculturation* or *socialization*.

It seems clear that using the word *society* in the singular is simplistic and misleading, since everyone lives within multiple groupings whose cultures are not identical. An individual may simultaneously belong to the societies of sexually virile 20-year olds, English-language speakers, Catholics, residents of Arizona, college undergraduates, feminists, environmentalists, microcomputer enthusiasts, third-generation Chinese-Americans, and the Martin and Ethel Ching family. The individual shares certain attitudes, values, and modes of social interaction with the other members of each of these groups.

The problems that bring clients for counseling are often associated with these multiple societies' cultural expectations. One source of problems is a conflict between the norms of one social group and the norms of another. Values traditionally held within the Ching family, for example, may conflict with certain of the values that are common among sexually virile college undergraduates. Traditional Catholic values may conflict with those of feminists. Hence, the client may come to the psychologist for help in resolving the conflict between these incompatible expectations.

In social systems that are undergoing rapid transition, generational gaps can contribute to personal/social problems. Among adolescents and young adults, family disorders often arise from youths' wanting privileges before parents wish to grant those privileges—permission to drive a car, to stay out late, to drink alcohol, to use drugs, to choose companions, and to groom themselves in unconventional ways. Parents who grew up believing that the state of marriage is the proper qualification for sexual intercourse can be disturbed by their sons' and daughters' treating any pleasant acquaintanceship as sufficient license for copulation. The controversy arising from such intergenerational clashes can produce the personal/social disorders that carry one or more of the antagonists to the counselor's office.

Whereas, in many cases, the client's problem derives from the incompatibility between one group's standards and another's, in other cases the difficulty arises from tension between a society's standards and an individual's needs. A teenager's sexual drives often conflict with the manner in which the society believes such drives should be expressed. A 70-year-old man who has been forcibly retired from 50 years of a satisfying occupation can suffer a feeling of worthlessness and despair at the new state of inactivity that society has assigned him.

In other instances, expectations regarding physical attributes underlie a client's problem. A very tall female or a very short male can suffer distress in a society which holds that men should be taller than women. During the years of adolescence, concern over such discrepancies in height are especially prominent, since girls typically enter puberty two years earlier than boys, so that the average girl will be taller than the average boy between ages 11 and 14. Other common physical characteristics during adolescence also frequently conflict with a society's ideals regarding desirable appearance in males and females. A teenager who suffers acne, has protruding teeth, or is considered inordinately chubby or thin may feel miserable enough to seek counseling.

A personal-adjustment disorder can also be seated in a discrepancy between people's talents—as judged by their performance—and what their society values. Perhaps the most frequent example is poor academic performance. Students who lag behind the majority in achievement are the ones singled out for remedial measures by their families, by school authorities, or by both. In other cases, the individual's disappointing performance is not academic but, rather, is social or occupational. The unduly belligerent youth (and less often, the inordinately shy and retiring one) fails to fit the society's expectations and thereby appears to require the attention of a counselor.

In effect, personal/social-adjustment difficulties are often related to the kinds of expectations commonly held by members of the societies that an individual inhabits—such societies as the person's age cohort, family, school, athletic team, religious denomination, place of employment, and the wider community.

A particularly important aspect of societal pressures is the attitude that the client adopts toward others' expectations. Consider a case in which parents have taught their daughter that feelings of resentment, envy, or jealousy toward family members is sinful, so that such feelings are proper sources of guilt and shame. It will then make a significant difference in the counseling process if the girl has accepted this teaching as valid rather than as false or at least as very questionable. Thus, it is first useful for a counselor to understand societal norms—that is, to know about the expectations held within societies in which a client is a member. Then, in the counseling sessions, it is useful for the therapist to discover which societal expectations the counselee accepts as valid and desirable, which expectations the client considers improper or unfair, and which ones are viewed with ambivalence.

In summary, a counselor's knowledge of attitudes commonly held in the societies with which a client interacts can alert the therapist to issues that are profitably investigated by means of the counseling sessions. In other words, the data about societal norms become the basis for questions that the therapist poses during counseling sessions in order to discover the way in which those norms may bear on the case at hand.

"How do you think your Black friends and your family feel about your going with a white woman?"

"When you've applied for jobs, have you told prospective employers that you've been in prison?"

"When you were considering abortion, what did you feel would be the advantages and disadvantages of it?"

"Your parents are from Japan? Then how do you think they feel about the way in which you should spend your leisure time, compared with how parents of other kids at your school would feel about their boys' and girls' use of after-school time?"

ADOPTING SUITABLE COUNSELING TECHNIQUES

An Appropriate Counseling Approach

How can the level of physical, cognitive, emotional, and social development of clients at this life stage, of this gender, and of this cultural type help determine the counseling techniques that will likely be most suitable for solving their problems?

There is perhaps no therapist who treats each case in precisely the same way. Many counselors are true eclectics, intentionally using quite different techniques with different clients. Even therapists who subscribe primarily to one approach, such as psychoanalysis or behavioral therapy, alter their practice somewhat to fit the nature of the case at hand.

Therapists can use at least three methods for deciding which techniques will likely succeed best with a given client: (1) the logical analysis of characteristics of the client and of the client's social setting, (2) normative information about how different techniques have succeeded in the past with counselees of this type, and (3) the progress of the present case.

Logical Analysis. The first method—logical analysis of a client's characteristics and social ecology—is illustrated in some detail in Chapter 3, where brief descriptions are offered of different approaches to counseling that are suited to different types of clients. However, the general nature of logical analysis can be demonstrated at this point with the example of two counselees who seem to face the same problem but whose personal characteristics and social settings could logically suggest that the counselor should adopt a somewhat different approach with each of them. One counselee is an 11-year-old, 6th-grade girl who has been referred to the school psychologist by her teacher because of the girl's moods of depression that interfere with both her school work and her relations with classmates. The other client is a 21-year-old college woman who has come to the college counseling center because of strong feelings of unworthiness that affect her ability to concentrate on her studies. In these cases, the initial counseling session suggests that in both instances a very dominating, criticizing mother has exerted a significant influence on each client's feeling inadequate to manage either academic or social demands. How, then, can this information, combined with the psychologists' perception of the clients' characteristics and social settings, affect the selection of counseling techniques? Consider the following lines of reasoning that a therapist might pursue in the two cases.

Two significant differences between the 6th-grade girl and the college student are their levels of intellectual maturity and their levels of independence. Compared with the 11-year old, the college student has had an additional decade of experience with the world, so she is likely to be more apt at generating a variety of options for solving her problems and more adept at analyzing the strengths and weaknesses of those options. Also, because of her age and experience, the college student is probably more employable than the sixth-grader. The 11-year old will be legally bound to her mother for some years to come and is therefore obligated to continue living at home. Even in a nonlegal sense, the child is economically and emotionally dependent upon the mother's support. In contrast, the 21-year old is legally free of the mother. Furthermore, while attending college, the young woman has lived away from home, so she is accustomed to being on her own, not depending on parents for daily nurture. In college, she has held a part-time job, so she is not entirely dependent on her parents for economic support, and she could conceivably become entirely independent by taking a full-time job, though that might slow her progress toward graduation. From the viewpoint of the psychologist, these several differences between the two clients could suggest that:

1. It is important to involve the 11-year old's mother in the counseling process, whereas it is less important and probably impractical to involve the 21-year old's mother.
2. The counselor of the 21-year old may be less directive, placing more responsibility on the client for proposing likely solutions and for carrying these proposals through. The counselor of the sixth-grader may offer more suggestions for possible solutions.
3. To help each client recognize the amount of freedom that her social situation allows in her choice of solutions that are most feasible, the college counselor might focus more on how the college student could become additionally independent of her family and yet maintain amicable relations with them, while the elementary-school counselor might emphasize how the sixth-grader could adapt to her family, how the mother's child-rearing practices might be improved, and how the school staff could help to enhance the girl's sense of adequacy.

Normative Data. The second method of selecting a counseling approach (as guided by normative information about the results of past cases of the same kind) appears in a variety of places in Chapters 4 through 9. However, as an introduction to such matters, an example from a study of prisoner recidivism can illustrate a typical form that such normative data may take.

When we as counselors consult normative studies as a means of estimating the likely effectiveness of a given treatment, we are addressing ourselves to the question of causality. In other words, we are trying to judge how that treatment is likely to influence the outcome of the case at hand. Attempting to make such a judgment about cause is a rather hazardous undertaking that requires caution if mistaken conclusions are to be avoided. Among the factors that make cause estimation a risky business is that of multiple causation. The term *multiple causation* refers to the conviction that no event in life is the result of a single cause. Every happening has derived from the confluence of a variety of causal elements. Therefore, the task of deciding why a counseling case turned out as it did involves estimating how much the counseling treatment contributed to the outcome, as compared to contributions from the other factors that were present. Thus, when normative data are consulted about cases like the one we currently face, our task of drawing a convincing conclusion about how much good the reported treatment did is usually difficult indeed. This problem is illustrated by the results of the following study.

To estimate the effect that college-degree programs (conducted in New York State prisons) had on inmate reincarceration rates, a research team traced the careers of 276 released prisoners who had completed such programs while in prison. Over the five-year period 1979-1983, the annual average rate of return to prison of college-degree holders (one-year certificate graduates, two-year associate-of-arts graduates, four-year bachelor-degree graduates) was 14%, as compared to 20% for the general prison population. Furthermore, the higher the degree, the lower the rate of recidivism (16% at the certificate level, 12% at the associate level, 11% at the bachelor level). At first glance, these figures might suggest that counseling prisoners into college-degree classes will reduce the likelihood of their returning to prison after their release. However, the authors of the study were more cautious in their interpretation: "Since [college classes were] only one component in an inmate's overall prison experience, it is difficult to conclusively identify the separate effect of the college program on post-release behavior. Furthermore, it may be argued that those inmates who successfully complete college programs are more motivated and/or competent than those who do not complete these programs and that these same factors are related to their future adjustments on parole.... As such, the lower return rate of the sample of offenders who completed college programs may be jointly attributed to both the offenders' motivation and capabilities and the impact of the program" (Thorpe, MacDonald, & Bala, 1984, p. 87).

The third method of judging the efficiency of counseling procedures involves not the initial selection of a method but, rather, the assessment of how well present counseling sessions are succeeding. This method will be discussed in the next section.

The Progress of Counseling

What are efficient ways to assess how well the counseling process is advancing for clients who face such adjustment problems at this stage of life?

During each counseling session, and from one session to the next, therapists typically are alert to signs of success or failure in the therapeutic process. They often use four types of evidence for determining how the case is progressing.

One type is the extent to which the counselee is cooperating with the particular approach that the therapist has proposed. For example, in a program of career planning, counseling is judged to be more successful if the client willingly and promptly completes the recommended aptitude tests and questionnaires than if the client balks at such tasks or postpones them. With a psychoanalytic approach, progress is considered to be satisfactory if the counselee attends all sessions and freely pours forth the recollections of childhood experiences that the therapist regards as the source of the individual's current problems.

The second variety of evidence is the testimony of clients about how much the counseling sessions are helping them to cope with their lives. As the sessions advance, do clients say that they worry less, are more confident about facing daily responsibilities, have fewer physical aches and pains, sleep well, and the like?

A third kind of evidence is derived from attitude tests or adjustment inventories which the client fills out. When a counselee's scores upon entering the counseling relationship are compared with scores at a later time, conclusions may be drawn about how well the process is succeeding.

The fourth type of evidence is the extent to which the symptoms that brought the client to the therapist in the first place have abated. Do objective observations of the client's behavior show that maladjustment has diminished or disappeared? Does the young woman no longer appear painfully shy when she is meeting strangers? Does the third-grade boy no longer wet his pants? Has the stockbroker stopped smoking? Is the wife's criticism of her husband less frequent and less strident? Has the elderly man taken up a hobby so that he no longer spends much of the day lying in bed?

To some degree, the assessment techniques most suitable for a particular case can be age-related. Clearly, very young children cannot be expected to give sophisticated testimonials about how well their problems have been solved. Hence, the most appropriate way to judge the progress of the counseling process may be to observe these children in order to identify changes in their symptomatic behavior. Also, engaging a child in play activities with dolls may reveal the way the child feels about others, when direct questioning would not elicit those feelings.

Normative data can be useful throughout this evaluation process by informing the counselor of what assessment methods have proven most suitable in the experience of other counselors who have handled similar cases. The data can also suggest the types of reactions that are typical of clients in these kinds of cases at different stages of the counseling process.

Evaluating the Solution of the Client's Problem

What are suitable methods for evaluating how well the counseling has solved the problems of clients of this age, gender, and cultural background?

This evaluation task is allied to Step 5, in which the progress of the counseling process was continually assessed as a guide to the counselor's subsequent decisions. This new task, however, occurs at or near the end of the counseling program, rather than periodically during the sessions. In effect, Step 6 is a summative evaluation of the apparent outcome of the entire process. Therefore, it is appropriate to collect evidence not only about the client's condition at the close of the sessions but also about the counselee's attitudes and behavior some weeks or months or even years later. In other words, at this step, the therapist is interested not simply in judging the immediate effects of the counseling effort but also in learning whether long-term effects show up some time after the relationship has ended. Consequently, appropriate sources of evidence consist not only of the four used for Step 5 but also of follow-up evaluations that draw on formal reports of the client's behavior (such as reports from the school, police, probation officer, or social agency) and on interviews with the client and his or her acquaintances. At this step, normative information apprises the therapist of assessment techniques used with similar clients in the past and of the immediate and long-term outcomes of comparable cases.

COMPLETING THE COUNSELING PROCESS

Terminating Counseling

How, why, and by whom is counseling best terminated with individuals of this age, gender, and cultural condition?

In arriving at this culminating decision, therapists can be aided by normative reports of ways in which the counseling relationship has been closed out with similar types of counselees.

In summary, the professional literature on counseling and psychotherapy, along with publications about demographic characteristics of populations, provides a great store of normative information that can contribute to the psychologist's, psychiatrist's, or social worker's decisions throughout the foregoing seven steps of the counseling relationship. However, some normative data are far more useful than others because of their precision and their suitability for particular clients. It is to these matters of precision and appropriateness that we turn next.

The Precision of Normative Statements

All normative statements offer quantitative information about an aspect of life—the frequency of different causes of death among people over age 60, the incidence of masturbation during early adolescence, the proportion of divorced people who remarry their former spouse, the success rate of behavior-modification therapy among overweight women, and the like. Furthermore, normative statements vary greatly in their level of precision. The least precise are statements in which the quantity is expressed as a nonnumerical adjective *(many, a few, most, several, some)*, as an adverb *(occasionally, unduly, typically, slightly, often)*, or as a noun *(a majority, a small number, a substantial portion)*. As an illustration of such differences in precision, the information offered earlier in this chapter on the frequency of drug use by American youths was more specific than the nonnumerical generalizations about the reactions of young children to the death of a close relative.

Most normative statements on which counselors base their practice are rather imprecise, often because the information on which the statements are founded was not collected in a systematic fashion that would permit a more specific description of the quantities involved. Such is the case when normative generalizations are based on a counselor's casual observations of people in everyday life or on a clinician's recall of clients whom he or she treated in the past.

Imprecise statements can also result from a counselor or a textbook-writer's inspecting a variety of research studies, then trying to summarize the gist of the studies in an easy-to-remember form. For instance, one study may report that 20% of clients recovered from a minor phobia as a result of aversive therapy. Another study may report a 36% recovery rate, a third a 23% rate, and a fourth a 61% rate. From these figures, an easy-to-recall verbal summary might be drawn: "In most cases a strong minority profit from such treatment." Slightly more precision can be lent to the statement if it is rephrased as: "The rate of recovery from the disorder ranged from nearly one-quarter to slightly over one-half of the clients."

Another reason that quantities are so often expressed in nonnumerical terms is that those who issue the statements are unsure about how faithfully the data collected on the normative sample of people will apply to the client who is now before the counselor. (In the following section, this matter of sampling will be inspected in some detail.)

While most normative descriptions that bear on counseling are verbal rather than numerical, it is obviously more desirable to have data in numerical form. For instance, it is important to know that the term *most* or *a majority* refers to 97%, rather than 53% of a category of people—or that *relatively few* means 18% of the group, rather than 2%.

The four sorts of numerical information that are of most value to counselors are percentages, averages, measures of variability, and descriptions of the amount of relationship—or correlation—between two or more variables.

As demonstrated already in this chapter, *percentages* tell what portion of a group display a characteristic. Because percentages are easy to compute and easy to understand, they are especially useful for conveying normative information.

Averages tell how the group in general stands on some measure. The two most useful kinds of averages are the *arithmetic mean* (the people's totaled scores divided by the number of people) and the *median* or *50th percentile* (the score obtained by the person at the very middle of the group). Counselors are often interested in knowing how close a client is to the average on some characteristic, such as mental ability, weight, frequency of sexual activity, incidence of migraine headaches, and the like.

Measures of variability tell how much the group tends to spread out from, or cluster around, the average. Commonly reported measures of variability include the *standard deviation* and the *distance between percentiles*. Because most people do not score exactly on the average for the group, it is useful to know in what pattern the majority of the group spread out from the average. Such information helps a counselor to estimate how drastically a particular client deviates from the average.

Numerical descriptions of relationship, referred to as *correlation measures*, are very helpful, since they tell how likely it is that a client who has one characteristic, such as an inordinate fear of being alone, is likely to have other characteristics as well, such as a childhood spent with an overprotective mother or with an alcoholic father. Furthermore, a correlation figure can reflect the degree to which a test of mental ability predicts how well a high-school graduate is likely to succeed in college, or a correlation coefficient may suggest how well a client's score on a test of anxiety will reflect his or her efficiency in a stressful job.

(Because it is beyond the purpose of this book to explain the detailed characteristics of the statistical methods mentioned above, readers who wish to learn more about such matters are referred to the following authors, whose works are listed among the references at the end of this book: Hays, 1981; Johnson & Wichern, 1982; Marascuilo & Levin, 1983.)

As mentioned earlier, the contents of this volume are comprised primarily of normative information significant for the counseling process. Whenever I have been able to find current and reliable numerical data, I have cast the information in numerical form—that is, as statistics. But when I have been unable to find recent, trustworthy numerical information, I have given only imprecise verbal estimates of quantities.

Group Homogeneity and Representative Sampling

A crucial question in using normative information is: "How accurately does the information represent this particular client?" In other words, "how much will the information help me in working with this case?" The answer to such questions involves two considerations—the degree of homogeneity among the people forming the client's normative category and the extent to which the information accurately represents this type of client.

THE HOMOGENEITY OF THE GROUP'S CHARACTERISTICS

As explained earlier, the value of normative data lies in the guidance that it offers about what significant characteristics can be expected in a client who displays some such easily recognized traits as age, gender, or cultural background. Thus, for one type of case, we find it desirable to locate information about the proportion of girls who have not yet begun to menstruate by age 16. For a different case, we can profit from learning the percentage of Black families whose income is below the poverty level.

The information about menstruation can be useful when we are consulted by a mother who is distressed about her 16-year-old daughter's inordinate shyness and the girl's delicate physical build. Studies of the advent of menarche in girls tell us that by age 16, well over 90% of present-day North American girls already menstruate. Therefore, we may profitably ask this client about her daughter's menstrual condition, for if we learn that the girl has not yet experienced menarche, we recognize that she is notably different from her age-mates in a way that is typically important to adolescents. Such information, together with the mother's description of her daughter's physical appearance, would suggest that the girl is indeed slow in maturing and that her failure to fit society's expectations for normal physical growth may well be a factor contributing to her shyness. In this instance, the normative data have indicated a high degree of homogeneity within the category of 16-year-old girls (the great majority have passed menarche). We may assume from the data that if this girl has not yet reached menarche, she could well regard herself as undesirably "abnormal." Hence, we are prepared, during subsequent counseling sessions with the girl, to learn about her menstrual condition and about her attitudes toward it.

Consider next the frequency of American families living below what the government has defined as "the poverty level." For all American families, regardless of race, 17% were judged below the poverty level in the mid-1980s. However, there was a significant difference between whites and Blacks, with whites at 16% and Blacks at 37% (U.S. Bureau of the Census, 1987). Therefore, a Black client is more than twice as likely to be poor than is a white client. However, these figures about people's poverty status furnish a less secure foundation for speculating about a new counselee's characteristics than did the data about menstruation in the case of the 16-year-old girl. By age 16, the population of girls is far more homogeneous (over 90%) in terms of menstruation than are Black families in terms of financial welfare (63% above the poverty level). Hence, if we know that a girl is age 16, we can estimate with a far higher degree of confidence that she has passed menarche than we can predict that a Black family is above the poverty level.

In summary, the farther a percentage deviates from 50-50, the greater the homogeneity of a population on a given characteristic, and the more trustworthy our estimate can be that a new client is likely part of the majority. Likewise, the smaller the standard deviation (so that the entire group bunches closely around the average), the more useful the average score will be in predicting the likely score or status of a newly met member of the group whose characteristic has been measured or tested.

THE SUITABILITY OF THE NORM SAMPLE

Whenever we use either formal or informal normative information as a foundation for speculating about a client, we are assuming that the people in the normative sample faithfully match our client in ways important for the counseling process. To the extent that the sample does not accurately represent this client's condition, our speculation will be misguided. As a way of estimating the soundness of our assumption, we can attempt to answer two questions: (1) "Which characteristics of individuals and their environments do we believe are particularly significant as causes of the kind of problem that our client suffers?" and (2) "Which characteristics of individuals and their environments do we believe determine which kind of treatment can best solve the client's problem?" In these questions, the phrase *characteristics of individuals* refers to such factors as the client's age, gender, mental ability, cultural traits (language, attitudes), and personal habits (diligence in performing assignments, ways of investing leisure time, use of drugs or alcohol). The phrase *characteristics of environments* refers to such factors as the family's socioeconomic status, attitudes of the surrounding society toward people of the client's age and ethnic status, and the degree of the client's economic, emotional, and decision-making dependence upon others.

With these two sorts of significant characteristics in mind, we are prepared to inspect the demographic structure of a normative sample so as to estimate how well our client's characteristics match those of the people on whom the norms were founded. The better the match, the greater our confidence in using the normative information to speculate about our client.

Fundamental to this process of speculating is the set of convictions that the particular counselor holds about what factors in life most influence the sort of problem experienced by the client. For example, in the case of a teenage client who has come for help because of poor academic performance, do you believe his or her genetic endowment (inherited mental capacity) could be a significant causal factor? Might the youth's socioeconomic status also be important as a cause of his or her academic failure—or, if it is not a direct cause, is such status at least usually correlated with a learner's level of academic success? Can the nature of a student's close companions exert a strong influence? Can parental attitudes toward school be important? If any or all of these factors are considered to be significantly related to academic success and failure, then normative information will be most useful to the counselor if it has been drawn from a sample of students similar to the client in these respects. In other words, the judgment about how suitable the normative data will be for the case at hand depends upon the counselor's theory about what personal and environmental characteristics most potently influence the type of problem faced by the counselee. Furthermore, when a therapist reviews the professional literature to learn which counseling techniques have succeeded with clients who have had this same type of problem, it is appropriate to estimate how closely the therapeutic conditions in the cases reported in the literature compare with the conditions in the counselor's present case.

Among the variables found in normative studies, age is the one most often reported. The usefulness of age data derives from the fact that age—particularly during the first two decades of life—so often suggests a person's level of physical maturation (including the maturation of the neural system) as well as the amount of an individual's life experience. Data on gender are also frequently reported, especially because societies have traditionally expected males and females to assume different roles in life, and these differences have influenced individuals' personal/social adjustment. Furthermore, reports often identify ethnic and cultural characteristics of the normative sample because people's life experiences and their life chances are commonly affected by their cultural status. Thus, in Chapters 4 through 9, much of the normative information has been described in terms of these three variables—age, gender, and cultural characteristics—to aid readers in estimating how well such information matches conditions of counseling cases that readers themselves may face.

CONCLUSION

The contents of this introductory chapter—indeed, the contents of the entire book—derive from two fundamental convictions about the process of helping others to solve their personal/social-adjustment problems. The convictions are:

1. That data about the status of people who compose a population (which is defined by such variables as age, gender, certain cultural characteristics, and type of personal/social problem) can enhance the efficiency of counseling a client who qualifies as a member of that population. Such data assist the therapist by reducing an infinite number of possibilities about the nature of the client to a limited set of probabilities. In other words, normative information can give sharper focus to the therapist's opening estimate about clients' problems and about clients' potentials for solving those problems.

2. That normative descriptions cannot tell what a particular counselee is *really like*, since each person is indeed unique. Hence, while descriptive group data can suggest questions to pose and areas of counselees' lives to investigate, the success of treating any case depends ultimately on how artfully the counselor discovers—by means of interviews, observations, tests, and intuition—how the variables in each client's life are woven together to form that person's special pattern of individuality.

2

Normal Development and Life-Span Stages

As noted in Chapter 1, normative information describes characteristics shared by members of a group, such as an age-group or a cultural group. One of the important questions faced by counselors when comparing a client to such a description is: "What do these data tell me about how 'normal' my client's behavior is?" The answer depends on how the counselor interprets the word *normal* and how this interpretation may be related to the term *desirable behavior*. The first section of Chapter 2 addresses these issues.

The second section offers an overview of normative information during successive stages of the life span. This overview is intended to introduce the kinds of developmental characteristics to be presented in Chapters 4 through 9.

The third section distinguishes age cohorts from age stages and suggests how this distinction can affect a counselor's perception of clients' problems and their social-psychological environments.

The chapter closes with a brief discussion of how a conception of life-span development is related to the practice of developmental therapy.

WHAT IS NORMAL?

A frequent concern in counseling—as well as in social work and law enforcement—is the question of what is meant by *normal development* or *normal behavior*. Since there is much confusion about this matter among both professionals and the public, we can profitably inspect the question in some detail, particularly as it relates to the use of normative data.

In the field of human development, there are two common uses of *normal*—(1) statistical similarity or frequency and (2) desirability or acceptability. The first use refers to how much a person's condition is like the condition of other people in the same category or how frequently other people in that category are like the individual whose normality is being questioned. The decision about an individual's normality in this instance involves two steps: (1) knowing how a group of people are distributed in terms of the characteristic being judged (height, aggressivity, moodiness, verbal fluency, time of menopause) and (2) deciding how close to the average or in what percentage category a person needs to be in order to be judged normal rather than abnormal. Step (1) is a matter of objective statistical description. Step (2) is a matter of subjective judgment, based on the judge's values and on a rationale which is adduced by that judge.

The second use of *normal*—desirability or acceptability—refers to how closely the client's condition matches the value system of the person making the judgment about normality. In this sense, *normal* means *approved, admirable, satisfactory, acceptable, proper*, and the like.

It is possible for a person to be normal in the first sense and abnormal in the second, or vice versa. A 6-year old with an intelligence quotient of 150 could be judged statistically abnormal but normal (or supranormal) in terms of desirability. A 16-year old could be judged statistically normal in the use of marijuana (when 70% of the age-group in the community have used marijuana) but abnormal in the sense of desirable behavior.

There are also alternative uses of *natural/unnatural*—(1) statistical similarity or frequency and (2) whether development can proceed satisfactorily without special intervention, as implied in the phrase "She's just growing up naturally" or "It's just natural to pass through a phase like that."

Consider, then, the kinds of evidence required for deciding whether a person is developing normally in terms of similarity and in terms of desirability.

Normal or Natural as Similar or Frequent

The first kind of evidence needed for this decision is a description of a category of people along a particular dimension (such as weight by age or height, smoking habits by gender and age, child abuse by gender, or English-language fluency by ethnic designation). The description is most helpful if it is in the form of a distribution showing the percentage of people at different points along the dimension. The distribution can be equally helpful when it is summarized in the form of the group's average (mean, median) and extent of variability (standard deviation, distance between percentiles 20 and 80). Or, when information is offered in dichotomous or trichotomous form (*Yes, No* or *Often, Sometimes, Never*), the results are typically in the form of percentages of people in each subcategory.

The second kind of evidence needed is a description of where the individual stands in relation to the group, such as the client's height, weight, degree of moodiness, incidence of experiencing abuse at the hands of an adult, or score on an English oral-language test as compared to the group's status or *norms*.

The third kind of evidence is the line of reasoning that establishes the cutting point on the distribution, or that sets the percentage level in dichotomous data, in order to distinguish normal from abnormal (natural from unnatural), or that stipulates degrees of normality (such as *very normal, somewhat normal, slightly abnormal, very abnormal*). This is not an objective judgment but, rather, a decision reflecting the values held by the judge, so it calls for support in the form of the line of logic that explains the values on which the judgment is founded.

Normal as *Desirable* or *Acceptable*

The criteria used to identify normal in this sense can differ greatly from one person to another. Thus, defining *normal* as *desirable*, or at least as *acceptable*, is a subjective act. Its basis is the set of values held by the definer and, as such, requires clarification (1) of the elements that go into the definition and (2) of the proper sources of evidence for making a decision about the normality of a given case. It appears likely that many people's bases for assessing normality in this sense are rather vague and intuitive instead of specific and rational—with *rational* meaning *under conscious cognitive control*. I am proposing that it is important for counselors not to be satisfied with holding only vague, subliminal, intuitive conceptions of normality (in the sense of desirability or acceptability) but, rather, that they should clearly identify the components of their definitions so that their conceptions of normality can be intentionally applied in specific cases and so that these conceptions can be communicated accurately to clients and colleagues.

One way to begin identifying the components of such a conception is to offer a general definition of *normal*, then to explain the line of logic supporting each component and the interactions among components. The following general definition of *normal development* in the sense of *desirable or acceptable development* illustrates this process:

> People are developing normally (properly, desirably, satisfactorily, acceptably) when: (1) they feel that they are fulfilling their own needs at least moderately well, (2) their behavior does not unduly encroach upon other people's rights and opportunities, (3) they fulfill the responsibilities typically held as reasonable for people of their ability (physical and mental) and social environment, and (4) their personal characteristics do not cause others to treat them in ways which harm them physically, psychologically, or socially or which deny them opportunities [equal to those of their peers of the same age, gender, and physical, intellectual, and/or social behavior] to pursue their ambitions.

This definition is the one to which I subscribe, so it now becomes my obligation to explain the set of values on which I base the four components. My rationale, then, is as follows:

1. FULFILLING ONE'S OWN NEEDS.

A large proportion of the people who come voluntarily for counseling do so because they feel that their needs are not being satisfied. Whether or not others see them as well adjusted, they themselves feel distressed.

The kinds of needs going unfulfilled may vary from time to time and from one person to another. An unmet need may be physical—a lack of proper nourishment or of sexual gratification. The problem may also be psychological—not being appreciated and respected by others, not accomplishing anything worthwhile, not having valued friends with whom to exchange confidences, failing to find a worthy mission in life, being stuck in a depressing occupation, or being misunderstood by others.

Thus, I believe that people who suffer unmet needs are not developing in an optimal way. In such cases, counseling is intended to reveal ways to fulfill such needs, thereby contributing to more desirable development.

2-3. RESPECTING OTHERS' RIGHTS AND BEARING ONE'S OWN RESPONSIBILITIES.

In contrast to the introspective nature of the first criterion, the second and third standards represent perceptions from society's viewpoint. The rationale supporting these two standards holds that no one lives alone, except the rare hermit. Instead, people live in interdependent groups, sharing common territories, working together, dividing up the labor of daily living, engaging in continual cooperation and competition. Under these conditions, if the greatest good is to result for the greatest number, individuals cannot be concerned exclusively with fulfilling their own desires without regard for others. It thus becomes a matter of enlightened self-interest for people to recognize that, in the long run, their own needs will be best met if they permit others to exercise the same rights that they themselves want to enjoy. Furthermore, their own needs will be best satisfied if they, and all others in the society, bear a fair share of the responsibility to perform the tasks that make the society operate efficiently.

Criteria 2 and 3, in effect, represent the social aspect of satisfactory development. People who are failing to meet these criteria sometimes come voluntarily for counseling. However, it is perhaps more common for them to be sent for counseling by a friend or relative, the courts, the school, an employer, a social worker, or a physician. Clients who are most obviously failing in social responsibility are those in conflict with the law because of drunk driving, child neglect, spouse abuse, assault, theft, forgery, rape, and the like. Other less dramatic problems of rights and responsibilities are cases involving marital dissension, family disputes, occupational conflicts, and difficulties at school.

Normative data are particularly important in judging how well clients are respecting others' rights and are bearing their own responsibilities because societal expectations about responsibilities can vary from one age level to another. Expectations are also influenced by a person's gender, although this is less true today than in the past when greater distinctions were made between male and female rights and responsibilities. Furthermore, the degree to which an individual's physical and mental development is considered normal (in the sense of average) affects judgments of the person's ability to respect rights and carry responsibilities. Less is expected of the physically and mentally handicapped than is expected of others the same age.

For clients whose development is deemed unsatisfactory in terms of criteria 2 and 3, the purpose of counseling is to help them learn to respect others' rights and to bear their share of responsibilities.

4. THE SIGNIFICANCE OF SOCIETAL ATTITUDES AND SOCIOECONOMIC OPPORTUNITIES.

Oftentimes people's failure to achieve optimal development is the result of their being treated in prejudicial ways by others. Restrictions are placed on their opportunities to achieve their potential. The fault, in many instances, lies in other people's basing their judgments of an individual on false normative impressions. This can occur when a general conclusion about an easily identified group—Catholics, Jews, Blacks, Latin-Americans, Irish, adolescents, wealthy people, the homeless—is applied to every member of the group in equal measure. In effect, individuals who bear the group label are not judged on their own individual characteristics but are branded with a generalization about "those kinds of people." Such normative impressions (stereotypes) as "women make decisions emotionally rather than logically" or "Blacks are poorly educated" or "the Irish have quick tempers and like to fight" can suggest that all women, Blacks, and Irish display such traits. As a consequence, opportunities for individual women, Blacks, and Irish who do not fit such stereotypes can be restricted by those people in the society who hire employees, enroll students in schools, admit youths to clubs, invite guests to parties, permit their adolescent children to date members of the opposite sex, and the like.

In short, the failure of a person to develop in the most desirable way can be due to prejudicial attitudes of people in the environment who control opportunities for growth, self-expression, and need fulfillment. If people come for counseling because their chances for optimal development are frustrated by others' stereotypical attitudes or by socioeconomic conditions, the counseling task is that of discovering how such conditions might be changed. This sometimes can be accomplished by the individual's moving into a different environment that is free from prejudicial attitudes. Or, in the case of parental prejudices regarding a child's or adolescent's opportunities, the counseling may involve working with the parents to alter their perceptions. Often, however, the social environment cannot be changed, so that counseling consists of helping the client learn to cope with unfavorable conditions, even though such conditions continue to diminish the chance for optimal development.

A further effect of societal attitudes concerns the significance placed by society on deviations from the statistical average. Thus, it is important to recognize what attitudes the society, or subgroups within the society, hold toward each kind of deviation. Knowing that a person is precocious or is average or is retarded tells us nothing about the desirability of that individual's condition until we know which particular realm of life is involved and how society views that realm. For example, in most present-day cultures, a child's being ahead of the group in academic or athletic skills is generally admired. In contrast, a child's being precocious in sexual activities and in the use of alcohol is deplored by most adults, though not necessarily by the child's peers. However, even in those aspects of life in which giftedness is generally lauded, such as in academic and artistic performance (music, drama, dance), individuals who deviate quite markedly from the norm may suffer social-psychological difficulties because of the wide gap between them and their more average age-mates. Ordinary children can misunderstand and envy precocious age peers, and they can express their resulting distaste by taunting or socially isolating the gifted ones. Also, the gifted may judge their age-mates to be boring, slow-witted, and lacking in talent, and, as a result, the gifted can openly express disdain, thereby generating enmity between the precocious and the average.

At the other end of the scale of talent, those who fall notably below their age peers often experience personal/social-adjustment problems because of attitudes expressed by people toward such deviance. Normative data can aid the counselor in estimating the nature and extent of such attitudes in the social environment of the handicapped client who has come for help.

Not only is the importance of deviation affected by societal values, but it is also influenced by how a given form of deviance influences the person's ability to carry out the tasks which arise at the current stage of life. The handicapped are typically unable to perform all the tasks that nonhandicapped age-mates can carry out, a shortcoming that frequently leads to personal-adjustment difficulties which call for the aid of a counselor.

Sources of Data About Desirable Development

In the foregoing paragraphs, I have sought to present a pattern of reasoning that explains the values on which my definition of *desirable development* is founded. The purpose here has not been to suggest that my definition is *the right one*. A review of others' writings about personal/social adjustment and mental hygiene reveals that there are other definitions reflecting different values. My purpose, then, has only been to illustrate a process of stating a definition and defending it by a line of logic.

A definition at such a level of specificity can also serve as a guide to the types of information that a counselor will need for answering a parent or teacher who asks about a child or adolescent: "Is his behavior normal? Am I expecting too much of her, or is she okay? Shouldn't he be doing better than that? Do I really have anything to worry about?" In Table 2.1 below, the components of my earlier definition are listed at the left, and suggested sources of information are proposed at the right. In the right-hand column, items preceded by an asterisk (*) provide a standard against which the individual's condition can be compared, whereas those preceded by a triangle (Δ) furnish information about the individual's condition.

The assumption here is that gathering evidence about the four components of the definition enables a counselor to estimate the degree to which the client's behavior is normal, in the sense of desirable or acceptable. If development is judged undesirable, this scheme aids the counselor in estimating the kinds of interventions that might improve the client's condition. For example, the intervention would be different if the undesirable or unacceptable component is in item 1 instead of item 3, or if it is in both 1 and 4.

The judgment to be made on the basis of such evidence is not whether the person's development is absolutely desirable or undesirable but, rather, it is made on (1) the *extent* to which development is desirable or acceptable and (2) whether or not this extent appears to require some intervention in addition to, or in replacement of, the "natural" influences in the individual's current life. *Natural* in this sense refers to the pattern of life that the client has been experiencing and will continue to experience unless intentional changes are attempted.

Frequently, when people inquire about the normality (desirability, acceptability) of a child's or adolescent's current developmental status, they are concerned primarily with what such a status portends for the future. In other words, they may not be pleased with present conditions (such as bed-wetting or stammering or having nightmares or temper tantrums), but they can consider these conditions to be nothing to worry about if they can be assured that "It's just a stage that nearly all kids this age normally pass through, and the problem usually clears up naturally." To make the desired estimate of the

Table 2.1 Information About Desirable Development

Components of Desirable Development	*Sources of Information*
1. Individual fulfills own needs.	*1.1 Interview the individual to discover his or her perceived needs.
	Δ1.2 Interview the individual to discover how well the needs are satisfied.
	Δ1.3 Interview acquaintances of the individual to receive their estimates of how well the client's needs are being met.
2. Individual does not encroach on others' rights and privileges.	*2.1 Obtain normative data on rules, laws, and customs of the societies the person inhabits.
	Δ2.2 Read school, police, court, social-worker, employment records.
	Δ2.3 Observe the individual's behavior in social situations.
	Δ2.4 Interview others who are acquainted with the individual's social behavior.
3. Individual fulfills responsibilities at a level typically considered reasonable for people of similar developmental status and social environment.	*3.1 Obtain normative information about expectations regarding the type and level of responsibilities for people of similar developmental status and social condition.
	Δ3.3 Interview the person's acquaintances.
	Δ3.4 Read school, social-worker, employment, police, court records.
4. Individual's characteristics do not result in others treating the person in ways that are harmful or that deny the individual equal opportunities.	*4.1 Obtain normative information about stereotypes, prejudices, and discriminatory rules and practices in the society.
	Δ4.2 Interview the individual.
	Δ4.3 Interview the individual's acquaintances.
	Δ4.3 Read school, police, court, social-worker, employment records.

future, the additional type of normative information that the counselor needs is predictive data. The counselor seeks to learn the prognosis for the future for people of the client's type when nothing special is done to intervene *(the child naturally grows out of it)* or when some special treatment has been instituted at the present stage of life *(remedial measures are applied).* Examples of such predictive information are provided in Chapters 4 through 9.

CHARACTERISTICS OF LIFE-SPAN STAGES

One of the perennial debates in the field of human development is over the question of whether growth proceeds very gradually by imperceptibly small increments or if, instead, it moves ahead by major steps or stages, with each new stage significantly different from the previous ones. In this book, I am adopting an intermediate position. While admitting that development does indeed advance by extremely slight changes from one day to the next, I am accepting as well the notion that during certain periods between conception and death, people are markedly different than they were in earlier years— physically, intellectually, socially, and emotionally. A key problem encountered when we seek to delineate stages arises from the difficulty of identifying the length of a given stage and the borderlines between stages. This problem is less troublesome early in the life span and near the end, since the observable changes that occur during those segments of life can be more readily used as stage markers. For example, infancy is typically distinguished from early childhood by the child's achieving upright locomotion and gaining some command over expressive speech. Hence, when the young can walk and talk, they have left babyhood and have entered early childhood. Rather clear markers also separate later childhood from early adolescence. Around age 11 to 14, the growing child displays primary and secondary sex changes which signify that a new phase of life has arrived—girls menstruate, boys produce spermatozoa, height and weight increase rapidly, body contours change, body hair appears, and boys' voices lower in pitch. All of this happens during a relatively short space of time, so the notion that the person has rather suddenly moved up to a new plateau of growth is well-founded.

At the other end of the life span, people beyond age 60 or 70 exhibit physical, social, and mental changes that are sufficiently sudden and noticeable to signal the advent of a new stage beyond middle adulthood. Physically, the aged suffer more ailments than do younger adults, and recovering from injuries takes more time than it did in the past. Acuity of sight and hearing decreases, physical strength declines, reaction time diminishes, and the ability to recall recent events and the names of people newly met can wane. Most of the aged who were employed during their adult years have now retired from their regular jobs, thereby adding a social criterion to the physical and mental indicators of the stage of old age.

Whereas physical, mental, and social changes furnish rather obvious markers between stages during the first decade-and-a-half of life and during the final years of the life span, we face far more difficulty in marking stages between late adolescence and old age. From age 18 or 20 through age 60 or so, neither physical nor mental abilities need to deteriorate significantly. As a consequence, knowing the age of a client who is between age 20 and age 60 is of less help to a counselor in estimating how to work with the client than knowing the age of one who is under 20 or over 60 or 70.

Chapters 4 through 9 have been organized with the foregoing considerations in mind. The first decade of life has been divided between two chapters because the marked changes that occur during these years can make the task of counseling with preschool children (Chapter 4) significantly different from that of counseling with elementary-school pupils (Chapter 5). Problems of adolescence are treated in a single chapter (6). Chapters 7 (early adulthood) and 8 (middle age) encompass the long span of 40 or 50 years between the end of adolescence and the onset of old age. Finally, characteristics of the waning years of life, age 60 or 70 and beyond, provide the topics in Chapter 9.

Each of the six chapters—4 through 9—begins with a brief review of general traits exhibited by people at their particular stage of life, along with a description of societal expectations often held regarding people of that age range. Following this introductory overview, the chapter offers normative information about several types of personal/social adjustment problems that are prominent during that period. For example, in contemporary American society, problems of anorexia nervosa (eating disorders that are occasioned by the individual's fear of gaining weight) usually begin during early adolescence. Therefore, data about anorexia are presented in the chapter on adolescence. Likewise, problems of selecting a spouse or love partner are most prominent in early adulthood, so that normative information about marriage and related issues is located in Chapter 7. And because retirement from active employment generally occurs near the end of the life span, data bearing on retirees are offered in Chapter 9.

A Sketch of Life-Span Cognitive Development

As an example of types of age-stage characteristics to be found in Chapters 4 through 9, Table 2.2 illustrates some ways in which the

Table 2.2 Development in Seven Cognitive Categories

Early Childhood	Later Childhood	Adolescence
EGOCENTRISM		
Sees everything in terms of self. Cannot see other's viewpoints. Not as likely to empathize with others.	Begins to see others' viewpoints, but may still blame or credit events to one's own wishes and behavior.	Able to place self in others' situations and understand their points of view.
PERCEPTIONS OF CAUSE		
Casual correlations accepted as cause. Magical rather than logical interpretations of causality.	Slightly better at interpreting causal relations, but may use magical and phenomenological reasoning. Does not see causes that underlie appearances.	Can understand multiple causation and the need for a line of logic to differentiate casual from causal correlations. Starts to recognize underlying causes. Some magical thinking may persist with belief in supernatural forces.
FANTASY VERSUS REALITY		
Cannot readily distinguish fantasy from reality—goblins, ghosts, monsters, Santa Claus. Often thinks dreams are part of reality.	Better able to differentiate the real from the unreal in the physical world	Distinguishes the real from unreal in the physical world. May not recognize the true from untrue in social relations, as in "true friends."
LITERAL VERSUS FIGURATIVE USE OF LANGUAGE		
Tends to accept words at their face value. Does not understand metaphorical or figurative speech.	Starts to develop skill in the symbolic use of words. Begins to draw implications, not just literal meanings from language.	Achieves marked progress in symbolic, abstract use of language, as in math, stories, jokes, proverbs. Infers implications and hidden meanings.
VOCABULARY BREADTH AND COMPLEXITY		
Average vocabulary grows from 300 words at age 2, to 1,500 at 4, 2,100 at 5, and to 2,500 at 6.	Average of 3,000 words at age 7, and 1,000 words per year thereafter.	High-school senior knows 14,000 to 15,000 words.
UNDERSTANDING CLASSES AND RELATIONSHIPS		
Barely starts to recognize classes of objects or people and relationships	Recognizes classes of objects and their relationships when they are seen or heard, and also begins to classify things that are imagined.	At Piaget's formal-operations level, not only recognizes classifications and relationships among objects directly seen, but also (1) of imagined objects and events and (2) classification and relationship systems themselves (as in algebra, natural science, and social science).
PROCESS OF STORING AND RETRIEVING MEMORIES		
Few experiences to store. Tends to store events as visual and auditory images.	Begins to store experiences as verbal symbols or concepts as language abilities advance. Metamemorial skills advance.	Stores experiences primarily as verbal symbols. Memory bank becomes more complex, with more interrelationships among contents. Metamemorial skills are refined.

Table 2.2 (cont'd.)

Adulthood	*Old Age*
Has more experience with diverse viewpoints so as to understand others' perspectives.	Reduced involvement in the workaday world. May be more egocentric, seeing only own viewpoint.
Has more experience with life situations in which causal relations are demonstrated. Is more realistic about what is possible in practical life situations. May attribute cause to supernatural forces, such as God or the devil.	May retain causal logic from middle adulthood, or may revert to less logical analyses of events. May attribute cause to ill-fate or to supernatural forces.
Recognizes the real from unreal in the physical world. May hold beliefs about supernatural powers, particularly as part of religious convictions.	In very advanced years, may not distinguish real events from imagined ones. This may be related to difficulties in accurately recalling events.
Ability in figurative use of language and in drawing inferences advances in proportion to experiences that focus attention on such skill.	May maintain skill in figurative use of language, but also may lose agility in these skills, particularly after age 75 or 80.
College senior knows 18,000 to 20,000 words. Vocabulary grows in adulthood in relation to how useful new words are in the person's life.	Vocabulary is very resistant to loss with advanced age.
As life's experiences (occupation, avocation, community participation) require, sophistication in classifying and recognizing relationships among events, people, and objects grows, varying considerably from one person to another on the basis of both native endowment and nature of experiences.	In advanced old age—particularly when the brain's blood supply and the individual's energy decrease—skill with classes and relationships can be impaired.
Memory bank grows with experience. Metamemorial skills progress.	Memory for recent events declines. Memory for long-past events remains, though sometimes altered in accuracy. Retrieving memories takes more time and effort.

level of a client's mental development exerts an important influence on the counseling process. The table summarizes some general trends in cognitive growth for five stages of the life span: early childhood (ages 2-6), later childhood (ages 7-12), adolescence (ages 13-21), adulthood (ages 22-65); and old age (65+). These age divisions are somewhat arbitrary, since not everyone passes through the stages at the same rate. Furthermore, not every adult achieves the more advanced levels of thought listed under *Adulthood* but, instead, some become fixated at an earlier stage—or at least they appear to operate primarily at a less mature cognitive stage. Far more detailed analyses of such developmental characteristics are offered in Chapters 4 through 9.

Significant Life Periods and Critical Events

An important aspect of a life-span perspective is that the effect of critical events on an individual's personal/social adjustment may be different during one period of life than during another.

In the present context, the term *period* refers to a stage of life, such as late childhood or middle age, during which the accumulation of a person's experiences day after day exerts a marked influence on the individual's personal/social adjustment. Examples of people involved in adjustment problems related to significant periods include those of (1) a late-maturing, overweight, junior high school boy who is remarkably shorter and heavier than his age-mates, (2) a young wife confined at home in child care (a six-month-old boy and twin girls age two) after she had begun a promising career in advertising, and (3) a middle-aged spinster living with a nagging elderly mother who disapproves of any man in whom the daughter displays interest.

The term *events* identifies incidents or sudden occurrences that precipitate unusual stress in the person's life. In the professional literature, the phrases *life events, life changes*, and *life incidents* are used as synonyms. Hurme (1981: p. 2) has suggested that: "There is no absolute rule for calling an occurrence a life event or a life change, but usually [such incidents] have a clearly discernible beginning and they are abrupt, sometimes even dramatic. The most salient feature is, perhaps, that they do not pass without attention or without leaving a trace."

In an effort to account for the effects of such happenings, psychologists in recent times have devised *stress theories* intended to explain:

> the relationships between a stressor, the physiologic and emotional reactions to it, and the resulting health consequences, if any.... Holmes and Rahe [1967]... developed a quantitative technique for assessing the relative stress imposed by various types of life events, including loss and bereavement. They considered loss of a spouse the most severe change in adult life; other life events (both positive and negative), such as sickness of relatives, marrying, moving, or loss of a job, were also considered stressful but were weighted less heavily. Although both the reliability and validity of the original scale (and numerous other life-events scales modeled after it) have been challenged, the findings from hundreds of studies have generally supported the proposition that life stressors of all types place individuals at greater risk for a variety of physical illnesses and mental disorders (Osterweis, Solomon, & Green, 1984, p. 9).

The influence of a given event on an individual can differ from one stage of life to another. When psychologists and social workers in Finland's child-guidance clinics were asked to judge how seriously different life events affected children's development, they ranked 16 of the events under four age groupings, with the most serious life change ranked as 1 and the least serious as 16 (Table 2.3). The technique of presenting the data in Table 2.3 in the form of ranks fails to reveal the magnitude of many of the estimated effects at different age levels. For instance, a mother's starting work was judged to be three times more significant for children ages 1-3 than for ones ages 11-13, whereas the death of a close friend was deemed four times more serious at ages 11-13 than at ages 1-3. A marked drop in the family's financial status was increasingly more traumatic with the increase in the child's age. On the other hand, the death of a parent was considered to have equally serious consequences across all four age periods.

It is apparent that critical events and significant periods can be intimately related. Such an event as changing jobs, moving to a different city, or suffering the death of a loved one can inaugurate a new significant life period. Throughout Chapters 4 through 9, attention is directed to the effect both of critical incidents and of significant periods.

Table 2.3 The Seriousness of Events in Children's Lives

	Ranks by Age Levels			
Events	0-3	4-6	7-10	11-13
1. Death of mother	1	1	1	1
2. Death of father	2	2	2	2
3. Mother's serious illness or injury	3	3	5	7
4. Divorce of parents	4	4	5	6
5. Serious illness or injury of child	5	5	5	4.5
6. Adoption	6.5	8	7	3
7. Marital separation of parents	6.5	7	8	9
8. Parent in prison for more than one year	8	10	10.5	11
9. Father's serious illness or injury	9.5	9	9	8
10. Death of brother or sister	9.5	6	3	4.5
11. New marriage of mother	11	11	10.5	10
12. Mother starting work	12	14	16	16
13. Child in hospital for more than one week	13	15	15	15
14. Birth of brother or sister	14	12	13	13
15. Strong decrease in family financial status	15	16	16	14
16. Death of close friend	16	15	12	12

Adapted from Hurme, 1981, pp. 24-25

Age Periods and Age Cohorts

In people's progress through life, an important factor that sometimes goes unrecognized is the distinction between age periods and age cohorts. As noted above, an *age period* is a segment of the life span that extends over several years, identified by such terms as *early childhood, adolescence,* and *middle adulthood.* In contrast, the phrase *age cohort* refers to that set of people born in the same year or within the same decade. People in a given cohort, such as those born in 1975 or those born in the decade of the 1950s, pass through the age periods together.

This distinction between periods and cohorts is important in counseling, because some characteristics of clients are the result of their being in a given age period, whereas other characteristics have been influenced by their membership in a particular cohort. Reaching the period of early adolescence (with its puberty) or later middle age (with its menopause for women) tends to affect all people—or at least most people—in similar ways, no matter whether they entered that age period in 1910, 1950, or 1990. This is because the source of their life change has, to a great extent, been biological. However, societal conditions at the time when a person's age cohort passes through such a period as adolescence or middle age can be significantly different from conditions at the time when earlier or later cohorts reached the period. The experience of being an American college student in the early 1930s was, in many ways, different from that of the typical student in the mid-1940s, mid-1960s, and late 1980s. The economic depression of the 1930s, the World War in the 1940s, the free-speech movement and Vietnam War of the 1960s, and the economic conditions and AIDS-virus sexual atmosphere of the 1980s all exerted different influences on the problems faced by the cohorts of youths during those times. As a consequence, it is useful for counselors to recognize that both age-period information and cohort information can help in estimating the problems experienced and the attitudes likely to be held by a client of a particular age. To help with this task of estimating, the normative data throughout this volume contain descriptions of trends from one era to another in societal patterns, including trends in people's attitudes, experiences, personal problems, and attempted solutions.

By way of illustration, the following statistics on trends in marriage and divorce in the United States suggest attitude differences between one cohort and another. These differences can contribute to the social-adjustment conflicts between generations that cause clients to seek counseling.

In the United States in 1935 there were 10.4 marriages annually per 1,000 inhabitants and 1.7 divorces. In 1960 marriages dropped to 8.5, while divorce advanced to 2.2. By the mid-1980s, there were 10.5 marriages and 5 divorces. Thus, marriage was as common in the mid-1980s as in the mid-1930s, but divorce had become nearly three times more frequent. The number of married women who became divorced in 1965 was 10.5 per 1,000, a figure that would nearly double in less than 20 years (21.7 in 1983).

Between 1960 and the mid-1980s, the median age of first marriage for males increased from 22.8 to 24.1 years and for females from 20.3 to 22.3. Between 1965 and the mid-1980s, the median age of remarriage for divorced or widowed males declined from 39.6 years to 35.7 and for females from 35.5 to 32.5. Hence, the trend was for people to wait longer for first marriage (approaching their mid-20s) but to remarry at a younger age (approaching their mid-30s).

The likelihood of a divorced woman's remarrying in 1965 was markedly higher than in the early 1980s. Of 1,000 divorcees ages 14-24, over half (512) in 1965 remarried, but less than one quarter (264) did so in 1982.

The incidence of unmarried couples sharing the same household more than tripled over the 15-year period of 1970-1985 (523 per million to 1,983). By the mid-1980s, the greatest proportion of these (61%) were in the 25-44 age range, with 22% under age 25, another 12% in the 45-64 range, and 6% beyond age 64. Less than one-third (31%) of the unmarried couples had children under age 15 living with them. (U.S. Bureau of the Census, 1987, pp. 42, 81).

LIFE-SPAN DEVELOPMENT AND DEVELOPMENTAL THERAPY

In recent years, the terms *developmental therapy* and *developmental counseling* have been used synonymously to describe counseling approaches that give particular attention to suiting treatment methods to stages of human development. Some writers stress the importance of a therapist's recognizing the stage at which a client is currently operating so that the therapist can view the world from the perspective of that stage and thus better understand how the client is interpreting life (Ivey, 1986). Other writers advocate the identification of a client's present stage so that proper techniques can be selected to advance the counselee to the next higher stage of perception and behavior. In one version of this approach, Gazda (1985, p. 1385) proposes that: "the therapist is concerned with the client's deficits in each of his or her developmental areas. Once the deficits ... are ascertained, the therapist attempts to adapt the treatment/interventions to the age/stage level of the client."

How, then, do such conceptions of developmental counseling relate to the contents of this book? I see the connection to be this: The sorts of normative information in which this book focuses are useful to practitioners of developmental therapy by alerting them to (1) characteristics commonly displayed by clients at different age stages (and often by gender and cultural categories), (2) types of personal/social problems often experienced by those types of clients, (3) causal factors that often underlie such people's problems, and (4) therapeutic techniques that have succeeded with those kinds of clients in the past. In effect, the contents of the present book should be useful at several junctures of the counseling process for improving a developmental therapist's initial estimate of how best to work with a client.

CONCLUSION

The first purpose of this chapter has been to direct readers' attention to the diverse ways in which people use such terms as *normal development* and *natural development* and to suggest the desirability of counselors' defining rather precisely for themselves what they mean by these terms. The second purpose has been to illustrate life-span stages that have implications for counseling over the life span, with special attention directed at significant life events and life periods. The third objective has been to distinguish age periods from age cohorts and to identify the importance of this distinction for counselors. The final aim has been to sketch briefly the nature of developmental therapy and developmental counseling.

3

Types of Counseling Techniques

Throughout the following chapters, counseling techniques are frequently mentioned, with each type identified by such labels as *behavioral counseling, a psychoanalytic approach, rational-emotive therapy, relationship counseling, bibliotherapy, genetic counseling,* and the like. I assume that not everyone is acquainted with all of these types. Furthermore, not everyone applies the same meaning to each labeled type. Therefore, to orient readers to the meanings assigned to counseling techniques mentioned in Chapters 4 through 9, the present chapter describes a collection of representative techniques in terms of (1) a label or name, (2) assumptions about the kinds of clients and counselors for whom the technique is appropriate, (3) the expected role of the counselor, (4) the expected role of the client, and (5) the times of life when a given technique is most often suitable.

The illustrative counseling approaches are presented according to categories that represent eleven principal functions served by the different techniques. The functions are those of: fostering emotional catharsis, providing a catalytic setting, offering hope and assurance, furnishing information, altering reciprocal relationships, reliving forgotten events from the past, rearranging consequences to produce new habits, confronting and analyzing reality, focusing on *being* and on creating goals, addressing make-believe situations, and altering body chemistry.

As the following discussion advances, it will become apparent that I have rendered the counseling process unduly simplistic by separating functions into discrete categories. In real life, counselors typically perform several different functions at successive steps in a case—perhaps first fostering catharsis, then confronting reality, and later promoting cooperative planning. Still, for purposes of analysis, I find it useful to divide counseling techniques into such function-categories so as to illustrate the fact that most of the labeled counseling approaches or schools of thought depend primarily upon one or two of the functions and give little or no attention to the others. For instance, educational counseling is heavy on information-giving, while counseling the bereaved depends more upon offering assurance and hope.

FOSTERING EMOTIONAL CATHARSIS

Being a good listener may be all that is required for providing someone the opportunity to achieve emotional catharsis. This approach requires no special training. It merely involves listening in a sympathetic, understanding manner to a person's feelings and problems. A key assumption underlying this approach is that as the client verbally unloads his worries to a receptive listener, he or she obtains relief from the emotional pressure that he or she has suffered. As a result, the client may be able to go ahead with his or her life in a more productive—or at least a more bearable—fashion. This technique is suitable at life periods beyond infancy—that is, from early childhood through old age.

What is required of the listener is a degree of patience and an attentive, nonjudgmental attitude. What is needed from the client is the ability to express feelings verbally and a willingness to confide in the listener.

As is true with nearly any counseling approach, the extent to which sympathetic listening has achieved its aim of emotional catharsis is typically gauged by the client's testimony: "Thanks for hearing me out. I feel much better now." Or "This may have been boring to you, but it's done me a lot of good." A further way to assess the method is to compare the individual's actions prior to the counseling encounter with his or her actions following it in order to estimate whether positive behavioral changes have resulted.

PROVIDING A CATALYTIC SETTING

Counseling approaches that extend beyond simple listening are ones in which the counselor assumes a somewhat more active role, one that is intended to produce a catalytic atmosphere in which the client can work through his problems. Illustrations of labeled counseling techniques that fit this description are *client-centered counseling* and *relationship therapy*.

Client-Centered Counseling

Client-centered counseling is also known as *Rogerian technique* because Carl Rogers first explicated and popularized the method. The terms *client-centered* and *person-centered* replaced an earlier label, *nondirective counseling*, after critics claimed that every counseling technique necessarily gives some direction—if not explicitly, at least by implication—to the counseling process and because the phrase *client-centered* accurately identifies where the main responsibility for solving the client's problem is placed—on the client, not on the therapist. The goal in client-centered counseling is to help the person *self-actualize*, which means that the individual realizes all of his or her capacities and potentialities.

In this approach, the task of the counselor is to encourage a client's expression of beliefs and feelings, to listen attentively, to mirror those feelings, to display a nonjudgmental understanding of the client's situation, and to encourage the counselee to move through the steps of analyzing his or her problems, suggesting solutions to them, and appraising the worth of the possible solutions. The therapist allows counselees to select their own life goals, to express any opinions they wish, to generate their own options for action, and to assess their own progress. In a pure form of the client-centered approach, therapists do not criticize their clients' beliefs or ambitions, do not furnish information or advice, and do not offer a counselee any assessment of the success of the counseling endeavor. The counselor is expected to display acceptance of the client, genuineness, and understanding (Meador & Rogers, 1979).

As to the kinds of counselees for whom this particular method is suited, person-centered therapy assumes that clients have reached a level of rational maturity sufficient for meaningfully expressing their beliefs and feelings and for working out solutions to their problems. The approach also assumes that clients have sufficient economic, legal, and emotional independence to put into action solutions that have been generated during the period of counseling. These assumptions are most often warranted in cases of young and middle-aged adults—that is, among clients who are beyond late adolescence but have not yet reached the debilitated condition of advanced old age.

The success of client-centered counseling is often determined by how well the counselee has achieved the goals that he or she set for himself or herself as reflected either in his or her testimonial or in his or her manner of confronting problems in his or her life.

Relationship Therapy

In the relationship-therapy school of thought, the improvement in a client's condition does not result from some intended role of treatment applied by the counselor, such as giving information, offering advice, or tracing emotional problems into the past. Instead, any good that results from counseling sessions derives from the human relationship involved (Allen, 1942, p. 47). It is the interested, supportive, caring human relationship provided by the counselor that enables the troubled client to grapple successfully with the burdens that brought him or her to the counselor's door. In other words, the theoretical position from which the counselor operates—such as psychoanalytic or behavioral—and the content of the counseling sessions matter far less than the caring relationship between therapist and client.

This assumption about the overriding importance of human emotional support makes relationship therapy suitable at all stages of life, from infancy through old age.

OFFERING HOPE AND ASSURANCE

Two key functions of many forms of counseling are those of offering clients hope for the future and of assuring them that they are worthy individuals, capable of surmounting the difficulties that concern them. Because providing hope and assurance are usually such prominent activities in pastoral counseling and bibliotherapy, we can usefully inspect these two approaches more closely.

Pastoral Counseling

What mainly distinguishes pastoral counseling from other forms of therapy is that pastoral counseling is furnished by members of the clergy. While it is true that the priest or minister or rabbi or imam who offers the service may be prepared to assist needy parishioners with any sort of problem, it is also the case that the types of difficulties posed by parishioners, combined with the typical pastor's view of life, make the technique of providing hope and assurance especially suitable to this type of counseling.

In regard to types of difficulties, counseling by the clergy is frequently sought in cases of death and bereavement, illness, divorce, an alcoholic or abusive spouse, a son or daughter turned wayward, or the loss of one's job or one's home. In these circumstances, clients who despair of the future or see little purpose in life are typically offered hope and assurance by the pastoral counselor.

The technique of providing hope and confirmation is particularly well suited to the conception of life and the universe typically held in the major Western religions. Specifically, the following beliefs are central to traditional Judeo-Christian-Islamic doctrine: (1) that life on earth is merely a preparation for eternal life after death, (2) that true believers who abide by God's commandments will be rewarded by eternal bliss in the life hereafter, (3) that the Almighty is a personal God, who looks after the welfare of each individual, (4) that God works in mysterious ways not comprehended by humans but ways designed to promote the ultimate welfare of the individual, if not immediately on earth, then at least in the afterlife, (5) that difficulties suffered in the present life are a test of the believer's faith, and (6) that bearing life's difficulties with courage and faith will be rewarded by a carefree life after death, so that everything will turn out all right in the end. The hope and assurance that the parishioner is offered in pastoral counseling is typically founded on these convictions.

Counseling techniques include citing quotations from the holy books as well as recounting anecdotes about other people who have suffered similar problems and, through faith and courage, have gained control over their lives. The anecdotes serve as modern-day parables.

The expected role of clients is that of accepting the pastor's interpretations as a foundation for bearing the trials they face and for abiding by their religion's tenets, thereby making the most of their lives while awaiting the advent of eternal bliss.

Providing hope and assurance is a technique appropriate at all stages of the life span, with the methods of assurance including nonverbal (hugging or caressing) as well as verbal techniques, particularly during infancy and childhood. The efficacy of this technique is usually gauged by the client's testimony about how much the counseling has helped and by the client's ability to pursue a more productive life than was the case at the outset of the counseling sessions.

Bibliotherapy

As a counseling procedure, bibliotherapy is the process of using reading material to help people solve their problems of personal/social adjustment and development. A client who reads about the lives of other people who have suffered problems like his or her own may gain renewed hope for the future by witnessing how people in the written accounts conquered the obstacles that they faced. Bibliotherapy has several advantages over a client's talking directly with a psychotherapist. First, bibliotherapy can protect one's privacy. With a book serving as the counselor, the reader avoids the risk of the humiliating self-exposure that might occur if he or she told another person of his or her secret fears, loves, hates, and cravings. Second, reading material is available when needed, and it can be reviewed time and again if necessary. Furthermore, for many people, the printed word carries an air of verisimilitude that an orally related anecdote may not. However, in contrast to a counselor, a book cannot respond to a client's moods and questions with a sensitively designed reaction—empathy, blunt reality, reassurance about a specific matter—as the moment requires.

Bibliotherapy is suitable for all ages beyond infancy. For young children not yet literate, an adult reads the stories aloud. School-age children and people beyond childhood can pursue the reading on their own. To be most successful, a book's contents need to match the client's own situation so that he or she identifies with the characters in the account and accepts their solutions as suitable for his or her own case.

FURNISHING INFORMATION

The three most common forms of counseling that feature information-giving are (1) career or vocational counseling, (2) educational guidance, and (3) genetic counseling.

Career or Vocational Counseling

The phrases *career counseling, vocational guidance,* and *occupational counseling* all refer to the process of helping people select, prepare for, and adjust to employment. A key goal of career counseling is to achieve a good match between society's job opportunities and the characteristics of counselees. This means furnishing clients with information (1) about the requirements, working conditions, and rewards of different careers and (2) about such pertinent characteristics of clients as their aptitudes, physical and mental skills, background knowledge, values, motivations, interests, and ambitions. Data about job opportunities are provided in the form of job descriptions, brochures on occupations, and lists of the types of jobs available in various areas of the country and the world. Information about the client's characteristics is gathered by means of interviews, questionnaires, vocational-interest inventories, and achievement and aptitude tests.

The period of life when career counseling is sought extends from mid-adolescence into late middle age, and sometimes beyond. However, within this range, the nature of counseling typically differs from one period to another. Youths from their mid-teens into their twenties are newly choosing a career. People in their late twenties through their fifties are frequently seeking to change their careers, leaving one field of work for another because of injury or illness, dissatisfaction with the nature of a job or its compensation, technological unemployment (changes in the job market), a desire to move to a new geographical location, and the like. Women in their thirties and forties who were homemakers during the years when their children were growing up may now wish to spend time outside the home in a vocation. Or, with the increasing incidence of divorce, women who were homemakers while they were married but are now divorced must find a job in order to support themselves and, perhaps, to support their children. Furthermore, people in their later fifties and into their seventies who have retired from one career may wish to enter a new field of employment for the latter years of their active life span. To fulfill the needs of each of these types of clients, counselors are obliged to furnish substantial amounts of information.

The success of career counseling is typically determined by whether clients (1) arrive at an informed career decision which they accept as realistic and, if possible, satisfying and (2) actually enter the career that they have selected.

Educational Guidance

As the term *educational guidance* is used here, it means helping learners plan a program of study—choose classes for the coming semester, select a major field of emphasis, decide on a college to attend, locate a program in which to train for a vocation, and the like.

Educational guidance involves furnishing information about educational opportunities and about how well the client's characteristics (interests, aptitudes, past experience, financial condition, family status, geographical preferences, occupational plans) match the array of opportunities.

The greatest call for educational guidance occurs during adolescence and early adulthood. However, as more middle-aged and older adults engage in lifelong learning, educational guidance becomes increasingly important for people beyond age 25. Educational guidance may also be sought by parents engaged in planning their young children's future from the preschool years on up the educational ladder.

Genetic Counseling

Genetic counseling is typically sought by couples who are considering having a child but who suspect that factors in their own genetic makeup might produce unfortunate characteristics in such a child. Or, perhaps, the couple fear that the wife's health could be threatened by her becoming pregnant and giving birth (Capron et al., 1979). Thus, the type of information that can aid them is normative data about the probability that the wife's pregnancy would result in the outcomes that they fear or in other undesirable outcomes of which they are not aware.

Clients for genetic counseling may also be parents who already have a child who suffers a genetically based handicap. In this event, the parents usually are seeking information about suitable child-rearing practices and about expectations that they can reasonably hold for the child's future. Thus, the life stages when genetic counseling is most common are those of young and middle adulthood, people age 20 or so through ages 40 or 45.

To qualify for offering genetic counseling, a psychologist, physician, or social worker is expected to be well-versed in the medical facts of genetic disorders, including the diagnosis, frequency, probable cause, and available management of such aberrations. The success of genetic counseling is usually estimated by the degree to which the clients reach a well-informed decision with which they feel comfortable.

ALTERING RECIPROCAL RELATIONSHIPS

Group counseling consists of a therapist's working with several people at the same time. There are at least three different goals behind group approaches—to alter an interpersonal-relationship configuration (as within a family or organization), to provide counselees with a peer setting, and to optimize a counselor's time and energies. The first of these goals is the primary aim in the group treatment of family, workplace, and athletic-team problems.

In most forms of counseling, and particularly when the client is an adult, only the client appears for treatment. Significant people in the client's life do not appear for counseling. Therefore, if something is awry with the client's interpersonal relations, such as within the family or on the job, the opportunity for the counselor to try altering the nature of these relations is limited to the client's role in that interpersonal network. However, more opportunity is provided for altering the reciprocal relations of the members of a family, work group, or athletic team when significant members of the group attend counseling sessions together.

Marriage and Family Therapy

The typical goal of group marriage and family counseling is to stimulate the members of the group to alter their attitudes and behaviors in relation to each other so that they can function more amicably and productively together. Or, if the family cannot reasonably stay together, the goal becomes that of equipping the members to separate in a manner that enables each one to pursue a constructive future alone or in a new relationship with others outside the family (Minuchin, 1974).

The role of the counselor is to assist the family members in expressing their feelings about each other, in sharing their own hopes and needs, and in seriously considering the attitudes and needs of the others. The counselor often asks family members to suggest ways for solving their interpersonal conflicts. The counselor may also propose alternatives for the family to consider. Such methods are intended to provide opportunities for catharsis, to promote interpersonal communication (clarify for the members of the group how they feel about themselves and about each other), and to generate new, more profitable options for behaving toward each other than they have used in the past.

In their role as clients, all the family members are expected to participate seriously in the counseling sessions and to continue in the counseling relationship until they have adopted reasonably acceptable ways of resolving their problems.

In terms of life periods, marriage counseling that mainly involves a wife and husband is most common among young and middle-aged adults. However, personal/social problems of children and adolescents or of the elderly also may be the stimulus for family therapy sessions. The child or the elderly grandparent may be the initial center of attention, but then the group that becomes engaged in counseling also will include the young and middle-aged adults who are part of the family configuration.

Organizational Counseling

The aim in counseling members of a work group, such as an industrial or business organization, is to improve interpersonal relations so that members of the group function more productively together. The roles of counselor and of clients are similar to those in family-therapy situations.

The period of life during which organizational counseling is most common is from the time when young adults enter the full-time work force until they retire, so the age range is typically from 20 or 25 to 65 or 70.

Team Counseling

A relatively new specialization in the counseling field is *sports counseling*. This can involve aiding individual athletes to solve their psychological problems and maximize their performance, or it can involve working with a group—an entire team or a segment of a team—to resolve interpersonal difficulties that affect the team's mental health and performance. Team counseling, therefore, is a special form of organizational counseling. The period of life when team counseling is most common is from middle adolescence until around age 35 or 40, the time at which most people who have engaged in serious team sports are no longer competing.

CONSTRUCTIVELY RELIVING THE PAST

Some approaches to therapy are historically oriented, in that their focus is on discovering earlier events in the client's life that have produced the individual's present difficulties. The prototype of this approach is psychoanalysis.

Psychoanalytic Forms of Counseling

A conviction undergirding types of counseling derived from Freudian psychoanalysis is that the seeds of the client's disorder lie in events in the person's childhood, particularly in events involving sexual relationships within the family (Brenner, 1955; Freud, 1946). The assumption is that these events were psychologically so painful that they were repressed. In other words, the distressing incidents were buried in the individual's unconscious where they still continue to fester, creating the symptoms the client now suffers. The goal of therapy is to unearth the hidden conflicts so that they can now be psychologically lived through—in the sense of talked through—in a more constructive, acceptable fashion. In effect, psychoanalysis assumes that when the disordered past is recast in a new perspective, the conflicts become resolved and the client's symptoms will abate, freeing him or her to lead a more constructive, more bearable way of life henceforth.

The counselor is expected to encourage the client to speak freely about past and present concerns, letting all feelings and thoughts flow out uncensored. The counselor's task is to select from this stream of free associations those items that seem symbolic of repressed conflicts from the past. The counselor explains to the client the meaning of these utterances, encouraging the individual to view such past events in a new light, thereby dispelling the destructive feelings of fear, guilt, and shame that were originally attached to the incidents in childhood.

Psychoanalytically oriented therapists sometimes also employ projective techniques, such as Rorschach ink blots or sentence-completion tests or pictures (as in the *Thematic Apperception Test*) to elicit clients' expressions of their world view.

Traditional methods of psychoanalysis are used most often with young and middle-aged adults. Some forms, such as the approach devised by Erik Erikson, are also applied during adolescence (Erikson, 1968), Psychoanalysis with children often takes the form of play therapy, since play situations are usually more effective than direct dialogues for evoking children's view of the world and their opinions of themselves and of members of their family.

REARRANGING CONSEQUENCES
TO PRODUCE NEW HABITS

Adherents of the psychological school known as behaviorism contend that it is unprofitable for therapists to concern themselves with such unobservable entities as *mind, conscience,* and *psychological needs*. Instead, behaviorists hold that counselors should concentrate on the publicly observable ways in which people act. According to behaviorist theory, the ways in which people habitually act are influenced by the types of consequences that follow the actions. Acts that are followed by consequences which a person finds rewarding *(reinforcing)* increase the likelihood that the same action will be used in the future when the individual is in similar circumstances. Behaviors followed by consequences experienced as unpleasant *(punishing)* or at least unrewarding *(nonreinforcing)* are not likely to be used in the future under similar stimulus conditions (Skinner, 1974).

Social-learning theorists generally accept such notions about the significance of consequences, but they also are willing to speak about people's thinking processes. These theorists propose that a highly important aspect of human behavior is that of imitation. A large percentage of people's actions result from their modeling their behavior after that of other people whom they observe in daily life or ones they read about or hear about (Bandura, 1977).

The terms *behavioral counseling* and *behavior therapy* refer to techniques founded on behaviorist and social-learning principles. The focus of attention in such approaches is not on the client's past experiences—as is the case in psychoanalysis—but, rather, on the types of consequences that are maintaining the client's present unsatisfactory behavior. In simplified form, the therapeutic process consists of four steps:

1. Identify the specific behavior you wish to substitute for the presently unacceptable acts.
2. Arrange for the client to try out this new, desirable behavior. There are several ways in which this can be done—simply wait for it to occur spontaneously, provide a model, verbally explain what the desired behavior is, shape it through gradual approximations to the desired actions, or use several of these techniques.
3. Determine what sorts of consequences will be strongly rewarding or reinforcing for the client and what sorts will be punishing.
4. Manipulate the consequences so that the desired behavior, when it

appears, will yield greater reinforcement than does the undesirable behavior. In other words, arrange a schedule of reinforcement and/or punishment that will make it profitable for the client to give up the old behavior in favor of the new.

To foster this process, the counselor explains the purpose and the steps to the client, proposes options regarding the behaviors to eliminate and those to adopt, suggests alternative consequences that can be used to effect the desired substitution, helps the client decide which options to attempt, and aids the counselee in monitoring the behavior-modification process in the weeks ahead. The role of the client is to understand this process and to cooperate in carrying it out.

In relation to the life span, behavioral counseling has been deemed suitable for all age periods. However, the specific way in which it is applied can vary somewhat from one period to another, particularly between childhood and adulthood. Young children are unable, and often unwilling, to actively support the changes that are deemed appropriate by parents or teachers, so the therapist takes full responsibility for selecting the behaviors to be eliminated and those to be adopted, and the therapist identifies and manipulates the consequences without the cooperation of the child. The process is also more firmly in the hands of the therapist in cases of antisocial adult behavior, as with the treatment of criminals who do not willingly choose to change their habits.

CONFRONTING AND ANALYZING REALITY

A large number of counseling approaches are founded on the assumption that a significant part of a client's problems arises from the individual's not understanding or not accepting reality. *Reality* in this sense refers to an "objective" picture of the client's (1) true abilities, attitudes, and potentials, (2) physical and social environments, and (3) available options for actions. While a focus on the nature of reality is significant in many conceptions of counseling, the emphasis on the client's confronting reality is far greater in some approaches than in others. Two examples of counseling methods that display such emphasis are rational-emotive therapy and reality therapy. These two are described solely for the purpose of illustration and do not nearly exhaust the number of such cognitively focused psychotherapies. For example, Mahoney and Gabriel (1987) identified 17 variants of cognitive therapies current in the late 1980s.

Rational-Emotive Therapy

This variety of counseling was originated in 1955 by Albert Ellis, after Ellis judged psychoanalysis to be an inefficient mode of treatment (Ellis, 1985b). Ellis has contended that "people's emotional disturbances and dysfunctional behaviors largely (not completely) stem from their irrational and unrealistic thinking and can be efficiently helped by their making a profound philosophic change" (Ellis, 1985a). The counselor's task is to teach clients—and to have them practice—a number of cognitive, emotive, and behavioral methods of self-control. More precisely, the approach "first employs a number of cognitive methods—including the scientific disputing of irrational ideas, the use of coping statements, cognitive distraction and focusing methods, modeling techniques, semantic procedures, and several psychoeducational techniques. Second, the therapy employs various emotive-evocative methods, such as shame-attacking exercises, rational-emotive imagery, forceful coping statements, role playing, and unconditional acceptance of people with ineffectual behavior. Third, use is made of several behavior methods—especially active-directive homework assignments, in vivo desensitization, reinforcement and penalizing contingencies, skill training, and problem solving" (Ellis, 1985a).

Practitioners of rational-emotive therapy deem the approach suitable for nearly all age levels beyond the earliest years. However, the particular techniques that will be successful are not identical at all stages in the life span, since what works best with clients depends on the level of their analytical skill, their emotional maturity, and their degree of independence (legal, financial, intellectual, emotional) (Ellis & Bernard, 1983).

Reality Therapy

Reality therapy as a counseling method was devised by a psychiatrist, William Glasser, while Glasser was working in a facility for delinquent adolescent girls. Two underlying tenets of Glasser's system are: (1) that innate human drives include the need to love and belong and the need to compete for worth and recognition and (2) that the reason why people often fail to satisfy these needs is that they misperceive their life condition and thereby fail to devise realistic strategies to attain suitable goals.

The practice of reality therapy is comprised of eight steps (Glasser & Glasser, 1985). The counselor:

1. Establishes a warm, trusting relationship with clients, so that the therapist can successfully insist that the clients examine the life that they are currently choosing to live.
2. Asks clients how they are currently living their lives—"What are you doing?"
3. Urges clients to consider how helpful their current behavior is in achieving their desires—"Is what you are doing helping you?"
4-5. Helps clients plan more effective behavior and make a commitment to carrying out the plan.
6-8. Accepts no excuses, does not punish clients, and insists that clients never give up trying to improve.

Glasser's approach has been judged suitable at all age levels from the elementary-school years to old age. In particular, he and his followers have written extensively about the use of reality therapy with children, adolescents, and youths (Glasser, 1969; Glasser, 1981; Cates & Gang, 1976).

FOCUSING ON *BEING* AND ON CREATING GOALS

The concern of some counseling methods is more on the present and future than on the past, and more on one's attitudes toward the environment than on the environment itself. Such methods are often subsumed under the title *existential approaches*. Convictions that different existential techniques share in common include:

1. That the essence of life is centered in one's perception of oneself. Thus, the core of human existence and of proper concern is not found in a person's overt actions or in material possessions or in the opinions of others but, instead, in the nature of one's sense of *being* or *experiencing*.
2. That people are not simply pawns moved around by fate but, rather, that they are responsible for their own actions, so that "external influences (heredity, environment, upbringing) are limiting but not determining" (Osipow, Walsh, & Tosi, 1984, p. 37).
3. That people are continually in a state of movement, of *becoming*. Hence, gaining an intense awareness of one's present *being* and of one's potential for future growth is a key outcome of the counseling process.

Counselors operating from an existential perspective may use any number of techniques for pursuing their goal—reasoning, analyzing, suggesting, instructing, interpreting. In relation to the life span, existential approaches are more suitable for people beyond age 10 or 12. However, some practitioners have adapted their techniques for use with primary-grade children (Castillo, 1971). Three varieties of existential counseling are known as logotherapy, gestalt therapy, and existential psychotherapy.

Frankl's Logotherapy

Logotherapy is the creation of Viktor Frankl, who generated his theory and techniques out of his experience as a prisoner in Nazi concentration camps for Jews during World War II (Frankl, 1962). A basic conviction that Frankl derived from observing which prisoners survived most successfully was that people must find meaning in their lives and that this meaning must transcend any circumstance that might constitute a threat to the individual. As a consequence, people "are capable of maintaining a sense of dignity and freedom even under adverse circumstances. It is this condition, and an awareness of one's right to freedom, that make life meaningful and purposeful" (Downing, 1985, p. 3139).

The techniques of logotherapy are intended to help people explore and clarify their value systems, to guide them toward finding worthy and self-fulfilling goals, and to direct their attention at positive opportunities in their life situation. Logotherapy is considered particularly suitable for people who find life boring or unbearably depressing and worthless. Thus, it is most suitable for people between adolescence and old age. Counseling is directed toward helping each client find meaning in life by identifying a mission to which the individual can enthusiastically dedicate his or her efforts.

Perls' Gestalt Therapy

As a reaction against more intellectual and analytical counseling methods, Frederick S. Perls in the mid-twentieth century created an approach that he labeled *gestalt therapy* (Perls, 1972). This method draws on a variety of counseling techniques that aim at moving clients out of what is called "the intermediate zone of experience, which is a neurotic condition fantasized by clients to avoid contact with their own internal reality or the reality of the world in which they find themselves. Clients maintaining this neurosis have a fear that catastrophic changes will occur if they open themselves to new experiences. They also imagine that they must manipulate those around them to provide environmental support even though they are perfectly capable of self-support" (Brown, 1985, p. 2040).

The counselor's task can involve frustrating and exposing clients' unrealistic conceptions of self and the world, so gestalt therapy serves also as a way of confronting reality. A central purpose of the approach is to convince counselees that they have control over—and thus are responsible for—the choices that they make. They are not simply buffeted about by environmental forces, but they themselves are the ones who determine if and how they will respond to what is happening around them. Any attention given in counseling sessions to past experiences in clients' lives is intended only to clarify their present condition, since the focus of gestalt therapy is on the *now* and on one's *current being*. The therapist serves as an instrument to give selective feedback about the effect that the counselee is having on the therapist. Such feedback is intended to be mainly descriptive, rather than interpretive or judgmental.

Because a gestalt approach requires that clients express feelings and opinions with some fluency and that they seriously consider ways to reconstruct their world view, the method is best suited to people beyond the age of childhood—that is, from mid-adolescence until old age.

May's Existential Psychotherapy

The main therapeutic function of Rollo May's existential approach is to "help the patient confront the normal anxiety which is an unavoidable part of the human condition" (May & Yalom in Corsini, 1984, pp. 355-356). The client selects the goal of being freed of distress, anxiety, or neurotic symptoms. The therapist selects the goal of uncovering the client's repressed conflicts, of altering unconstructive defense mechanisms, and of generating in the client a sense of being (I-Am) in order to achieve the client's goal of dispelling the unreasonable anxiety and neurotic symptoms.

The therapist assumes that the client experiences anxiety which issues from some existential conflict that is at least partially unconscious, so the therapist assists the patient in self-investigation with the aim of understanding the unconscious conflict, identifying maladaptive defense mechanisms, discovering their destructive influence, diminishing secondary anxiety by correcting these heretofore restrictive modes of dealing with self and others, and developing other ways of coping with primary anxiety. In contrast to psychoanalysis and other dynamic-psychology approaches, "the existential view of personality structure emphasizes the depth of experience at any given moment, [so] the existential therapist does not spend a great deal of time in therapy helping the patient to recover a personal past. The existential therapist strives for understanding...the patient's *current* life situation and *current* enveloping unconscious fears" (May & Yalom, 1984, pp. 373-374).

ADDRESSING MAKE-BELIEVE SITUATIONS

Three techniques that involve clients' participating in imagined incidents are those of (1) play therapy, (2) case discussions, and (3) psychodrama and sociodrama.

Play Therapy

Play therapy, as a counseling approach, is most appropriate during early and middle childhood, from around age 2 to 9, when children are unable or reluctant to discuss directly their feelings and problems, yet they are often able to reflect their concerns in the way in which they play with such toys as dolls or puppets that might represent members of their own family. The materials used for stimulating children's reactions are not limited to dolls but may also include blocks, construction materials, vehicles, easel paints, finger paints, clay or dough for modeling, and more.

The responsibility of the counselor is to furnish the child with stimulating toys, to establish a permissive and accepting emotional climate in which the child can play, and to offer comments and questions intended to elicit reactions from the child that can depict the child's perceptions of self, of parents, or school, and the like. The hope of the counselor is that the toys will stimulate the child to act and talk in a self-revealing fashion which helps clarify for the therapist the child's view of the world. The play setting is also intended to provide an outlet for the child's feelings of distress (promoting catharsis) and to offer an opportunity for the counselor to suggest to the child more constructive interpretations of reality than those that the child now harbors.

Case Discussions

The phrase *case discussions* is used here to identify an approach that consists of the counselor's furnishing cases from life for the client to comment about. Sometimes the participants in a case are carried only to a crisis point in the incident, and the client is then asked how the people in the case might best solve their problems. The client may also be asked to suggest different options for resolving a problem and then predict what the consequences of the various options are likely to be. In some instances, the cases will be carried through to an end point, illustrating the decisions reached by the people in the incidents and the consequences that resulted. In this event, the case serves as an example of a resolution which the client might copy in his or her own life or might evaluate for its desirability.

The cases for discussion can be of several types—protocols from the therapist's own records, examples from textbooks, incidents from published biographies, or events drawn from short stories and novels. Often the approach is used in group counseling, providing an opportunity for clients to hear varied interpretations of the cases so that a diversity of ways to react to problem situations is illustrated.

The task of the counselor in case discussions is to select stimulating cases, present them in an interesting manner, pose questions on which the clients' discussion can profitably focus, and react to the clients' comments in a manner that (1) promotes counselees' insight into their own and others' behavior, (2) offers new options for problem solving, and (3) furthers clients' understanding of the variety of consequences that their problem-solving decisions may produce.

The responsibility of clients is to engage seriously and willingly in the discussion of the cases and, when in a group setting, to respect—or at least politely tolerate—the opinions of the other participants.

Case discussions can be used at all periods of life from around age 3 or 4 to the end of the life span.

Psychodrama and Sociodrama

The terms *role playing, psychodrama,* and *sociodrama* are often used interchangeably because they appear to share much in common. Indeed, both psychodrama and sociodrama can suitably be categorized under the heading of role playing, since both of them involve people's acting out assigned roles in an unrehearsed, spontaneous simulated situation. But for purposes of analysis, it is useful to distinguish psychodrama from sociodrama in terms of the emphasis that they may represent in a counseling setting. Psychodrama can emphasize what is going on *inside the individual,* either while he or she struggles alone with inner problems or while he or she interacts with others in a social setting (Blatner, 1973; Moreno, 1969). Sociodrama, on the other hand, can emphasize how the actions of one person in a social setting affect the actions of the others. Both of these emphases—on the individual's inner struggle and on the pattern of transactions among people—can be useful in counseling situations.

Role playing can assume several forms and can serve different purposes. In one form of psychodrama, the client presents a problem that he or she currently faces, and other participants—such as the therapist and an assistant or other clients in a therapy group—then act out the apparent contending forces within the client's mind, with one person perhaps representing the client's conscience, another the client's anger, and a third the client's need for affection or success. The purpose in this case is to assist the counselee in exposing the contending inner forces that are involved in his or her psychological problem and in analyzing these forces so as to achieve a constructive resolution of the conflict.

In another form of role playing, a typical social-conflict situation from one or more clients' lives is introduced by either the therapist or a counselee, and different members of the group are then assigned to play the parts of the people in the conflict. In assigning the parts, the therapist gives each participant a different role than he or she typically assumes in life—such as giving an adolescent boy the mother's role to play and a middle-aged woman an adolescent boy's role. The intention of this form of reverse-role sociodrama is to encourage participants to understand more fully the motives, attitudes, and problem-solving attempts of the people whom they meet in daily life and, because of this understanding, to adopt more suitable modes of interaction with such people.

Another variation of the role-playing technique requires the counselee to imagine that an authority figure in his or her life is sitting in a chair. The counselee then expresses to the imagined individual the pent-up feelings that he or she has harbored toward that individual but has never before expressed. The authority figure may be the counselee's mother, father, employer, teacher, or lover. The purposes of this approach are to afford the counselee the opportunity for catharsis by venting fears and resentments, to bring into the open the client's feelings of both affection and anger so that these feelings may be put into a more constructive perspective, and to display to the counselor attitudes which the client holds that are important for the therapist to understand if the counseling process is to progress.

A further form of sociodrama involves placing clients in various roles to spontaneously act out psychosocial conflicts that they face in life, affording them the opportunity to play the scene over a number of times in order to practice different ways of interacting with others and thus to determine which of the ways seems most profitable.

Role playing can be used at all stages of life from middle childhood to old age.

ALTERING BODY CHEMISTRY

One way in which drugs are used in counseling situations is to artificially create "normal" biological effects that the individual seems unable to produce without chemical treatment. People whose life-styles or physical condition put them in a state of continual tension or pain often take drugs to induce relaxation and sleep. Although such treatment may constructively effect a temporary release from the distressing symptoms, it may also lead to an addiction which in the long run is destructive. As a consequence, drug treatment can lead to the necessity for further psychotherapy and perhaps to other drugs to counteract the addiction.

Drugs or a change in diet may also have a different purpose—to correct an imbalance of the substances that the body needs to operate properly. In other words, if the human body is viewed as an electrochemical organism governed by the types of fuel and building substances that the person ingests, then the food and drugs entering the body will influence the efficiency of the body's activity, both physically and mentally. Some nutritional and drug treatments of psychological or behavior disturbances are based on the conviction that psychopathology is the result, at least partially, of biochemical imbalances that affect the operation of the individual's neural system. The biological model on which these types of drug therapy operate proposes that messages, in the form of electrical impulses, travel through the brain via individual nerve cells or neurons. For an impulse to pass from one neuron to another, the first cell must release a neurotransmitting chemical substance into the space separating the two neurons, a space called the synaptic cleft. The neurotransmitting substance activates receptor sites on the receiving neuron, causing the receptor cell to electrically fire and carry the message to other neurons. Either too much or too little of a substance will alter perception, mood, thinking, or overt behavior. Therefore, malfunctions in the production, release, or reclamation of neurotransmitters are proposed as the cause, in part, of several types of abnormal behavior (K. E. Thomas, 1985a).

Over recent decades, therapists have increasingly turned to drugs and to changes in diet for the treatment of the types of problems brought before the counseling psychologist and psychiatrist. Such treatment has been applied at all stages of the life span, from early infancy until the end of life, and it has usually been accompanied by some form of psychotherapy.

ENLIGHTENED ECLECTICISM

As noted at the beginning of this chapter, counseling methods have been presented here as a series of different types, as a convenient way to review a variety of methods within a limited space. In so doing, it has not been intended to imply that most counselors adhere strictly to a single technique. Indeed, observations of therapists in action suggest not only that typical counselors adopt different techniques with different clients, but also that they may use different techniques at various stages in counseling the same client.

In writing about theories and "schools" of psychotherapy, Goldstein and Stein (1976, p. 4) have argued that:

> a one-true-light assumption has dominated much of our thinking about the conduct and conceptualization of psychotherapy. Stimulated by the unidimensionality or "unimethodology" of many clinical training centers, and abetted by the practitioner need to hang one's procedural hat on a consistent theoretical framework, most practitioners essentially know, practice, are committed to, and overtly champion a single therapeutic approach. While such singularity of orientation may be therapeutically beneficial for patients for whom the given treatment has been shown to be appropriate, concerns arise when it is utilized with patients for whom it is either inert or counter productive.

Evidence from a variety of sources suggests that these authors have probably overstated their claim that most practitioners are dedicated to a single counseling approach. While it appears to be true that most counselors have indeed had more experience with, and are particularly enthusiastic about, a given type or "school" of psychotherapy, in practice the majority apparently draw on a variety of techniques, adjusting their methods to the age level, type of presenting problem, and cultural characteristics of the client at hand. This strategy is sometimes called enlightened or skilled eclecticism. Such eclecticism seems particularly appropriate for the work of counselors whose clients are drawn from different stages of the life span.

As advocates of skilled eclecticism, Goldstein and Stein (1976, p. 3) propose that future research on the effectiveness of therapeutic approaches can profitably assume a form different from the dominant pattern of such research in the past.

> Researchers have but barely begun to ask, much less to answer, approximations to the proper therapy outcome question: Which treatment procedures, administered by which therapist to which patient, with which specific problems are predicted to yield which outcomes?

CONCLUSION

It should be recognized that the list of counseling approaches surveyed in this chapter has been illustrative, certainly not definitive. However, the illustrations that have been included should be sufficient for helping readers to understand the applications of techniques mentioned in Chapters 4 through 9.

PART 2

Life-Span Stages and Counseling

4

Infancy and Early Childhood: The Prenatal Period Through Age 5

The most rapid, dramatic developmental changes of the entire life span occur during the first half-decade. From the moment of conception—at the time when a sperm cell from the father enters an ovum in the mother—through age five, the newly created human changes from a single, undifferentiated cell into a physically agile, self-directed kindergarten child who talks, understands others' speech, solves problems, remembers events, sings tunes, draws pictures, counts, begins to read, reacts to television programs, expresses joy and sorrow, distinguishes between those social skills to use with adults and those to use with age-mates, and much more.

What a counselor knows about development during this early period of life is typically most useful in cases of:

—Pregnant women who wish to discover how their own behavior during pregnancy may affect the development of the unborn child that they carry.
—Parents seeking to learn what to expect of their young child and wanting to know what child-raising practices are best during the rapidly changing periods of growth in these early years.
—Parents who disagree strongly with each other about how to rear a young child, so that relationships within the family become fraught with conflict.
—Parents distressed by the way in which children in the family act toward one another. Sometimes this is a case of sibling rivalry arising from an older child's becoming disturbed by the arrival of a newborn brother or sister. Also, with the rise in divorce rates, more and more children of divorced parents are cast into new family constellations as their parents remarry and a new spouse brings a strange set of children to live with them.

—A child's parents or guardians, accused of child neglect or child abuse, who are sent for counseling by the court, a social agency, or a friend.   .

—A child whose development is judged as deficient, so the child is taken to a therapist for help.

The normative information about child development in Chapter 4 has been selected because of its usefulness in such situations as the above. The first half of the chapter offers an overview of developmental trends that helps to explain (1) the kinds of growth problems commonly occurring from conception through age five, (2) the causes of such problems, and (3) the characteristics that people often believe represent *normal* or *desirable* development at this stage of life. The second half of the chapter offers normative data bearing on two prominent types of difficulty that often bring clients to counselors during the early years of life: (1) child abuse and neglect and (2) childhood handicaps.

At the outset, it is important to recognize that when counseling is directed at solving problems of infants and young children, there is more than one client—the child and the child's principal caregivers. During the earliest years, the counseling encounter may be exclusively between the therapist and the parent or guardian and may not directly involve the infant at all. The purpose of therapy in this event is to guide the caregiver in providing an environment to promote the infant's optimal development. As the child grows older, approaching ages three to five, the therapist can increasingly work directly with the child or meet with the child and the parent together. When working with a young child, counselors typically employ some form of play therapy and adjust their mode of speech to the cognitive characteristics described in the following discussion of developmental trends during the first half-decade of life.

DEVELOPMENTAL TRENDS FROM
CONCEPTION THROUGH AGE FIVE

The following overview begins with a discussion of factors during the prenatal period that can affect an infant's start in life. Then the discussion traces growth trends from birth until the time when the child is ready to enter the first grade of elementary school.

Genetic Endowment and the Interuterine Environment

How well a newborn is equipped to begin life at birth depends both on the combination of genes contributed by the father and mother at conception and on the environment that the mother's womb provides throughout pregnancy.

PROBLEMS SEATED IN GENETIC FACTORS

Once conception has taken place, nothing can be done to alter the inherited genetic structure. However, as the initial impregnated cell rapidly divides, multiplies, and evolves into special parts to form an embryo and subsequently a fetus within the mother's uterus, information can be gained about genetically based conditions of the unborn child that may endanger optimal growth after that child's birth. Furthermore, from information about the parents' own developmental backgrounds, the probability of a child's inheriting undesirable characteristics can be predicted ahead of time. Counselors find that knowledge about such genetic influences is valuable in cases of women who wish to become pregnant or women who are already pregnant and hope to estimate ahead of time their unborn child's chances for normal development after birth. For example, the risk of bearing a child with Down's syndrome increases when the mother is beyond the age of 30, with the risk becoming even greater by the age of 40. A further example of genetic influence is found in the way in which the blood type that the mother inherited from her parents can interact with the blood types of the infants that she bears. As Blackman (1983, p. 188) has explained:

> A woman with Rh negative blood may have an infant with Rh positive blood. If minute amounts of blood from the infant enter the mother's circulation—which usually happens at the time of delivery—they are recognized as foreign by the mother's system; her body reacts by developing an immunity to that type of blood. Antibodies against Rh positive blood remain in the mother's circulatory system and, in subsequent pregnancies, pass through the placenta to the fetus. Unless the unborn child has Rh negative blood like the mother, these antibodies will destroy the child's red blood cells, causing severe anemia.

As a preventive measure, a mother with Rh negative blood should be advised to have a special injection immediately after each delivery

to counteract the destructive response of her antibodies to Rh positive blood cells from the infant.

PROBLEMS OF THE INTERUTERINE ENVIRONMENT

Even more important than knowledge of genetic influences is
knowledge about ways in which the mother's habits during pregnancy can influence the child's developmental fate. While the mother
can do nothing to affect the child's genetic structure either during
pregnancy or after birth, she can do much to influence the interuterine environment inhabited by the embryo and fetus.

A variety of conditions affecting the interuterine environment can
bode ill for the infant's start in life. One source of damage to the fetus
is the mother's ingesting harmful substances classified as *teratogens*.
Prominent among the substances are illicit drugs (cocaine, heroin),
tobacco smoke, alcohol, caffeine, and certain legal drugs used as
tranquilizers, antibiotics (especially tetracycline and streptomycin),
anticonvulsants, and anticoagulants (including aspirin) (Eriksson,
Catz, & Yaffe, 1973; Howard & Hill, 1979).

The mother's blood system transports nutrients to the fetus by
means of blood vessels in the umbilical cord that pass into the
placenta, which is a layer of membranes connecting the mother's
circulatory system with that of the fetus. The placenta permits only
small molecules to pass through, so there is no direct connection
between the mother's blood and that of the fetus. However, many
drugs passing through the mother's circulatory system can penetrate
the placental barrier, thus directly affecting fetal development.
Infants born of mothers addicted to heroin or cocaine arrive in the
world already addicted, and they suffer withdrawal symptoms that
can be fatal (Brazelton, 1970). A mother's cigarette smoking can cause
a variety of difficulties for the unborn child, including a shortage of
oxygen which results from nicotine's constricting the mother's blood
vessels. Smoking may also contribute to miscarriage, to the malfor-
mation of organs (heart, lungs), to nervous-system damage when
carbon dioxide rather than oxygen passes through the placental
barrier, to low birth weight, and to fatal birth defects (Himmelberger,
Brown, & Cohen, 1978; Naeye, Ladis, & Drage, 1976; Niswander &
Gordon, 1972).

Women who are undernourished and suffer unusual stress while
pregnant are also likely to damage their unborn child in ways that
will last over the child's lifetime. Brazelton (1986, pp. 520-521) has

reported that "As much as 40% of the potential DNA content of the brain and other vital organs may never be made in the developing human fetus if the mother's protein intake is below a critical level during pregnancy." In one study, infants born at full term from undernourished, stressed mothers were immature in development and behavior—"more difficult to arouse . . . and bring to responsive states for interaction . . . we could predict with 80% certainty in the neonatal period which infants would suffer from marasmus [thinness, dry skin, poor muscle development, irritability] in the latter half of the first year or from kwashiorkor [retarded growth, changes in skin pigmentation, potbelly, anemia] in the second year of life" (p. 521).

Expectant mothers who contract rubella (German measles) during the first three months of gestation, particularly when the fetus is growing rapidly, are likely to bear deaf, blind, or mentally retarded babies. Rubella can be prevented by vaccination. If the mother was not vaccinated for German measles as a child, she can be vaccinated as an adult, but it should be done at least three months before pregnancy to provide complete immunization. A vaccination during the first three months of pregnancy has the same effect on the embryo-fetus as does rubella itself.

A mother infected with syphilis can also produce a deformed infant, one suffering from blindness, deafness, or mental retardation. However, if the intended mother is successfully treated for the disease within the first 18 weeks of pregnancy, the fetus will probably not be infected (Bee, 1981, p. 57).

Other diseases in which the agent is small enough to pass from the pregnant woman's bloodstream into that of the unborn child are rubeola (another form of measles), diphtheria, influenza, typhoid, and chicken pox.

From Birth Until Primary School

It is apparent that one aspect of an individual's life, such as physical growth, does not operate independently of other aspects, such as intellectual, social, or emotional development. Instead, all are interconnected. However, when discussing growth, it is not possible to consider all aspects simultaneously. So for convenience sake, the following overview of the early years is organized under five categories that seem particularly useful for guiding counseling decisions: (1) physical size, appearance, and functions, (2) cognition and language, (3) social relationships, (4) sexual behavior, and (5) self-perception.

PHYSICAL SIZE, APPEARANCE, AND FUNCTIONS

A common concern among parents of a newborn is whether the baby is physically normal. They want to know if all the organs are in place and functioning properly, if the infant's energy level is high, and if the child is free from disfiguring features. These questions about a neonate's physical well-being are usually addressed to a medical doctor or a nurse, but counselors also are asked about such matters, especially when parents want to know what a particular characteristic, such as a physical handicap, may portend for the child's future. Parents also ask which child-rearing methods they should adopt in order to foster the infant's optimal development.

The pattern of general physical growth over the first two decades of life is reflected in Figure 4.1. The steep increase in physical size and complexity during the prenatal period continues into the early post-natal years, then begins to taper off in middle and late childhood, only to display a new spurt of rapid growth in early adolescence, a trend which again tapers off in the late teen years until the ultimate height, weight, and strength of age 20 is reached. During infancy, when the child's growth changes noticeably by the month, parents typically seek normative information about growth to determine whether their baby is progressing as well as should be expected. In this endeavor, they often consult height and weight charts to see how their child compares with the average. If they discuss these matters with a counselor, the counselor may be of aid by suggesting several considerations that they can keep in mind as they use norma-tive data in making judgments about their child.

Typical height and weight charts in the past have offered average heights and weights at each age level. People using such charts have usually interpreted the average for an age as being *normal* height and weight, with the inference that *normal* in such cases meant *desirable*. Such charts, however, may fail to reflect several·important factors that can influence the interpretation of what the data imply for an individual child. These factors can include gender, parental stature, extent of variability within an age-group, and time of year.

In the case of gender, it is clear that there are significant differences between girls and boys in their patterns of physical growth. Tanner (1978, p. 15) has noted that "... the typical girl is slightly shorter than

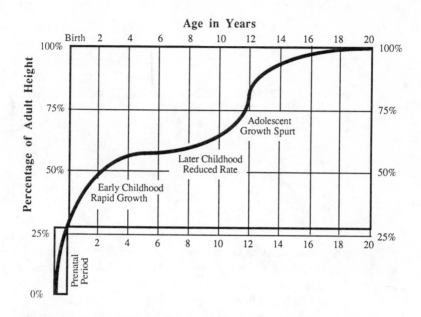

Figure 4.1. Physical Growth Rate—Conception to Age 20

the typical boy at all ages until adolescence. She becomes taller shortly after 11.0 years because her adolescent spurt takes place two years earlier than the boy's. At 14.0 she is surpassed again in height by the typical boy, whose adolescent spurt has now started, whereas her's is nearly finished. In the same way, the typical girl weighs a little less than the boy at birth, equals him at age 8.0, becomes heavier at age 9 or 10 and remains so till about age 14.5."

As for parental stature, shorter parents, on the average, have shorter children than do taller parents. In effect, the genetic endowment, as well as the health care and nutrition that today's parents provide their offspring, tend to make children somewhat similar to their parents in stature. For instance, the correlation between parents' and children's heights is around +.5. Recognizing this, some producers of height charts have offered different averages for children whose parents are short than for ones whose parents are tall. Table 4.1 illustrates a chart of this variety.

Table 4.1 Heights of Children from Birth to Age 6 Based on Averaged Height of Parents

| | BOYS | | | GIRLS | | |
| | Parents' Averaged Height | | | Parents' Averaged Height | | |
Child's Age in Years	163 cm*	171 cm	178 cm	163 cm	171 cm	178 cm
Birth	47.1 cm	48.3 cm	51.4 cm	48.9 cm	48.8 cm	47.5 cm
1/2	65.1	65.8	70.3	64.7	66.5	73.2
1	73.1	73.4	77.8	73.0	75.2	73.2
2	85.4	87.8	91.3	84.0	88.8	87.6
3	93.2	97.2	99.9	90.4	97.1	96.2
4	99.5	104.6	107.0	96.8	104.9	104.3
5	105.6	111.5	113.8	103.5	111.6	111.7
6	110.9	117.4	119.8	110.2	118.2	118.8

*NOTE: To convert centimeters to inches, multiply by .39.
SOURCE: Data adapted from Lowrey, 1978.

In regard to variability, it is clear that not all children score exactly at the average on any measure. In fact, relatively few are precisely average. Therefore, it is useful to learn how an age group is distributed around the average. In judging the significance of the height of a given child, it makes a difference if the entire age group is bunched closely around the middle or is spread out widely from the average. Therefore, information about the extent of variability of an age group is helpful. Tables 4.2 and 4.3 display such variability in terms of the percentage of children at, below, or above a particular height or weight at a given age. For example, numbers under the 5th percentile in Table 4.2 give the height below which the shortest 5% of children fall at each age level. Numbers under the 50th percentile show the height that divides the shorter half of the age-group from the taller half. Numbers under the 90th percentile show the height above which the tallest 10% of children in an age-group fall. A similar mode of analysis is used for interpreting the weights in Table 4.3.

During the early years of life, when changes occur so rapidly, the time of the child's birthday becomes a significant consideration in judging how close the child is to the figures on growth charts. In the preparation of age-based statistics, it is usually the case that the children on whom the average for a particular age was based are all those who reached that age on their last birthday, whether the birthday was last week or 50 weeks ago. Therefore, the reported

Table 4.2 Heights of Children by Percentiles; Birth Through Age 5

Sex and Age	5th	10th	25th	50th	75th	90th	95th
			PERCENTILES				
GIRLS							
Birth	45.4 cm*	46.5 cm	48.2 cm	49.9 cm	51.0 cm	52.0 cm	52.9 cm
3 months	55.4	56.2	57.8	59.5	61.2	62.7	63.4
6 months	61.8	62.6	64.2	65.9	67.8	69.4	70.2
9 months	66.1	67.0	68.7	70.4	72.4	74.0	75.0
12 months	69.8	70.8	72.4	74.3	76.3	78.0	79.1
18 months	76.0	77.2	78.8	80.9	83.0	85.0	86.1
2 years	81.3	82.5	84.2	86.5	88.7	90.8	92.0
3 years	90.0	91.0	93.1	95.6	98.1	100.0	101.5
4 years	95.0	96.4	98.8	101.6	104.3	106.6	108.3
5 years	101.1	102.7	105.4	108.4	111.4	113.8	115.6
BOYS							
Birth	46.4 cm	47.5 cm	49.0 cm	50.5 cm	51.8 cm	53.5 cm	54.4 cm
3 months	56.7	57.7	59.4	61.1	63.0	64.5	65.4
6 months	63.4	64.4	66.1	67.8	69.7	71.3	72.3
9 months	68.0	69.1	70.6	72.3	74.0	75.9	77.1
12 months	71.7	72.8	74.3	76.1	77.7	79.8	81.2
18 months	77.5	78.7	80.5	82.4	84.3	86.6	88.1
2 years	82.3	83.5	85.6	87.6	89.9	92.2	93.8
3 years	91.2	92.4	94.2	96.5	98.9	101.4	103.1
4 years	95.8	97.3	100.0	102.9	105.7	108.2	109.9
5 years	102.0	103.7	106.5	109.9	112.8	115.4	117.0

*NOTE: To convert centimeters to inches, multiply by .39.
SOURCE: Data dapated from Hamill, 1977.

average for age 3 is most applicable to children who are halfway through their third year of life. That average is not as applicable to a child who has just turned 3 (and by comparison will appear small) or one who is about to turn 4 (and by comparison will look large). This matter of birth date is particularly important in judgments of physical growth in infants born prematurely. For example, in comparisons of pre-term infants to normative data, "A child born at 36 weeks instead of 40 should not, 6 months after birth, be plotted at age 6 months, or 26 postnatal weeks, but at 22 postnatal weeks. Failure to do this can result in considerable error in the first year after birth" (Tanner, 1978, pp. 184-185).

Therefore, while normative data about physical growth, reported by age levels, provide a useful basis of comparison in judgments of an individual child, such data need to be interpreted with considerable

Table 4.3 Weights of Children by Percentiles; Birth Through Age 5

Sex and Age	5th	10th	25th	50th	75th	90th	95th
				PERCENTILES			
GIRLS							
Birth	2.36 kilo*	2.58 kilo	2.93 kilo	3.23 kilo	3.52 kilo	3.64 kilo	3.81 kilo
3 months	4.18	4.47	4.88	5.40	5.90	6.39	6.74
6 months	5.79	6.12	6.60	7.21	7.83	8.38	8.73
9 months	7.10	7.34	7.89	8.56	9.24	9.83	10.17
12 months	7.84	8.19	8.81	9.53	10.23	10.87	11.24
18 months	8.92	9.30	10.04	10.82	11.55	12.30	12.76
2 years	9.87	10.26	11.10	11.90	12.74	13.57	14.08
3 years	11.60	12.07	12.99	13.93	15.03	15.97	16.54
4 years	13.11	13.84	14.80	15.96	17.56	18.93	19.91
5 years	14.55	15.26	16.29	17.66	19.39	21.23	22.62
BOYS							
Birth	2.54 kilo	2.78 kilo	3.00 kilo	3.27 kilo	3.64 kilo	3.82 kilo	4.15 kilo
3 months	4.43	4.78	5.32	5.98	6.56	7.14	7.37
6 months	6.20	6.61	7.20	7.85	8.49	9.10	9.46
9 months	7.52	7.95	8.56	9.18	9.88	10.49	10.93
12 months	8.43	8.84	9.49	10.15	10.91	11.54	11.99
18 months	9.59	9.92	10.67	11.47	12.31	13.05	13.44
2 years	10.54	10.85	11.65	12.59	13.44	14.29	14.70
3 years	12.26	12.69	13.58	14.69	15.59	16.66	17.28
4 years	13.64	14.24	15.39	16.69	17.99	19.32	20.27
5 years	15.27	15.96	17.22	18.67	20.14	21.70	23.09

*NOTE: To convert kilograms to pounds, multiply by 2.2.
SOURCE: Data adapted from Hamill, 1977.

caution so that unwarranted conclusions are not drawn about how adequately the child is developing physically. As Tanner (1978, p. 10) has warned, cross-sectional data based on measuring groups of children at successive age levels "have one great drawback; they can never reveal individual differences in rate or velocity of growth or in the timing of particular phases such as the adolescent growth spurt." Children can be somewhat off the average in basic physical characteristics yet be progressing quite satisfactorily in terms of their health, energy level, regularity of growth, and their ability to cope with tasks suited to their present size. Therefore, judgments about the desirability of a particular child's physical-development pattern require attention to the consistency in that child's own growth rather than simply basing these judgments on how that child's height, weight, musculature, and agility compare with the average for his or her age.

Not only do parents wish to assess their child's current physical growth, but frequently they also want to know what these present growth characteristics suggest for the child's future size, strength, and agility. In other words, they seek evidence about the correlation between physical traits of infancy or early childhood and the same traits in adolescence and adulthood. Normative data about such matters are available. Although predictions of adult height based on an infant's length (compared to that of its age-mates) are not very accurate during the first two years of life, when the child reaches age 3, the correlation with adult height advances to around +.8 (Tanner, 1978, p. 125). Thus, in general, a 3-year-old girl who is taller than her age-mates will likely be taller than other women when she is an adult. However, a prediction made on the basis of a +.8 correlation still leaves considerable room for error. When this child reaches adulthood, she could be as much as 8 centimeters (3.15 inches) above or below the predicted height. Therefore, it is again important to recognize that predictions need to be interpreted with care, since they are based on group averages that do not accommodate adequately for all the factors that influence the growth of an individual. Yet, such correlations, if they are relatively high, can improve estimates about a child's future status and, in this way, may prepare parents to adopt a constructive child-rearing attitude as the child moves toward his or her future physical status. For example, if a boy is somewhat below average in height at age 4, it is likely—though not inevitable—that he will be below average as an adolescent and adult as well. A counselor may aid parents in preparing for this expectation by guiding them toward treating their son in ways that encourage him to develop a strong sense of self-worth and to make the most of his potential in the future. Counseling techniques for accomplishing such a goal are considered later in the chapter under the topics of childhood handicaps.

Keeping in mind the foregoing cautions about individual differences in growth rates, an estimate of the stature that a child ultimately will reach in adulthood can be based on normative data about the average percentage of adult height for children at different age levels. For example, in a study of California children, boys age 3 had 53.5% and girls had 57% of their ultimate height. At age 6, the percentages were 65.3 for boys and 70.3 for girls; at age 9, 75.6 for boys and 81.2 for girls; at age 10, 84 for boys and 92.6 for girls; and at age 15, 94.6 for boys and 99.3 for girls. A study of children from Boston yielded very similar results (Malina & Roche, 1968, Vol. 1). Thus, at all age levels, girls were approaching their ultimate height more rapidly than were boys.

Whereas the foregoing discussion has centered on height and weight as physical characteristics, the same kinds of considerations about multiple factors affecting growth need to be kept in mind when judgments are made about the desirability of other facets of a young child's physical development, such as musculature, strength, dexterity, agility, body proportions, and the like. Table 4.4 displays the average ages (50th percentile) at which infants accomplish various psychophysical tasks and the range of variability between the earliest and latest ages (5th and 95th percentiles) for illustrative items on the Bayley Scale of Infant Development. A comparison of the 5th and 95th percentiles for successively advanced tasks demonstrates the general phenomenon of increased variability with increased age that obtains for all sorts of physical and psychological measures. The earlier maturers progress farther and farther ahead of the later maturers.

COGNITION AND LANGUAGE

Adults often appear to believe that the naive thoughts expressed by the young result simply from children's lack of experience. Hence, the remedy for children's faulty thinking should be to give them the kind of instruction that will set their minds aright. However, studies of mental growth demonstrate that children are not merely uninformed adults. Instead, over the first dozen years or so of life, children advance through successive stages of thinking, with each stage displaying its own characteristics. During these years, children think differently than do older children and adults. So, unless adults adjust their expectations and their instruction to fit these periods, they are bound to fail in the attempt to "smarten up" the child. In understanding early cognitive development, we need to recognize that progress through the cognitive-growth stages is determined by a combination of the internal maturation of the nervous system and the child's daily experiences.

The researcher most influential in delineating stages of children's mental growth was the Swiss psychologist Jean Piaget (1896-1980). One popular version of Piaget's system casts cognitive development into four main periods that range from birth into adolescence (R. M. Thomas, 1985a, pp. 272-284). The first two periods—called the sen-

Table 4.4 Ages at Which Infants Perform Common Tasks

		Percentiles		
	Task	5th	50th	95th
		Earliest Age	Median	Latest Age
Head held vertically erect and steady		0.7 months	1.6 months	4.0 months
Sits with slight support		1.0	2.3	5.0
Sits alone momentarily		4.0	5.3	8.0
Sits alone steadily		5.0	6.6	9.0
Early stepping movements		5.0	7.4	11.0
Stands up by furniture		6.0	8.6	12.0
Walks alone		9.0	11.7	17.0
Throws ball		9.0	13.3	18.0
Walks up stairs alone, both feet on each step		18.0	25.1	30+

SOURCE: Data adapted from Malina & Roche, 1983, Vol. 2, 11-12.

sorimotor and the preoperational stages—occur during the years of infancy and early childhood. The third and fourth periods appear during the elementary-school and junior-high years.

Sensorimotor Period—Birth to Age 2

In the first two years of life, infants achieve only a very rudimentary command of language. Therefore, evidence of their cognitive growth during this time must derive from observations of how they increasingly pay attention to objects and events (sensory acts) and how they physically respond to the events (motor acts). Within this period, Piaget identified six substages which mark infants' progress from only performing reflex actions, to gradually perceiving the effect of their actions on objects, then to distinguishing between self and objects, to anticipating people and objects, and finally to representing objects mentally and thereby cognitively combining and manipulating them.

The Preoperational-Thought Period—About Age 2 to About Age 7

In Piaget's system, the term *operations* means manipulating objects in relation to each other. However, this is not just any sort of manipulation. In order to qualify as operations, actions must be internalizable, reversible, and coordinated into systems which have laws that apply to the entire system and not just to the single action itself. By *internalizable*, Piaget meant that the actions can be carried out in thought without losing their original character of physical manipulations. By *reversible*, he meant that they can readily be inverted into their opposite—two groups of apples that are combined (added together) to form a whole group can as easily be reduced (subtracted from the whole) to their original status as two groups. As the phrase *preoperational-thought period* implies, the child before about age 7 is not yet able to carry out mental operations in the above sense but is still in the stage of preparation for performing true operations (Piaget, 1972, p. 8).

Several characteristics of young children's thought processes which adults often fail to recognize are those of egocentrism versus objectivity, fantasy versus reality, the internalization of action, relationships and classes, language development, and literal versus figurative language. The following examples illustrate how such matters can affect adults' child-rearing practices and the counseling process.

Egocentrism Versus Objectivity. Young children are highly self-centered, in that they interpret the world entirely from their own perspective. They fail to understand that other people may see things differently or that others deserve to have the same rights that they themselves desire. They find it difficult or impossible to imagine themselves in someone else's shoes. When the nursery-school teacher explains that "We're going to take turns so that everyone has a chance to use the paints," the typical child expects to get the first turn and to use the paints as long as he or she likes. A teacher or parent who presents a logical argument for fairness and equal rights to the young child and then expects the child to abide willingly by the principles of the argument is usually disappointed. Moral principles of even-handed justice and compassion can become meaningful during the elementary-school years and can be very important to adolescents, but, during the first half-decade of life, they generally fall on deaf ears. It is not that young children are seeking to be wicked; it is simply that their cognitive limitations do not enable them to understand others' viewpoints or to grasp the broader, long-term consequences of self-centered behavior.

In counseling cases that involve parent-child conflicts, an important cause behind such conflicts is often the adult's failure to understand that egocentrism is natural in preschoolers. As a consequence, parents' arguing at length with the child about matters of fairness and objectivity is a futile endeavor. In the realm of social relations and moral behavior, the young child is guided more by whether a given act will result in an immediate reward or punishment than by principles of "rules should be obeyed" or "treat others as you would want to be treated."

Fantasy Versus Reality. One of the important tasks in life, from the viewpoint of counseling, is for people to distinguish which things are real and which are imaginary. This is a particularly demanding endeavor during early childhood, when children lack skills of judging what tests to apply in order to determine whether something is true. The young child who watches television does not know that the frightening monsters in cartoon programs are simply drawings and do not exist in reality. Furthermore, the young do not know how likely it is that the violence of crime and war portrayed in so many television dramas might occur in their own neighborhood. And when conflicts between mother and father result in the parents' abusing each other verbally or physically, the young cannot accurately judge how much they themselves are at fault and thus deserve blame for their parents' fights, separation, and divorce.

Therefore, counseling with the young often involves attending to children's confusion, fears, and feelings of guilt and shame that are seated in their mistaking fantasy for reality. In such cases, it becomes the therapist's task to help the preschooler distinguish the real from the imagined, a task frequently best accomplished in a play-therapy setting.

The Internalization of Action. During the early years of life, children are still not adept at manipulating ideas solely in their minds. They generally need to see and hear directly the things that they are to think about. Only later, as their cognitive apparatus becomes more mature, can they internalize actions—that is, act on objects and ideas that are represented entirely in their minds.

This phenomenon of early childhood can be illustrated with speech. During the years 1-4, the child begins to talk a lot, and the talk is of two varieties. Some of it is *social communication*—asking parents to reach for a toy that one cannot reach by oneself, telling one's sister that one wants one's doll back, or telling one's mother that one wants to go to the toilet. A far larger proportion of the child's talking and listening is *egocentric*, a running oral commentary that accompanies what the child is doing at the moment. It is not intended to communicate anything to anyone else. Since this kind of talk often appears in social situations, such as in a group of children at play, it can, at first glance, be mistaken for social communication. However, on closer inspection, it becomes apparent that everyone is talking to herself or himself without listening to the others. For this reason, Piaget labeled such speech *collective monologues*. An important factor behind this discourse, in Piaget's opinion, is the child's lingering self-centeredness. The child still views life from his or her own perspective and has difficulty seeing things from the viewpoint of others. Hence, he or she does not try to comprehend what others say in order to respond from the perspective that those others express.

To check this hypothesis, Piaget observed preoperational children in situations requiring them to explain something to another child, and then noted, from the other child's behavior, how well the explanation had been understood. The observations revealed a systematic egocentricity, in the sense that the child who was giving the directions had great difficulty adopting the other's viewpoint in order to make the explanation readily comprehended from the second child's perspective (Piaget & Inhelder, 1969, pp. 120-122).

A Russian psychologist, Vygotsky, noted that such egocentric speech was no longer observed in children by age 7. He speculated that such "thinking out loud" had not really disappeared but that, rather, it merely had been internalized. Vygotsky believed that the children still talked silently to themselves as they went about their work and play. In an experiment that he devised to test his hypothesis, Vygotsky gave children play activities in which a problem always came up—a missing bit of equipment or some other puzzling matter. Although the children had ostensibly passed the stage of egocentric speech, when they came across the problem, they usually started talking aloud to themselves again. Vygotsky interpreted this as confirmation that the "thinking out loud" had not disappeared but that it had been internalized and could be revived by a frustrating problem which caused the child to revert to the earlier pattern of observable oral thinking (Vygotsky, 1962, pp. 16-17).

Relationships and Classes. Preschool children have difficulty understanding many of the relationships and classifications referred to in the speech of older children and adults. For instance, the young are often confused about the relationship intended in such terms as grandparent, great-grandmother, cousin, uncle, stepfather, foster parent, and the like. A four-year-old girl inquired about a neighbor's wife, "Is your mother making cookies today?"

Young children are also puzzled by references to time—a few minutes and a couple of hours, last year and next year, older and younger, sooner and later. When a three-year-old boy begged his father for a skateboard like the ones that the neighborhood teenagers used, his father said, "When you're older, maybe. But now you would fall off and hurt yourself." The boy then pled his case with what he thought was a convincing argument: "Once when I was older I didn't fall off, so I need one now."

Young children's drawings further illustrate that their conception of objects in their environment is not the same as an adult's. When asked to draw a picture of a person, the typical three- or four-year old is content to make a circle with several lines extending out as limbs and perhaps two or three dots inside as a face (Harris, 1963). If an adult tries to explain why such a portrayal is inadequate, the child fails to grasp what the complaint is all about. As children grow older, their drawings reflect an evolving recognition of which elements to include in the drawing to produce a good match between the sketch and people's actual appearance.

Knowing about children's perceptions of relationships can aid counselors in diagnosing and treating children's personal/social adjustment difficulties that are seated in misunderstandings about such matters. Frequently, this means helping the child's caregivers to recognize the nature of children's thought processes and to see how such ways of thinking can affect children's social interactions and their misinterpretations of their world. To illustrate, a common difficulty that parents face when they try to teach their young child to read, count, or understand physical phenomena is the parents' failure to understand a child's typical modes of thought at different age levels. For example, in a popular Piagetian experiment, a child watches an adult pour all the water from a bowl into a tall glass. The child is then asked if there was more water in the bowl than there is now in the glass, or was the amount the same. Before age five or so, the typical child will say that there is more water in the glass. This is because the child centers attention on only one dimension of the containers—the height—and fails to understand that the width of the bowl compensates for its lack of height. In a similar demonstration, the child sees the adult break up a single ball of clay into four smaller balls and then is asked whether there is more clay in the four small balls than in the single large ball, or vice versa. The typical preschool child will say that there is more clay in the four small balls. Again, the child has centered attention exclusively on one dimension—the number of balls—failing to see that the greater mass of the single large ball compensates for the greater number of small balls. Thus, child thought during the preschool years is dominated by visual appearances rather than a pattern of logic that accommodates more than one element of a situation. Parents who do not understand that such preoperational thinking is normal during the preschool years can become frustrated when their young children fail to think like adults. When children fail to accept their parents' logical explanations, the adults frequently show their anger at what they conceive to be the child's stubborn stupidity. Then a family conflict ensues, leaving the child feeling guilty and rejected without understanding what he or she has done wrong.

Language Development. To even the most casual observer, it is apparent that children's vocabulary and the complexity of their sentences increase rapidly over the first half-decade of life. Providing generalizations about the size of children's vocabulary at different age levels is a tricky business that results in imprecise figures because of the conditions involved. For instance, children's passive vocabulary (words which they understand when others speak to them) is larger than their active vocabulary (words which they utter themselves), with active vocabulary being the easier of the two to measure. In addition, there are different levels of understanding a given word. Some children can use a word in only one of its grammatical forms (*salt* as a noun), while others can use it in a variety of forms (*salt* as a noun and verb, *salted, salty, salting, saltier, saltiest, salt-free*). In addition, there are marked variations in the number of words understood by different children who are the same age. M. K. Smith (1941) found that among six-year olds, children's vocabularies ranged from 5,500 to 32,000 words.

Although, in recent years, researchers in the field of language development have concentrated on aspects of language other than vocabulary word counts, data from the past suggest something of the rate of vocabulary growth. M. E. Smith (1926) found in a group of children that she studied that the average number of words which children could use at different age levels was around 300 at age two, 950 at age three, 1,550 at age four, and over 2,000 at age five. Bloom (1964) summarized a variety of vocabulary counts by proposing that by age six, children have 50% of the vocabulary that they will have at age eight, and at age eight, they have 50% of the vocabulary that they will have at age 18.

Not only does vocabulary grow rapidly over the preschool years, but children also make remarkable progress in their command of grammar and syntax. When young children first begin to string a few words together to form rudimentary sentences, their utterances can be labeled *telegraphic speech*, since their speech resembles an adult's telegram which, for the sake of brevity, leaves out articles *(a, the)*, coupling and "helping" verbs *(is, will)*, some pronouns *(my, their)*, and the like. As a result, the one or two year old may say "Mommy go?" or "cookie fall" to represent "Is Mommy going to go away?" and "I saw the cookie fall to the floor." In children's earliest talk, their utterances are pretty well limited to nouns and verbs, the parts of speech most essential to convey meaning. Then, gradually, they acquire such prepositions as *in* and *on*, some present progressive verb inflections (Martha's *eating*), and some plurals and possessives. The role of these grammatical morphemes is to modulate or embellish in a simple way the basic content of what the child at the prior stage said with just a noun and verb (Brown, 1973).

Information about young children's language development can imply at least two suggestions for the conduct of counseling. First, when talking with young children, therapists can be careful to use simple vocabulary and simple sentence structures. Counselors who have recently completed their graduate studies or have worked mainly with adults and only then encounter a child client often fail to adjust their terminology and syntax to suit the child's level of language use. Hence, it is safest for a therapist to begin by talking in quite simple terms with the child (yet avoiding the insult of using telegraphic "baby talk") and then to estimate from the child's responses how sophisticated that child's command of the language is. The therapist's subsequent conversation with the child can be adjusted to the child's observed level of language sophistication.

Second, information about children's language development can assist the counselor in guiding a parent's child-rearing techniques. As noted earlier, parents' conflicts with their young children are often seated in the adults' failure to recognize how a young child perceives the world and how a child's language command can differ from that of most adults. When a counselor observes a mother interacting verbally with her daughter, it may become apparent to the counselor that the two are operating on different levels of language usage, so that the incongruity of their language contributes to their failure to understand each other. In such cases, the therapist may find it useful to demonstrate to the mother a mode of talking with the child and of interpreting the girl's speech that is better suited to the daughter's level of language development.

Literal Versus Figurative Language. The young tend to interpret words in terms of concrete, literal meanings rather than symbols and abstractions. A four-year old asked her father, "Is God bloody?" When her father inquired about why she asked such a question, she replied, "Mama said God lives in our heart, so isn't he bloody?"

Because children tend to be literal, therapists can properly stick to the literal use of words as they talk with young clients. And, when someone else uses a figurative term in talking with a preschooler, it is helpful if the counselor explains to the child what the term was intended to mean and why. For example, in speaking with a nursery-school boy, a therapist can say, "The teacher didn't think you were a pig. When she said, 'You're eating like a pig,' she just meant that pigs eat very fast. She thought you were eating very fast. She really knows you're a fine boy, not a pig."

SOCIAL RELATIONS

Our inspection of social relations centers primarily on the way in which the young interact with family members, age peers, and strangers.

From birth through early childhood, those with whom a typical child lives most intimately are family members, chiefly parents and siblings. The home environment exerts a particularly strong effect on the child's personal-social relations because it is from family members that the young derive their first taste of what the social world is like. For instance, does the infant experience the world as comfortable and protecting or as abusive, as stable and predictable or as neglectful, as indulgent or unsettled and likely to change without notice, or what? Family members also offer children their first role models, their first examples of how to act toward others. And the family teaches the child the kinds of consequences—rewards and punishments—to be expected for different kinds of behavior. These initial learnings form a template for the growing individual's later patterns of social interaction unless strong forces intervene at further stages of life to alter the perceptions established in the early years. Hence, counselors often face the task of helping the child's caregivers to recognize how the models that they provide and the consequences that they impose are affecting the young one's social development.

It is also the case that caregivers can fail to understand the difficulties that the child has in identifying the characteristics of different social environments which call for adjustments in one's behavior. As a consequence, adults may hold unrealistic expectations for the young and may lack the patience and skills of guiding the child's evolving social perceptions. For instance, how society expects a girl to act can vary according to whether she is at home, is a guest in someone else's home, is at nursery school, is in church, is on the playground, or is in a restaurant. Typical of this problem is children's use of "dirty words" in public. Preschoolers hear their parents and older siblings say things at home that get the young in trouble when they themselves say those things at school, in front of a friend's parents, in church, or at the market. The objectionable phrases range from the slightly nocuous *pee-pee* and *pooh-pooh* through *dammit* and *Oh, my God* to what kindergarten teachers call "the F words"—*fuck* and *fart*. Thus, counseling parents of young children may include offering them information about typical social behavior of the young at different age levels and about techniques for helping children learn how to act acceptably in different social settings. In a counselor's work with the children themselves, therapy can often involve engaging them in sociodramas so that they can practice how they might properly respond in different social settings.

During the first five or ten years of life, children's symptoms of social maladjustment can vary markedly—extreme aggressivity, chronic disobedience, painful shyness, lying, stealing, damaging property, injuring other people, and more. As already noted, the most significant causes behind such behaviors are frequently the parents' unsuitable child-rearing practices—unrealistic standards of behavior, harsh discipline, overindulgence, improper role modeling, exploitation of the child for the parents' benefit, emotional rejection, inconsistent reward-and-punishment patterns, physical and emotional neglect, or others. Clinical studies have demonstrated that improper child-rearing methods can lead to extensive, long-term social-development consequences.

> By far the most disturbing and consistent finding in observations of young children who have been abused and neglected is the delay, or arrest, of their development.... The most devastating effect is the inability to adequately relate to oneself or to others.... The lasting effect is that this loss of skill prevents any semblance of reasonable parenting skills from developing. The next generation is affected, and the cycle continues (Kempe, 1976, pp. 64-65, 73).

Because most children must continue to live under the jurisdiction of their parents, counseling a socially maladapted child typically requires counseling the parents as well if improvement of the child's condition is to be expected.

Other common causes of social maladjustment in the young, in addition to unsuitable parenting patterns, are critical events that require drastic changes in the established modes of coping with life. Examples of such incidents can be the death of a family member, moving to a new city, or first entering school. In these instances, counseling may take the form of aiding the caretakers in making an extra effort to give the child personal attention, affection, consolation, and an opportunity to express distress to a sympathetic listener.

SEXUAL DEVELOPMENT

A century ago, the Viennese neurologist Sigmund Freud shocked Western society when he proposed that from the time of birth children exhibit sexual drives. He further suggested that parents' inappropriate responses to children's sexual expressions were the cause of much of the neurotic behavior that people suffered during adolescence and adulthood (Freud, 1938). According to Freud, the initial erotic experiences of the infant are centered on the act of sucking at the mother's breast. Thus, what Freud termed the oral zone—lips, tongue, gums, teeth—became the center of sexual gratification. Frustrations suffered during the process of eating and of indulging the sucking desire become a source of distress for the infant and lead to a distrust of the world, a distrust that can cause problems at later stages of psychological development (Erikson, 1963). During the second year of life, the primary focus of the child's psychosexual attention shifts from the mouth to the excretory functions of the body. In Freud's interpretation, the child gains erotic pleasure from both expelling and retaining feces and urine. At the same time, parents typically try to toilet-train the toddler by urging him or her to expel feces and urine only in a toilet and only at times convenient to adults. Freud contended that conflicts between children and their parents over the timing and methods of toilet-training can further frustrate children's satisfying their anal-erotic needs and, as a consequence, can establish another cause for children's developing a distorted perception of self and of the world, a distortion that can be displayed as neurotic behavior in later life.

According to Freud, by ages three to five, the child's erotic desires shift once more to a new object, the primary genital organs—the vagina and clitoris in girls and the penis in boys. Now the child gains pleasure by fondling these body parts, oftentimes in the presence of other people. The others—parents, older siblings, friends, nursery-school teachers—typically disapprove of such behavior, frequently in very strong terms, threatening the child with serious consequences if the practice does not stop. In connection with this genital period of psychosexual development, Freud constructed a theory about son-mother, daughter-father love relationships which he felt explained many of the neuroses that people exhibit in adolescence and adulthood. It is not my purpose here to elaborate on this "family romance" portion of Freudian theory but, rather, to note only that today the notion that children do derive pleasure from oral, anal, and genital activities during the first half-decade of life is pretty well accepted among psychologists, whether or not they accept other Freudian proposals. Psychologists also generally agree that the way in which parents respond to preschoolers' oral, anal, and genital interests can have an important influence on the children's psychosocial adjustment. Hence, therapists find that in cases of young children whom they treat, conflicts within the family can often involve problems of weaning a child from the breast or bottle, of the success or failure of toilet-training, or of ways of dealing with children's fondling themselves, exhibiting their genitals to others, or seeking to examine others' sex organs. Or, in cases of child exploitation, an adult may engage the young child in sex play or some variety of intercourse.

Thus, it is appropriate for counselors to recognize that young children derive pleasure from oral, anal, and genital zones of their bodies and that the types of responses which adults make to children's attention to these erogenous areas can affect children's social adjustment and feelings of self-worth. Parents who do not understand normal processes of development can adopt destructive methods of toilet-training and of reacting to children's sexual curiosity. Counseling such parents can involve teaching them ways of responding that do not cause children to feel unwarranted guilt, yet ways that will guide children to express themselves in a manner not publicly offensive. For example, parents can tell children that fondling their own genitals is not a wicked act but, nevertheless, it is a private act, one that should be indulged only when the child is alone and thus not observed by others.

SELF-PERCEPTION

Therapists who consider themselves humanistic or existential psychologists will usually focus their primary attention on how the child is developing a sense of self. Theorists who write about such matters describe the self in various ways. Combs and Snygg (1959, p. 124) have proposed that the *phenomenal self* "is the individual as he seems from his own vantage point." Rollo May (Reeves, 1977, pp. 286-287) has called the self "the organizing function within the individual ... consciousness of one's identity ... as a thinking-intuiting-feeling and acting unity."

An important characteristic of infancy is the process by which children begin to differentiate themselves from the rest of the environment and develop a concept of "who I am." The newborn apparently has no notion of self in the adult sense of the term. However, by trial and error, the infant gradually recognizes that his or her fingers and toes are part of him or her, while the toy dog and baby bottle are not. Furthermore, how adequately young children meet parental expectations—the rewards and punishments they receive, the attention and neglect they experience—helps them to define who they are in relation to the world. This process of self-identification and differentiation from the environment becomes gradually refined as the early years advance, so that by the time the child enters nursery school, a recognizable self-concept has evolved. A variety of terms containing the word *self* reflect factors that people have come to associate with this evolving personality construct—self-identity, self-confidence, self-adequacy, self-control, self-denial, self-reference, self-centered, self-assertive, self-effacing, and more.

Whether or not psychologists concur on exactly how to define *self*, they all appear to agree that the early years of life play a crucial role in forming the kind of self-concept that a person will display throughout the rest of life. The following three child-raising principles are ones that I am convinced can promote the development of a positive self-concept in children:

Affection and Protection

The child's caregivers freely offer physical affection. They protect the child from physical harm as well as from confusing and frightening experiences. They fulfill the child's needs for food and warmth, and they provide comfort when the child is distressed.

Suitable Expectations

Caregivers suit their expectations for the child's behavior to the rate of development that can properly be expected at that child's stage of life. The term *suitable expectations* during early childhood can mean that parents and teachers do not require toilet-training, physical strength and agility, cognitive skills (speaking, counting, reading, writing), social behavior, displays of conscience, and emotional control that are beyond the ability of the child at the present stage of growth. When caregivers continually expect a higher level of performance than the child can achieve, they are undermining the young one's sense of confidence. Such children can come to perceive themselves as unworthy, and thus they will face the future with a sense of never being good enough.

Not only are unduly strict expectations conducive to an inadequate sense of self, so too are unduly lenient standards. Young children can be overindulged and overprotected in ways that prevent them from performing the tasks and achieving the skills warranted by their evolving abilities. Parents who hasten to meet the child's every whim and desire without requiring any effort on the part of the child are robbing the child of chances to develop self-reliance. Caretakers who continually prevent the child from taking chances or from trying new ventures for fear that the child will fail or be injured are reducing the young one's opportunities to gain skill, exhibit bravery, and overcome adversity—qualities required for a sound sense of self-adequacy throughout life.

A Predictable Environment

People's feeling of confidence—their belief in being able to cope with the world—seems strongly affected by how accurately they can predict what to expect of their environment. Consistency in child-rearing practices helps to build in children an early foundation of trust, a belief that they can predict what is likely to happen. In contrast, inconsistent child-rearing methods foster anxiety, fear, and self-doubt. When parents on one occasion punish a type of behavior that they overlook or laugh at on another occasion, they contribute to children's doubt about the predictability of life. On the other hand, when adults make clear to children what to expect and then the adults consistently follow through to make their predictions come true, they enhance children's feelings of security and self-confidence.

Whenever counselors are faced with cases of overly shy, fearful, or aggressive young children, it is possible that one factor contributing to such children's disturbing behavior is the parents' inappropriate child-rearing methods. In such instances, it may prove useful for a counselor to inquire about how adequately the child's caregivers are applying the three principles described above. The treatment of such cases may include directing the caregivers in applying these principles.

CONCLUSION

The purpose of the first half of this chapter has been to offer generalizations about development during the first years of life that can be of aid to counseling psychologists, social workers, psychiatrists, and nursery-school teachers who are asked to help with personal/social-adjustment problems that cause distress for young children and their families. The topics selected for discussion have been ones that appear to be of particular importance for counseling practice.

We continue now with the second portion of the chapter, which furnishes more specific normative information about two kinds of developmental disorders that may often be encountered by counselors who work with young children.

KINDS OF COUNSELING CASES IN EARLY CHILDHOOD

Among the numerous types of presenting problems that bring young children to counselors are two that seem particularly prominent: (1) child abuse and neglect and (2) handicapping conditions. The remainder of the chapter offers normative information that may aid counselors in estimating what to expect in these types of cases.

Child Abuse and Child Neglect

There have always been people concerned about the abuse and neglect of children, but never has attention to these problems been so intense and widespread as during the last four decades. It is true that during the nineteenth century in industrialized societies there was a dramatic awakening of public solicitude for the plight of the young. Such novelists as Charles Dickens, with his stories of *David Copperfield* and *Oliver Twist*, helped to stimulate interest in reducing the exploitation of children, an interest reflected in the establishment of the first two English Societies for the Prevention of Cruelty to Children in Liverpool and London in the 1880s (Lynch, 1985, p. 10). However, efforts to correct child abuse and neglect were never so great as they have become in recent years. As a result, more and more cases of children's needing protection are appearing in counseling practice.

The matters on which the following overview focuses are those of identifying (1) types of abuse and neglect, (2) the extent of the maltreatment of children, (3) causes of maltreatment, and (4) methods of treatment and rates of success.

DEFINING TYPES OF CHILD MALTREATMENT

A continuing problem among workers in this field is that of agreeing on what is meant by *abuse* and *neglect* and of distinguishing between the two. Gil (1980, p. 120) has offered what is likely the broadest definition by comparing the treatment of children against a standard of "optimal development" opportunities:

> any act of commission or omission by individuals, institutions, or society as a whole, and any conditions resulting from such acts or inaction, which deprive children of equal rights and liberties, and/or interfere with their optimal development, constitute, by definition, abusive or neglectful acts or conditions.

As admirable as Gil's definition may be, it seems unduly idealistic for the practical needs of addressing serious cases of child maltreatment. In other words, it is likely that every parent will, on at least a few occasions, do or say something to a child that can interfere with the child's "optimal development," but all parents do not require counseling. Thus, what counselors need are more precise criteria for distinguishing between minor incidents of neglect or abuse, which may have little if any long-term influence on the child's welfare, and major incidents that are truly damaging and call for professional intervention. The following three examples illustrate typical attempts at establishing such criteria.

In a British research project, Oliver, Cox, and Buchanan (1978, pp. 122-123) defined *severe abuse* as consisting of physical injury to a child that required serious medical treatment. The label *moderate abuse* was applied to lesser degrees of assault or injury and of suffocation (putting a child's head under water, covering a child's head with polythene bags). *Neglect* included depriving a child of food, fluids, freedom, warmth, and medical treatment as well as the imposition of unnecessary psychological stress and various mental assaults. Abandonment was also considered to be neglect.

Researchers in Rhode Island collected opinions about what constituted serious abuse from seven types of professionals (general-practice and emergency-room physicians, school counselors and principals, clinicians, social caseworkers, and police officers). Over 95% of the respondents believed that willful malnutrition, sexual molestation, and intentionally inflicted trauma qualified as abuse, while 82% considered locking a child in a dark closet as abusive as well. Over two-thirds said that parents were abusive if they injured a child while administering corporal punishment. Half of the respondents believed that child injury due to parental carelessness was abusive. Less than 20% of the professionals believed that children were abused if they were injured as a result of poor housing conditions, if they suffered malnutrition due to the family's financial limitations, or if they lacked health care when health services were unavailable (Gelles, 1982, pp. 5-8).

Meddin (1985, pp. 60-61) studied the judgments made in abuse and neglect cases by 315 social-caseworkers in the Midwestern United States, where one public child-welfare agency estimated that it received around 300 child-abuse reports a day, 100 of which were judged as warranting professional action. The 315 caseworkers were asked what factors they considered in assessing the potential risk of harm to the child from further abuse or neglect. The workers reported that they did not base their assessments solely on one or two factors but, rather, on a combination of elements in each case, including: (1) the child's age (younger children were judged to be at greater risk), (2) the functioning of the child (especially the child's ability to protect himself or herself), (3) the cooperation and functioning of the prime caretaker, (4) the intent of the perpetrator involved (deliberate intent to harm the child as contrasted to an accidental event or a misunderstanding), (5) current access of the perpetrator (easy, frequent access to the child was considered to pose greater risk than difficult, rare access), (6) the severity of the incident, and (7) the existence of previous incidents suggesting continual danger to the child.

In view of the limited resources available for intervention to promote children's welfare, the foregoing set of seven criteria appear to be appropriate in distinguishing those cases in which professional action, including counseling, is most clearly warranted.

THE INCIDENCE OF MALTREATMENT OF YOUNG CHILDREN

Statistics on the extent of child abuse vary markedly because of differences in definitions of what constitutes significant maltreatment and because so many cases go unreported. As a result, by the mid-1980s estimates of abuse and neglect ranged between one and six million children a year in the United States. Several surveys in the United States and Britain have suggested that each year 1 out of every 100 children will be sufficiently maltreated to require professional intervention. However, a variety of specialists in the field place the number closer to 1 in every 10. "The '1 in 100' figures for child victims represent the proven apparent cases.... The '1 child in 10' usually just suffers, and his plight is only apparent to conscientious people who spend an appreciable part of the day with him, ... and he is the likely parent of the blatantly battered baby in the next generation" (Oliver, 1978, p. 114).

CORRELATES OF ABUSE AND NEGLECT

When correlates of abuse and neglect are identified, counselors can improve their predictions both of (1) the kinds of people—both adults and children—who may be involved in child abuse and (2) the type of counseling aid that such people may need. The following examples illustrate kinds of normative data that offer such information.

An initial question of interest is whether useful predictions can be made prior to a child's birth about the likelihood that one or both parents will abuse or neglect their expected offspring. In an investigation of this issue, 587 expectant mothers were interviewed through use of a Family Stress Checklist developed at the University of Colorado Health Sciences Center. Two years following the children's birth, the charts of 100 children whose mothers had been considered "at risk" were compared with charts of 100 children whose mothers had been judged "at no risk." The incidence of apparent child abuse/neglect among the at-risk mothers was 52%, and, among the no-risk mothers, it was 2%. Whether a mother was single or a teenager was not a feature distinguishing between child abusers and non-child abusers. The researchers concluded that the Family Stress Checklist "proved a remarkably accurate predictor, with a sensitivity (percent correct negatives) of 89%" (Murphy, Orkow, & Nicola, 1985, pp. 225-

235). The authors recommended the use of such scales prenatally or even before conception as a step toward developing preventive measures with the prospective parents. Results equally impressive as those derived with the Colorado instrument have been reported for the use of the Michigan Screening Profile of Parenting (Schneider, 1982).

A review of 6,532 cases of child abuse in Britain over the period 1977-1982 indicated that the parents or caretakers of abused children were characterized by their early parenthood, marital instability, large families, criminality, and mobility (Creighton, 1985, p. 441).

Another question of relevance for counselors concerns the effect of maltreatment on children's psychosocial adjustment. Although the number of research studies conducted on this issue is limited, and the methodologies have sometimes been flawed, Lamphear's (1985, p. 262) analysis of such studies led her to conclude that abused children are likely to display behavior problems (noncompliance, tantrums, aggression), poor peer relationships, unsatisfactory social skills, less empathy than other children, and poor school achievement and adjustment. Such results help to identify the types of presenting problems that abused children often bring to the counselor's office.

The matter of how abuse is related to children's self-concept has also been investigated. A review of studies of children who have suffered abuse over a period of time indicates that they typically manifest a general air of depression, unhappiness, and reduced self-concept (Kinard, 1980). Such evidence suggests that counseling is warranted for both the caretakers—who are usually the parents or foster parents—and the child. "This should first include a careful assessment of the child's developmental and emotional status followed by a long-term program for the child which aims at improving the child's skills in interpersonal relationships and in building up self-esteem" (Oates, Forrest, & Peacock, 1985, p. 163).

Two further correlates of abuse and neglect are tendencies toward delayed language development and poor intellectual functioning in the young child. In a comparison of two sorts of mother-child pairs (abusing mothers versus nonabusing mothers), Allen and Wasserman (1985, pp. 338-339) noted that "Abusing mothers are more likely to ignore their infants, and are less likely to use verbal means to teach the infant about the workings of the world. The mother fails to display the kinds of verbal stimulation and availability which encourage language development. . . . While she may indeed provide for the child's physical needs, her interactional pattern is one of *covert neglect.* . . . The data on child abuse certainly suggest a recursive cycle. Maternal nonstimulation and ignoring may contribute to the delayed or disordered emergence of child language skills (which may be influenced in part by congenital or acquired neurological disability). The failure of the child to develop age-appropriate language skills leads to continuing disturbances in parent-child relationships, peer interactions, symbolic intelligence, school performance, and self-esteem." Counseling in such cases can thus include helping the mother to learn, by means of demonstration and role playing, ways of talking with the young child that encourage normal progress in verbal and cognitive skills.

To summarize the information reviewed in the above paragraphs, we can note that the correlates are of two varieties—environmental and personal. Environmental factors are conditions surrounding the child, conditions that may be either causal or only casual, such as early parenthood, family stress, large families, poverty, criminality, and mobility. Personal characteristics are those traits of children that are associated with abuse and neglect, including tendencies toward problem behavior, low self-concept, poor social skills, unsatisfactory peer relationships, delayed language development, and poor school achievement.

CAUSES OF CHILD MALTREATMENT

The causes of child abuse and neglect are quite complicated because of variations from one case to another in the form of abuse, its frequency, and the way in which influential factors combine to precipitate the maltreatment. Nevertheless, there are several conditions reviewed by Bowles (1980) that appear prominently in many cases of abuse and neglect.

One frequent condition is that of family stress, which results from parents' facing demands that overtax their energy, patience, and coping skills. Parents who are on the lower rungs of the economic ladder can be particularly prone to suffer stress as they must strain to meet the family's needs, especially if their employment is insecure and the family is large. Children who are hyperactive or suffer handicaps are frequently difficult to manage, thereby increasing the frustrations of child rearing that parents face. Unexpected life changes, such as illness or death in the family or change in employment, add to tension within the family. When parents' ability to cope adequately with these pressures is severely diminished, they may neglect their child-rearing responsibilities or may display their distress by verbally or physically abusing their children.

A further condition frequently contributing to child abuse is the parent's own experience of having been mistreated when young. The parenting model learned during an abused childhood is often reproduced in the way in which a formerly abused person will, as an adult, treat his or her own children.

Another variable affecting the type and extent of abuse is the cultural acceptability of different methods of punishment. In those societies where hitting children, locking them up, withholding meals, and verbally denigrating them are common practice, more cases of abuse can be expected. Smith and Hanson (1980, p. 250), in a study of 214 parents of battered children, concluded that the "demanding behavior of battering parents did not exceed that which generally characterizes low social class populations. In a few specific respects it was excessive: maternal over-involvement, demands for obedience and use of physical punishment. Of greater explanatory value was the finding of inconsistency and unreasonableness," which sometimes could be traced back to similar treatment that the parents had experienced in their own childhood.

Parents' unreasonable expectations for their children can also lead to abuse. Incidents of bed-wetting, which are quite normal at certain ages and of longer duration in boys, can be interpreted by parents as misbehavior, so the parents resort to punishment that is abusive. Furthermore, "Some parents (mothers are most frequently mentioned) expect emotional support and responsiveness from a child which is beyond that child's capacity, and abuse may occur when the child fails to provide it" (Bowles, 1980, p. 5). In such cases, counselors may find that normative data are useful in teaching parents what can reasonably be expected of children at different stages of growth.

There is also a higher incidence of abuse and neglect in families that are isolated from social networks that can offer them support. Apparently this is because families which do have such support available find that the stress of parenting is reduced—friends and confidants provide occasional relief from child care, serve as sympathetic listeners to whom parents can unburden their concerns, and provide warnings when parents' display abusive child-treatment methods. Counselors may assist socially isolated families by suggesting ways in which parents can establish social contacts through discussion groups, clubs, churches, community agencies, cooperative nursery schools, and the like.

The question of how defects in parents' personalities may contribute to their abusing children is an issue of continuing controversy. In a classic 1961 article in which the term *battered child* was originally used, the authors reported from a nationwide survey of child-abuse cases treated in U.S. hospitals that:

> Parents who afflict abuse on their children do not necessarily have psychopathic or sociopathic personalities or come from borderline socioeconomic groups, although most published cases have been in these categories. In most cases some defect in character structure is probably present; often parents may be repeating the type of child care practiced on them in their childhood (Kempe, Silverman, Steele, Droege, Mueller, and Silver, 1980, pp. 49-61).

So, even though many adults who abuse children may not manifest major personality disorders, there is still evidence that personality shortcomings are often involved because "Individuals can differ significantly in their capacity to organize and meet the demands of their daily environment. These differences affect the capacity to provide adequate child care and to deal with the stresses produced by child care" (Bowles, 1980, p. 5). This point is illustrated in a study of 152 neglectful mothers, both Black and white, living in somewhat impoverished rural and urban settings in a southern section of the United States. They complained that their neighbors were unfriendly and failed to assist them with their child-rearing problems. The neighbors, however, described the neglectful mothers as deviant, antagonistic, and unlikely to reciprocate help. These apparent shortcomings seemed to derive from the neglectful mothers' deep-seated personality traits: self-derogation, shyness, fear of intimacy, and abrasiveness. In contrast, a matched group of nonneglectful mothers living in the same socioeconomic circumstances displayed personality traits and social skills that enabled them to establish supportive relationships with neighbors. Thus, the personalities of the neglectful mothers caused them to be abrasive with others, which caused neighbors to avoid or reject them. As for suitable counseling approaches in such cases, the research team recommended that: "Social skills training may be a necessary part of the intervention for some; others will be ready for making close friends only after extended casework treatment. But there is no doubt that when the social environment becomes more forthcoming, the demand for basic change in the mother is thereby lessened" (Polansky, Gaudin, Ammons, & Davis, 1985, p. 275). Thus, in addition to offering mothers help in developing better social skills, treatment can properly involve enlisting the aid of community groups that enhance the environmental support for such parents, groups found in churches, clubs, and cooperative child-care projects.

Handicapped children are particularly prone to suffer abuse and neglect. In a survey by Gil (1970), developmental disabilities prior to abuse were found in 29% of 6,000 abused children. A study of nearly 100 battered children indicated that 70% had earlier developmental problems (Johnson & Morse, 1968). There are a variety of reasons that the handicapped are maltreated more often than the normal. Parents often feel resentment, shame, or guilt when a faulty child is born to them, so they may respond by spending as little time as possible with the child, even to the extent of abandoning the infant. In other instances, parents who sincerely love the child may not be equipped—in terms of time, knowledge, or patience—to provide the extra care that a handicapped infant can require for optimal development, so the child inadvertently suffers neglect. Furthermore, a study by Sandgrund, Gaines, & Green (1974) showed that the behavior of children with intellectual and neurological deficits is likely to be provocative or unmanageable, thereby increasing the chance of these children's being abused.

In summary, a variety of interlinked causes can contribute to child abuse and neglect. Common among these are family stress, cultural traditions that tolerate the maltreatment of children, unreasonable parental expectations for children, parents' repeating abusive practices that they themselves suffered when they were young, a family's isolation from social-support groups, defects in the parents' personalities, and traits in children (such as handicaps) that cause parents inconvenience and embarrassment.

METHODS AND SUCCESS OF TREATMENT

Specialists in this field propose that the goal in treating cases of child abuse and neglect is not simply that of stopping caregivers from injuring their young charges. Rather, the goal is far more positive—to direct caregivers in providing children with constructive nurturing treatment that stimulates healthy development rather than inhibiting children's growth and well-being (Bowles, 1980, p. 2).

Programs of counseling with parents to reduce the incidence of their abusing very young children have had mixed results. In one study of 71 cases of physical abuse to children under the age of two, nearly all of the families were referred for mental health counseling and parent training, but only one-third of the group complied. Half of the children were subsequently abused again, with nearly one-third of them abused after their parents were referred to a counselor. Reabuse appeared to be unrelated to whether the parents had gone for counseling. Half of the families were deemed to be functioning poorly, and only nine were judged to have made good progress in their counseling (Rivara, 1985, p. 81).

The limited effect of counseling in such programs as the above raises the question of how successful counselors can expect to be in altering abusing and neglectful caretakers' treatment of children. One follow-up evaluation of short-term voluntary primary-prevention programs, aimed at enhancing specific coping skills of at-risk single mothers of young children living on government assistance, suggested that "competencies were not improved by the programs and that the modest attitudinal shifts and changes in social supports which did occur were not sustained over the longer term. The [discouraging] research findings may be almost completely due to the limited exposure that subjects received from the programs and the high attrition of subjects from the study. These events occurred despite a large number of incentives to keep subjects attending the programs and the great effort expended by the researchers to track subjects over the 18-month period" (Resnick, 1985, pp. 486-487). In short, it was extremely difficult to engage the caretakers in counseling, particularly over the extended period of time likely to be needed to effect positive changes in their child-rearing habits.

One of the difficulties in providing treatment for cases of child maltreatment occurs at the first step of the process—that of identifying which children are being abused. An unknown percentage of child-abuse cases remain concealed, unrecognized, or not reported. "In particular, the more subtle and difficult-to-treat forms of child abuse do not readily come to the attention of adults who are prepared to intervene. When society cannot or will not report victimization, it has always been found necessary to encourage victims to report on their own behalf" (Ney, Johnston, & Herron, 1985, p. 47). One device created to encourage children to report abuse to authorities has been a special telephone crisis service. Such a service has been operating since 1982 in Christchurch, New Zealand, under the label Childhelp Line, bearing the slogan "Hurting doesn't have to be a way of life. You can trust us" (Ney, Johnston, & Herron, 1985, p. 48). The counselors who answer calls are trained volunteers under supervision, who work mostly from their own homes via a telephone answering service. When a call comes in, the counselor: (1) seeks to establish a trusting relationship so as to facilitate communication, (2) identifies the name and address or phone number of the caller, (3) estimates the severity of the reported abuse, and on the basis of this estimate may counsel the child over the phone, refer the case to a proper agency, or call the police to intervene, (4) contacts the family (with the child's permission) so as to provide coping help for the parents, and (5) phones back one week later, for the safety of the child and the benefit of the family (Ney, Johnston, & Herron, 1985, p. 49).

It should be apparent that rarely would a child below age six use a crisis line. In the Christchurch service, the bulk of the children calling on their own behalf were between ages 8 and 16, with only a few in the 5 to 8 range. However, older children may call for the sake of a younger sibling who is being abused. As a result, a crisis line can provide assistance for children and youths over the entire first two decades of life.

Evidence from a variety of studies indicates that abused and neglected preschoolers often display maladaptive social skills. This is apparently due, at least in part, to the poor models of social interaction that they have seen in their homes. One approach to improving children's social skills has been that of demonstrating to parents how to interact more constructively with their children. In addition to the usefulness of such counseling, a study by Howes and Espinosa (1985, p. 402) of abused children in a day-care center indicated that placing a child in the center markedly enhanced the abused child's social behavior. "Abused children observed in well-established peer groups [of children who consistently attended the day-care facility] were similar to normal children in their complexity and frequency of peer interaction and in their expression of positive emotion." Thus, it would appear desirable for counselors to consider recommending to parents the placement of abused or neglected children in established day-care or nursery-school programs where the abused gain daily experience in interacting with normal peers.

In conclusion, research in recent years suggests that efforts to improve the child-rearing methods of abusive and neglectful parents are likely to succeed in only a limited number of cases. The greatest improvement can be expected for those families in which the parents are willing to engage in extended counseling and can be provided social-support resources that help reduce stress within the family. In addition, placing the abused child in a well-organized, permanent child-care program may enhance the child's self-concept and social skills. However, in a great many instances, the apparent causal factors of abuse and neglect are so deep-seated and continuing that there can be relatively little hope of effecting significant change in abusive and neglectful child-rearing conditions by means of short-term counseling.

At this point, we leave cases of abuse and neglect and turn to normative information about children who suffer physical and mental handicaps.

Handicapping Conditions in Early Childhood

In the present context, the word *handicap* refers to any physical or mental characteristic of children that prevents them from developing as adequately as the majority of their age-mates. The detrimental influence of a handicap can be either direct or indirect. The influence is direct when the handicapping condition negatively affects children's ability to perform tasks as well as most others their age. Such is the case of a malformed leg that inhibits the child's walking, a brain defect that retards language development and adaptive behavior, or a faulty auditory mechanism that reduces the ability to hear. Influence is indirect when a condition causes people to treat the child in ways that diminish his or her chances of developing physically, socially, or emotionally as well as would normally be expected. Examples of such characteristics are an infant born with a facial birthmark that people consider disfiguring or a three year old whose level of hyperactivity strains the patience of those responsible for his or her care. The unfortunate developmental consequences of some childhood conditions can be both direct and indirect, as in the case of a girl born with cerebral palsy, who not only lacks the physical agility of others her age but also has parents who openly show their disgust at being burdened with such an offspring.

The significance of a handicapping condition can differ at different age levels. When a girl is born with a cleft palate and harelip, the condition is immediately recognized. Remedial surgery may be attempted at that time or later. When the girl begins to speak, during the second year of life, her enunciation will likely be distorted. Furthermore, people's reactions to her appearance and speech will affect her self-concept, her social opportunities, and her social skills. In contrast, a boy's hyperopia (farsightedness) may not be discovered until he enters school and begins having trouble doing close work, such as reading and writing. Up to that point, his self-perception and social skills were probably not influenced at all by his handicap. Therefore, it is far more probable that the girl with the cleft palate will become a counseling case than will the boy with hyperopia. The girl and her family will apparently be in far greater need of professional help.

If the family has applied constructive methods of raising their child from birth onwards, then the need for counseling may not arise until the child moves into a wider, unprotected social sphere where taunting, rejection, and unreasonable expectations damage the child's self-image and social adjustment. For the young child, this can occur with enrollment in nursery school or kindergarten. At that time, parents may seek professional help in guiding the child toward developing attitudes and skills for coping with prejudicial social environments.

The following discussion addresses four topics that may aid counselors in estimating what to expect from cases concerning childhood handicaps: (1) types of early handicaps and their frequency, (2) correlates of handicapping conditions, (3) counseling the caretakers of handicapped children, and (4) counseling the handicapped child.

TYPES OF HANDICAPS AND THEIR FREQUENCY

Handicaps labeled *physical* are usually ones involving a person's appearance and recognizable damage to body organs. Examples include malformed limbs, unusual body proportions, a skin condition or facial features that might be considered disfiguring, a heart or kidney disorder, and malfunctions of visual, auditory, or speech organs. Handicaps labeled *mental* or *psychological* are ones displayed as immature or undesirably strange behavior, as represented in such terms as *mental retardation, neuroses,* and *psychoses*. Oftentimes a child will exhibit symptoms of both physical and psychological handicaps.

Types of specific handicaps and their causes are great in number and complexity. For instance, Hayden and Beck (1982) estimate that there are 500 different anomalies related to mental retardation alone, more than 4,000 separate causes of severely handicapping conditions, and over 220 recognized types of malformations. Space does not permit describing the incidence of all variations of handicap, but the following samples do illustrate the frequency with which some of the more common disorders may be found in the general population. For convenience of discussion, the handicaps are described under two major types—physical and psychological—even though the two may not be entirely separate, and some children will suffer both varieties at the same time.

An impression of the comparative frequency of various handicaps among young children receiving public aid in the United States in the mid-1980s is provided by the following figures on the number of children, ages 3-5, who annually were given assistance—including counseling—through the U.S. government's Education for the Handicapped Act (U.S. Department of Education, 1987, p. E-5). Figures in parentheses show the percentage of handicapped children represented by each type of disorder. Speech impaired 182,880 (70%); mentally retarded 21,068 (8%); learning disabled 19,355 (7%); multi-handicapped 11,531 (4%); orthopedically impaired 7,786 (3%); emotionally disturbed 6,279 (2%); hard of hearing and deaf 5,484 (2%); other health impaired 4,523 (2%); visually handicapped 1,935 (1%); deaf-blind 144.

Physical Handicaps

The two most prominent forms of sensory disabilities seen in childhood are visual and auditory disorders. The extent of visual impairment can range from mild refraction distortions (nearsightedness, astigmatism, farsightedness) and muscular imbalance (strabismus, as in "crossed" eyes) to complete blindness. In North America, an estimated 80% of children have reasonably normal vision, slightly less than 20% have a vision defect that could be corrected, as with glasses. Two children out of 1,000 are still classified as *partially seeing* even after as much attempted correction as is possible, and, in school, they will need the type of teaching and materials provided in sight-saving special-education classes. Five out of 10,000 children are blind (Baker, 1959, p. 297).

Auditory disorders can range from slightly-hard-of-hearing to complete deafness. About 4% of school-age children have a hearing impairment that calls for special help. Of this group, around 5% have been handicapped since very early childhood, so that without specialized treatment they will not achieve spoken communication. An estimated 40 to 60% of childhood hearing loss results from genetic or chromosomal abnormalities, while the remaining causes are disease-related (Bricker, 1986, p. 148; van Uden, 1985).

Orthopedic handicaps are defects that cause interference with the normal use of bones, muscles, or joints. The exact percentage of children suffering from orthopedic handicaps is not known, partly because different investigators have used different definitions of crippling conditions. Estimates have ranged from 1 child per 1,000 to 10 per 1,000 (Garrison & Force, 1959, p. 309). These estimates focus on the more serious conditions, so if slighter degrees of lameness or deformity are included, the incidence will be higher.

Seizure disorders are classified here as physical handicaps because they often assume the form of dramatic physical displays. A seizure disorder or epilepsy is caused by a transitory disturbance of electrical discharge in the brain that results in altered states of consciousness and/or disturbed sensory-motor activity. In its mildest form, the child merely "blanks out" momentarily, with the observable evidence no more than a flickering of the eyelids. In its severe form, the child writhes, falls unconscious, uncontrollably expels urine and feces, bites its tongue, and chokes. Seizures often have a genetic foundation or result from brain injury. The number of people suffering from epilepsy is not known for certain; but an analysis of World War I and World War II draft figures suggests that out of 1,000 people in the general population, 6 or 7 are epileptic (Hoch & Knight, 1947, p. 46).

Other physical deficiencies that can bring clients for counseling include heart conditions (congenital defects or the result of rheumatic fever), malnutrition, allergies, and disfigurements that cause the child to become, in others' eyes, the object of dislike, distaste, or ridicule.

Psychological Handicaps

For convenience sake, psychological handicaps are often divided into three types: (1) mental retardation, (2) learning disabilities, and (3) behavioral disorders, emotional disorders, or mental illness. The term *mental retardation* is applied to children whose intellectual development lags behind that of the majority of their age-mates. The phrase *learning disabilities* is usually applied to children whose general mental ability appears to be normal or above but who have trouble with specific forms of learning, such as learning to read, write, or compute. The terms *behavioral disorders, emotional disorders,* and *mental illness* identify children whose mental growth may advance at the same pace as that of most of their age-mates, but who act in ways regarded as undesirably deviant. They display extreme shyness, depression, aggressivity, physical self-destructiveness, fear, feelings of persecution and rejection, and the like. Some children are diagnosed as suffering from both mental retardation and behavioral disorders.

In describing the incidence of mental retardation, I am using the classification developed by the American Association on Mental Deficiency and based on intelligence-quotient levels derived from children's scores on standard intelligence tests. The entire category of mental retardation is comprised of children with intelligence-quotients (IQs) below 70, a category that includes 5 or 6% of the general population. Mental retardation is deemed *mild* for children whose test scores range between 50 or 55 and 70, *moderate* for those with scores between 35-40 and 50-55, *severe* for the range between 20-25 and 35-40, and *profound* for children with scores below 20 or 25 (Hallahan & Kauffman, 1982). Estimated percentages of the mentally retarded population that fall within each of these categories are: 85 to 87% mild, 6 to 10% moderate, 3.5% severe, and 1% profound (Cartwright, Cartwright, & Ward, 1984). However, when estimating how well a child will be able to get along in the world, counselors should view these figures with caution. Since the figures are based solely on IQ scores, they may fail to reflect children's actual ability to care for themselves and adapt to social situations. Recognizing this fact can be important in counseling parents of the retarded, so that additional observations of how well the child learns personal-care and social skills should be collected to aid in predicting the child's potential and in determining the sort of child-rearing methods that parents and teachers should adopt.

In around 25% of children diagnosed as mentally retarded, a biological cause can be identified as accounting for the disability. The causes for the remaining 75% are attributed to unknown or environmental factors, with the environmental factors including lack of cognitive stimulation during the early years, poor nutrition, and abuse (Bricker, 1986, p. 148).

The time in children's lives when they first are diagnosed as retarded usually differs with the degree of retardation. Severe and profound retardation, and such types as Down's syndrome that display distinctive observable characteristics, are typically recognized very early, whereas very mild retardation may not be identified until the child is already in primary school or nearly so. Consequently, a therapist is likely to be consulted earlier by parents of severely or moderately retarded children than by parents of the mildly retarded. In addition, the more severe the handicap, the more likely it is that the cause can be identified as biological as opposed to environmental.

One problem faced in arriving at a proper diagnosis of mild retardation is that some children who will eventually achieve normal status are developing at a slower rate, particularly if they have been born prematurely. Hence, during the earliest years of life, it is often difficult to estimate whether a child is truly retarded and will never catch up with his or her age-mates intellectually, or whether the child is simply a late developer.

As noted above, the term *learning disabilities* identifies children who are not mentally retarded but, nevertheless, have an unusually difficult time with certain learning tasks. Because these disabilities are usually not manifest until the child is in the primary grades, discussion of them will be postponed until Chapter 5, where problems of the elementary-school child are considered.

The third major category of psychological disorders—behavioral difficulties, emotional disorders, or mental illness—includes a variety of forms of maladjustment, some of which have distinctive symptoms and labels. Among the distinctive types that may appear in early childhood is infantile autism, a form of psychosis appearing in children before 30 months of age. The incidence of infantile autism is about 4.9 per 10,000 (Wing & Gould, 1979). Between 70% and 80% of autistic children score in the mentally retarded range on standard tests of intelligence, so that psychologists have sometimes found it difficult to distinguish the autistic child from those suffering from other types of deficiency. However, Ungerer (1985, pp. 137-138) reports two features as consistently critical for distinguishing infantile autism from other disorders. These are profound impairments of social relatedness and communicative speech: "Autistic children have always been considered socially aloof and incapable of forming normal attachments and social relationships. Originally, this deficiency was attributed to inadequate parenting ... but research has failed to support this relation. The parents of autistic children do not demonstrate more psychopathology than parents of children having clear organic disorders with or without psychosis, and their parenting skills have not been shown to be deficient."

Another distinctive psychotic disorder is childhood schizophrenia, which may appear at any point during childhood. Typically it is manifest in the child's inability to develop and maintain satisfactory social relations (especially with peers), a distortion in emotional expression (a display of feelings unsuitable to the present situation), an inability to judge reality accurately, and a high level of anxiety. Sherman & Asarnow (1985) have hypothesized that the cognitive portion of the schizophrenic's disorder results from limitations in the child's mental capacity, particularly in the cognitive system that governs the way in which the child directs and controls his or her attention.

> If the child does not have sufficient cognitive capacity to perform and practice more complex cognitive functions, those functions will not become automatized.... Certain strategies and skills that will become automatized, and therefore demand only modest amounts of attention in the child's normal peers, will remain unpracticed and therefore highly capacity-demanding for the schizophrenic child.... Schizophrenic children are preoccupied with internally generated ideas, and they engage in the performance of stereotyped behaviors. Both of these types of [mental-capacity] allocation deviances will interfere even further with the child's cognitive functioning by draining his or her resources to nonproductive ends. These allocation problems will further impede the schizophrenic child's development of peer relations by interfering with the amount of cognitive capacity directed outward. (Sherman & Asarnow, 1985, pp. 165-167)

In addition to autism and schizophrenia, there is a broad array of other emotional disturbances, many of them less well-defined and less dramatic, that interfere with children's intellectual and social development.

Psychophysical Handicaps

Some handicapped children display primary physical as well as psychological deficiencies. One such disorder is cerebral palsy, which is caused by damage to the brain's motor-control system and is manifest in a disorganization of motor control as a result of brain injury experienced prenatally or in the first three years of life. Because of their neuromuscular dysfunction, children with cerebral palsy may also exhibit difficulties in learning, behavior, speech and language, and sensory functioning. In the United States, an estimated three children out of 1,000 suffer some degree of the disorder. Around 40%

of the cerebral-palsied population exhibit some measure of mental retardation (O'Connor, 1985, p. 100).

Speech malfunctions are difficult to classify as a single type of handicap, because the causes and symptoms can differ from one kind or speech problem to another. The speech of a child with a malformed hard palate (roof of the mouth) or an unconventional jaw and teeth structure will be abnormal because of such physical characteristics. In contrast, stuttering apparently does not result from a physical condition but, rather, from psychological causes or from both neurological and psychological factors. In early childhood, it is difficult to distinguish between what will become a lasting speech disorder and what is simply normal speech among preschoolers. A large proportion of young children occasionally stammer, lisp, mispronounce words, enunciate in strange ways, and use *baby talk*. The majority of them will "naturally grow out of it" during their kindergarten and primary-grade years, as their neural development and more astute attention to adult and peer models bring their speech closer to the cultural norm. However, some young children's speaking difficulties are sufficient to require professional attention during the early years. Counselors who have specialized in speech disorders may be able to diagnose such conditions and offer therapy. Counselors without such expertise can aid parents by referring them to a speech specialist.

CORRELATES OF HANDICAPPING CONDITIONS

As handicapped children reach school age, they increasingly compare themselves with their age-mates. In addition, they become more conscious of how other people react to them. A common result of the comparisons and reactions is that the handicapped view themselves as inferior to others and as objects of teasing, scorn, and rejection. A personality correlate that often derives from years of such experiences is a negative self-image, which makes it difficult for the handicapped to accept themselves as worthy of love, respect, and admiration. Hence, two central tasks in counseling the handicapped are usually those of (1) helping caregivers to learn to foster their child's positive self-acceptance and self-regard and (2) helping the handicapped child to accept the reality of his or her disability and, at the same time, recognize ways of making the most of life and of taking pride in those successes that such conditions permit.

In addition to the self-acceptance problems that accompany most handicaps, there are other correlates often associated with specific disabilities. For instance, most deaf children score in the normal range of intelligence on nonverbal tests, but their average scores or verbal tests are somewhat lower than those of hearing children. The lack of hearing does not seriously reduce a child's play with objects during the first two years of life. However, at later ages, when play involves communicating with peers whose hearing is not impaired, the deaf child advances through successive stages of play at a slower rate than does the hearing child. Thus, deaf children tend to continue in parallel play when their age-mates have progressed to cooperative play. The deaf child's play is also often solitary and unimaginative (Fewell & Kaminski, 1988, p. 152).

Blind children score in the normal range of general intelligence, but "the distribution of their scores is bimodal. That is ... compared to sighted peers, there is a slightly higher percentage of blind children in the superior range and a considerably larger percentage in the below average range" (O'Connor, 1985, p. 101).

Some correlates of mental retardation are rather obvious, since they are often elements in the defining syndrome of the condition. One correlate of this type is the retarded child's deficiency in communicating with both adults and peers. The retarded have difficulty in understanding what others mean and in expressing their own needs, beliefs, and feelings. This communication deficit poses problems for therapists as they seek to learn how the child views the world and as they try to help the child understand his or her own and other people's actions.

Emotional development in mentally retarded children, such as those suffering from Down's syndrome, is highly correlated with cognitive development. Displays of pleasure, fear, distress, and the like in the retarded child under age 5 lag noticeably behind such displays in children of normal mental ability (Vietze, 1985). This delay in emotional response often contributes to parents' disappointment with their retarded offspring.

Children who suffer major seizures are often retarded. Ninety percent or more that suffer infantile spasms are seriously retarded mentally. In a study by Keith (1963), 40% of children with grand mal seizures were retarded, but most children with only petit mal seizures scored within the normal range on intelligence measures, although they showed poor school performance, as was true also for children who had partial or focal seizures (Thompson & O'Quinn, 1979). The play behavior of children with autism and other emotional disorders and of ones within multiple handicaps generally is in keeping with such children's cognitive, language, and social skills. As mental and social abilities advance, so does the complexity of play activities (Fewell & Kaminski, 1988, p. 152).

COUNSELING CARETAKERS OF HANDICAPPED CHILDREN

Two of the most common types of parents that will appear for counseling are (1) those who voluntarily seek guidance in child-raising techniques and (2) those sent for counseling because they have been accused of child abuse or neglect. The prognosis for success in counseling is usually greater for the ones who come on their own initiative than for those sent by the court, by a social-welfare agency, or by a concerned relative.

Probably no parents are pleased to have a handicapped infant born into the family. Nor are they glad that a normal son or daughter becomes handicapped through accident or illness. However, they do have a choice in how they will respond to the child's condition, and it is the particular response that they adopt which becomes important to the counselor. While reactions of children's caretakers can be quite varied, research in this field suggests that there are four dominant kinds of responses that caretakers exhibit—acceptance, overprotection, rejection, and denial (Kanner, 1952, p. 26; Cruickshank, 1955, pp. 255-259). It is true that in a given parent these reactions may not appear in pure form. Instead, the response can be a mixture of two or more varieties. However, it is also the case that one of these reactions often dominates a parent's attitude toward the defective offspring. When counselors are aware of the four types, they can seek to identify which type is operating in a given case and, as a consequence, more precisely estimate what their counseling task will involve. In some instances, the mother represents one type and the father another, thereby complicating the child's life more than would be true if the parents agreed on how to respond to the handicap. The four varieties, then, are as follows:

Constructive Acceptance of the Handicap

This attitude typically leads to the healthiest personality development for the child. The parents have accepted the handicap in an objective way. They neither reject nor overprotect the child. They say, "He's our son; he has this defect, and together we'll make the best of it." They plan realistically for the boy's education and his future. They do not express guilt or anger at the handicap, and in social situations, they do not display shame, nor do they apologize for the child's condition.

Somewhere in their lives, such parents have developed a philosophy to care for this situation. Researchers conducting a study of parents of blind children concluded that "in most cases religion gives [the parents] mental and spiritual support" (Cruickshank, 1955, p. 256). Counseling, whether in a pastoral or secular setting, may contribute to parents' assuming such an attitude.

Overprotection of the Child

Mothers, more often than fathers, exhibit this reaction. They are overcome with feelings of pity for the child or of guilt for having produced an offspring so poorly equipped to face the world. Wolfensberger (1972, p. 330), in reviewing studies of parental reactions to a retarded child, found that the most frequent reaction was guilt. Such parents may protect the child too carefully, do too much for her, and prevent the child from making decisions or carrying responsibility by herself. In response to overprotection, the child can remain infantile and overdependent. She avoids trying many of the tasks that she is quite capable of performing. In some cases, the child becomes domineering. Her parents (usually the mother) become the child's slaves. Mothers who adopt this role may actually be assuaging their own guilt feelings through their penitent dedication; or perhaps they fulfill their need for a person in whom to invest their love. Olshansky (1970) observed that chronic sorrow may persist throughout the lives of these parents.

Sometimes the caregivers' oversolicitous attitude is really a disguised rejection of the child. They consider the handicap a disgrace, but because society takes a pitying attitude toward such children and because the parents suffer from their own punitive consciences, they cannot outwardly reject their child. Hence, they play the overprotective role. In doing so, they may damage the child's personality as much as if they expressed undisguised dislike for him. For instance, some parents of this type make it obvious to the child that they are denying themselves a normal life by their dedication to him. This causes the child to heap destructive guilt and shame on himself for being faulty.

Overt Rejection of the Child

This type of parent openly resents the handicapped child. Such people are aware of their own resentment and dislike but assuage their guilt feelings by projecting the blame onto the environment: onto society for its negative attitude toward the handicap, onto the physicians who have not seriously tried to help the child, onto the teachers who are prejudiced against the handicapped one, and onto the child himself for resisting normality—"He doesn't half try to succeed the way other children do."

Denial of the Handicap

Some caregivers will not accept the fact that the young one is handicapped and requires somewhat different aims and treatment than do other children. These people typically set overambitious goals for the child, insist on high achievement, and fail to accept the guidance of others in planning a realistic future for the young one. Therefore, the child suffers because too much is expected of her, and the child is not given the special aid that might improve her adjustment. At least, when parents display this attitude, the child is permitted to try participating in the activities of more normal age-mates. She is not overprotected.

Counseling Decisions

As implied in the above descriptions of parental attitudes, an initial task of the counselor is to estimate which attitude, or combination, is held by the parents of the case at hand. On the basis of this estimate, a decision can be made about what counseling techniques will be most appropriate and about the sequence in which the techniques should be applied.

One technique useful in nearly all such cases is the encouragement of *catharsis*—that is, providing an opportunity for caregivers to unburden themselves of their worries, resentment, and guilt. In many instances, parents need accurate *information* about what can reasonably be expected of their handicapped child, both now and in the years ahead. They may also require information about books to consult, about ways to provide constructive care and activities for their child, and about community agencies that can help. On the basis of such information, counselors can also assist in devising a realistic plan for the child's future. For parents who either reject the child or deny the handicap, a counselor may adopt an approach that confronts the clients with reality and with the responsibility that society expects them to assume—such an approach is *gestalt, rational-emotive,* or *reality* therapy. To equip caregivers with specific techniques of interacting constructively with their child, the therapist may apply *behavioral* methods. The largest amount of research on work with parents has focused on teaching them behavior-management skills. The results indicate that parents can indeed learn specific skills for influencing the handicapped child's behavior, but it is not clear how well most parents can generalize what they have learned to new situations (Bricker, 1986). Because having a handicapped child usually places extra demands on the patience, ingenuity, and energy of caregivers, counseling may include offering comfort and *consolation* to help them bear their burden (Stewart, 1986).

COUNSELING THE HANDICAPPED CHILD

As noted earlier, the older the child, the more likely it is that the counselor will work directly with the child, rather than solely with the parents. Counseling with handicapped children usually is directed toward three goals.

The first goal is to remedy those aspects of the handicap that can be corrected. In some cases, the counselor may be equipped to provide the therapy directly, such as with speech training. In other cases, the counselor refers the client to a qualified specialist, such as an orthopedic surgeon for a child with a malformed arm or a nutritionist for one who is chronically exhausted.

The second goal is to help the child accept her handicap realistically so that she recognizes both the limitations that it imposes on her activities and the positive opportunities still open to her. To accomplish this task with the kindergarten child or with those who are older, counselors may tell the child stories of others who have been handicapped and yet made positive adjustments to their condition. Furthermore, play therapy can include the counselor's providing dolls that represent family members and the child's peers, offering an opportunity for one or more of the peers to display a disability, such as a bandaged leg or a patch over one eye. As the play session evolves, the child can be encouraged to tell how the other people treat the handicapped doll and also to tell what that doll thinks about the others and about herself. The session may thus serve as a diagnostic tool for revealing the child's perception of her world and of herself, both as an avenue of catharsis for the child's feelings of distress and as a way for the therapist to suggest how the handicapped doll could act so as to feel better about herself. Hand puppets can be used in the same fashion.

The third goal is to provide the child practice in acting in constructive ways in situations that have caused him distress in the past. The counseling techniques can involve both behavior therapy and role playing. In behavior therapy, the counselor engages the child in tasks in a play situation, then arranges the reward-and-punishment contingencies in a manner that encourages the child to adopt more mature behavior than has been his or her habit in the past. In role playing, the counselor sets up "let's pretend" situations, then participates with the child (perhaps the parent also takes part) in a manner that gives that child practice in trying new, more constructive ways of interacting with others. For children too shy to engage directly in these spontaneous playlets, using puppets may provide them sufficient psychological distance from directly revealing themselves to become willing to engage the puppets in the "let's-pretend" situations.

Counselors have discovered that trying to interview young children directly often proves unproductive, because children may be shy or may find the counselor's questions and remarks uninteresting or confusing. Thus, it is well to provide media in which the children can invest their interest. Then the counseling conversation can be conducted in relation to the media. Magazines or storybooks that picture handicapped people or animals can serve this purpose. Easel paints, crayons, colored marking pens and drawing paper, plasticine, or play dough may also be suitable.

CONCLUSION

The dual purpose of this chapter has been to summarize general developmental characteristics of young children that can influence counselors' decisions and to describe in greater detail normative information related to two types of cases—children who have suffered abuse or neglect and children who suffer handicaps. A point made frequently throughout the chapter has been that the clients in such cases are both the children and their caregivers, with the success of counseling depending primarily on how well it improves the caregivers' treatment of their young child.

5

Later Childhood: Ages 6 to 12
The Elementary-School Years

Children at this stage of life rarely seek counseling on their own initiative. Instead, they are taken to a therapist by someone who is concerned about their behavior and welfare. Consequently, counselors who receive children in this age range often end up with more than one client, since the adults who send children for help may themselves become actively involved in the counseling process. The counselees in a case may be a mother and son, a stepfather and stepdaughter, a teacher and pupil, or a child's entire nuclear family.

Cases frequently met during the elementary-school years are ones involving children:

—Whose academic progress fails to equal that of the majority of their age-mates. Parents or school personnel have referred the pupil for counseling to discover why the child fails to keep up with classmates in school work, and they wish to identify ways to correct or at least ameliorate the child's learning difficulties.
—Who are distressed by their place in a changed, and ofttimes poorly defined, family constellation as a result of the separation or divorce of their parents. Such distress may be expressed in phobias, depression, aggressivity, school failure, or lawbreaking.
—Who suffer a physical handicap or an illness that affects their appearance, their ability to engage in the typical activities of their age-group, and their feelings of self-worth.
—Who continue to act like children who are considerably younger. Such developmental lag is manifest in failure to control urination or defecation, in the use of "baby talk," in crying or engaging in temper tantrums when frustrated, or in preferring younger children as companions.
—Who have become distraught as the result of a traumatic event, such as the death or serious injury of a parent or sibling, the breakup of the

parents' marriage, a sexual assault on the child, an alcoholic father's abusing the mother, the child's suffering a serious injury, or the family's moving into a frightening neighborhood.

—Who inordinately display such characteristics as depression, cruelty, shyness, aggressivity, self-deprecation, disdain for others' rights, irresponsibility, lack of self-confidence, fear, anger, weeping, or the like.

—Who have been referred by a social agency or the courts as a result of their suffering abuse or neglect on the part of parents or guardians.

In the present chapter, the normative information that bears on counseling children of elementary school age is presented in two sections. The first contains general developmental characteristics for years 6 through 12. The second offers information especially relevant to three types of problems: (1) unsatisfactory school performance—dyslexia, (2) nontraditional family constellations, and (3) developmental lag—enuresis.

DEVELOPMENTAL TRENDS
AGES 6 THROUGH 12

The following overview of general growth trends is organized under four categories: (1) physical size, appearance, and functions, (2) cognition and language, (3) social relationships and sexual development, and (4) self-perception.

Physical Size, Appearance, and Functions

In terms of physical development, later childhood is an interim of decreased growth rate that falls between the rapid growth rates of early childhood and early adolescence. Obviously, later childhood is not a growth plateau, in the sense of a time of no increase in height, weight, and musculature. It is merely a reduction in the pace at which growth proceeds. Some figures on average heights at different ages can illustrate this trend. Among boys in the United States, the average increase in height over the three-year period of ages 3 through 6 is 21.2 centimeters. For the age period 7 through 10 years, the increase declines to 15.7, then rises to 19.3 centimeters for the age period 12-15 (Hamill, 1977).

In the upper reaches of later childhood—ages 10 through 12—the difference in growth rate between boys and girls becomes apparent. On the average, girls arrive at puberty one-and-one-half or two years before boys. Thus, girls can begin their early-adolescent growth spurt in the upper-elementary and early junior-high grades, as reflected in rapid increases in height and weight and in changes of body contours. As a result, the pattern of average height increase for girls is similar to that among boys for the age period 3-6 years (20.5 centimeters), but exceeds that of boys in the period 7-10 (17.7 centimeters), and has already declined by the end of the 12-15 period (10.3 centimeters) (Hamill, 1977).

Later childhood is also a period of consolidation and progress in muscular coordination and strength. Between ages 6 and 12, children become noticeably more agile in both their large-muscle movements (running, jumping, hopping, twisting, throwing, catching) and their small-muscle activities (handwriting, drawing, painting, cutting with scissors, fitting small objects together). This is the period of life when children typically play the greatest variety of games, trying out many types of physical activities as if preparing to select the ones they wish to concentrate on during adolescence.

Cognition and Language

Marked advances in children's cognitive abilities, combined with society's expectations that children will achieve academically, are central features of mental development during later childhood. Developmentalists of a variety of theoretical persuasions have emphasized the importance of intellectual accomplishments during these elementary-school years.

Erikson (1964, pp. 115-134), in his theory of psychosocial stages, has proposed that the key developmental crisis of ages 7 through 12 centers on the child's learning to accomplish tasks well, including intellectual tasks. In Erikson's view, school-age children still need and enjoy hours of make-believe games and play, but they become dissatisfied with too much of this and want to do something worthwhile. They want to earn recognition by producing something and gain the satisfaction of completing work by perseverance. In Erikson's opinion, if adults pose tasks for children that they can accomplish and that they can recognize as interesting and worthy, and if the adults furnish the guidance needed for completing the tasks, then children have a better chance of coming through this period with a sound sense of industry. However, if the family has not prepared the child well for school life and if the child does not achieve the tasks faced in school, later childhood can produce the opposite of self-confidence—a sense of inadequacy and inferiority. Feelings of inferiority may also occur if the things the child has already learned to do well are considered insignificant by the teacher, parents, and class-mates. Furthermore, Erikson contends that the child may have potential abilities which, if not evoked and nurtured during these years, may "develop late or never" (1959, p. 87).

From a different theoretical position, such Soviet psychologists as Vygotsky and Elkonin have conceived of child development in terms of stages, each dominated by a *leading activity* (Davidow, 1985; Elkonin, in Cole, 1977; Vygotsky, 1962). A leading activity is marked by three features: (1) It is the chief factor establishing a given period in the child's psychological development, (2) it is within the field of this activity that particular psychic functions emerge, and (3) the climax of the activity forms the foundation for the next leading activity. The leading activity for infancy is intuitive and emotional contact between the child and adults. For ages 1 through 3, it is object manipulation. For ages 3 through 7, it is playing games. For the years 7 through 11, the leading activity is *learning*. The principal formal setting for pursuing this activity is the school. Within this stage, children develop theoretical approaches to the world of things, a function that involves their considering objective laws of reality and beginning to comprehend psychological preconditions for abstract theoretical thought (intentional mental operations, mental schemes for problem solving, reflective thinking).

Quite in keeping with both Erikson's and the Soviets' views are Piaget's discoveries about the advance of mental processes during later childhood. As explained in Chapter 4, Piaget posited two major periods of mental development prior to age 6 or 7—the sensorimotor (birth to age 2) and the preoperational (ages 2 to 7). The third period—that of *concrete operations*—appears during the elementary-school years (around ages 7 through 11). The fourth and final period—called *formal operations*—begins around age 12, although there are noticeable individual differences among children in the time when this may occur.

CONCRETE OPERATIONS

Consider now those features of the concrete-operations stage that can yield implications for counseling. As noted in Chapter 4, in Piaget's system the term *operations* means manipulating objects in relation to each other. At the concrete-operations stage, children become capable of performing mental manipulations directly related to objects. In the next stage—that of formal operations—they will learn to perform operations on verbally stated hypotheses and propositions that are not limited to particular objects (Piaget & Inhelder, 1969, p. 100). The term *concrete* does not mean that children must see or touch actual objects as they work through a problem. Rather, *concrete* means that the problems involve identifiable objects that are either directly perceived or imagined. In the later formal-operations period, children are able to solve problems that do not concern particular objects. This difference can be illustrated with the following two problems. The first is suitable for the concrete-operations child and the second for the more-advanced, formal-operations child or adolescent:

Concrete: If Bill has two toy cars and Frank gives him three more, how many cars will Bill have altogether?

Formal: Imagine that there are two quantities which together make up a whole. If we increase the first quantity but the whole remains the same, what has happened to the second quantity?

Although children at the concrete stage do not need to see the objects in order to carry out the operations, in their early-transitional phase of entering this period, they will be aided by viewing the actual objects or pictures of them. Hence, in helping children grasp concepts in mathematics, science, and social studies, primary-grade teachers find it particularly important to illustrate the concepts with objects and pictures and to provide children opportunities to manipulate these items, either physically or in discussion.

As mentioned in Chapter 4, in order for actions to qualify as operations, the actions must be internalizable, reversible, and coordinated into systems which have laws that apply to the entire system and not just to the single action itself. By *internalizable*, Piaget meant that the actions can be carried out in thought without losing their original character of physical manipulations. By *reversible*, he meant that they can readily be inverted into their opposite—two groups of apples that are combined (added together) to form a whole group can as easily be reduced (subtracted from the whole) to their original status as two groups. Examples of *coordinated system* are the sets of operations that make up such disciplines as mathematics, biology, chemistry, and physics.

A further characteristic of operations is that they are not unique to an individual child but are common to all people of the same intelligence level. In addition, an operation assists children not only in their own private reasoning but also in those "cognitive exchanges" with others that bring together information and combine it in various ways.

One of Piaget's most significant discoveries about the development of children's intelligence is reflected in the question: "When something is transformed, what aspects change and what aspects remain the same?" That is, when an object is moved or transformed in some way—in a transformation that qualifies as operatory—not everything about the system changes. Some aspects remain constant. Piaget gave the label *conservation* to this feature of constancy or invariance of objects. How adequately the child's conception matches that of adult logic or "reality" can be judged if we assess which aspects of objects the child believes have been conserved during a transformation.

Piaget's investigations have shown that the particular features that a child sees as being conserved depend on the child's age, or more accurately, on the child's cognitive-development level. For example, when two lumps of clay the same size and shape are shown to a child and then one lump is rolled into a sausage form, the typical child age 7 or 8 recognizes that the substance has been conserved—it is still clay. But not until 9 or 10 does the child discover that the weight has been conserved as well. And not until 11 or 12 does he or she identify the conservation of volume that occurs when an object, such as a clay ball, is immersed in water and the displacement measured (Piaget & Inhelder, 1969, p. 99). Thus, during the elementary-school years, children discover more and more of the properties of objects and transformations, and thereby they master an increasing number of mental operations that can be applied in understanding their world.

The egocentrism that causes preschool children to see things only from their own viewpoint also changes as the elementary-school child gains language facility and becomes more *allocentric*, meaning that the child can now better understand others' perspectives. Children's notions of causation also mature, so they are more likely, at this stage, to abandon explanations based on magic ("the elves did it") and casual-correlation ("the clouds moved to make the wind blow") in favor of descriptions of cause based on the same criteria as those used by most adults.

FORMAL OPERATIONS

From around age 11 or 12 to middle and late adolescence, children are no longer limited by what they directly see or hear, nor are they restricted to the problem at hand. They can now imagine the conditions of a problem—past, present, or future—and develop hypotheses about what might logically occur under different combinations of factors. For example, if we begin a problem with "Imagine that water in the river ran uphill; then what would happen if . . . ," children younger than 11 will typically claim that water does not run uphill. By the close of the formal operations period, teenagers can accept the hypothetical condition of upward flow and can apply it in solving the posed problem.

One of Piaget's favorite examples further illustrates the difference between the concrete-operations child and the one who has attained formal-operations ability. This is the problem of *transitivity*, meaning that a relationship between two elements or objects is carried over to other elements that are logically related to the first two. For instance, children have solved the problem of transitivity if they recognize that when A=B and B=C, then A=C. Or if A<B and B<C, then A<C. So the question posed to children is this: "Edith is fairer than Susan; Edith is darker than Lily; who is the darkest of the three?" Piaget (1950, p. 149) found that children before age 12 could rarely solve the puzzle. Instead, they engaged in such reasoning as: "Edith and Susan are fair, Edith and Lily are dark, therefore Lily is darkest, Susan is the fairest, and Edith is in between." However, by mid-adolescence, students could solve the problem accurately, for they comprehend the transitivity that it involved.

Finally, an important fact that counselors can profitably recognize is that, while all children advance through the same major phases of thinking in essentially the same sequence, the pace of their progress can vary significantly from one child to another. Children whose rate of mental growth deviates significantly from the average for their age cohort will frequently become the object of psychological counseling. Pupils whose mental development trails behind that of classmates are the ones whose deviance is most often viewed as a problem by parents, school personnel, and the pupils themselves. However, sometimes those who have sped ahead of their age-mates in mental growth will "get into trouble" out of boredom or disrespect for authorities, and, thus, they may be brought for counseling.

In summary, Piaget's conceptions of children's intellectual development during later childhood—conceptions generally corroborated by a large body of evidence gathered by other researchers—demonstrate that children, in their thought processes, are not merely uninformed adults who will think like adults if they are simply "told the facts." Rather, children naturally think differently than do adults. Over the first decade of life, children's modes of thought advance in a regular fashion toward the formal-operations abilities displayed in mature adult thought. Understanding these progressive steps in mental growth is important for counselors in working with children and in helping parents to understand why sons and daughters think and act as they do. A typical 6-year-old whose parents are getting a divorce cannot understand as well as a 12-year-old the reasons for the family breakup, since the young child is less capable of viewing the event from the perspective of the parents or an outsider. A slow-maturing 8-year-old, whose grasp of conservation lags behind that of his more gifted age-mates, will have difficulties with third grade mathematics, science, and social studies concepts that his classmates are already equipped to comprehend.

VOCABULARY GROWTH

The size of children's vocabularies is ·no longer studied extensively. However, investigations from the past still provide an impression of the diversity in children's rates of language development. In a study of the vocabularies of school-age children grades 1 through 11, M. K. Smith (1941) learned that within a single school system the first and second graders who achieved the highest vocabulary scores knew more words than did the poorest students in every grade above them, including grade 11. Reading ability varies in a similar way. Tests of reading skill among third graders in two California elementary schools showed that the poorest readers succeeded no better than an average beginning first grader, whereas the best readers succeeded as well as average seventh graders (Thomas & Thomas, 1965, p. 307). In effect, at every age level throughout childhood, there is great variation in individuals' command of language. As a consequence, in counseling a child, it is useful in the early sessions for the therapist to converse in simple vocabulary until the child's apparent understanding and the richness of the child's spoken vocabulary suggest that the child operates easily with a more varied, sophisticated range of words. If the counseling involves the administration of reading comprehension measures or aptitude tests (such as the Stanford-Binet or Wechsler Intelligence Scale for Children), then the results of these measures can serve as a guide to the vocabulary level on which the child can communicate.

MEMORY

The term *knowledge base* refers to the quantity of contents stored in people's long-term memory. Compared to the preschool child, the typical school-age child has compiled a greater number of memories of events and relationships as a result of more years of experience and a more mature neural system. Besides having a greater fund of items in their knowledge base, older children have a greater number of associations among the items than do younger ones. For example, the typical older child recognizes more ways in which the concepts *father, mother, stepmother, cousin, grandparents,* and *remarriage* can be connected than does the younger child.

Furthermore, the older child has a greater command of mnemonic processes (techniques for remembering and recalling material) than does the younger one, and the older child uses these processes in a more sophisticated manner. For instance, if children are asked to memorize a telephone number or a list of street names, first and second graders are likely to depend on one strategy, such as rehearsal (saying the number list over and over). However, this is "by no means the most effective mnemonic strategy available to a sophisticated and resourceful information processor" (Flavell, 1977, p. 195). By the end of the elementary grades, children not only rehearse the items but also begin to cluster or group them according to some common factor, such as their ordinal or alphabetical sequence. Children also may intentionally associate the items with others already in memory, such as comparing a phone number to their own phone number or to a similar number from history. Children can be taught mnemonic strategies, but, in the lower grades, they will not often automatically transfer the use of a strategy to remembering items other than those involved with the instruction that they received. The older child and adolescent can make such a transfer. In effect, the ability to transfer generalizations or processes from one situation to another increases during the years in school.

Counselors who recognize these trends in cognitive development can profitably adjust their expectations and techniques to the realities of (1) how accurately children may recall events from the past that bear on their present counseling problem, (2) how well children can understand and retain what is discussed during counseling sessions, and (3) how well children can transfer strategies practiced in the counseling setting to solving comparable problems in their daily lives.

Social Relationships and Sexual Development

The most significant event affecting most children's social development in the years of middle childhood is their entering school. Not only does school attendance require that the child adjust to a large number of age-mates of diverse social backgrounds, but the school's routine requires that the child abide by rules that may seem strange and restrictive. For girls and boys who attended child-care centers or nursery schools during their early childhood, the transition to primary school is less distressing than for ones whose initial encounter with a crowd of peers occurs only in kindergarten or first grade. The experience can be particularly trying for children, who, before reaching school age, have lived only with their parents or with no more than one or two siblings and who have had few if any neighborhood playmates.

Entering school often exposes children to unfamiliar language, behavior patterns, and attitudes that may conflict with those experienced in their own family. From their new classmates, children may learn words which, when used at home, are censured by parents as "dirty talk—don't ever let me hear you say that again." Or, in contrast, phrases commonly used in a child's own family, which he or she then carries to school, may be condemned by the teacher as "nasty" or "filthy" or "ungodly." Furthermore, methods of settling arguments or of getting their own way that children are accustomed to using at home may conflict with the expectations and ways of acting held by the teacher or classmates. Whining, crying, kicking, threatening, cheating, lying, or sulking may not succeed as well at school as they have at home, thereby confronting the child with a choice of either revising long-standing social habits or facing a school career of unpleasant consequences.

Cultural differences in social expectations can cause problems for children whose ethnic or social-class backgrounds have fostered behaviors different from those considered suitable by school personnel. Children who have learned at home to remain quiet unless their opinion is directly requested are not likely to volunteer ideas during class discussion, and this reticence may be mistaken by the teacher and classmates as dim-wittedness. Such misunderstandings are compounded if the child comes from a home where the language spoken is not that of the school, so that the child is handicapped in explaining clearly what he or she means.

However, the expanded social world of the school does not just confront children with problems. It offers many positive opportunities as well—the chance for making new friends, for hearing about other people's beliefs and their ways of life, for engaging in new games, for exchanging jokes and riddles and rhymes, and for trying out new skills. Not only are children's social perceptions broadened by their direct encounters with an expanded community of peers and school personnel, but the social-studies portion of the curriculum opens broader social vistas, including ways of life of people in other places and at other times. The ready accessibility on television and videotapes of life in cultures around the world brings such matters more graphically to present-day classrooms than was possible in the past, when books and oral descriptions were the main media for describing social events from beyond pupils' immediate experiences.

Television programs, however, are clearly a mixed blessing in terms of their contribution to the school-age child's social development. By the 1980s, the average U.S. American child spent more time watching television (3 to 4 hours a day) then engaging in any other activity. As a result, television viewed at home has had an influence on children's conceptions of proper social behavior that may equal or exceed the influence of school experiences. The damaging effect on children's social values exerted by growing amounts of violence and explicit, casual sex on television has now been well documented, with the evidence indicating that viewing television increases the probability of violent action (Parke & Slaby, 1983; Singer & Singer, 1983). As a result, child-welfare activists advocate that parents carefully monitor the television fare that their children are permitted to consume.

Children's conception of the nature of rules and regulations tends to change during middle and later childhood. Piaget's (1932/1948) study of children's game-playing behavior illustrates one interpretation of such changes. Between ages 2 and 15, he identified three stages of rule conception. He called the first stage *egocentric* (around age 2 to 5 or 6), when children begin to recognize rules imposed by others but do not abide strictly by the rules, whether playing alone or with others. In effect, the child more or less imitates rules described by others but does so in a purely individual, unabashedly self-serving fashion. Stage 2 (age 7 through 10) is a period of *incipient cooperation*, when players begin to concern themselves with mutual control and unification of the rules, but the rules are not yet stable, nor is children's understanding of the rules entirely clear and consistent. Stage 3 (ages 11 to 15 and beyond) marks a period of *rule codification*, when every detail of the game is fixed and the code of rules is known throughout the society of players. Children in the upper levels of these stages can recognize that rules are not inviolate but, rather, that they can be altered through consent of the members of that society. Counselors who recognize that rules do not have the same meaning for children at different age levels are prepared to investigate how a child client who has broken rules may perceive the significance of what he or she has done. Learning the nature of the child's perception may then aid the counselor in deciding what approach to take in the case.

A further, oft-mentioned characteristic of the elementary-school years is children's tendency to keep company primarily with age-mates of their same sex. This period of social development is often referred to as the *gang age*. Incidents of taunting and expressing disrespect between boys and girls during these years should come as no surprise. Freud termed it the *latency* or *homosexual* period, with *latency* suggesting a stage of apparent disinterest in sexual matters and *homosexual* signifying children's preference for spending their time predominantly with others of their own sex (Freud, 1938). The term *homosexual*, in this context, is not intended to imply that children necessarily become involved in physical sexual relations. However, research into such matters has revealed that children approaching puberty often do engage in some mutual genital fondling with same-sex age-mates. Studies in recent decades have suggested that in the United States these sorts of exploratory homosexual encounters increase gradually during later childhood, so that, by age 14 about 35% of girls and 50 to 60% of boys have engaged in the activities at some time (Broderick, 1966; Martinson, 1974). Such sex play does not seem to predict adult sexual preference, since, in many cases, the early experimentation is dropped and attention thereafter is directed toward the opposite sex.

Differences in maturation rate between girls and boys near the close of later childhood can cause differences in social interests and relationships in the upper-elementary grades. As girls, on the average, mature 1½ to 2 years earlier than boys, some girls by ages 10-12, begin to experience pubertal development that not only alters their appearance but also stimulates their interest in matters more typically adolescent. Thus, by the final years of elementary school, some divergence of social interests may be observed between early-maturing girls and their classmates who are approaching puberty at a slower pace, particularly the boys. Problems associated with these differences in social interests may come to the attention of counselors.

Self-Perception—The Child's Personal Identity

The personality factor identified as *self-concept* or *self-perception* in Chapter 4 is also often referred to as one's *personal identity*. It is the individual's notion of "who I am" or "what I am like." Brody (1980), in writing about personal identity, has suggested that when, from one month to the next, the essential characteristics of a person remain constant, this constancy represents the individual's identity. The phrase *essential characteristics* has been included here to show that everything about a person need not stay the same over time for the individual to have an identity. Instead, only certain aspects need to remain unchanged (Hirsch, 1982). These aspects are the ones Boer and Lycan (1986, p. 155) have called *important properties*. An 8-year-old girl's level of self-confidence would typically be regarded as a more important characteristic of her identity than would the length of her toenails. Furthermore, the properties considered important can vary from one context to another. During a church service, an 11-year-old boy may regard his beliefs about God, sin, and death as important properties of his identity, whereas, on the football field, he may consider his physical agility, strength, and courage more consequential for his identity than his relationship to God and his beliefs about sin and death.

Identity can be viewed from both internal and external perspectives. By means of introspection, a girl may see her own identity (properties she considers most important) as including her sense of insecurity around boys, her love of romantic poetry, and her desire to please her parents. This is her self-concept. In contrast, other people may cite different properties as the significant indicators of her identity—her height and weight, her name, her facial features, her academic achievement, and her manner of talking with adults. Some writers have applied the label *personal identity* to the introspective view and *social identity* to the external view. Erikson (1959) adopted both the internal and external perspectives in defining *ego identity*, contending that ego identity has been achieved when the internal and external views become congruent, so that others see us the same way we see ourselves.

The sense of ego identity, then, is the accrued confidence that one's ability to maintain inner sameness and continuity is matched by the same sameness and continuity of one's meaning for others. Thus, self-esteem . . . grows to be a conviction that one is learning effective steps toward a tangible future, that one is developing a defined personality within a social reality which one understands (p. 89).

By speaking of a *defined personality*, Erikson implies its reciprocal, which can be called an *ill-defined* or *diffuse* or *nebulous* personality. Such terms suggest that people's identities can vary in their degree of clarity, sharpness, or precision.

Linked to, but not identical to, this matter of clarity or precision is a *conscious-unconscious* variable. Even when people's behavior suggests that they have an "accrued confidence" in their ability to "maintain inner sameness and continuity," they may differ in the degree to which they can verbally express the nature of this confidence. In other words, when viewing themselves or when viewing others, they may or may not be able to explain clearly the properties they believe to compose their own or others' identities. Thus, the term *conscious*, as used here, refers to people's skill in describing the nature of their own or someone else's identity within a given context. When a girl's description of her own identity is only vague and intuitive, we would say that she is "unconscious" or "not conscious" of the components of her identity. Young children, in particular, are unable to explain such matters.

In summary, personal identity can be conceived to be a multifaceted core of the personality, whose evolution during the elementary-school years is effected both by the increasing maturation of the neural system and by those daily interactions with the social environment that influence the identifications which the child acquires. From the earliest weeks of life, two opposing psychological processes appear to contribute to people's developing a personal identity. The first process is identification; the second is differentiation.

Identification is taking place when a person assumes that some object, person, or idea in the environment is part of himself or herself. In effect, identification is the extension of one's personal identity to include phenomena from the world. An introspective emotional test which enables us to recognize our identifications consists of inspecting how we feel at the successes and failures of objects in the environment. The objects may be human (mother, a school athletic team, the nation's armed forces), nonhuman (a dog, a teddy bear), or nonmaterial (a religion). If we feel pleased at their successes and distressed at their failures, then we conclude that we have encompassed such phenomena within our personal identity or sense of self. If we feel no pleasure at their successes and no disappointment at their failures, we conclude that we have not identified with those phenomena.

Furthermore, the power or strength of our identifications can be estimated from the degree of pleasure or distress we feel. Becoming very angry when someone speaks ill of our nation's top leader signifies that we have established a strong identification with that leader, whereas feeling only slightly piqued at someone's criticizing a teacher of our acquaintance signifies our weak identification with that teacher. The term *negative identification* can be applied to phenomena which arouse our dislike, fear, or hate at their success and arouse pleasure at their failure. Hence, in counseling encounters, the therapist can estimate the type and strength of a client's identifications by the kind of emotional reactions that the client displays at the success or failure of phenomena in the client's experience. The situation is made more complex by the fact that a child may hold ambivalent identifications, simultaneously liking and disliking the same object. Parents, teachers, siblings, and companions often elicit such alternating emotional reactions. This process of deciding "which things are me" (and to what degree) and "which things are not me" is at the core of the lifelong process of identity development.

During infancy and early childhood, the phenomena with which children have identified and which they have thereby incorporated into their sense of self were multiplied rapidly as they acquired language, expanded their world of experiences, and matured in their modes of thought. However, throughout the first five years of life, children still have been limited in their ability to differentiate themselves from others. Although they recognized that others are different from themselves in appearance, they still have tended to be egocentric in failing to understand that other people may not perceive the world as they themselves do. This egocentricity can make it difficult for them to understand such moral concepts as fair play or to comprehend why the activities that they themselves enjoy may not be preferred by others.

However, throughout the elementary-school years, children's expanding range of social interactions while attending school is combined with their exposure to the wider world of knowledge through books and television, thereby increasing the number of options for establishing identifications and defining the self. At the same time, school-age children's growing mental ability to adopt an allocentric rather than egocentric perspective helps them to differentiate themselves from others. They acquire an increasing sense of individuality, which they can contrast with the individuality of others whom they know. During these years, the identifications that become integrated into children's identities are partially reflected in the words that they use to tell "who I am." "I'm an American school girl, I'm a good singer, I'm pretty good at riding a horse, I love dogs, I like to read, I hate math, and I like to fix my hair like some of those rock stars on TV."

Counselors' estimates of school-age clients' sense of identity can be derived in several ways. The most obvious is that of observing the clients' modes of social interaction with the counselor and with others. "Are clients self-deprecating or self-adulating? Do they apologize, or do they brag a lot? Do they readily engage in conversation or shyly hold back? Do they willingly attempt new tasks or hesitate to try anything new?" and the like? Other means of estimating children's sense of self can be part of a classroom writing assignment, such as creating essays entitled "Who I Am" or "What I Would Like to Be" or "What My Life Has Been Like." Opportunities to write short stories and poems may serve the same purpose. A sentence-completion activity can consist of the teacher or counselor's offering a series of sentence stems which the child finishes either orally or in written form. The following types of stems may produce identity revelations:

What I like best about myself is _____ .
I'm very good at _____ .
If I could change my looks, I _____ .
What most people don't know about me is that _____ .

It is perhaps obvious that children's responses to such stimuli should not necessarily be taken at face value. To protect an identity which they do not wish to reveal, school-age children may falsify the conception of self that they present to the world. Therefore, it is useful to gather evidence of a child's personal identity from a variety of sources—observations of behavior in social situations, interviews with the client, others' impressions of the client in a variety of settings, projective techniques—in order to establish a convincing picture of the child's personal identity.

With the foregoing overview of key characteristics of development from age 6 to age 12, we turn now to selected kinds of counseling cases often met during these years.

KINDS OF COUNSELING CASES
IN LATER CHILDHOOD

The three types of cases chosen to illustrate personal/social difficulties among elementary-school children are ones involving (1) unsatisfactory academic performance—dyslexia, (2) nontraditional family constellations, and (3) developmental lag—enuresis.

Unsatisfactory Academic Performance—Dyslexia

Children can appear for counseling for various reasons that are related to school—to remedy their unsatisfactory academic progress, to treat the emotional distress that they display in the school setting (inordinate shyness, crying, temper tantrums), to improve their social interaction with peers, or to correct their failure to abide by school rules (truancy, disturbing the classroom learning climate, challenging the authority of teachers and staff). Frequently, the problem that brings the child to the counselor's office involves more than one of these. Because an inspection of all such difficulties would require far more space than these few pages allow, the following discussion of children's school-related difficulties is limited to one puzzling disorder, *dyslexia*, which diminishes pupils' progress in all academic areas by impairing their ability to read.

DIAGNOSING DYSLEXIA

The term *dyslexia* was coined to identify a reading handicap displayed by children or adults whose general mental ability is average or above, whose senses of sight and hearing are normal, whose physical health is adequate, and who are not significantly disadvantaged by their social/cultural environment (as would be true if the child had missed a great deal of school, if the family spoke only a foreign language, or if the parents were notably abusive). Thus, the delayed development of reading skill in a child whose general intellectual ability is well below average (warranting the designation of *mental retardation*) does not qualify as dyslexic. Neither does the far-sighted or deaf child or one whose general ability is normal but who suffers emotional problems that distract him or her from concentrating on such school tasks as learning to read.

Dyslexia, then, is a *specific* learning disability, limited to the skill of reading. Other specific learning disabilities in the use of language and numbers bear other labels. *Dyscalculia* or *acalculia* identifies a deficiency in performing arithmetic operations, and *dysgraphia* means a disorder of writing skill. Sometimes a child will suffer more than one of these handicaps.

The above defining characteristics of dyslexia serve as the basic guides to identifying children who suffer the condition. Diagnosis requires information about the pupil's reading skill, general intellectual ability, sight and hearing, past and present opportunities to learn to read, language environment and child-rearing practices in the home, and emotional stress sufficient to affect school progress. The following are typical ways in which each of these factors is appraised.

Reading Achievement

There are several common ways for assessing children's reading skills. One is to have them read aloud, then answer questions about the content of the passage. Oral-reading performance reveals the extent to which a child miscalls words, reverses letters, or inserts or deletes words or letters. The follow-up questions indicate how well children have grasped the meaning of the passage. There are also numerous standardized reading tests, as well as tests accompanying reading textbooks typically used in classrooms.

General Intelligence

Judgments of general intellectual ability are typically based on a child's performance on an individually administered intelligence test. The most frequently used evaluation device has been the Wechsler Intelligence Scale for Children—Revised (1974). The Wechsler test is divided into two major sections, verbal and performance, with each section containing subtests. The verbal subtests concern general information (30 items), similarities (17 items), arithmetic (18 items), vocabulary (32 items), comprehension (17 items), and digit span (repeating series of numbers—14 items). The performance subtests involve picture completion (16 items), picture arrangement (12 items), block design (11 items), object assembly (4 items), coding (45 symbols for below 8 years, 95 symbols for above 8 years), and mazes

(9 items). Separate intelligence quotients can be derived from the verbal and performance parts of this test. A skilled psychometrist, inspecting the pattern of scores over the various types of items, can draw useful conclusions about a child's more specific strengths and weaknesses in the separate subtests. Since the WISC-R is standardized for ages 6 through 16 years, 11 months, psychologists testing children ages 4 through 6 commonly use the Wechsler Preschool and Primary Scale of Intelligence or WPPSI (Wechsler, 1967).

The third revision of the Stanford-Binet Intelligence Scale (Terman & Merrill, 1973) and the Columbia Mental Maturity Scale (Burgemeister, Blum & Lorge, 1972) are also suitable measures of general intelligence. However, they are employed less frequently than the Wechsler scales, which, according to a survey of school psychologists, have been used nearly 80% of the time for assessing intelligence in school children (Goh, Teslow, & Fuller, 1980).

A more recent psychometric device, the Kaufman Assessment Battery for Children—KABC (Kaufman & Kaufman, 1983), has certain advantages over the WISC-R and Stanford Binet, in that it depends less on language and verbal skills in testing. It also evaluates different types of reading skills, enabling the tester to identify which factors in the child's array of reading abilities are more deficient than others. The Kaufman Battery, however, still needs to prove itself additionally in practice by having a greater number of research studies conducted with it to determine its advantages and disadvantages. For example, a comparison of the use of the WISC-R and the KABC with 117 first- and second-grade pupils showed that the WISC-R successfully predicted the pupils' level of performance on two novel learning tasks, whereas the KABC did not (Ayers, Cooley, & Severson, 1988).

Because scores on an intelligence test are determined not only by children's genetic endowment but also by environmental influences, it is important when interpreting scores to estimate how conditions in the children's lives may have affected their opportunity to learn the sorts of skills that are measured by test items. Growing up in a language-impoverished environment or under family conditions that prevent children from a wide range of experiences can serve to depress the scores that children earn on such tests.

Sight and Hearing

For estimating a child's visual acuity as it relates to reading, the popular Snellen Chart (viewing letters of different sizes at a distance of 20 feet) is unsuitable, because a child who is farsighted (hyperopic) can pass the Snellen test yet see nothing but fuzzy images when looking at print in a book. The most accurate assessment of visual acuity is made by an opthalmologist or optometrist. However, a psychologist or teacher can gain hints about a possible visual disorder by observing how the child approaches close-up school work. Behaviors that may indicate a vision problem include holding a book at arm's length, squinting, cocking the head to the side while reading, appearing to brush away a blur, and complaining of sore eyes or headaches after close work.

Hearing ability is best tested by a specialist using an audiometer. However, as in the case of sight, a psychologist or teacher can make initial estimates of hearing ability by watching for symptoms, such as a child's frequently mistaking oral directions, appearing inattentive when spoken to, asking for the speaker's comment to be repeated, cocking the head to the side or leaning forward to hear people speak, and having wax in the ears.

Opportunities to Learn to Read

Particularly in the case of children who have transferred into their present school from another district, it is important to discover what sort of reading instruction they have received in the past and what reading opportunities have been provided in their family. If a child has not had a fair chance to learn reading or was given instruction before his or her neural system was sufficiently mature, then assuming that the child is dyslexic is unwarranted. The pupil's reading deficiency may result from the lack of proper instruction at the proper time. Information about these matters can be sought through interviews with the child, with parents, and with school personnel. Records of the pupil's past school achievement may also prove useful.

The Child's Social Environment

Information about how well conditions in the child's home foster academic progress can be obtained through conversations with the child and members of the family. Evidence from these interviews can help the diagnostician to estimate whether the pupil's reading deficiency is caused, at least partially, by emotional distress or by patterns of family life that do not encourage reading.

As elementary-school children advance through the grades, the negative effects of a reading disorder can be expected to increase, thus progressively damaging children's self-perception and making them the possible targets of classmates' derogatory comments and social rejection. In effect, emotional distress may contribute to a reading deficiency, but it may also be the result of such a deficiency.

Debated Issues

Among numbers of workers in this field, when the foregoing factors have been eliminated as likely causes of a child's reading disability, then the typical conclusion is that the child is dyslexic. In other words, the term *dyslexia* is a label for the residue of cause that remains after the factors of intelligence, sensory acuity, opportunity, and environment have been dismissed as likely causes. However, Miles (1983, p. 18) has disagreed with this "residue" viewpoint, contending that in addition to the absence of the above conditions, several positive signs are also needed to warrant a reading disorder's being dubbed dyslexia. These additional signs, Miles proposes, are revealed in a test which he created that assesses children's skills in performing tasks which involve repeating digits forwards and backwards, distinguishing left from right for parts of the body, repeating polysyllabic words, doing mental subtraction, repeating times tables, saying the months of the year forwards and backwards, reversing the letters *b* and *d* in writing, and having a history of reading difficulties in the family (Miles, 1983, pp. 22-23, 203-207). Thus, there continues to be a measure of disagreement among professionals about the most suitable way to identify cases of dyslexia.

The question of whether it is desirable to distinguish subtypes of dyslexia, and what should be the basis of the subtyping, is also a matter of debate. For example, Boder (1973) has suggested classifying children by their type of reading errors, thereby producing three subgroups: *dyseidetic, dysphonetic,* and *mixed.* Dyseidetic pupils appear to suffer a visual-perception disorder that renders it difficult for them to recognize the pattern formed by a group of letters, so they read and spell words by their sounds—"hows" for "house" and "ruf" for "rough." Such children read very slowly because they must sound out every word rather than immediately recognizing sight words that they have memorized. "As they go along in school, these children generally remain slow readers, but they can become relatively good spellers" (Batshaw & Perret, 1986, p. 281). Dysphonic pupils have difficulty matching the sight of a word to its sound, so they are able to read words they have memorized but cannot apply phonetic rules for sounding out new words. "A child with this disability may be able to approach grade level in reading but is usually a poor speller," while the child with a mixed type of dyslexia "has the worst of both worlds" (Batshaw & Perret, 1986, p. 281).

In sum, answers to some of the key questions about the nature of dyslexia remain controversial.

THE INCIDENCE AND CORRELATES OF DYSLEXIA

Figures on the frequency of dyslexia in the child population range from around 1% to nearly 20% (Goldberg, Shiffman, & Bender, 1983, p. 143). The wide discrepancy in these estimates is caused mainly by differences in the criteria used for identifying dyslexics. Some people have classified as dyslexic all children whose reading skill is two years or more below their grade in school or their apparent mental age. When such a broad definition is used, the numbers of dyslexics can be as high as 15% or 20% of school children. However, when the more specific criteria described above are applied, the figure comes closer to 1% or 3%. One thing is clear, however—dyslexia is more common in boys than in girls, in a ratio of about 4 to 1 (Miles, 1983, p. 160).

In the attempt to recognize and understand the dyslexic child, diagnosticians and teachers are aided somewhat by knowing a series of characteristics that are frequently—but not invariably—associated with such learning disorders as dyslexia. The Foundation for Children with Learning Disabilities (1984) has provided a guide for parents of children with learning disorders. The guide includes the following kinds of behavior that may be displayed by school-age children who have at least average mental ability but still suffer learning difficulties.

Visual-Perception Problems:	Difficulty distinguishing shapes and sizes
	Difficulty coloring, writing, cutting out
	Lack of established "handedness"—uses either right or left hand to perform a task
	Letter and word reversal
Attention/Memory Problems:	Difficulty concentrating, does not listen well, forgets easily
	Cannot follow instructions that involve many steps
Language Deficits:	Delayed language development
	Difficulty forming sentences or finding the right words

Reading Problems: Trouble sounding out words
Difficulty understanding word meanings
Misreads letters or puts them in incorrect order

CAUSES OF DYSLEXIA

The causes of dyslexia are not well understood. There is some evidence that dyslexia is more common in some families, so that a genetic component may be involved. But exactly what this component is and why it affects some family members and not others is as yet unknown. Studies of brain functions suggest that areas of the brain which govern language syntax (i.e., the parietal lobe) display certain abnormalities in children who suffer such learning disorders as dyslexia. However, the detailed relationship of these abnormalities to language functions, the sources of such abnormalities, and the question of whether visual-perception training can reprogram the faulty neural connections are still unclear (Batshaw & Perret, 1986, p. 282).

TREATING DYSLEXIA

What hope is there, then, that the child diagnosed as dyslexic in the early primary grades can be cured or at least can improve appreciably? Miles's (1983) study of the progress of dyslexics over a period ranging from one to seven years led him to conclude that:

> dyslexic subjects can improve their performance in all kinds of ways as they grow older, and that, even at reading and spelling there can be appreciable gains if the conditions are right. Even so, however, it is clear that traces of the handicap remain; and it seems that these are particularly likely to show themselves in difficulty over saying [arithmetic] tables and difficulty over remembering digits. It is therefore incorrect simply to describe a dyslexic child as "behind" at reading or spelling and able, or partially able, to catch up; a less misleading formulation is to say that he is handicapped but can achieve considerable success in learning to compensate. (p. 155)

There is no one educational treatment that can be applied successfully to all cases of dyslexia. What works well with one child may not work well with another. Therefore, it is useful for the remedial-reading expert or classroom teacher to have available more than one technique to try. Generally, a dyslexic child's learning problem can be approached in two ways, direct and indirect. The direct approach involves seeking to improve the child's reading skills. The indirect approach involves providing ways for the pupil to progress in academic work despite the reading disability.

Direct Approaches

The most common direct means for teaching reading focuses on helping children to associate the sight and sound of words. Among these visual-auditory methods are the following:

Basal Reader. The basal-reader approach consists of using a series of graded textbooks that introduce words and sentence structures at a gradual, systematic rate, then repeat these words in subsequent selections to give pupils practice in using them. Such systems often furnish workbooks that engage children in activities intended to consolidate their reading skills. Basal reading programs typically include training in phonics, so that children gain skill in sounding out words that they meet in print.

Language Experience. Under the language-experience approach, the teacher offers children an experience—a TV program, an animal brought to class, a game to play, a set of pictures, or the like—and the pupils discuss the event. Then they are asked to dictate a story about the experience. As they dictate, the teacher prints their story on a large sheet of paper displayed on an easel before the group. Finally, the pupils learn to read their story, with the expectation that, in the process, they will memorize the sight of the words that they have included in their composition.

Initial Teaching Alphabet. Words in the English language, unlike those in such languages as Spanish and Malay, are oftentimes not spelled in a consistent phonetic pattern. For the child who is newly learning to read, these frequent exceptions to the rule are a cause of confusion, as illustrated by the phoneme *ough* in such words as *rough, through, cough, plough,* and *although.* To simplify the problems of the beginning reader, several systems have been devised to regularize the spelling of English for the early lessons in reading. One of these, called the Initial Teaching Alphabet, makes a temporary change in the orthography of English for beginning readers by creating a consistent phoneme-grapheme relationship. That is, words that do not fit the usual phonetic patterns are printed in a simplified spelling that conforms to basic phonics rules. Then, after children have gained some mastery over reading, they are guided through a transition period to standard English orthography. A disadvantage of this system is that some children are confused in trying to make the transition.

Color Coding. Another technique for attacking the inconsistent orthography of English is that of printing vowels in colors that consistently represent a given sound, no matter what the visual form of the vowel or vowel combination may be. Thus, children memorize the sounds associated with the colors, using the color rather than the letters as their principal guide for pronouncing words that they meet in their beginning reading lessons.

Linguistic Delay. A further approach to the orthography problem is to limit the words in early reading to ones that follow consistent phonetic rules, then gradually introduce words of irregular phoneme-grapheme relationship at a later stage of reading.

Visual, Auditory, Kinesthetic, Tactile. Two well-known systems of instruction for disabled readers, the Fernald and the Orton-Billingham methods, employ not only visual and auditory stimuli but also engage children in exercises of touching and manipulating letters and words in an effort to effect a secure connection between sight and sound in the brain's neural network. For example, as pupils say and hear a word, they trace the form of the word with their fingers, perhaps on sandpaper or on their desk, so as to get the "feel" of the letters.

Some reading therapists also engage children in physical activities intended to increase their balance, sense of direction, and awareness of parts of the body and of body positions. The assumption underlying such treatment is that kinesthetic awareness is one of the necessary foundational skills behind the visual scanning and visual-auditory interpretation abilities required for learning to read.

Teachers and reading specialists who are acquainted with the foregoing array of instructional techniques are equipped to adopt whichever combination they decide may be of most help to the particular dyslexic child that they currently face.

Indirect Approaches

When pupils' reading disabilities prevent them from learning adequately from texts and periodicals, teachers sometimes circumvent dependence on reading by utilizing other teaching media—lectures, discussions, demonstrations, debates, student oral reports, charts, mounted pictures, television or radio programs, and tape recordings.

These nonreading methods can be fitted together with reading approaches in a variety of ways. For example, the teacher who assigns the class to read about a topic in the textbook may later emphasize once again the main points about the topic by means of illustrated lectures and discussions. Thus, pupils who did not master the assigned reading will understand at least the main elements of the lesson.

As another technique, one of the better readers in the class can occasionally be asked to read passages orally into a tape recorder so that a dyslexic classmate can later listen to the tape and grasp the contents of the lesson. A dyslexic pupil can also take books home, where parents or a sibling may be willing to read the material aloud.

A poor reader may profit from small-group projects as well. If the pupil is part of a trio conducting a science experiment, the better readers in the group can read aloud the procedures that they are to follow, and together the trio can carry out the experiment and observe the results. Small-group discussions enable the inept reader to learn the subject matter from the comments made by fellow group members about what they have read.

In effect, dyslexic pupils can be aided in coping with their reading disability by means of both direct and indirect methods of fostering academic progress.

Disturbed, Nontraditional Family Constellations

It is clear that children from both traditional and nontraditional family patterns can suffer personal/social difficulties serious enough to warrant the aid of a counseling psychologist, social worker, or psychiatrist. However, because of the marked increase in nontraditional family structures over recent decades, information about the incidence of such family arrangements, their variety, and their relationship to children's problems have become particularly important to therapists. To provide such information, the following review focuses solely on unconventional family structures, giving only incidental attention to traditional families that are comprised of a father, a mother, and their children within an intact first marriage.

In North America during the closing decades of the twentieth century, the term *unconventional* as applied to family structures still meant *nontraditional*, but it no longer meant *unusual* or *infrequent*. By the 1980s, half of all first and second marriages could be expected to end in divorce. At the same time, the frequency of remarriage nearly matched the divorce rate, with 83% of divorced men and 80% of divorced women remarrying. After their divorce, women with children experienced a substantial decline in their standard of living. Divorces and remarriages were occurring earlier in the life cycle and with a decreasing interval between the divorce and the subsequent new marriage. As a result, more children were living in stepfamilies, with the most common type of stepfamily comprised of own-mother and stepfather. Half of the young children alive at the close of the 1980s could be expected to spend at least some time in a single-parent family before the age of 18 (Glick, 1980; Gecas, 1987). Divorces in the United States tripled between 1960 and 1982 (.39 to 1.22 million); since then, they have leveled off somewhat but still remain high. In 1987, both marriages and divorces dipped slightly, but the decade-long trend still found divorce on the increase. At this same time, the birth rate continued to increase. In view of growing divorce rates and the high incidence of remarriage, the stepfamily could become the predominant family form in North America within a few years (Robinson, 1984, p. 381).

Not only have divorce and remarriage become common, but the informal arrangement of children living with unwed adults has become more frequent as well. Sometimes the adults are the biological parents of the children, but, in many cases, only one of the adults is a biological parent (usually the mother) and the other a live-in companion.

The incidence of single-parent families has also increased, with an unwed, divorced or widowed mother in charge of the children (90% of the cases), or, far less frequently (about 10%), a divorced or widowed father will head the household. By the mid-1980s, 26% of U.S. families were headed by one parent, which is twice the percentage of 1970. Over the same period, two-parent families had decreased by 13% (from 87% to 74%). The proportion of Black family households maintained by women alone was more than three times the proportion among whites, with the increase in single-parent Black households advancing since 1970 at a more rapid pace than that of whites (Hanson & Sporakowski, 1986). The proportion of Black single-mother households grew from 30% to nearly 50% between 1970 and the mid-1980s (Norton & Glick, 1986).

Boys are more likely than girls to live with their father, particularly if the father is over age forty-five. Boys are generally more difficult to raise than girls and often prefer to be with their father, especially during later childhood and adolescence (Norton & Glick, 1986).

Throughout the first half of the twentieth century, the typical father worked to provide the income while the mother served as the homemaker, responsible primarily for child care and household tasks. By the closing decades of the century, this dominant pattern had changed significantly. In the 1980s, over 50% of mothers with pre-school children and 60% of mothers with school-age children worked outside the home (Gecas, 1987).

In effect, during recent times, family constellations have undergone dramatic changes. Numbers of analysts have suggested that these changes have resulted in "deficiencies in nurturant socialization" of children.

> Poor cognitive and emotional development, low self-esteem, low self-efficacy, antisocial behavior, and pathologies of various kinds are some of the consequences.... The social environment most conducive to nurturant socialization is an adult-child relationship characterized by intimacy, affection, stability, and security.... Contemporary trends ... make it increasingly difficult for families to perform this function well (Gecas, 1987, p. 435).

Yet, however interesting the changing patterns may be, information about them is of no practical use to counselors unless particular family constellations are found to be more often associated with variables important for counseling. It is to this matter of pertinent correlates of family structures that we now turn.

CORRELATES OF FAMILY STRUCTURES

The two-part question addressed in the following paragraphs is: "What kind of normative information about family constellations can aid counselors in estimating characteristics of clients who are elements in those constellations, and how can such information influence counseling procedures?" Of particular significance are the ways in which characteristics of school-age children are related to different family patterns. The types of family configurations discussed below are those of stepfamilies, one-parent families, working parents, and unwed parents.

Stepfamilies

At the outset, it should be recognized that most of the research on stepfamilies has been conducted only since the mid-1950s. And while the number of studies has been increasing, there is still "a paucity of information regarding the socio-demographic characteristics of these families, the structural and functional differences among various types of stepfamilies, the processes involved in establishing an effective stepfamily, and the kinds of support systems most facilitative of stepfamily functioning" (Esses & Campbell, 1984, p. 415). Nevertheless, summaries of the studies reported in the professional literature do provide the basis for several tentative conclusions.

In a review of 38 studies of the effects of remarriage on children, Ganong and Coleman (1984, p. 389) reported that "In general, there was little evidence that children in stepfamilies differ from children in other family structures on such variables as school grades, academic achievement, field independence [depending on one's own judgment rather than others' opinions], IQ, psychosomatic symptoms, personality characteristics, social behavior, family relationships, marriage attitudes, problem behavior, or negative attitudes toward self and others."

However, other studies have shown differences between stepfamilies and non-stepfamilies on several dimensions. For example, child abuse appears more likely to occur at the hands of stepparents than of biological parents, with stepfathers more frequently abusing children than stepmothers (Giles-Sims & Finkelhor, 1984).

One-Parent Families

As styles of conjugal relationships and child bearing have changed over the past three decades, the number of one-parent families has markedly increased. The most common form is a mother and her child or children. In some cases, the children in the mother/child family are from different fathers, since the mother had separated from a sequence of two or more spouses with whom she bore children. Less frequent than the mother/child combination, but also growing in number, is the father/child family.

The problems that bring school-age children of single-parent families to the counselor can be manifold and complex. They can include child neglect, child abuse, the imposition of undue responsibilities on the young, loneliness, and personal-identity confusion for the child.

In regard to educational attainment, single parents are much more likely than married parents to have less than a full high-school education, and married parents are much more likely to be college graduates. In the mid-1960s, 28% of lone parents of children under age 18 (usually mothers) had finished high school, and only 9% had a college diploma. However, between 1970 and 1984, there was a marked increase in the number of single mothers who graduated from high school (52% to 72%) and completed at least some college education (13% to 25%). The educational attainment of lone Black mothers was similar to that of their white counterparts, whereas twice as many Hispanic than Black single mothers had not finished high school (Norton & Glick, 1986, pp. 12-13).

Single-male parents generally had more education than single-female parents and therefore had better-paying jobs, enabling them to realize greater economic security than single-parent mothers. Around 88% of men and 69% of women in one-parent families were in the work force by the mid-1980s (Norton & Glick, 1986, pp. 12-13).

Research on parenting and occupational performance has revealed a particularly clear-cut relationship between being a female single parent and job tension.

> These women are typically both the sole parent in their household and the main, if not exclusive source of household income. The work/family role strain inherent in this position is compounded by the fact that single female parents generally enter or reenter the labor force under unfavorable circumstances such as separation, desertion, or death of a spouse. They also tend to be concentrated in low paying sectors of the labor market (Kelly & Voydanoff, 1985, p. 372).

A survey by Burden (1986) of 293 employees of a large corporation supported the observation that single female parents are at particular risk for high job/family-role strain. But even with this strain, the single mothers expressed a high level of job satisfaction and showed no significant difference in absenteeism from that of their married and single-nonparent coworkers.

Types of help that counselors can offer the single working parent who is suffering a high level of job/family stress include: (1) assisting such clients in revising their schedules to provide more outside support for both household tasks and job responsibilities, (2) teaching clients stress-reduction techniques (relaxation exercises, meditation, biofeedback methods), (3) helping clients locate community agencies (children's clubs, child-care centers) that furnish constructive activities for children, and (4) conferring with employers to suggest types of support which they might offer to reduce the stress that their growing quantity of single-parent employees experience (flexible work schedules, time off for family emergencies, child-care assistance, counseling services).

Of particular interest to therapists who work with school-age children are the questions of (1) how the family responsibilities borne by children in two-parent households compare to those borne by children in one-parent households and (2) how such responsibilities affect children's welfare. Numerous studies have shown that the burden of responsibilities carried by children in single-parent families are greater than those in two-parent homes (Peters & Haldeman, 1987). Weiss (1979) notes that children in single-parent families "grow up a little faster" because they are likely to make a greater contribution to family functioning than their peers in two-parent households. The child in the single-parent home is often obliged to care for younger siblings, shop for groceries, prepare meals, clean house, and serve as the parent's main confidant—that is, as a receptacle for the parent's load of worries and complaints. However, in certain family configurations, such may not be the case. Greif's (1965) study of 1,136 single fathers who were raising children alone revealed that a large proportion of the fathers were not at all overburdening their children with home maintenance tasks.

> Fathers who believe they are helping children adjust by not having them carry an appropriate share of the housework are placing an unfair burden on themselves and giving the children the wrong message about home responsibility and life in a single parent family. ... Some of the children may be counted on too much for emotional support from a parent who has no one else to talk to. ... But there is a difference between a child being overburdened emotionally and underburdened in housework (Greif, 1965, p. 356).

Greif suggests that in such cases the counselor may find it desirable to encourage fathers to expect more of their children in household responsibilities. Fathers may also need help in: (1) relieving some of the guilt that they feel about the dissolution of the family and (2) dispelling the notion that they must prove to the world their competence as a single parent by performing so many of the household maintenance chores on top of their regular job.

A problem that therapists can face with single-parent families is the blurring of the intergenerational boundary between parent and child. When a girl or boy is in late childhood or adolescence, the single parent—typically a mother—may abdicate the traditional parental role and begin functioning as a peer/partner of the child. This can lead to the mother's failing to furnish sufficient guidance to the child and placing on the child an undue burden of decision making and emotional stress. Glenwick and Mowrey (1986) have proposed that in such cases counselors can help the mother (1) return to her parental role and learn better ways of resolving conflicts in family matters, (2) permit the child to express thoughts and feelings appropriately, and (3) modify parent-child communication patterns.

Whether the child is a girl or a boy generally makes a difference in household assignments. When children help with housework, daughters typically are assigned more of the load than are sons. This is a version of "the Cinderella phenomenon"—the girl functioning as a parental child by taking care of father and brothers, a relationship that is becoming less acceptable in societies in which women are successfully seeking rights more equal to those traditionally enjoyed by men, so it may become an issue to be negotiated through family counseling (Weltner, 1982).

The question then arises about what type and quantity of family responsibilities are good or bad for the child's welfare. It should be apparent that there is no simple answer, for the answer depends on a complex of variables in each case, including the child's level of physical and mental development, the amount of work required to keep the family functioning (which varies with the number of house- hold members and their abilities, as well as the physical size and complexity of the household), the socioeconomic support available to the family (poor families have a more difficult time), how much time the parent is at home, and the energies and abilities of the parent. A counselor, through observation and interviews with family members, can investigate these variables in order to estimate how the type and amount of responsibilities assigned to a child are affecting the child's school progress, self-reliance, social skills, physical growth, compe- tence in solving out-of-school tasks, and feelings of self-worth. On the basis of this estimate, the counselor can decide what, if anything, should be done to alter the family role that the child has been performing.

Working Parents

Although clinicians have long recognized the strain that conflicting work and family roles have placed on working parents, normative studies of the conditions and effects of such strain are rather recent, chiefly since the latter 1970s (Kelly & Voydanoff, 1985). From the growing quantity of research in this area, several generalizations have been drawn. One obvious conclusion is that conditions on the job or at home which cause parents stress can effect the quality of their child-rearing roles. Children of parents who are under family/ work stress are more likely to be neglected or treated harshly than children whose parents do not feel strain between home and job responsibilities. Work factors that tend to contribute to job tension include too little responsibility (boredom) or too much responsibility (pressure), lack of flexibility in the work schedule, increased overtime hours, responsibility for dealing with the public (particularly over the phone, as is true in public relations occupations), unpleasant work environment, and a low level of job satisfaction. Home factors that can contribute to family/work strain include the number of children in the home (the more children, the more strain) and, for working husbands, the wife's skills in mediating conflicts in work/family responsibilities (Kelly & Voydanoff, 1985).

Several implications for counseling can be drawn from these findings. When interviewing parents of a school child who suffers personal/social-adjustment problems, a therapist may discover that parents' child-rearing practices have likely contributed to the child's difficulties. The therapist may surmise that these unsuitable practices are ones deriving in part from family/work-role conflicts (lack of time or patience to help the child with homework, assigning the child unreasonable kinds or amounts of family responsibility, arguments between the parents that cause the child emotional distress). Thus, counseling can include helping the parents to reevaluate their family/ work relationships so as to reduce the strain that they themselves have been experiencing. As a result, they may endeavor to rearrange work schedules or to change jobs, to adopt personal stress-management practices (relaxation activities, exercise), to alter their time commitments, to be more tolerant of their spouse's and children's needs, and to secure more outside support in child rearing (constructive child-care arrangements when both parents are at work, tutoring for children who face difficulties with school tasks, supervised recreational pursuits offered by boys' and girls' clubs).

The phrase *latchkey children* has been applied to the growing number of pupils who are without adult supervision for part of each school day. They typically return home from school to an empty house. Studies indicate that they often must cope with fear, loneliness, boredom, unsafe conditions, transportation problems, and decreased academic achievement because they lack supervision with homework. However, the extent to which they suffer such difficulties can depend on mitigating factors. Those who live in relatively safe areas have been found to be more self-sufficient, capable, and responsible. Whereas kindergartners and first-graders have been found to prefer their mother's care, pupils in upper-elementary grades are more content with staying alone or with someone else. Although siblings and peers can reduce loneliness, they also can cause stress and increased responsibility for the latchkey child. A therapist can assist latchkey children by aiding teachers in assessing such pupils' needs, with the therapist helping teachers either case-by-case or by means of newsletters and workshops. Counselors can also direct parents to child-care facilities and supervised recreation and can inform parents of ways to relieve children's fears, loneliness, and boredom (Little, Rosen, & Toenniessen, 1989).

Unwed Parents

The term *unwed parents* is used here to mean a household in which there are children under age 14 living with a female and male who are not married to each other. The unmarried couple in such cases can be the biological parents of the children, or one of the couple can be a biological parent (usually the mother) and the other a live-in companion who performs more or less in a parenting relationship to the children. In recent decades, these living arrangements have been on the steady increase. In 1970, there were an estimated 196,000 households of this type. By the mid-1980s, the number had grown more than 350% to nearly 700,000 (U.S. Bureau of the Census, 1987).

Children in households of unwed parents experience personal/social difficulties that often call for counseling aid. One obvious problem is the way in which such an unconventional relationship between the adults is viewed by the child's classmates and their parents and by school personnel. The unwed-couple arrangement usually produces confusion about the family name that the child bears—a name that may be the same as the woman's in the household, the same as the man's, or perhaps different from both. In this situation, children's sense of identity can be affected, as they are not sure to whom they belong. Even more difficult for children is the ephemeral character of many of these arrangements. Since there is no commitment to marriage, the man in the household may easily be replaced by another man or perhaps by a series of other men, for indeterminate periods of time. Family life, erected on such shifting foundations, can be the source of constant anxiety for children, as they are troubled by the unpredictability of intrafamily relationships, by the chance that they will be moving from one location to another, and by financial and emotional instability.

The clients in such cases should be both the children and the unmarried couple, since the family constellation, rather than only the children, is in need of revision. However, when either one or both of the adults are unwilling to participate in counseling, the clients will be only the children, whom the therapist seeks to help despite their having to continue living in an unsatisfactory family setting. Such children may be ones sent for counseling by the school, a social agency, or the courts.

Developmental Lag—Enuresis

The phrase *developmental lag* refers to a delay in a child's cognitive, physical, social, or emotional growth in comparison to the growth of children of the same age and sex. Such a delay may be caused primarily by the individual's genetic structure, by environmental conditions, or by the interaction of genetic endowment and the environment.

The illustrative type of developmental lag reviewed in the following section is that of *enuresis*, a label identifying a child's failure to control urination. The term is usually not applied to infants' involuntary voiding, since lack of bladder and bowel control in infancy is universal and thus considered normal. Instead, the word is used to label what is socially regarded as a problem condition—urinary incontinence when most age-mates have gained bladder control during both daytime and nighttime hours. The label *enuresis* is limited to those cases of involuntary wetting in which no apparent organic pathology is involved. When there is an organic cause, the term *incontinence* is commonly applied. Cases of enuresis brought to a physician's or a counselor's attention usually concern children between the ages of 4 and 7, but older children, adolescents, and adults can also be enuretic.

Most children can control daytime bladder functions at an earlier age than they can control nighttime functions. Thus, nocturnal enuresis (bed-wetting) is far more common than diurnal (daytime) enuresis. In discussions of the disorder, a distinction is often made between primary and secondary varieties. The phrase *primary enuresis* identifies the condition when bladder control has never been achieved. *Secondary enuresis* or *onset enuresis* identifies the reoccurrence of involuntary urination following a period of control, as in a return to bed-wetting after a period of dryness.

Estimates of the number of bedwetters among U.S. American children in the 1970s and 1980s ranged from 3.5 million to 7 million children between age 3½ and the close of adolescence. Around 50% more males than females suffer the disorder. A relatively large-sample study in Britain reported that 15% of children age 4.5 were bed wetters, with the incidence declining to 2.5% by age 15. Studies in several countries have demonstrated that about 10% of all 6-year olds continue to wet their beds, with the annual spontaneous-cure rate thereafter around 15% (Baller, 1975; Scharf, 1986).

CORRELATES OF ENURESIS

Conditions regarded as correlates of enuresis include a mixture of those that are apparently myths and those supported by evidence. Three supposedly causal factors that Baller (1975) condemns as destructive myths are people's beliefs that children use bed-wetting to (1) get attention, (2) vent their spite, and (3) substitute for masturbation. People who have studied enuresis extensively are nearly unanimous in rejecting these three as causal factors. An unfortunate result of adults' subscribing to such convictions is that they typically attempt to cure the bed-wetting by punishing the child. However, the punishment usually not only fails to stop the bed-wetting but also damages the child's self-concept and breeds mutual dislike and distrust between adult and child.

Another widely held proposal about the cause of bed-wetting is that the neural mechanism governing bladder control matures more slowly in the enuretic child. And, indeed, this may be a cause for bed-wetting in some children. However, researchers have questioned whether late maturation is a causal factor in most cases, since a large number of children who wet the bed experience occasional dry nights or month-long dry periods before they resume bed-wetting. A variation of the maturation hypothesis is one suggested by MacKeith (1968), who proposed that around age 3, the confluence of several developmental changes produces a "sensitive period." At this age, the child is expected to be gaining mastery over a variety of physical and mental skills, including bladder control. Thus, the period "makes for a relatively high degree of vulnerability where stress producing conditions exist. A child who at three years of age is caught up in this combination of circumstances (vulnerability and stress) may be seriously handicapped in gaining the controls that are considered 'normal' at four years, or more especially, at five" (Baller, 1975, p. 11).

A hypothesis that has been investigated in considerable detail is the proposal that enuretic children are particularly deep sleepers, so that they are still physiologically in deep sleep when their bladder feels full, and they inadvertently wet the bed. However, studies of brain-wave activity, based on EEG (electroencephalogram) reports, cast serious doubt on the assumption that the problem is simply a matter of deep sleep. EEG recordings have suggested that enuretics are often physiologically awake during the bed-wetting episode, though they appear to be still asleep. One proposed explanation of this seemingly contradictory state is that enuresis is not so much a disorder of sleep as it is a disorder of arousal.

> Like somnambulism, night terror, and nightmares, enuresis generally occurs during *arousal* from State IV (or III) of EEG activity to Stage II, I, or to wakefulness. These four types of disorders of arousal are all characterized by a mental state with, for example, confusion and disorientation, automatic behaviours, and retrograde amnesia. This particular state, aptly called ... *ivresse de sommeil* [sleep intoxication], could regularly be produced [experimentally] when a subject was awakened ... from Stage IV or III. (Wiklund, 1978, p. 54).

However, the evidence bearing on the possible role of deep sleep in enuresis is still not conclusive, so that further research is needed to settle the matter. Also in need of further study is the proposal that there is a higher incidence of enuresis in certain family strains, with the possibility that genetic factors may be at least partially involved.

TREATING ENURESIS

Among the useless and harmful treatments that Baller (1975, pp. 35-36) mentions are the practices of having the bedwetter sleep on a hard surface (the bare floor), on open bedsprings, or with a rope tied around the waist and a large knot at the back, so that the child will sleep lightly and thus respond to his or her full bladder by awakening in time to avoid wetting the bed. Other ineffective and ofttimes inhumane treatments include "bladder and rectal irrigations; constriction of the urinary orifice; elevation of the bed so as to have the feet much higher than the head; severe restriction of liquids not only before going to bed but, sometimes, during the day as well" (Baller, 1975, p. 36).

In contrast to unsuitable treatments are several approaches that have been reported as appropriate, with some of them more effective than others. They can be categorized as *psychodynamic, conditioning,* or *drug* techniques.

Psychodynamic methods, when used as the exclusive form of treatment, are typically based on the assumption that enuresis is a symptom of a more basic, hidden, psychological conflict. Proponents of psychodynamic theory contend that a cure is effected only when the conflict is identified and resolved. Efforts to get rid of bed-wetting directly, without unveiling the underlying cause, can be expected to fail. And, when such efforts do appear to succeed, the result is merely a matter of *symptom substitution,* meaning that bed-wetting is replaced by some other expression of maladjustment—aggressivity, depression, delinquent acts, and the like. Many psychiatrists and clinical psychologists subscribe to such a mode of treatment. Their technique consists chiefly of conducting psychological interviews during which they delve into the client's past and present conflicts in an effort to learn what initiated the bed-wetting and what factors continue to maintain it.

Conditioning methods aim at directly eliminating the bed-wetting rather than seeking any underlying psychological disorder. Some conditioning techniques involve the use of a special pad that is positioned on the bed beneath the child's lower back and upper thighs. Electrodes located in the pad are activated whenever water touches the pad, resulting in an immediate warning being sounded, which wakens the child. There are several versions of the pad on the market. With some, the warning is a bell. With others it is a hooter, a light that shines on the child's face, a slight electrical stimulus to the skin, or some combination of these (Baller, 1975). The principle on which this manner of treatment is founded is that of *classical conditioning,* a principle first derived by Pavlov from his animal experiments. A key assumption is that the onset of urination occurs at about the peak of distension of the bladder. In the enuretic child, the sensation of distension is not sufficient to waken the child before urine is released. However, the bell or hooter or light is a stimulus adequate to waken the sleeper. Thus, the purpose of the treatment is to have the bell ring or the light appear as close in time as possible to the peak distension of the bladder. This is accomplished by the first drops of urine's setting off the warning mechanism, with the expectation that the sensation of a full bladder will, after a series of experiences with the system, become so closely associated in the child's subconscious mind with the ringing or flashing that the distension itself will henceforth waken the child, even without the bell or light. In short, the feeling of a full bladder becomes substituted by conditioning for the light or bell as a sufficient stimulus to waken the child.

One mode of conditioning that does not involve apparatus is that of training patients "to take in, and hold, increasingly large amounts of liquid during the day. The hope would be that such a practice would result in an increase of bladder capacity and an increase in control which would be carried over into the individual's nighttime sleep" (Baller, 1975, p. 45). There are several variations of this approach, which often include providing rewards to the child for successes in increasing bladder control.

Drug treatment has typically consisted of administering such a substance as imipramine (Tofranil) to the enuretic patient.

A question that now arises about these diverse treatment approaches is: "How do they compare as cures for bed-wetting?" The answer is not a simple one, since the conditions of the individual and the social environment can differ from case to case. However, from a substantial body of research on enuresis, several normative statements can be drawn. For unknown reasons, a certain percent of enuresis cases "cure themselves," in the sense that, as time passes, the individual attains dryness without special interventions. It appears that the enuretic "grows out of it." Thus, the technique of simply waiting will succeed in certain cases. However, simply waiting on the chance that time will eliminate the problem means taking two risks—(1) that during the waiting period personality damage (low self-concept, guilt, self-punitive behavior) may result and (2) this particular case may not be one in which automatic remission will take place.

This brings us, then, to our three categories of intentional intervention—psychodynamic counseling, conditioning, and drugs. Of the three, the best record of success has been compiled by conditioning techniques, both in gaining initial dryness and in maintaining it. The second most effective appears to be drug treatment, so long as the drug continues to be used. Evidence of how well dryness is maintained after the drug has been withdrawn is generally lacking. Psychodynamic counseling approaches, when used as the sole treatment, have the poorest record of cures. However, some studies suggest that psychodynamic techniques may serve as a useful adjunct to conditioning or drug treatment by revealing conditions in the enuretic child's life that have produced stress which may contribute to the disorder (Baller, 1975; Wiklund, 1978).

CONCLUSION

Later childhood, as depicted in Chapter 5, is a time of slowed physical growth but one of advanced cognitive and social development. A crucial element in children's lives is the requirement that they attend school, where they are expected to engage in serious, formal study of the written word, of mathematics, and of the social and scientific worlds. School attendance also places new demands on children's ability to participate in increasingly complex social settings. Children's problems of personal/social adjustment that are occasioned by developmental changes during these years are often serious enough for parents and school personnel to seek help from the counseling profession.

6

Adolescence: Ages 12 to 21
The Secondary School and
Post-Secondary Years

People who have studied adolescence closely have often observed that, for many young people, it is a particularly stressful period of life. Lewin described it as a stage of instability, a time of locomotion from one stable period (late childhood) to another stable but, as yet, poorly comprehended stage (adulthood). Lewin proposed that the adolescent's conception of life was forced into a fluid state by the puzzling bodily changes brought on by puberty, by the youth's growing intellect, and by new opportunities for social freedom offered by society. To compound their problems, teenagers in the modern Western world are not quite sure about how much freedom they really have or want. In short, after late childhood, the terrain ahead is poorly mapped in the youth's mind. The "cognitively unstructured character" of the new situation can cause the adolescent to be shy, sensitive, or aggressive. Emotional tensions arise from the conflict between the attitudes, values, and styles of life of the period being left behind (childhood) and the period vaguely seen ahead (adulthood). Adolescents are apt to take extreme attitudes in politics or social behavior and to shift positions radically. They are like emigrants into a new culture—the sociologist's *marginal man*—living with both old and new cultures but not completely accepted by either (R. M. Thomas, 1985a, p. 161).

The adolescents who are sent for counseling or come on their own initiative are often those:

—Who continue to break the law or habitually fail to abide by school rules. On frequent occasion, they are involved in such activities as using illicit drugs or alcohol, engaging in sex play, shoplifting, telling lies, being

truant from school, abusing their age peers or younger children, tortur-
ing animals, destroying property, carrying weapons, and the like. Such
clients usually have been sent to the therapist by their school, by the
juvenile court, by a social-service agency, or by their own parents.

—Who lag behind their classmates in school achievement and need help
in coping with their learning problems.

—Who cannot get along amicably with their parents or other family
members, so that their behavior produces frequent conflict within the
family.

—Who suffer personal-identity difficulties and engage in practices that
parents or school personnel—and perhaps even the adolescents themselves—believe are contrary to the teenagers' welfare. Such practices
can include eating and drinking habits, the use of tobacco, the choice of
companions, hobbies and recreational pursuits, and modes of dress and
grooming.

—Who need guidance in making suitable educational and career choices
for the years ahead.

—Who suffer mental, physical, or social handicaps that interfere with their
academic and social development and cause them problems of self-
acceptance.

—Whose sexual attitudes or behavior have brought them to the counselor
for help. Such clients may include pregnant teenagers, youths suffering
from sexually related diseases, those concerned or confused about their
sexual identity (particularly homosexual propensities) and ones whose
parents consider them out of control in their sexual proclivities, so that
parents wish to have them adopt more *normal* (in the sense of *more
desirable* or *traditional*) behavior for their age level.

The first portion of this chapter offers an overview of general
characteristics of adolescence that are of use to counselors. The
second portion focuses on four common varieties of counseling cases
that appear during the teen years, cases involving (1) educational
guidance, (2) accepting one's physical self—anorexia, (3) sexual relationships—teenage pregnancy, and (4) juvenile crime—drug abuse.

GENERAL CHARACTERISTICS OF
ADOLESCENT DEVELOPMENT

The following overview of adolescence begins with physical characteristics, then continues with cognitive abilities, sexual development,
and social development and personal identity.

Changes in Physical Size, Appearance, and Functions

The marked physical changes that occur at the onset of adolescence are determined primarily by the individual's genetic structure, which controls an internal maturational timing system, and by hormones. The most dramatic of these changes is the development of sexual maturity during the period called *puberty*. At the beginning of puberty, the testes in the male and the ovaries in the female enlarge. Then, over the following months and years, secondary sexual characteristics appear. In girls, the secondary features include rapid growth in height, weight, strength, and breast development, as well as the growth of hair in the armpits and pubic area. Among boys, puberty brings rapid increases in height, weight, and strength, accompanied by the growth of body hair and facial hair and a lowering in the pitch of the voice. In both girls and boys, skin blemishes often appear because of the changed activity of sebaceous glands beneath the skin. Muscles grow in strength and size, heart and lungs enlarge in relationship to total body size, systolic blood pressure rises, the pulse slows, and the blood's capacity for carrying oxygen to the muscles increases.

> ... the individual becomes not only stronger but able to endure hard physical work over a longer period of time. There is no justification for the popular belief that boys outgrow their strength in puberty. They become progressively stronger, although their maximum strength may not be reached until their growth in height and sexual development are more or less complete. There may be a period during which a boy looks like a mature man but has not yet developed the strength and stamina suggested by his appearance. Nevertheless, he is considerably stronger than he was the previous year (Marshall & Tanner, 1986, p. 203).

Pubertal changes occur in girls one-and-one-half to two years earlier than in boys. For example, the average girl is taller and heavier than the average boy between ages 11 and 14, and girls usually achieve their full height between ages 16 and 17, while boys reach their full height between 18 and 20 (Roche & Davila, 1972).

The need for a balanced diet with substantial amounts of minerals, protein, and carbohydrates is particularly great throughout adolescence, especially during the time of the growth spurt. This requirement is considerably higher for tall youths than for their peers.

"Many adolescent boys carry rather small amounts of fat, so one must decry the efforts of some high school wrestling coaches at encouraging them to lose weight in preparation for contests. Strenuous exercise demands energy, so the young athlete must have a sufficient energy intake" (Forbes, 1986, p. 139).

Although the types and sequence of physical changes during adolescence are common to all teenagers, the time at which the changes appear can vary markedly from one youth to another. The range of the first occurrence of nonpathological menstruation in girls—the *menarche*—is from 9 to 16 years of age (Bullough, 1981). Penis growth in most boys begins at age 13 but can start as early as 11 or as late as between 14 and 15. This growth spurt may end before age 14 in some boys or as late as 17 in others (Stolz & Stolz, 1951). A similar range of differences is observed in the timing of other aspects of physical growth during adolescence—height, weight, musculature, body hair, and body contour.

Early-maturing boys are physically stronger than late-maturing ones from preadolescence throughout adolescence, with the greatest difference occurring at ages 13-16. To a somewhat smaller extent, early-maturing girls are also stronger than their late-maturing agemates during adolescence, particularly in the age range of 11-15, and becoming less apparent thereafter (Malina, 1986, pp. 94-95).

Whether the physical maturation of a teenager is early, average, or late can affect the youth's psychological adjustment. Studies of personal/social characteristics suggest that early-maturing boys may have a social advantage over late-maturing ones. In one study, adults tended to view early-maturing boys as more masculine and more attractive. Late maturers were seen to be tense, childish, and rebellious attention-getters. Other adolescents saw late maturers as bossy, unattractive, and lacking in leadership qualities (Jones & Bayley, 1950). In a follow-up study of the same boys when they were in their thirties, differences between the early and late maturers could still be identified. Late maturers tended to display a lower self-concept, less self-control, and more rebelliousness, yet they were also more assertive and insightful than their early-maturing peers (Jones, 1957). By the time the same group had reached age 40, differences between early and late maturers had generally evened out, though early maturers tended to be more rigid and conforming, while late maturers exhibited greater insight and flexibility, as reflected on personality tests (Jones 1965, Peskin 1973).

Research into effects on girls of early and late maturing have resulted in conflicting interpretations. Some researchers have found early-maturing females less likely to suffer anxiety than late-maturing ones (Weatherly, 1964) and more likely to be better adjusted by age 30 (Peskin, 1973). Yet, other studies have shown no personal/social differences between early and late maturers (Jones & Mussen, 1958).

In the foregoing surveys, any personality differences between early- and late-maturing adolescents were only slight tendencies or hints rather than trends that were true of all early and late maturers. In the case of individual teenagers, the patterning of other influences in their lives may override any such tendencies that could arise from the timing of their maturation. Thus, it would be unwise for a counselor to expect every early or late maturer to exhibit these tendencies, particularly since the data were derived from the study of relatively small groups. Yet, the possibility that adolescents' physical deviation from the average might affect their personal/social adjustment can alert counselors to the desirability of investigating how an early- or late-maturing client's social adjustment and self-perception might have been influenced by maturation rate.

Although a teenager's genetic inheritance is the prime determinant of when puberty will occur, the timing and progress of physical changes are affected somewhat by such environmental influences as nutrition, medical care, and exercise. Over the past several generations, the onset of puberty and the completion of the adolescent growth spurt have been occurring at progressively earlier ages. This phenomenon has been called a *secular trend*, meaning a trend that extends over a considerable period of time, such as from century to century. In 1840, Norwegian girls typically experienced menarche around age 17, but now the average is age 13, which is a trend also found among American girls (Katchadourian, 1977). Furthermore, in a variety of nations, each generation of youths has been growing taller and heavier. Improved nutrition, sanitation, and medical care have been credited for such changes.

Evidence collected in recent years suggests that vigorous exercise in girls may retard the onset of puberty. Girls involved heavily in gymnastics and ballet have been found to reach menarche as much as three years later than age-mates. In addition, strenuous exercise has been found to disrupt women's menstrual cycle (Warren, 1980; Bullen et al., 1985).

In summary, the dramatic physical changes of early and middle adolescence can alter the abilities and motivations of youths in ways that call for stressful adjustments of attitudes, expectations, and activities that warrant the aid of a counselor.

Cognitive Abilities

In Piaget's stages of mental development, the highest stage—that of formal operations—is entered during or sometime after the arrival of puberty. As teenagers achieve an increasing command of formal-operational thought, they are able to grasp concepts and employ cognitive strategies which eluded them during childhood. Now they can manipulate abstractions, apply generalizations, and comprehend relationships in mathematics, linguistics, history, science, and social affairs that would have puzzled them in earlier years. Now they can see the sense of such a statement as "Let x represent one unknown quantity and y another unknown" or "Let's say z is any number." They can explain the binary system and its importance in the operation of electronic computers. They can understand that "Chinese is a tonally inflected language, whereas inflections in English are produced by structural changes in words and sentences." They are able to interpret poetic figures of speech. They can explain why 1992 is in the twentieth century, why 55 B.C. came before 12 B.C., and what is meant by the term *light-year*. They can describe the role of genes and chromosomes in heredity, of sperm and ova in human reproduction, and the nature of cell structure. They can grasp the notion that all matter is composed of atoms comprised of such charged particles as electrons and protons that spin about a nucleus to form a kind of submicroscopic solar system.

These advanced cognitive abilities are not all achieved suddenly, nor are they displayed evenly across subject-matter fields. An adolescent may begin to think in the abstract terms of formal operations in algebra class but still continue to think in concrete, less-sophisticated ways in history or general science. In other words, thought processes may be somewhat compartmentalized, with the patterns of logic applied in understanding cell structure in biology not employed when the young student is asked to compare Darwin's theory with a biblical explanation of the origin of human and animal species. Piaget assigned the label *horizontal decalage* to this unevenness of thought processes across different phenomena.

There are also marked individual differences among youths in the time when they arrive at the period of formal-operational thought. Furthermore, there are significant differences in the degree to which youths will ever achieve the ability to manipulate ideas in abstract, complex patterns. These differences in cognitive abilities are frequently at the core of problems which adolescents experience in the academic program of the secondary school. Students faced with the task of mastering algebra, geometry, calculus, physics, biology, chemistry, history, literature, music theory, and the like, before they are intellectually ready, are bound to be in academic difficulty. Their scholastic shortcomings often lead to a diminished self-concept, introversion, aggression, truancy, or delinquent acts. As a result, they frequently end up in a counselor's office. When treating such cases, it is therefore important for the therapist to obtain an assessment of the youth's cognitive skills, either by means of formal tests or by estimating the teenager's mental ability on the basis of how the youth analyzes problems posed in counseling interviews. This estimate can then serve as the basis for offering academic and vocational guidance as well as for judging what form of treatment will best suit the client's cognitive level and style.

Piaget's proposal that the highest of his stages of mental functioning appears in early or mid-adolescence has attracted a variety of critics who are unconvinced that the pinnacle of cognitive development is reached so early in the life span. They contend that intellectual growth does indeed continue well beyond the teens, as evidenced by the obvious intellectual accomplishments of people in early and middle adulthood. In responding to such criticisms, Piaget observed that the most obvious distinction between adolescent and adult thought is the greater lingering egocentrism displayed by adolescents. Teenage youths, with their acquired skills of logical thought, are idealists who expect the world to be logical. They fail to recognize or accept the reality that people do not operate solely on the basis of logic, so youths become reformers and critics of the older generation, foreseeing a glorious future in which the young and their peers will right today's wrongs. In Piaget's opinion, the egocentrism and idealism of youths are rendered more realistic and social by the young people's entering the occupational world or by their taking on serious professional training.

The adolescent becomes an adult when he undertakes a real job. It is then that he is transformed from an idealistic reformer into an achiever. In other words, the job leads thinking away from the dangers of formalism back into reality (Inhelder & Piaget, 1958, p. 346).

Other theorists have proposed somewhat different explanations for cognitive development beyond the formal-operational thought of adolescence. Klaus Riegel (1973) accepted the Piagetian stages as being reasonable as far as they went, but he then suggested a dialectical scheme whereby one set of psychological forces struggle against other sets to produce development beyond the middle-teen years. Dialectical theory is founded on the assumption that each time a person achieves a new insight or a new concept or belief, it soon becomes apparent that the insight or concept is incomplete or simplistic, for it appears to conflict with other beliefs. The initial insight is called the thesis, and the subsequent conflicting beliefs are called the antithesis. The dialectical confrontation of thesis and antithesis is experienced by the individual as a problem, a puzzle, a kind of cognitive dissonance that needs to be resolved. The person then struggles to remedy the conflict and, when successful, achieves a satisfying synthesis of the opposing factors. The synthesis represents a more mature, sophisticated insight. According to Riegel, this dialectical process continues on and on throughout adolescence and adulthood, accounting for the advances in intellectual maturity that appear over the life span until old age. Thus, according to a dialectical view, people can continually grow in knowledge, decision-making strategies, and judgment by constantly engaging in problem solving. Counseling with adolescents may therefore be seen as an occasion for promoting cognitive development by helping them resolve the conflicts that frustrate their present attempts at personal/social adjustment.

It is clear, however, that people do not necessarily apply their cognitive skills in an objective, unemotional manner as they attempt to solve life's problems. This is apparent during adolescence, when youths' reasoning skills can be very advanced, yet their judgments are often colored by such strong emotions that their elders are dismayed by their apparently illogical decisions and behavior. This emotional warping of logic is often a factor with which counselors must contend among clients of any age, but certainly among adolescents.

Sexual Development

E. F. Jones (1986, pp. 64-65) has offered a description of the conflicting messages about sexual behavior that have caused adolescents distress throughout the closing decades of the twentieth century:

> If teenagers are not sexually active by their late teens, they are viewed as odd and out of step by their peers. If they have a contraceptive on hand before a steady relationship is established, they may be considered promiscuous by revealing that they expected to have intercourse. If they don't use a method, they are called irresponsible. Many adolescents cannot talk with their parents about sex and contraception, and if they try to get a method on their own they may be afraid that their parents will find out.... If they get pregnant and decide to have an abortion, they cannot remain unaware of the newspaper articles about organized opposition to abortion ... they may have to pass through pickets or demonstrators to get into the abortion facility.

Thus, the matter of how to manage sexual drives that have newly been stimulated by the arrival of puberty is an issue of serious concern for adolescents. One common solution to the problem of sexual expression has been the self-stimulation of masturbation. It is true that genital stimulation is not limited to the teen years. Masturbation often provides pleasure and self-solace for infants and young children, but in adolescence it achieves a new importance, serving as a way of:

> expressing and managing powerful sexual urges ... a method whereby the experience of sexual excitement is allied with fantasies about sexual involvement. Pubertal masturbation is a way station on the road to adult sexuality. Through masturbation, a boy, particularly, may learn to master a seemingly uncontrollable body. Erections are more frequent as puberty proceeds and arouse awareness of the feeling that a part of the body is, and his feelings are, out of control. The masturbatory act helps to control tumescence and detumescence (Group for the Advancement of Psychiatry, 1986, pp. 8-9).

Some ethnic and religious groups continue to perpetuate the conviction that masturbation is sinful, so the young are warned of dire consequences that will result from the practice. When such beliefs conflict with the strong sexual drives of the teen years, the resulting distress can contribute to the personal confusion that brings adolescent clients for counseling.

Children's curiosity about the private equipment of the opposite sex begins in early childhood, but such interest is notably heightened in adolescence, when new opportunities and strong erotic drives contribute to increased heterosexual exploration. Kastenbaum (1979) has suggested that the purpose of this groping activity is usually more that of seeking to understand one's own new sensations than to establish an intimate loving relationship. The beginning and extent of heterosexual exploration is often hastened by peer pressure, by a sense of competition and a desire to be accepted and admired in a teen society that presses for adult experience and privilege at an early age. Since the 1950s, more permissive youth-rearing practices and a shift in societal moral values have contributed to adolescents' engaging in sexual intercourse at increasingly younger ages. In a study by Chilman (1978), over the decade 1965-1975, the rates of premarital intercourse increased by 50% for white males and 300% for white females. By age 16, one-quarter of white males and females had engaged in coitus, as had 90% of Black males and nearly 50% of Black females.

Adolescence has often been pictured as a testing period during which youths measure themselves against the world as they attempt to discover the extent of their physical and mental abilities, their interests, their goals, and their appeal to others. Sexual exploration is part of this self-testing. Both girls and boys seek to assess their powers of attracting the opposite sex or—in a society that permits greater open recognition of homosexuality—of attracting members of their own sex. The outcome of this appraisal of themselves as sex objects contributes to their sense of personal identity that evolves over the teen years. Feeling neglected, rejected, or scorned in sexual relations can be expected to lead to a diminished sense of adequacy, whereas feeling accepted and sought-after can contribute to a sense of confidence and power. Confusion, disappointment, guilt, fear, and shame that may arise during this process of sexual exploration can result in the adolescent's being sent, or voluntarily coming, for counseling aid. This has been particularly true during the post-World-War-II period of shifting moral values, intergenerational disagreements about acceptable sexual conduct (including homosexuality), coitus at increasingly younger ages, teenage pregnancy and venereal disease, and the specter of AIDS.

Part of the difficulty that teenagers may experience in their sexual identification and relationships is caused by their individual differences in rates of maturation. As noted earlier, the first occasion of nonpathological menstruation in girls—the *menarche*—is from 9 to 16 years of age, and penis growth in most boys begins at age 13, but it can start as early as 11 or as late as between 14 and 15. An individual's position in late-childhood's parade toward sexual maturity affects that person's sex drives and emotions, treatment by age-mates, and self-esteem. By age 13 or 14, late-maturing boys and girls may still feel, act, and be treated like children, whereas early-maturing ones may feel, act, and be treated like older youths on the verge of adulthood. Counselors are often asked to help adolescents solve personal/social problems that derive from these differences in maturation rate.

In summary, the physical, psychological, and social changes that accompany sexual development pose some of the greatest concerns of adolescence and, as such, become crucial elements in the problems that teenagers bring to counselors.

Social Development and Personal Identity

During the years prior to puberty, as children's physical and mental skills have regularly improved, their interactions with the social environment:

> contribute . . . to a more realistic self-esteem. This self-esteem grows to be a conviction that one is learning effective steps toward a tangible future, and is developing into a defined self within a social reality. The growing child must, at every step, derive a vitalizing sense of actuality from the awareness that his individual way of mastering experience (his ego synthesis) is a successful variant of a group identity and is in accord with its space-time and life plan (Erikson, 1963, p. 235).

In Erikson's (1963) proposed stages of psychosocial development, a major threat to the older child's established sense of identity occurs with the advent of adolescence. At the onset of puberty, marked changes arise in the child's biological nature—the ripening of the sexual functions, rapid growth in height and weight, alterations in body contour, and growth of body hair. Parental social and moral values, which usually continued strong during later childhood, often diminish significantly during adolescence as peers and the images furnished by mass-communication media—films, television, videotapes, magazines—become increasingly important models for teenagers' social behavior. Strained relations can develop between parents and their adolescent offspring as the youths seek privilege and independence sooner than parents believe these to be suitable. Parents often doubt the teenager's ability and willingness to accept the responsibilities that accompany the privileges of incipient adulthood. At the same time, the youth's perception of the options offered by the world expands significantly, and the problem of selecting and preparing for a life career looms large. The confluence of these forces can precipitate what Erikson has called an identity crisis, which is displayed in what he first termed *identity diffusion* and later replaced with *identity confusion* (Erikson, 1968, p. 212).

The identity problem of adolescence differs from that of early childhood. Young children's amorphous sense of self is caused by their immature cognitive skills and lack of experience with the world. In contrast, adolescents' identity confusion results from their being overwhelmed by body changes and by a flood of alternatives from the environment at a time when their judgments are guided by an unanchored, drifting value system. The typical adolescent's identity (at least in modern industrialized societies) is considered to be deficient in stability, appropriateness to context, and clarity. "To keep themselves together, [youths] temporarily overidentify, to the point of apparent complete loss of identity, with the heroes of cliques and crowds" (Erikson, 1963, p. 262). Therefore, a major task of adolescence becomes that of resolving the identity crisis, so that youths can enter adulthood with an increasingly secure set of values and a clearer conception of their appearance, physical and mental abilities, interests, social relationships, potentials, ambitions for the future, and individuality.

This is not to say that all teenagers search for identity in the same manner, nor that all of them experience the search as a crisis to the same degree. For some of them, the task is easier than for others. James Marcia (1980), in an attempt to distinguish differences in identity development among teenagers, has proposed four principal types of identity status, which he labeled *achievement, foreclosure, moratorium,* and *diffusion.* As the first of these types, Marcia postulated that those adolescents who have achieved identity are ones who have faced doubt (crisis) in personal values and self-identification, have weighed alternatives, and intentionally have subscribed to a set of values. Under the second type are youths who have reached identity foreclosure. At first glance, they appear to have achieved identity, because they exhibit a commitment to a set of values. However, they did not reach this commitment through considering alternatives and consciously choosing a defensible position. Instead, they have uncritically accepted someone else's values, oftentimes those of their parents. Third, Marcia attached the label *moratorium* to the adolescent who has questioned goals and values and weighed alternatives but has not yet made a commitment and therefore is continuing the search. Fourth, Erikson's term *identity diffusion* has been applied to teenagers who are making no serious attempt to consider issues of personal goals or values, and thus they express no conscious belief system or realistic plan for the future. Thus, as Marcia's typology implies, there can be significant differences among teenagers in the form of their identity search, its timing, and its success.

Youths who are experiencing particular difficulty with establishing a satisfactory identity may display symptoms that bring them for counseling, such symptoms as indecision, depression, outlandish behavior, rebellion, and the like. It then becomes the counselor's assignment to recognize the nature of their problem and assist them in their search.

With the foregoing brief overview of key characteristics of adolescence as a background, we now consider representative kinds of adolescent clients often met by counselors.

KINDS OF COUNSELING CASES DURING ADOLESCENCE

The four illustrative types of cases selected for more detailed discussion in the remainder of this chapter are ones involving (1) educational counseling and guidance, (2) adolescents' problems of accepting their changing physical self, with the condition of anorexia nervosa used as a specific instance of this problem, (3) sexual relationships during adolescence, with teenage pregnancy inspected as one possible outcome of such relationships, and (4) juvenile crime, particularly the use of illicit drugs.

Educational Counseling and Guidance

Educational counseling or *educational guidance* is a process of helping people (1) identify the educational options available to them, (2) make wise selections among the options, and (3) adopt productive steps for pursuing the options that they have chosen.

Educational guidance can be called for at any stage of the life span. Parents of a preschooler can seek advice about what sort of nursery school or child-care center will be best for their child. At the elementary-school level, a teacher may ask for help in deciding whether a boy who has performed poorly during the current school year should be kept back to repeat the grade. Parents may turn to a counselor for estimating whether to have their daughter transfer from her present classroom to the room of another teacher or whether to move their daughter to a different school. Parents may also wish to learn what opportunities outside the regular school program might be available for broadening the experiences of a gifted child in the arts (drawing, painting, dancing, music) or in science.

Adults may also seek educational counseling for themselves, either to prepare for an occupation or to enrich their lives in a more general way—adopt a hobby, try out their creative skills, understand more about the social and scientific world, learn computer technology, and the like.

However, even though clients for educational guidance can be young children and adults, the greatest need for such counseling occurs during adolescence. The school's curriculum, which is essentially the same for all children at the elementary-school level, becomes more diversified in the secondary school. Junior- and senior-high-school students are often obliged to enter particular curriculum tracks or streams that are identified by such labels as general, college preparatory, vocational, science-math, social sciences, or the arts. Or if students are not assigned to an established curriculum track, they at least have elective subjects among which they must choose. And the closer students approach adulthood, the more their decisions about electives are influenced by their vocational ambitions. As a result, by the latter years of adolescence, educational guidance and career counseling typically overlap. Thus, an important service furnished by school psychologists and counselors is that of providing educational and career guidance. Frequently, this service is linked to the counseling function of diagnosing and treating learning difficulties.

The need for efficient educational counseling is reflected in a variety of normative data about students who experience difficulties in school. In the United States in 1970, the number of high-school dropouts (youths who did not remain in school through grade 12) ages 14 through 24 was 4.7 million. The number rose to 5.2 million in 1980, then declined to 4.3 million by 1986. Thus, the dropout rate had diminished from 12.2% of the youth population in 1970 to 10.8% by the mid-1980s. In terms of race, the percentage of white youths (10.3%) who were dropouts in 1985 was slightly less than that of Black youths (12.8%). However, the improvement in Black youths' remaining in school between 1970 (22.2% dropouts) and 1985 (12.8%) was far greater than that of whites (10.8% dropouts in 1970 and 10.3% in 1985) (U.S. Bureau of the Census, 1988). Therefore, even though the trend for students' completing high school improved over the 1970-1980 period, there were still over 4 million youths in the 14-24 age bracket who, by the mid-1980s, had not obtained the basic level of education needed for competing successfully in the world of work or for progressing into advanced schooling. I am not assuming here that the reason why all these youths did not finish high school was that they had not received proper educational counseling. Indeed, the reasons for their quitting school were varied and complex, often beyond the ability of school personnel to remedy the causes. However, included among the difficulties experienced by many of these youths is a lack of suitable educational guidance. Therefore, the dropout rate is to some extent a reflection of inadequate educational counseling.

A second demographic symptom of insufficient guidance is the illiteracy rate. The U.S. Department of Education has estimated that 25 million American adults—one in seven—are functional illiterates, since they are unable to read, write, calculate, or solve problems at a level enabling them to cope with essential daily responsibilities. A further 47 million are judged to be borderline illiterates, ones who can somewhat handle the written word and numbers but not proficiently (Goddard, 1987, p. 73).

> An estimated 45 million adults holding jobs today are either functional or marginal illiterates. One study shows that half of our nation's industrial workers read at or below the eighth-grade level and each year another 2.3 million functional illiterates age 16 or older join the nation's employment pool.... The U.S. Department of Education... estimates the functionally illiterate now account for 30% of unskilled workers, 19% of semiskilled workers, and 11% of all managers, professionals, and technicians (p. 73).

Other sources of estimates—using different criteria for judging levels of literacy—propose different totals of Americans who cannot read well enough to fill out a job application, write a check, read a poison-warning label, or follow directions in a manual for operating or repairing a machine. Such totals range from 47 to 72 million adults (Schoultz, 1986, p. 45); but, whatever the exact figure may be, the number is very high.

When the entire child population of a nation is obliged to attend school for 10 to 12 years yet many do not learn to read, write, or compute with at least modest skill, then the school's instructional and educational-counseling functions both appear to be at fault. Clearly, the school is not solely to blame for people's lack of reasonable fluency with written words and numbers. Also at fault are parents' child-rearing habits and modern society's heavy dependence on television and radio for news and entertainment. However, insufficient educational counseling is still part of the problem.

In addition to high dropout and illiteracy rates, less formal evidence of the need for proper educational guidance is found in the frequent cases of parents and pupils who do not understand the curricular choices available in the secondary school, who do not know what kind of educational preparation is needed for various occupations, and who do not recognize what can be done to remedy students' academic shortcomings. These problems are particularly prominent among families on the lower socioeconomic level, where ethnic minorities and recent immigrants are overrepresented. Compared to such families, parents of middle- and upper-social-class status are better acquainted with how schools operate and with how to draw the attention of school personnel to their children's needs, including the need for effective educational guidance.

THE TASKS AND MEDIA OF EDUCATIONAL COUNSELING

If the purpose of educational counseling is to help students and their parents make wise educational decisions, then the activities comprising the counseling process can be of two general varieties— (1) those intended to influence the student and the student's family and (2) those intended to influence the school or other educational agencies.

Counseling tasks focusing on students and their families include: (1) identifying those who need help in planning a teenager's present and future education, (2) assessing students' aptitudes and interests, (3) informing them of the array of available educational opportunities appropriate for such aptitudes and interests, (4) describing how to take advantage of such opportunities, and (5) helping them to set criteria that they wish to use in choosing among the options.

Counseling tasks focusing on the school and other educational agencies include: (1) obtaining information about school opportunities and about how to take advantage of them and (2) convincing the school bureaucracy to make reasonable adjustments in its routines so as to meet the educational needs of individual students.

If these are the tasks of educational counseling, then by what people and what techniques are they most suitably performed? The answer is that the roles assumed by professional counselors, teachers, and other school personnel vary from one school to another, since the most appropriate way to carry out educational counseling depends on such factors as the preparation and experience of school personnel, the number of students to be served, the complexity of students' problems, and parents' interests and skills.

The task of analyzing students' aptitudes and interests is typically carried out by a psychometrician, school psychologist, counselor, or teacher who has had experience with tests of ability and interests. Tests may be administered in either group or individual sessions.

The function of providing information to teenagers and their parents about educational and vocational opportunities is typically performed by a counselor or a teacher armed with a list of the school's curriculum offerings, brochures about occupations, college catalogues, and videotapes. The information is distributed in either group or individual settings, oftentimes as an activity of a regular school class.

As noted above, not only do educational counselors work with students and parents, but they also function as the student's advocate in altering the usual school program to accommodate needs that are not well met by the school's ordinary procedures. Thus, the counselor may seek tutoring for a pupil who has been ill, arrange for a gifted student to take an advanced mathematics class in a nearby college, or petition for a skilled musician to be excused from the school's required music-appreciation class.

Accepting One's Physical Self—Anorexia and Bulimia

Parallel to the marked physical changes following puberty are teenagers' heightened concerns over their physical appearance. Adolescents are especially sensitive to how their looks are judged by their age-mates. Styles of dress and grooming during these years often reflect youths' attempts to appear more adult than their age warrants. Typical symptoms are girls' early use of cosmetics and boys' attempts to shave or to grow a mustache. In contrast, dress and grooming can become symbols of rebellion against adult authority, serving as marks that distinguish the young from the old—multicolored punk-rock hair styles, mottled blue jeans, miniscule swim suits, and tee-shirts embellished with provocative pictures and sayings.

Commercial advertising and popular heroes in movies, television, and magazines contribute significantly to the images that adolescents seek to emulate in their own appearance and behavior. Prominent among these images is that of the ideal teenage girl—thin, with unblemished golden skin and shining hair. The acceptance of this image as an ideal to achieve has been a significant factor in the increase among American girls of an eating disturbance that comes to the attention of counselors and physicians with growing regularity. Because such a restricted ideal is unrealistic for so many girls, a very large number of them are distressed about how they fail to match it. For example, studies from North America and Western Europe, cited by Kelly and Patten (1985, pp. 191-193), show that the majority of teenage girls worry about being overweight. In one investigation, 80% of them wanted to weigh less, although only 43% could be categorized as above average in weight on the basis of measurements. Their concern about weight can become an obsession, resulting in a disorder known by such a variety of labels as anorexia nervosa, self-starvation, bulimia, and the binge-purge syndrome. This condition of extreme distress about weight serves as the example of problems of physical self-acceptance that we will inspect in some detail. Other physical problems that can bring adolescents to the attention of counselors include acne, obesity, height that deviates markedly from that of age-mates, lameness, disfiguring birthmarks, unusually formed facial features, defective posture, and protruding or crooked teeth.

THE NATURE AND INCIDENCE OF
ANOREXIA NERVOSA AND BULIMIA

Typical symptoms of anorexia nervosa, as listed in the *Diagnostic and Statistical Manual of Mental Disorders* of the American Psychiatric Association (1980, p. 69), include:

(1) Intense fear of becoming obese, which does not diminish as weight loss progresses.
(2) Disturbance of body image, such as claiming to feel fat even when emaciated.
(3) Weight loss of at least 25% of original body weight; if under 18 years of

age, weight loss from original body weight plus projected weight gain expected from growth charts combine to make the 25%.

(4) Refusal to maintain body weight over a minimal normal weight for age and weight.

(5) No known physical illness that would account for the weight loss.

(6) Amenorrhea [no menstrual flow].

The disorder occurs far more often in girls than in boys, in a ratio of 9 to 1, and usually begins during adolescence, with one out of every 250 girls between the ages of 12 and 18 suffering from the disease (Gross, 1982, p. 1). The symptoms in both girls and boys are essentially the same, except for the addition of the disturbed menstrual periods in girls. The incidence of anorexia has advanced sharply in recent decades, probably as a result of increased social pressures within the adolescent peer culture. Romeo (1986, p. xiii) reports that approximately two-thirds of anorexics recover, while the remaining one-third continue to be chronically ill, with an estimated 5% ending in death. Gross (1982, p. 2) states that "Sometimes patients die of infectious disease because of deficits in their immunological systems. The results of several studies show a mortality rate between 15% and 20%."

The word *anorexia* literally means loss of appetite and thus is something of a misnomer, since those who suffer from the illness usually do not lose their appetite until the very late stages. In the early stages, the anorexic forces himself or herself to fast or eat very little despite the desire to eat more (Gross, 1982, p. 1).

Whereas *anorexia* and *anorexia nervosa* are the most common terms used for this eating condition, other terms have also been created to distinguish among related varieties of this general class of eating disorders. For instance, *bulimia* and *binge and purge* identify a pattern of behavior in which the client, after eating (often to excess), seeks to eliminate what has been eaten, with the most common technique being self-induced vomiting, though laxatives are sometimes also used. Gross (1982, p. 154) reports that an estimated 80% of female college students have used vomiting at least once to avoid gaining weight or to assuage their feelings of guilt for having eaten too much. Powers and Fernandez (1984, p. 6) note that about 50% of patients with anorexia nervosa have experienced episodes of binge-eating, while 50% of patients with the bulimia syndrome have a past history of anorexia nervosa. Thus, in terms of symptoms, the two conditions are related but not identical. Both involve fear of obesity and the adoption of unreasonable methods for becoming thin.

Romeo (1986, pp. 5-6) has observed that during the early stages of anorexia nervosa, the anorexic's dieting is no different from normal dieting. But, as time passes, the anorexic's beliefs turn irrational as she fears becoming grossly obese. Thereafter, the anorexic constantly seeks to become thinner and experiences such high levels of anxiety whenever she eats that she cannot resume normal eating habits. Hunger pangs increase, producing a painful conflict between an intense desire to eat and an equally intense fear of becoming fat.

CORRELATES OF ANOREXIA AND BULIMIA

From his study of the conditions under which anorexia nervosa occurs, Gross (1982, p. 1) concluded that:

> At the onset of the disease there is often evidence of a stressful life situation, such as conflicts in the family or at school and peer-group pressure. These patients have a tendency to be perfectionists and usually have a history of being model children. About one-third of the patients may have begun dieting because they were slightly overweight but then adopted obsessive, compulsive eating habits, with weight loss as the primary goal. Once they succeed in losing weight, they continue relentlessly, to the point of severe emaciation. When a substantial amount of weight is lost, they become fearful of regaining it and resist any pressure from their parents to eat.

Other frequent concomitants of the disorder in its advanced stages are reduction of body temperature and blood pressure, slowed pulse rate, severe dehydration, swelling (edema) of the ankles and legs, and gastritis. Occasionally, the patient also displays abnormal liver function, low white blood cell count, loss of hair, and reduced resistance to diseases. A further common correlate is hyperactivity, with the anorexic exercising beyond the amount conducive to good health (Anderson, 1985).

Anorexia nervosa is often associated with particular family patterns (Romeo, 1986, pp. 3-4). The majority of anorexic girls are from families in the middle and upper-middle socioeconomic classes. Their parents are well educated, emphasize academic achievement, value physical fitness, encourage their children to engage in sports, and are frequently on a diet. Wilson's (1983, p. 46) psychoanalytic study of 50 families of anorexics led him to conclude that the parents exhibited (1) overconcern with dieting and fears of being fat, (2) overconscientious perfectionism, which the anorexic adolescent adopts, and (3) repression of emotions. The anorexic tends to be an obedient, model teenager, a good student, and a pride to both parents and teachers. Although anorexia and bulimia are traditionally most prominent in the middle and upper social classes, in recent years these disorders have become increasingly apparent in the lower strata of the social-class structure as well.

Schwartz's (1987) review of studies analyzing the families of bulimics identified three general family types, with each type exerting social-adjustment pressures on the adolescent girl. First was the "Americanized" family described above—perfectionist and striving to achieve such dominant values of contemporary American culture as slimness and educational achievement. Second was the protectionist family with foreign ethnic roots, in which the daughter was pressured to maintain the woman's traditional role and stay close to home. Third was the transitional family in which daughters were caught between the Americanized and ethnic traditions. Most of the bulimic families studied by Schwartz manifested a lack of impulse control, in contrast to the emotional restrictiveness observed in many anorexic families.

TREATING ANOREXIA NERVOSA AND BULIMIA

Some cases of anorexia and bulimia recover spontaneously, with *spontaneously* meaning that no special treatment has been provided, so that the causes underlying the recovery are unrecognized. Oftentimes, anorexia appears only as a single extended episode that is followed by full remission, particularly when treatment has been provided early in the course of the disease. In other cases, however, patients may relapse, even following extensive treatment (Gross, 1982, p. 2).

One of the most popular forms of treatment has been behavioral therapy in both respondent and operant modes. Under the respondent mode, therapists apply systematic desensitization and response prevention to reduce patients' anxiety about food. Under the operant mode, therapists seek to alter the consequences that are reinforcing the clients' present attempts at self-starvation, such as providing positive reinforcement for adaptive eating behaviors or weight gain. Studies of behavioral therapy versus traditional techniques (psychoanalytic, informational, person-centered, and others) suggest that behavioral approaches have been superior to traditional methods in terms of reducing both hospital stays and long-term residual problems of life adjustment. However, behavioral and traditional approaches have been nearly equal in producing normal eating habits, the maintenance of appropriate weight, and a return of menstruation. An estimated half of anorexic patients suffer interpersonal difficulties after treatment, partly because of a negative self-image carried over from their earlier perception of their weight condition, so that behavioral methods are recommended for improving their assertiveness and communication skills (Hatsukami, 1985, pp. 107-116).

Gross (1982, p. 86) contends that most therapists who treat anorexia nervosa have found psychoanalysis ineffective for inducing weight gain or changing patients' attitudes toward food and health, since psychoanalysis focuses on patients' narcissistic concentration on the body and fails to achieve the goal of preparing the individual for more mature, self-reliant coping with life.

Some counseling psychologists and psychiatrists advocate insight-oriented treatment, in which the therapist reflects to the patient the types of difficulties that the patient is suffering and points out various solutions from which the individual can choose. It is then the patient who selects the most suitable solution, since she is considered to be the one who best understands her needs. Some professionals also report success with versions of rational-emotive and reality therapy, combined with information about nutrition and exercise (Gross, 1982, pp. 95-96).

Family therapy is often recommended in order to correct family members' misperceptions of the illness and to aid them in changing their behaviors that maintain or reinforce the patient's eating disorder.

Group therapy has been used for a variety of purposes: (1) as a diagnostic tool to reveal patients' interpersonal skills and their feelings about themselves, (2) as preparation for entering the hospital among patients who require intensive, controlled treatment, (3) as a support and refresher source for those who have left intensive individual or hospital treatment, and (4) as an inexpensive mode of outpatient-therapy.

While psychological intervention has been the principal treatment for anorexia and bulimia, drug therapy has recently been found to be useful with certain individuals, although the evidence about the effectiveness of psychopharmacology is still meager. Since depression is often a characteristics of anorexics, antidepressant drugs "may prove useful for at least a subgroup of patients" (Johnson, Stuckey, &

Mitchell, 1985, p. 146). It is also possible that anticonvulsant medications can help in some bulimic patients.

Gross (1982, p. 126) has reported hypnotherapy to be useful for perhaps 10% of anorexics. While the client is hypnotized, the therapist suggests improvements in health, strength, and appearance that the client could experience, with the implication that such advantages would accrue under improved eating habits.

In conclusion, experts in the realm of eating disorders appear to agree that anorexic and bulimic patients are often difficult to treat and that the best approach can be one that integrates various treatment techniques in a manner that seems best suited to the conditions of the particular case at hand (Eckert & Labeck, 1985, pp. 152-168; Reece & Gross, 1982, pp. 103-109). In other words, a therapist may appropriately combine behavioral techniques with aspects of person-centered, insight, and reality methods, which, in some cases, may be supported by drug therapy.

Sexual Relationships—Teenage Pregnancy

Radical changes have appeared since 1960 in the sexual habits of American adolescents. The changes have included higher rates of premarital intercourse, an earlier age for the first incident of intercourse, a higher frequency of teenage pregnancy, more single teenage mothers attending high school or college, and more unmarried teenagers living openly with someone of the opposite sex. National survey data indicate that the majority of U.S. Americans by the mid-1980s saw premarital sexual relations as acceptable. According to the Gallup Poll in 1969, only 24% of U.S. adults thought it was not wrong for a man and woman to have sexual relations before marriage. By 1973, the fraction had increased to 47%, and, by 1985, to 57% (E. F. Jones, 1986, p. 60). This period also witnessed a growing frequency of *casual sex*, a term referring to intercourse with someone of brief acquaintance or with a variety of different partners on one or two occasions, in contrast to engaging in a sexual relationship with only one partner over an extended period of time. Freer sexual practices that did not include suitable protective contraception measures also led to increases of such venereal diseases as syphilis and herpes simplex-2. However, in the 1980s, fears of contracting AIDS (Acquired Immune Deficiency Syndrome) began to discourage some people from indulging in casual sex, and it caused others to adopt the condom as a contraceptive device when they did engage in intercourse.

Furthermore, following the 1950s, homosexuality "came out of the closet" as members of the "gay community" openly represented their sexual lifestyle as a respectable alternative to heterosexuality.

As a consequence of the sexual conditions experienced by adolescents, counselors are often faced with the task of assisting teenagers with sex-related problems. To illustrate the way in which normative data may be useful in treating such problems, one of the foregoing issues—that of teenage pregnancy—has been selected for analysis in the following paragraphs. The discussion focuses on the incidence of teenage pregnancy, conditions correlated with motherhood during adolescence, and counseling services for such cases.

THE FREQUENCY OF TEENAGE PREGNANCY

In the popular mind, there appears to be the impression that teenage pregnancy has been steadily rising over recent decades. By the 1980s, the number of teenage pregnancies annually in the United States was reported to be 1.14 million. Of these, nearly one-half (49%) ended in live births. Adolescent girls accounted for nearly half of all out-of-wedlock births in the nation (Moore & Burt, 1982, p. 81; Romig & Thompson, 1988, p. 134), with the rate of teenage pregnancies in the United States much higher than the rates in other advanced industrialized countries (E. F. Jones, 1986, p. 228).

However, closer inspection of birth rates since 1940 reveal a somewhat different and more complex picture. According to Vinovskis (1988, pp. 25-27), by 1983, fertility rates among girls ages 15-19 were about the same as they were in the early 1940s (around 52 births annually per 1000 women). This was not the result of steady-state fertility over the 40-year period. Rather, after World War II, the rate rose rapidly to a peak of 97.3 per 1000 in 1957, declined to 52.8 in 1977, and leveled off at 51.7 by 1983.

In 1960 females ages 15 to 19 had 586,966 births while their counterparts in 1977 had 559,154 births—a decrease of only 4.7 percent. The reason for the relative stability in the total number of teenage births from 1960 to 1977 is that the number of female teenagers ages 15 to 19 in the population increased by 58.1 percent during this period. It is also important to observe, however, that the number of children born to teenagers [ages 15-19] declined by 13.3 percent from 1970 to 1977 and decreased another 12.5 percent from 1977 to 1983. In other words, since 1970 a substantial decrease in the number of births as well as in the birth rate for females ages 15 to 19 has occurred. (Vinovskis, 1988, pp. 25-26)

Such were the trends above age 14. In contrast, within the 10-14 age bracket between 1966 and 1970, fertility rates increased by one-third, then decreased by only 8.3% by 1983. Thus, while birth rates have declined among older teenagers, they have increased among the younger ones, whom teenage pregnancy affects most dramatically. Changing patterns of sexual behavior among young adolescents account for the rise. By the early 1980s, 20% of adolescents age 14-and-under were reported sexually active. "The rate of increase is most dramatic among white adolescent girls, whose sexual activity has doubled during the [first half-decade of the 1980s]. These teenagers are increasingly from the nonminority middle class, as well as from the traditionally sexually active lower socioeconomic groups" (Group for the Advancement of Psychiatry, 1986, p. 3).

There are notable differences between ethnic groups in the incidence of teenage birth rates. By the mid-1980s, nearly half of the first births of Blacks occurred to mothers under 20 years old, and almost all Black adolescents with children were unmarried. In a survey of census tracts in Chicago, where 20% or more of the population had family incomes below the federal poverty line, the percentage of Black women currently married did not exceed 35%, regardless of age. In the same survey, nearly 80% of Hispanic women and almost 70% of non-Hispanic white women were married, a finding consistent with other national trends (Franklin, 1988).

Whereas, in earlier generations, unwed teenage mothers—particularly those of middle and upper socioeconomic status—often gave up their babies for adoption, many were now keeping the infants, so that their problem was not only one of adolescent pregnancy but also one of baby-keeping and deficient motherhood.

CORRELATES OF ADOLESCENT PREGNANCY

Results of surveys conducted throughout the world are consistent with data from the United States in showing that high birthrates among teenagers are associated with low levels of educational attainment and with high rates of poverty and unemployment (Zimmerman, 1988, p. 320). The younger a woman was when she gave birth, the more likely it is that she came from an impoverished home.

The teenage mother faces economic dependence on some person or agency, has few educational and vocational options, and must rapidly develop an identity which includes being a parent (usually a single parent). Low self-esteem is almost inevitable. The adolescent is physically mature, yet emotionally deprived. Helplessness often characterizes her life due to her deep dependency on others after the baby is born. (Romig & Thompson, 1988, p. 135)

Compared to adult mothers, adolescent mothers are less likely to work and more likely to be on welfare, and most have neither full-time nor part-time jobs during and after giving birth. Many are poorly nourished, lack adequate medical care, and may be at risk for drug and alcohol use. Adolescent mothers who are not married usually do not receive financial support from the child's father. In 1981, among all mothers ages 18-24 in 1981 not living with the child's father, only 15% received support payments as compared to 39% of older mothers who lived apart from the father (E. F. Jones, 1986, p. 63).

Children born to mothers living in such conditions tend to receive a poor start in life. Franklin's (1988, p. 269) review of studies from the 1960s and 1970s indicated that children in low-income, female-headed households often display low self-esteem and limited affective and intellectual development. Such families are also described as producing children who develop early sexual proclivities and display tendencies toward violence and delinquency. Children whose mothers are older and those who spend more time in child care have scored higher on measures of mental ability than children of younger mothers or ones who spend less time with the child.

One of the important consequences of teenage pregnancy is the effect that the event has on the girl's family when the teenager bears a child. In the 1970s, nearly 90% of young mothers with their first pregnancy during their early-to-middle teens lived with a parent or close relative, and 77% were still doing so one year after delivery. Nearly half (46%) remained with their parents five years after delivery. Only one-quarter of teenage mothers married (Furstenburg, 1981).

Surveys of adolescent girls' family relationships suggest that "when parents (usually the mother) communicate openly and explicitly with their children about sex, irrespective of the context of this discussion, this communication seems to delay the start of sexual activity. Furthermore, once sex is initiated, explicit communication seems to be associated with more effective use of contraceptives" (Ooms, 1984, p. 218).

Moore and Burt (1982, p. 127), after reviewing studies of the outcome of adolescent marriages, concluded that:

> Marriage should not be advocated as a viable long-term solution in many cases. Although it resolves an unintended teenage pregnancy in a nominally profamily way, teenage marriages fail at alarming rates, and when they do, women are left with less education, fewer marketable skills, more children, and a high probability of resorting to welfare.

TEENAGE PREGNANCY AND COUNSELING

Counseling in cases of teenage pregnancy centers on the types of decisions faced by three kinds of clients—the pregnant girl, the boy or man by whom the girl is pregnant, and the family of the girl and, perhaps, of the boy. In any given case, one or more of these potential clients will be involved.

For the girl, the decisions to be considered can include: (1) whether to bear the child or to have an abortion, (2) whether to continue in school, (3) whether to marry the man by whom she is pregnant, (4) whether to leave home, (5) what to tell her parents and how to react to their response, and (6) if she does indeed bear the child, whether to keep it or put it up for adoption. After a teenager has borne a child, additional focal counseling issues become: (7) how to care for the infant, (8) what relationship to maintain with the child's father, (9) what employment to seek, if any, (10) what type of social life she should adopt for herself, and (11) how to plan for her own future and that of her child.

If the boy or man enters counseling, decisions to be considered include: (1) whether he should live with the girl, and, if so, whether it should be in a formal marriage relationship, (2) whether he should continue in school, (3) what responsibility—financial, social, emotional, educational—to take for the mother and child, and (4) what relationship he should establish with his own family and with the girl's family.

Because over 80% of teenage mothers live with their families, members of the girl's family—and sometimes the boy's family—can be important participants in the counseling process. With family members, decisions on which counseling sessions typically focus involve: (1) how to treat the girl and the boy, both privately within the family and publicly, (2) prior to the birth, should the parents recommend that their daughter bear the child or have an abortion, (3) if the child is to be borne, where should the girl live and who should furnish her financial and social support, and (4) should the girl continue in school during and after the pregnancy.

For each of these types of clients, the usual role of the counselor is to aid them in making wise decisions by helping them (1) identify alternative actions that they can take in relation to each question, (2) estimating the advantages and disadvantages of each alternative, (3) choosing the most suitable action, and (4) implementing it. There are a variety of media through which such counseling can be provided: school classes in social/sexual relationships and child rearing, hospital-based programs for adolescent mothers (mostly in a few inner-city hospitals), community-sponsored centers, private counseling services, and individual counselors (physicians, psychologists, social workers). Each of these settings can usually offer individual counseling, family counseling (teenagers and their parents), counseling with couples (the teenage girl and her mate), group counseling (several teenagers in the same condition), and bibliotherapy (reading material designed to assist the clients). The most common of these modes of intervention to serve adolescent mothers are school-based (Roosa, 1986, p. 313).

Secondary schools in the United States offer three principal types of courses intended to help students make constructive judgments about sex activity and parenthood. The largest number of these classes bear some such title as *Family Life Education* or *Modern Living*. Usually they are designed for both boys and girls, and they focus on a diversity of issues—choices of lifestyles, financial planning, occupational preparation, health and nutrition, sexual behavior, and child-rearing methods. The second type is entitled *Health Education*, with discussions of sexual matters frequently comprising part of the course of study. However, within most communities, a segment of the populace objects to providing sex education in the schools, on the assumption that discussion of such matters fosters sexual license among youths. The evidence to support or refute this assumption is, as yet, insufficient. However, Moore and Burt (1982, pp. 78-79), after reviewing available studies, estimated that:

> . . . it does not appear thus far that sex education encourages teens to engage in initial sexual activity. Taught from certain perspectives, it

seems likely to have the opposite impact. Curricula that help teenagers clarify their own values and goals, that explain the social and economic consequences of early parenthood, that develop decision-making skills so teens can evaluate their own behavior in means-end terms, that teach communication or assertiveness skills so teens can better explain and enforce their own values, seem likely to encourage a more considered and cautious approach among teenagers to the initiation of sexual activity.

Increasingly, secondary schools are also providing classes aimed at a more restricted clientele—pregnant adolescents and teenage mothers—with the classes typically labeled *Teenage Parenting Programs* (TAPP). The stated goals are to help young mothers continue their education, control their fertility, and become better parents. Such programs may include a nursery school or child-care facility which is located in the school and staffed by a trained director aided by high-school girls, who are usually the ones enrolled in the parenthood classes. It is within this setting that the counseling functions are performed, and having the child-care facility on the premises offers the advantage of providing teenage mothers guided practice in constructive child-raising techniques. Frequently the TAPP classes are conducted in a separate location, not on the regular high-school campus.

While a school-based program may serve the needs of pregnant adolescents who are currently in school, it fails to reach pregnant teenage dropouts. Roosa (1986, p. 314) cites a survey in a southwestern U.S. city which found that only 20% of the school-age mothers in the school district were enrolled in a Teenage Parenting Program. To identify ways that counseling services might be offered to these out-of-school mothers, Roosa has described three apparent subgroups within the dropout population. The first is composed of pregnant adolescents who left school as part of a subculture pattern. They were generally unsuccessful in school, already had as much education as their mother (or more), and were in neighborhoods in which adolescent motherhood is fairly common. "Girls in this group are elevated to adult status and receive abundant support throughout their social networks after becoming pregnant.... In such cases, interventions must be designed that better prepare adolescents for their adult roles without undermining those facets of the sub-culture (strong family ties and support) that are necessary for survival in that milieu (poverty, isolation, depressed economic opportunities)" (Roosa, 1986, p. 315).

The second subgroup is made up of teenage mothers who want to continue their education but drop out within several months after delivery. They have likely moved out of their parents' home and face such demanding financial, transportation, and child-care problems that they cannot manage their school responsibilities. Sometimes inflexible school regulations, which punish young mothers for being late to class or occasionally absent, precipitate their leaving school. Roosa (1986, p. 316) has proposed that this group could be aided if (1) programs for pregnant/parenting adolescents were located in neighborhood schools rather than in separate, out-of-the-way locations, (2) all TAPP programs included on-site child-care facilities, (3) schools' attendance policies were better adapted to the needs of young mothers, and (4) TAPP programs located in separate facilities did not require that young mothers transfer out of the program within one semester or one year after their pregnancy

The third subgroup is the smallest, consisting of adolescent mothers with high educational goals and strong support systems that suffice until their second pregnancy, when the young mother and her support network are overwhelmed by the added complexities of a second child, so that she leaves school.

> The most obvious intervention for this group is prevention of the second pregnancy which can be facilitated by education programs at school, parental support and understanding at home, and cooperation from the medical community. A commonly used measure of the success of TAPPs is the prevention of second pregnancies. (Roosa, 1986, p. 316)

It is apparent also that individual counseling can profitably be furnished outside of institutional settings. For instance, evidence suggesting the value of a nurse or child-development counselor's periodically visiting the home of unwed adolescent mothers has come from a comparison of the welfare of children of visited mothers versus nonvisited mothers ages 14-17 who are of low socioeconomic status. Measures of the physical and mental abilities of two groups of infants at age 9 months showed that the two were initially comparable. Members in one group were then occasionally visited by a professional worker who taught the mothers child-rearing practices designed to promote physical health and cognitive/affective growth. At age 30 months, children in the visited group showed moderately higher scores on the Stanford-Binet Intelligence Test and "only two of the 19 infants in the early intervention group, but nine of the 18 control infants, remained at risk. It is concluded that the intervention succeeded in preventing the decline from normal levels of functioning that is common in economically disadvantaged at-risk children. . . . (Cappleman, Thompson, DeRemer-Sullivan, King, & Sturm, 1982, p. 55).

Juvenile Crime—Illegal Drugs

If the incidence of law-breaking within an age category is used as the indicator of developmental confusion and social maladjustment of that age group, then the decade of adolescence can be regarded as the period of greatest confusion and socially unsuitable behavior of any decade in the life span.

There are several common ways of gathering data on juvenile delinquency, with each way suggesting juvenile law-breaking of different amounts. One way is to count the number of arrests of juveniles. Another is to survey teenagers to discover what delinquent acts they report having committed. Within each of these approaches, offenses can be divided into various types. Those acts judged to be serious crimes against persons and property are labeled *index offenses*. They include homicide, rape, aggravated assault, robbery, burglary, larceny, auto theft, and arson. In contrast are *juvenile status offenses*, a range of misbehaviors specific to juveniles which, if committed by adults, would not be considered criminal, such as wandering the streets at night, running away from home, and drinking alcohol. Status offenses include habitual disobedience or truancy by youths who are judged to be ungovernable and incorrigible. Other acts not fitting either of these categories are minor motoring infractions, which run rather high among youths, as evidenced by the elevated auto insurance rates for people between ages 16 and 25.

When data are gathered by adolescents' self-reports, the figures on juvenile law-breaking are far higher than when they are reported as the number of arrests. Self-report studies have shown that nearly 90% of teenagers have engaged in some form of delinquency, most of it undetected and chiefly of a less serious nature. Among 3,000 Illinois youths ages 14 to 18, who were interviewed several years ago, half said that they had smoked marijuana and two-thirds said that they drank alcohol frequently. One-third also reported committing one or more serious offenses, such as robbery or shoplifting (Finckenauer, 1984).

Arrest records place the prevalence of law-breaking far lower than do self-reports, since such records include only those people who were caught and formally charged. Arrest records also feature the worst offenders and the worst offenses, but the figures do attest to the fact that a substantial proportion of serious crime is committed by adolescents. In the early 1980s, 30% of those arrested in the United States for index offenses were under age 18, a percentage similar to that reported for Britain (Farrington, 1987, p. 35).

Although law-breaking is clearly a serious problem during the period of adolescence, the impression among the general public that it has been on the increase over the past two decades is in error. According to Finckenauer (1984), between 1973 and 1982, the number of people under age 18 arrested for all crimes decreased about 14%, while violent index crimes increased 9%, and property index crimes declined 4%. Over the period 1973-1980, the total number of personal crimes (rape, robbery, assault, personal larceny) attributed to juveniles decreased 27%. The main factor in this reduction of youth crime appeared to be the declining birth rate, so that there were fewer juveniles to be involved in crime. Finckenauer (1984, p. 5) has concluded that:

> Youth crime in this country has neither increased dramatically nor become more serious in recent years—in fact, just the opposite is true. Irrational public concern about this problem, especially when the concern is further fanned into fear and even hysteria by the media and some public officials, is unwarranted. Prudent concern and attention are what is needed. Hysteria is not a good basis for developing a sound juvenile corrections policy.

Juvenile crime is dominantly a male activity, with boys comprising 80% of those arrested and girls 20%. The incidence of arrests rises to a peak at age 17 for boys and at age 16 for girls, and it declines thereafter. While adolescent delinquency cuts across social class lines, it is most serious and pervasive among lower-class youth.

By the early 1980s, around 75% of juvenile arrests were of white youths and around 25% of Blacks at a time when Blacks made up 15% of the national juvenile population. Thus, there was a higher rate of arrests among Blacks. The Blacks were located chiefly in crowded urban centers and had lower socioeconomic status, less education, more one-parent families, and more unemployment than the whites (Finckenauer, 1984, p. 10).

In summary, delinquency during the adolescent years—in terms of index crimes, status offenses, and infractions of motoring laws—is widespread, and it is the source of many cases brought to counselors. Adolescent law breakers sometimes come voluntarily for aid, but more frequently they arrive unwillingly, sent for counseling assistance by the courts, their parents, or a social-welfare agency.

The one type of criminal offense analyzed in some detail in the following paragraphs is the use of illicit drugs. The topics treated are (1) the nature of illegal drugs, (2) the prevalence of drug use among adolescents, (3) correlates of illicit drug use, and (4) counseling methods that can be effectively used with drug-abuse clients.

THE NATURE OF ILLICIT DRUGS

The term *drug*, as intended here, refers to any chemical substance, other than food, introduced into a person's body that alters the individual's state of consciousness, sense of reality, or feeling of well-being. An *illicit drug* is one that, according to the law, is not to be used unless prescribed by a physician. Therefore, in the U.S., not only are such substances as marijuana and cocaine illicit drugs, but, for children and adolescents, alcoholic beverages are also illegal.

Drug abuse means using a chemical substance to the detriment of the individual's welfare. Abuse can involve either illegal substances (hashish, cocaine, heroin) or legal ones (aerosol products, lighter fluid, coffee).

For purposes of identification, drugs used by adolescents in an abusive manner can be placed in seven categories: alcohol, cannabis, depressants, hallucinogens, inhalants, narcotics, and stimulants (K. E. Thomas, 1985a, pp. 1463-1470).

Such alcoholic products as beer, whiskey, and wine (known by such street names as booze, hootch, sauce, and juice) are taken to produce a sense of euphoria or sedation. Their use can lead to a high degree of physical and psychological dependence. Immediate effects of drinking can include distortions of perception, judgment, coordination, and speech, and a loss of inhibition.

The word *cannabis* designates a class of substances known by the terms marijuana (pot, weed, grass, joint), hashish (hash, goma de mota), and tetrahydrocannibinol (THC). The immediate effects of these substances can be loss of inhibition and short-term memory, disoriented thought and action, and passivity or panic. The use of cannibis can result in moderate to high psychological dependence.

Depressants include barbiturates (downers, barbs, rainbows), benzodiazepines, methaqualone (quads, sopes, ludes), and other materials taken to produce drowsiness, sedation, and relief from physical or psychological pain. The use of depressants is sometimes experienced as an hypnotic state and a sense of euphoria or, on the contrary, as depression. Such drugs can result in slurred speech, distorted judgment, and the loss of inhibition, sensation, and coordination. Dependence varies from low to high.

Hallucinogens are such substances as lysergic acid diethylamide (LSD, acid, big D, trip), phencyclidine (PCP, angel dust, fuel, supergrass, killerweed), mescaline or peyote, and others. Hallucinogens effect an altered euphoric mental state. The extent of psychological dependence that they produce is undetermined.

Abused inhalants are usually legal substances not intended for human consumption, such as the fumes of aerosol products, gasoline, lead-based paint, cigarette-lighter fluid, nail-polish remover, and model-airplane glue. A person who inhales a quantity of the fumes of such products can experience a distorted conception of reality, disordered speech, anger, and violence. The use of inhalants can result in moderate to high physical and psychological dependence.

The class of drugs known as narcotics is comprised of such substances as heroin, opium, methadone, codeine, morphine, and others. Narcotics are used to produce relief from pain and to produce a condition of euphoria. Narcotics not only relieve pain, but they also may give rise to nausea, itching, loss of appetite, and poor vision. When taken by hypodermic injection, they can create infected sores and needle scars. Narcotics result in high levels of both physical and psychological dependence.

Stimulants include amphetamines (bennies, mollies, dexies, speed, uppers), cocaine (blow, coke, dust, rock, snow), caffeine (in coffee and cola drinks), nicotine (in tobacco), and others. Stimulants produce a heightened mood and reduced fatigue or sleepiness. Some stimulants can also aid in weight control. They lead to a high state of psychological dependence and sometimes to physical dependence as well.

DRUG USE DURING ADOLESCENCE

The teenage years are the most common time in the life span for people to first experiment with the foregoing substances, although, in recent decades, a growing number of children under age 10 have also tried them.

Prior to the 1960s, the use of such drugs as marijuana and heroin among youth was found in only a few large cities, principally New York, and mainly among lower-class Blacks and Hispanics. However, the mid-1960s inaugurated a new level of drug use fostered by leaders of what was called *the counter culture*, a nationwide phenomenon that included white middle-class adolescents and drew its inspiration from symbolic centers of youth rebellion in the San Francisco Bay region, Boston, and the East Village section of New York City.

> For the first time in modern history, there were pro-drug advocates, who, despite the illegality of some of the drugs, were enthusiastic proponents of the experiences they induced.... Users claimed that drugs enhanced sensuality, slowed time, enabled new solutions to old problems; for many users, drugs were reported to improve looking at art and listening to music.... Those young people who were preoccupied with drugs found support in knowing that the rest of the nation, hip or straight, was fascinated with the drama of new explorations into what was once forbidden behavior. (Mandel & Feldman, 1986, pp. 26-28)

The rapid spread of drug use among youth in the second half of the 1960s is partially reflected in nationwide figures on drug arrests, which rose from 29 per 100,000 people in 1963 to 162 per 100,000 in 1969. Teenagers under age 18 made up 6% of arrests in 1963 but 25% by 1969 (Mandel & Feldman, 1986, p. 31). However, the era of the counter culture was brief, as the social turbulence associated with the Vietnam War subsided and the traditional majority culture applied strong official measures to control the actions of rebellious youth.

By the middle and late 1980s, most drug use among teenagers had declined from the levels of the 1970s. Periodic surveys of U.S. highschool students showed that adolescents' use of marijuana, the most popular illegal drug, rose to a peak in 1978, then decreased markedly thereafter. The number of students who reported smoking marijuana during the 30 days prior to being surveyed declined from 37% in 1978 to 25% in 1983. Arrests of teenagers under age 18 for any type of drug use dropped by 50% between 1973 and 1983. However, the pattern of decline varied by ethnic groups. The most obvious reduction was among Anglo youth, whereas drug arrests among urban Black and Hispanic teenagers remained essentially the same (Johnston et al., 1984).

In the 1983 survey of high-school seniors, the illegal substance most commonly tried by students was alcohol, with 93% of respondents reporting they had used alcohol at some time in their lives. The next most popular substance was marijuana (57%), followed by stimulants (27%), cocaine (16%), such hallucinogens as LSD and PCP (15%), inhalants (14%), sedatives or barbiturates (14%), tranquilizers (13%), and opiates other than heroin (10%) (Johnston, O'Malley, & Bachman, 1984).

> [However,] ... even with the decline in arrests of young people in recent years, the number of persons under 21 years of age arrested for drugs in the 1980s, so far, averages about 250,000 per year. This level of arrests testifies to the continuing role of law enforcement in the lives of young people who, despite the constant protests of many responsible adults, continue to make drug use a part of their adolescent socialization rituals. (Mandel & Feldman, 1986, p. 39)

Furthermore, alcohol-related deaths (accidents, suicides, homicides) for the age range 15-24 have been cited as one cause for the increase in the death rate of this group since 1960, despite declining death rates over the same period for other age groups (Ried, Martinson, & Weaver, 1987).

In effect, by the close of the 1980s, adolescent drug use continued to produce substantial numbers of clients for counseling.

CORRELATES OF ILLICIT DRUG USE

Factors associated with drug abuse in the lives of teenagers are complex and can vary from case to case. Furthermore, it is difficult to determine which factors have influenced the adolescent to turn to drugs and which factors are perhaps a result rather than a cause of drug use. Yet, while each case requires its own analysis, there is also normative information about conditions frequently associated with drug use that suggest questions which can be profitably pursued by therapists in their search for causal factors when counseling a particular teenager. It is to this information that we turn now.

One factor correlated with drug use is the nature of adolescence itself. As described in the first portion of this chapter, the teen years confront youths with a variety of perplexing problems. Adolescents' maturing intellect equips them to recognize conflicts and complexities of life that were sensed only dimly, if at all, in childhood. Adolescents' bodies change in puzzling ways, and their sexual yearnings intensify. They seek the acceptance of both their peers and their family at a time when the values espoused by peers may well conflict with those of the family. They are expected to think ahead to a life career, yet career opportunities and their own talents are still insufficiently explored or tested. Furthermore, their vocational interests and lifestyle preferences have not stabilized. Hence, in their search for a clear identity and a satisfying future, adolescents may suffer an insecurity that contributes to their experimenting with drugs as a relief from confusion.

The condition of the teenager's family also affects the propensity to use drugs. For example, the model of adult behavior displayed by parents, particularly the mother, can either encourage or discourage a drug habit. Miller and Cisin (1983) found that teenage children of mothers who are either cigarette smokers or moderate drinkers are more likely to use a variety of drugs than are teenagers whose mothers do not smoke or drink. In a summary of studies of adolescents' families, Daroff, Marks, and Friedman (1986, pp. 196-198) concluded that teenage drug use is higher when (1) youths feel that they receive less love from parents, especially from the father, (2) there is a significant gap between what parents want their children to be and what the parents perceive them actually to be, (3) parents frequently criticize their children, (4) there is a low level of parental support of their children, and the children have a low level of self-esteem, (5) limits set by parents are inconsistent, (6) there is less shared authority and communication within the family, and (7) family members are prone to make incredible statements, such as unbelievable promises about how they will act in the future. Disruption of family stability through illness, death, separation and divorce, or loss of employment can also heighten adolescent drug use.

Peer influence is a further important element in youths' experimenting with illicit substances and continuing their use. Investigations have shown that students' drug use increases in rough proportion to the number of their friends who use drugs. In a nationwide Gallup poll of 13- to 18-year olds, 29% of the respondents stated that peer pressure to conform to group norms was the reason why so many young people tried alcohol and drugs (Ried, Martinson, & Weaver, 1987, p. 151).

From a study of the relationship between psychopathology and substance use among 232 high-school students in the Northeastern United States, investigators concluded that "it appears likely that there is an additive or cumulative-interaction effect in which having psychiatric symptoms (psychopathology) contributes to the tendency to use drugs, and using drugs adds to the tendency to have psychiatric symptoms. Among the nine types of psychic symptoms measured, obsessive-compulsive symptoms, hostility, paranoid ideation, and depression were found to be somewhat more predictive of later increase in substance use than . . . other types of psychic symptoms; phobic anxiety was not predictive at all" (Friedman, Utada, Glickman, & Morrissey, 1987, p. 233).

Finally, any factors that contribute to an adolescent's developing low self-esteem (unattractive appearance, inability to establish desired friendships, school failure, degrading sexual experiences) increase the likelihood that the youth will turn to drugs.

Also important for understanding the nature of teenagers' substance abuse is the identification of patterns by which youths generally are introduced to drugs and then progress from one type to another. Drugs that typically are the first kinds tried are referred to as *gateway substances*. The two most common are cigarettes and alcohol. A variety of studies have verified that by the beginning of the teen years, there are "surprisingly high levels of experimentation, regular use, and heavy use of the gateway substances. Even if these data are partially distorted by regional differences . . . a substantial portion indicates experimentation or use of alcohol and tobacco in sixth grade" (Grady, Gersick, Snow, & Kessen, 1986, p. 216).

Although the use of illicit substances has been found to be acquired in stages, the exact nature of the progression within various types of social groups and individuals has not been firmly established. However, one pattern that can obtain is illustrated in Newcomb and Bentler's (1986) eight-year longitudinal study of the sequence of drug use among 654 youths from early adolescence to young adulthood. The investigators found that cigarettes played an important role as a gateway to cannabis and hard drugs and that alcohol use significantly influenced later cannabis and hard-drug use.

> Cannabis use peaked during late adolescence; liquor, stimulants, and nonprescription medication increased steadily over the eight-year period; hypnotics and psychedelic use increased through late adolescence and remained stable through young adulthood; and early experimental use of cigarettes decreased to more committed use over the eight-year span. (Newcomb & Bentler, 1986, p. 101)

In conclusion, the above types of normative data about variables often associated with teenage substance use may help to guide therapists in their search for factors in the lives of youthful clients that should be addressed during counseling.

METHODS OF AIDING DRUG-ABUSE CLIENTS

The need for individualized counseling of drug users, rather than the prescription of the same treatment for all of them, is reflected in Mandel and Feldman's (1986) observation that: "However much an expert might know about the general consequences of a particular drug, it will be extremely difficult to advise or counsel a youth unless one knows the cultural background and life circumstances of that person. One cannot rely on uniform stereotype forms of treatment. In addition, treatment of Anglo youths having a problem with marijuana or PCP may not be applicable to black or Latino youths experiencing difficulties in their use of the same drugs" (p. 39).

The three most popular forms of therapy with adolescent drug-abuse clients are those of individual counseling with the teenager, group counseling with a collection of drug users, and family therapy.

Individual Counseling

The techniques applied in individual therapy can vary widely, depending upon the type and extent of drug use, on the therapist's estimate of the causes of a client's drug problem, on the therapist's skills and knowledge, on the client's attitude toward his or her drug use, and on the amount of time and money available. An impression of the diversity of treatments is suggested by the following examples.

A key factor determining a treatment mode is the therapist's estimate of how much a client's drug dependency is physiological and how much is psychological. If the dependency is judged to be heavily physiological, the treatment can include the administration of a drug. For example, patients diagnosed as physiologically dependent on opiates can be given methadone as a maintenance drug or as a transitional substance leading to detoxification.

Methadone is an orally effective, long-acting opiate drug that is used as a pharmacological substitute for short-acting illicit drugs such as heroin. During treatment, patients ingest a daily dose, usually under nursing supervision at a clinic dispensary, that maintains a stable level of opiate tolerance and dependence.... In addition to dispensing methadone, these treatment clinics provide counseling services in which cooperation with clinic requirements, elimination of illicit drug use, and participation in legitimate employment or other productive activities is emphasized.... Some clinics advocate time-limited maintenance and an eventual drug-free treatment goal, whereas other clinics advocate indefinite high-dose maintenance with social and personal stability as treatment goals.... The high relapse rate that is seen following treatment termination, even among otherwise well-adjusted patients ... suggests that long-term maintenance may be the better justified treatment goal for many opiate abusers. (Stitzer & McCaul, 1987, p. 340)

In contrast to the aim of methadone, the purpose of other drug treatment can be that of building into the client a distaste for opiates through the administration of such a *narcotic-antagonist* substance as naltrexone. The effect of the narcotic antagonist, as interpreted from an operant-conditioning perspective, is to block the euphoric effect of opiate injection and thus extinguish further desire for the opiate by eliminating the reinforcing pleasurable feelings that the narcotic had produced before treatment (Savage, Curran, & Doyle, 1978, pp. 313-320).

However, the most common approach to breaking physiological dependency is to have the client completely abstain from using the drug and simply bear the withdrawal symptoms until they disappear. Abstention alone is more frequently used to break a tobacco, alcohol, marijuana, or inhalant habit than to eliminate the use of opiates.

Diverse psychotherapeutic approaches have been applied in the effort to free clients from psychological dependence on harmful substances. Styles of therapy have included psychoanalysis, rational-emotive therapy, reality therapy, transactional analysis, person-centered counseling, teaching factual information about drugs and their effects, admonition in a Jewish or Christian pastoral-counseling setting, and behavioral therapy. Apparently, most counselors do not practice a pure form of any one of these interventions. Instead, they draw on elements of various approaches to produce an eclectic treatment that seems best suited to the conditions of the client currently at hand. There is no consensus regarding which approach may be superior to the others, since the success of any treatment depends on a complex of factors that obtain in each case. Such factors include the particular problem-conditions in the client's life, the type of illicit substance used by the client, the client's attitude toward treatment, the amount of treatment-support or -resistance the client's family and peers may provide, the counselor's skill in applying various therapeutic approaches, and the amount of time spent in treatment.

Group Counseling

Group counseling is the dominant treatment mode in drug-abuse cases, as well as in juvenile-delinquency corrections in general. Advocates of group counseling extol its value in helping participants: (1) obtain satisfaction from both giving aid to, and receiving it from, peers who are in their same condition, (2) learn about themselves through exchanging their perceptions with others, (3) vent feelings directly or vicariously through the testimonials of other group members, (4) gain security through the bond of mutual support established among group participants, (5) gain the acceptance of others in the group, and (6) improve their self-esteem (Perez, 1986, pp. 4-7). A further important advantage of group methods is their economical use of counselor time.

In Perez' (1986, pp. 7-20) review of forms of group therapy with alcoholics, he identified characteristics of five of the better-known approaches. While he judged the psychoanalytic concepts of unconscious motivation, repression, ego-defense mechanisms, resistance, and transference as being useful to therapists, he concluded that "The complex, intellectualized rationale of psychoanalysis, together with the lengthy time necessary for treatment, has alienated rather than attracted most alcoholics" (p. 7). Encounter-group therapy, as derived from the work of Carl Rogers, has been extensively used with alcoholics, valued particularly for its humanistic notions of empathy and unconditional regard among group members, of the encounter leader as a helper rather than healer, and of the importance of feedback and communication. Aspects of Gestalt therapy also have been incorporated into many group-treatment programs—such aspects as accepting and living each moment as it comes, facing reality, becoming responsible for one's own behavior, and being fully cognizant of one's feelings and statements. Eric Berne's transactional-analysis concepts have also influenced group therapy, particularly his proposal of three separate ego states in which people operate (child, parent, adult), *strokes* people give and take, rituals they perform, and *games* (adjustment attempts) people play. The fifth approach that Perez recognized is that of eclecticism, which incorporates selected elements of the other four, of behavioral techniques, and of common sense.

A widely publicized type of group treatment is the *therapeutic community*, which is a collection of former drug users who live together or periodically meet to engage in mutual confrontation and support as a means of coping with their drug habit. Alcoholics Anonymous is one form of this treatment mode (O'Brien, 1978, pp. 359-368).

Family Counseling

In a great many cases, it is desirable to include the adolescent's family in the counseling process, because both the causes and the potential remedies for the drug habit may reside, at least partially, in the relationships among family members. "Aside from other problems that may exist in the family, the impact on the parents' lives resulting from their adolescent child's drug abuse is often devastating. The youngster's drug-related problems (difficulties at school, involvement with the police, erratic and sometimes violent behavior) themselves create a family crisis" (Daroff, Marks, & Friedman, 1986, p. 198). As a result, revising family members' attitudes and behavior toward each other can become a key goal of therapy. Counseling sessions can be directed toward encouraging family members to try not to blame each other for problems, to adopt an objective and nondefensive viewpoint, and to search in their own attitudes and actions for ways in which they might be contributing to the adolescent's drug habit.

Frequently, the primary clients in teenage drug-abuse cases are parents who seek guidance in coping with their drug-using child. Therefore, the direct counseling is with the parents, who then serve as the instruments for treating an adolescent son or daughter who would refuse to see a counselor if urged to do so. The goal of counseling becomes one of directing the parents toward reacting to their child's drug habit in ways that are likely to yield positive results. For example, Silberman (1982) has proposed a set of behaviors representing what he conceives to be a constructive *assertive* stance that parents can display in communicating with their adolescent child, in contrast to unconstructive, *nonassertive* and *aggressive* stances. Table 6.1 depicts these three styles of response in terms of examples that can be used in analyzing the styles with parents.

Complete cures from drug use are sometimes attained. However, because drug-abuse cases so frequently involve both physiological and psychological dependency and are complicated by peer pres-

Table 6.1 Types of Parents

Nonassertive parents	Aggressive parents	Assertive parents
are evasive	blow up in anger	persist
beg	get into power struggles	listen to children's viewpoint
act flustered	endlessly argue	
try to "make things do"	accuse	reveal honest feelings
are confusing, unclear	discredit children's thinking	give brief reasons
let themselves be treated unfairly	trick, tease, put down	politely refuse to do something
worry about being popular	give harsh punishments	emphasize
are afraid of upsetting children	nag	carry out reasonable consequences
blame themselves	withhold information about what they expect	make clear, direct requests

Adapted from Silberman, 1982, p. 39.

sures and by clients' resistance and their complex personality problems, a high rate of complete therapeutic success cannot be expected. Oftentimes, the best that can be hoped for is not complete recovery but, rather, only a measure of improvement in clients' ability to cope with their responsibilities and to achieve some relief from social conflicts and feelings of inadequacy.

CONCLUSION

This chapter has pictured the second decade of the life span as a time of significant advances in physical and mental abilities. Yet, for many youths, it is an unsettling period, as it confronts them with marked physiological changes, shifting social pressures, diverse values from which to choose, expectations for school achievement, growing awareness of world problems, intergenerational conflicts, and the need to consider seriously an uncharted future. Counselors are frequently called upon to help such teenagers and their parents learn to cope with the difficulties encountered in their lives.

7

The Early-Adult Years: Ages 21 to 40

The two decades of early adulthood represent an initial rise to peak performance and then a decline in people's fitness, vigor, agility, and creativity. This is also the first major period of life in which society expects the young to display maturity by becoming economically self-sufficient and socially responsible. The impulsiveness, irresponsibility, and silliness of adolescence are no longer excused. Young adults engage in full-time employment, bear and raise children, purchase homes, vote in elections, hold political office, and fight the nation's wars. For many young people, this transition to a new level of maturity is not easily achieved, particularly in a modern-day society that is undergoing rapid change.

The trials suffered in trying to meet the demands of this portion of the life span bring substantial numbers of young adults to counselors' doors. Typical clients are those who:

—Need guidance in planning a career, finding satisfactory employment, and adjusting to job conditions.

—Are confused about their sexual and conjugal arrangements, including how to choose a partner (or a series of partners) and how to perform adequately in sexual relations.

—Have trouble managing their financial affairs to ensure that their income covers their expenses and that their economic future is reasonably secure.

—Experience child-rearing difficulties, including problems of raising children satisfactorily when the father and mother are separated.

—Feel inadequate in social relations, such as in making friends and feeling at ease in a group.

—Are in trouble with the law and either come voluntarily or are sent for counseling.

The first half of this chapter centers on general characteristics of early-adult development that can influence the counseling process. The second half reviews normative evidence about three classes of problems that are often brought to counselors by young adults— conjugal and sexual arrangements, career planning, and financial planning.

PATTERNS OF YOUNG-ADULT DEVELOPMENT

The following overview of significant characteristics of early adulthood focuses on physical and psychophysical growth, intellectual performance, social development, and personal identity.

Physical and Psychophysical Growth

The term *physical* is used throughout the following discussion in reference to gross bodily functions, such as strength and stamina. *Psychophysical* is used to mean observable behaviors that require combining perceptual skills—sight, hearing, touch—with physical movements, for example, the eye-hand or ear-foot coordination required in driving an automobile.

Whereas the nature of physical development during childhood and adolescence is determined primarily by biological-growth factors guided by a genetic timing system, physical status during early adulthood is more dependent upon the personal/social factors that make up an individual's style of life. Diet, exercise, communicable disease, the use or avoidance of drugs, family stress, type of occupation, residential environment (air pollution, noise level), and forms of recreation can all affect the young adult's physical well-being. For most physical attributes, the general tendency is toward a decrease in fitness after age 25 or 30. From their mid-twenties until the end of life, people typically experience a decline in muscle strength, reaction time, maximum work rate, stamina, oxygen intake, basal metabolic rate, blood flow to the brain, visual and auditory acuity, skin elasticity, and the filtration rate of the kidneys. Height decreases slightly as the connecting tissues between the bones are flattened by the pounding and grinding of physical activity. Weight can increase because abundant calories are no longer needed for the rapid physical growth of childhood and adolescence and the individual may fail to alter eating habits to suit an adult phase of reduced caloric need (Diagram Group, 1976).

However, it is important to recognize that the style of life which people adopt in the early-adult years can significantly influence the rate and degree of these trends. Attention to nutrition, regular exercise, sufficient rest, and periodic relaxation from stressful experiences all serve significantly to maintain fitness. The process of counseling adults who complain of physical disorders, lack of energy, and feelings of depression at their declining appearance and agility can profitably include an analysis of those aspects of their living habits and their environment which affect physical well-being. As experts in weight control attest, too many adults intend to "go on a diet" and "exercise to get back in shape" without accepting the fact that mere periodic dieting and exercising will fail to achieve the permanent state of fitness that they desire. As soon as they go off the diet and abandon an exercise regimen in order to resume what they regard as "normal living," their troubles return. The long-term solution to their problem is either that of effecting permanent changes in lifestyle or that of accepting their present condition without regret. In effect, the counseling process may be aimed either at helping clients to adopt lifestyle-change as a goal or at helping them to accept their current physical condition and future prospects as a satisfactory reality, so that they need make no attempt to alter their established pattern of living.

In conclusion, genetic endowment and the individual's growth experiences from the years of childhood and adolescence account for some of the differences among people in their physical condition in early adulthood. However, even more significant influences on fitness at this time of life are individuals' social and physical environments and the lifestyle factors over which they themselves can exert some control. These factors can become foci of attention in counseling with young adults.

Intellectual Performance

Evidence about the rise and decline of mental abilities over the adult years has been compiled from three main sources—biographical records of people's productivity in the sciences and arts, laboratory investigations of adult success on tests of aptitude and intelligence, and people's work performance.

Lehman's (1953, 1962) studies have furnished the most complete analyses of superior performances in the past. By consulting histories of the arts and sciences and biographies of famous persons, Lehman identified outstanding contributors in a wide variety of fields and then determined the ages at which these persons produced their most significant work. By this method, he learned that the publication of scientists' most notable contributions came in their early thirties for chemistry, mathematics, and physics. The peak age for publishing medical discoveries was around 37 or 38 in anatomy, bacteriology, pathology, physiology, and surgical technique. The same was true for psychology and American sculpture. Even younger (age 32 or 33) were the creators of well-known practical inventions and the composers of highly regarded German grand operas and German literature. Chess champions were also at their peak during their early thirties. Although these remarkable achievements were first exposed to public view when their creators were between ages 30 and 40, it seems apparent that the abilities which led to such productivity were already operating prior to age 30, during the gestation period that led to the publication of the creators' results. In effect, the decade of the twenties had to be a time of unusually rich intellectual activity for such people.

Studies of adults' performance on intelligence tests have been conducted by both cross-sectional and longitudinal methods. In cross-sectional investigations, the test scores for people in various age groups are collected all at the same time. In longitudinal research, the same individuals are tested at successive periods of their lives, such as at ages 20, 30, and 40. In both types of studies, the groups' total scores reflect the same general pattern—an increase in mental abilities until around age 22, a stable period until around age 30, and a steady decline thereafter. However, when the scores are broken down by subtests that compose the full test, a variegated picture of performance is revealed. The decline after age 30 occurs chiefly on measures of response speed, memory span, and nonverbal reasoning—skills that depend more on the current operating efficiency of the body's perceptual-neural system than on experience and education. In contrast, scores on measures of vocabulary knowledge, reading comprehension, and general information hold up well, and, in some cases, they increase over the decades of early adulthood and into middle age as people acquire broader experience and more education (Bee & Mitchell, 1984, pp. 473-480).

Investigations of work performance indicate that for jobs that have advanced education or training as an entrance requirement, people's scores on intelligence tests are not related to their job success. In these instances, the entrance requirement has already ensured that the job holders comprise a selected group of intellectually able candidates, so that differences in work performance within the group are determined more by diligence, motivation, and special abilities than by differences in the general intelligence of the group members. However, when there is no advanced educational requirement for entering an occupation, the specific characteristics of the job can affect how much people's tested intelligence will be related to their job efficiency.

> If the job has intellectual content (such as secretarial or bookkeeping work), the people with higher IQs tend to be more skillful and accurate. On the other hand, if the job lacks intellectual content (as it does for factory workers or package wrappers), then higher IQs are not associated with better performance. (Bee & Mitchell, 1984, p. 482)

The question of how much people's experience may affect their intellectual performance has been studied in some detail. Denney's (1982) research on problem-solving skills over the life span led her to propose that *optimally exercised* abilities maintain their strength far better than *unexercised* abilities. In effect, investigations of both physical and cognitive skills support the commonsense notion that if you work diligently at a type of skill, you not only reach a higher level of achievement but your performance also declines at a significantly slower rate than if you had not specifically exercised that skill. Consequently, consistent effort to improve selected mental abilities pays off in more years of efficient functioning in that realm.

Evidence also suggests that the strength of general mental ability can be sustained through active study and problem solving. In Guilford's (1967) theory of cognitive structure, he distinguished between *convergent* and *divergent modes* of thought. Convergent thinking involves bringing one's mental powers to bear on finding *the* correct answer to a problem, as is typically required in solving mathematics problems. Divergent thinking, in contrast, emphasizes the ability to devise unusual solutions by means of recognizing unorthodox connections between diverse concepts. Divergent thinking is thus seen as a key component of creativity. Horn's (1982) study of the relationship of creativity to intelligence showed that adults who scored high on divergent thinking skills also displayed continuing improvement on vocabulary scores and general knowledge. These results, along with studies of the relationship between people's educational level and their level of intellectual ability, suggest that active study and practice in divergent thinking can enhance and help to maintain general problem-solving skills over the life span.

Perlmutter (1986, p. 306) has noted that general knowledge about the world and *metacognitive memory contents* (knowledge of how to think and how to remember) increase over the years of early and middle adulthood, thereby compensating for declines in memory capacity. This seems true particularly for those realms of life which frequently require one's attention. In other words, in those life situations that are most familiar (such as one's occupation or avocation), new information is readily incorporated into what one already knows, so the new information is later more easily recalled than would be information bearing on less familiar areas.

In summary, although the average person's memory capacity appears to decline after around age 30, the decline can be counteracted by increased experience and study, the continuing exercise of cognitive skills, and the acquiring of new techniques of thinking.

Social Development

Changes in American social customs over the past century have furnished young adults a rapidly expanding array of choices among acceptable lifestyles. This growth of opportunities has necessarily been accompanied by people's increasing difficulties in deciding which of the options might lead to their success and happiness. Today, more than in the past, young adults are free to establish living arrangements with whomever they choose—as a married couple or simply as unwed companions, with the relationship platonic or sexual, heterosexual or homosexual. They can readily sever their relationship through separation or divorce. They find it acceptable either to bear children or not, to adopt children, to become stepparents, or to be separated from the former spouse with whom they share custody of their offspring. At the same time, the vocational structure of the society continues to evolve, with jobs in industry and agriculture still declining and positions in service and "information systems" on the increase. At a time when more varied types of education are required to prepare people for the diversity of jobs, continuing shifts in the society's occupational structure pose the likelihood that today's young adults will soon need to retrain for the new vocations that they will be obliged to enter in mid-life. Another significant development is the growing range of occupations open to women and the increasing number of women in the labor market. In effect, the early-adult years in modern-day America offer multiple alternatives accompanied by increasing demands for decision making. Consequently, the need for professional counseling has grown as well, to assist young adults in making such decisions and in adjusting to competing social values.

During young adulthood, social relations typically occur in four settings: (1) the family, (2) the occupational site, (3) recreational/avocational sites, and (4) locations related to daily living routines, such as traveling from place to place and shopping. In each of these settings, people fill particular roles, with *role* meaning a position which the individual assumes in a social system. Each position is marked by expectations about how the individual will act and about what privileges and responsibilities accompany the role. Everyone plays multiple roles which, in the early-adulthood stage of life, can be designated by such terms as *parent, sister, daughter, lover, employee, friend, voter, dog owner, tennis player, college student, auto driver, grocery shopper,* and more.

Associated with each role is a set of developmental tasks. A *developmental task* is a problem to be solved in learning to successfully perform a role. To illustrate, typical tasks accompanying the role of *new parent* include those of providing for the physical, emotional, cognitive, and social needs of a newborn. Tasks associated with the role of *employee* include getting to work on time, doing the job honestly and thoroughly, cooperating with fellow workers, and continuing to improve one's vocational skills. For certain roles in a society, the accompanying tasks are widely agreed upon and rather clearly defined, sometimes even delineated in written form (marriage contract, job description, labor-union contract, rules for student conduct) or at least by generally accepted custom. Other tasks are not so well defined, often because the social system is in transition from a traditional form toward some ill-defined future pattern or because several cultural styles and standards exist side-by-side. For example, in present-day North America, women's roles in family life and in the labor market are in transition, producing conflicting notions of the tasks that compose such positions as wife, homemaker, mother, and employee. The confusion faced by young adults in identifying and performing the tasks associated with their new roles can cause them to seek counseling aid.

A further useful concept for understanding social development is that of *attachment*, a term referring to the affectional bond between people which provides them emotional support, nurturing, encouragement, reassurance, assistance, and recognition of their worth. One's level of attachment can be located on a scale extending from complete emotional support at one end (strong attachment) to no support at the other (complete detachment). During the early-adult years, an individual's position on such an attachment-detachment scale usually undergoes significant change in different social interactions. For instance, the parent-child attachment that may have been surrounded by turmoil and ambivalence during adolescence will typically settle into a new form of parent-child attachment as young adults move out of the parental home to establish intimate attachments with peers and with the offspring that they themselves produce. While the strength of parent-child attachment typically diminishes as children enter adult life, the connections are often reaffirmed at times of personal crisis, when people turn again to family members for solace and support.

The foregoing concepts of roles, developmental tasks, and attachment/detachment furnish a framework for the following discussion of social adjustment in young adulthood. In the following discussion, attention is directed particularly toward the family and the workplace as social settings. The significance of these two has been emphasized by Lidz (1980, p. 23).

> During the early phase of young adult life, usually between the ages of 18 and 20, most [youths] consider that the time has come to make commitments which will greatly determine the course of the remainder of their lives. Some young people will feel, perhaps in an exaggerated way, that everything that has happened to them has largely been preparation, but now the time has come to start life in earnest. Sooner or later, though, the two critical commitments of choosing an occupation and a mate will start them on their way. Both choices will influence greatly the further development of their personalities and their chances for a happy future.

SOCIAL RELATIONSHIPS IN THE FAMILY

As noted in Chapter 5, the meaning of the concept *family* has become diversified and somewhat confused in recent decades by the marked changes in adults' living arrangements and their conjugal relations. The traditional nuclear family—wedded parents living with their own biological children—remains as only one of several major

Table 7.1 Duvall's Eight-Stage Traditional-Family Life Cycle

Stage	Typical Age Range*	Identifying Characteristics of Stages
1	20–23	Newly married couple without children
2	23–27	Parents with one or more children, infancy to 30 months old
3	27–30	Parents with preschool-age children
4	30–36	Parents of school-age children, last baby born
5	36–46	Parents of teenagers
6	46–52	Parents launch children as young adults
7	52–65	Parents alone again, with empty nest until retirement
8	66+	Old age, retirement for both spouses until their deaths

*The age for women is about two years younger than for men.
SOURCE: Adapted from Duvall 1977, pp. 140-148

forms of family, and, soon it may no longer be the dominant form. Therefore, it has become increasingly difficult to generalize about developmental patterns in family relations. Nevertheless, there are some identifiable trends for at least the traditional family. It is to these trends that we now turn.

The idea that the nuclear family usually displays life-cycle stages of its own has been proposed by a number of sociologists. Duvall (1977, pp. 144-157) has divided the family-life cycle into eight such periods, with the first five usually coming during the decades of early adulthood, ages 20 to 40. The periods and the typical times when those periods occur in the lives of parents are summarized in Table 7.1.

The concept of family-life-cycle stages is useful for directing counselors' attention to the sequence of changing roles typically met in the traditional nuclear family. Difficulties that young adults encounter in assuming these roles and in learning to perform their constituent tasks are what so often bring them for counseling. For example, as they enter marriage, newlyweds must adjust to each other's sexual desires, ways of handling money, beliefs about the division of labor in performing housekeeping chores, tastes in choosing close friends and companions, philosophical and religious persuasions, political preferences, recreational choices, and the need for private time alone. When their first child is born, a new set of developmental tasks is thrust on them, disturbing their established relationship by inserting another planet into the family constellation. The appearance of the newborn confronts the married couple with unfamiliar demands and restrictions. Not only must the parents learn to cope with the needs of a helpless being whose proper care they may only vaguely comprehend but the pattern of emotional attachment between the parents is altered as well by the child's arrival. The father may feel that the child has displaced him in his wife's affection, as the wife concentrates attention on the baby. In addition, the wife may be distressed by the demands of infant care, which limit her freedom to pursue a career or to continue "having fun."

When an additional child or two arrive over the next few years, the family social system is again disturbed by further requirements for readjustment. Adding one person to the family cycle does not mean that only a single new interpersonal adjustment is required. Rather, the total number of social interactions will increase in multiples computed by the following formula, in which x represents the number of interpersonal relationships and y the number of persons in the family:

$$x = \frac{y^2 - y}{2}$$

Thus, when the family consists of only a husband and a wife, the number of interpersonal connections is 1. With the addition of a single child, the quantity of interpersonal relations advances to 3. With a second child, the total becomes 6, and with a third child or perhaps a grandparent coming to live in the home, it is 10. Each of these additions evokes some shifting in the established emotional attachments within the family, a shifting that can result in jealousy, resentment, and feelings of rejection on the part of some family members. The feelings of ambivalence that the first child may feel toward a new sibling who appears to be capturing the parents' affection has been well documented in cases of children's displaying aggression toward the newcomer, rejecting the mother, and regressing to infantlike behavior. Counselors may be called on to help family members realign these unconstructive patterns of attachment.

Even when the family establishes its permanent number of members, new roles are cast on parents by the growth stages of their children. Clearly, the tasks involved in raising an infant differ from those required for properly rearing school-age children and adolescents. Diapering a baby or diagnosing its cries as signifying an earache is obviously a far different matter than deciding whether to let a 16-year old drive a load of friends to a party in the family car. All of the child-development stages, which tend to occur while parents are in the 20-to-40 age range and slightly beyond, periodically demand new skills and understandings if family life is to be conducted satisfactorily. Consequently, counseling during young adulthood is frequently directed toward helping parents cope with the tasks imposed on them by their offsprings' development.

Compared with the traditional family, nonconventional family forms hold even greater potential for creating problems of roles, tasks, and attachment. As one example, consider the increasing numbers of *blended families*, which bring together a husband and wife in their second marriage, accompanied by children from their first marriages. The kinds of difficulties that can be produced by blended families are reflected in such incidents as a child's saying "You're not my real father, so I don't have to obey you" or the husband's telling the wife "You keep favoring your Stephanie over my Allen, and that's going to cause trouble" or the wife's asking the husband "Why do you keep talking to your ex-wife on the phone and trying to solve her problems?"

In summary, the years between ages 20 and 40 require young adults to manage a sequence of social adjustments to the changes in family life that occur during these years. Later in this chapter, counseling issues related to certain of these adjustments are inspected in some detail.

SOCIAL RELATIONSHIPS IN THE WORKPLACE

Research on career patterns and vocational success supports the observation that more people fail in their occupations because of problems in social relationships than because of a lack of technical skill and efficiency.

Personal Identity

For most people, a stable identification of self appears to be reached during early adulthood, usually in the twenties. By this time, many young people have achieved a rather clear sense of the values that they hold, the extent of their abilities, the kind of future that they wish to pursue, and the types of relationships that they wish to—and are able to—sustain with others. In brief, these young people have established a style of life. Whitbourne's (1986) study of adults' sense of identity led her to conclude that the self-appraisals achieved by young adults in their family and occupational roles "permeate all other areas of identities. Together, the areas of family and work unite into an integrated sense of identity as an individual with a purpose in life; a purpose that is expressed in the everyday activities carried out in the home and in the workplace" (pp. 3-4).

PERSONAL IDENTITY AND THE FAMILY

In Chapter 5, an individual's personal identity was considered to result from the kinds of people, objects, and ideas with which the individual establishes identifications. For most people, the family is the most important source of such identifications. There appear to be several reasons for this. The newborn's introduction to the world occurs within the family, so that the infant makes its first emotional attachments with members of the family, on whom it must depend for physical and emotional sustenance. The family provides the chief models (people, objects, and ideas) with which the growing child can establish identifications. Moreover, family members not only control access to the models, but they also furnish the rewards and punishments that influence the child's decision about which models are good and should be embraced and which are bad and should be rejected. Thus, such early experiences serve as the foundation from which the individual's personal identity evolves. All subsequent influences (peers, school, church, mass-communication media) can alter and extend the identity of childhood and adolescence, but they do not erase it.

Traditionally, as maturing youths have entered their twenties and thirties, their identity has been expanded by their assuming the family roles of spouse and parent. However, with a greater diversity of conjugal and habitation arrangements spreading through American society in recent decades, the task of establishing a clear family-related identity in the early-adult years has become more complex. A growing proportion of young adults face the task of adjusting their conception of self to accommodate not only the roles of spouse and parent but also those of separated spouse, divorcee, live-in companion, weekend parent, and stepparent. Difficulties that young people experience in incorporating these roles into their established identity can bring them to the counselor's office.

PERSONAL IDENTITY AND WORK

The question of how an individual's personal identity influences occupational choice has been the focus of attention in at least two popular theories of vocational development. Super (1957, 1969) proposed that a key factor determining an individual's selection of a vocation is how closely the person believes that his or her self-concept relates to the characteristics of various occupations. In other words, Super has assumed that people view the vocational setting as one in which to express their personal identity. A young man who pictures himself as clever in working with machines will thus seek work of a mechanical nature. A young woman who conceives herself to be artistic will be drawn to an occupation that provides opportunities for creative expression.

In addition to founding his view of vocational choice on the self-concept, Super envisioned the typical individual's vocational career as being comprised of four stages. The first, occurring between ages 18 and 25, involves trying out various jobs which seem suited to the vocational self-concept that the young adult has evolved over the years of childhood and adolescence. During this tryout stage, the individual faces the realities of the world of work—the demands for punctuality, the intensity of the work schedule, the need to adapt to coworkers and superiors, and the satisfactions offered by different occupations. This initial stage may involve frequent job changes. From each of these experiences, the young adult discovers which occupational conditions seem best suited to his or her self-concept. In the process, the person's vocational identity may change somewhat when tested in real-life vocational settings.

The second stage in Super's scheme finds workers becoming established in an occupation appropriate to their self-concept. This process contributes to greater occupational stability after age 30 or 35 as the person achieves a realistic vocational identity, an intimate knowledge of how to do the job, and advancement up the occupational and salary ladder. The established vocational identity has now become an important element in the adult's overall self-concept.

The third and fourth stages occur during middle and late adulthood. The third, referred to as the maintenance stage, comes around age 45 to 55 and is marked by the individual's no longer striving to achieve significant career advancement but, rather, seeking to continue in the job until retirement. For most workers, their high level of productivity may have been reached in their forties. Thereafter, their job effectiveness may remain the same or decline. The final stage, that of retirement, is usually reached at age 60, 65, or 70. As noted in Chapter 9, this can be a traumatic event for many people as it can erode an overall self-concept that has been so strongly grounded in a work role over four or five decades.

In summary, Super's theory assigns the self-concept a central place in vocational choice, occupational stability, and satisfaction, since people's conceptions of "who I am" and "what I want to be" are intimately linked to their occupations.

When Super's approach serves as the basis for vocational counseling, the young adult's occupational self-concept is usually assessed by means of the person's statements about preferred work and leisure activities, perhaps as measured on such standardized instruments as the Strong-Campbell or the Kuder vocational-interest inventories. A further concern of the counselor is the degree of maturity of the client's vocational perceptions. Some young people are quite realistic in assessing their motivations, talents, and interests and in judging what sorts of working conditions will enable them to express these preferences in a satisfying way. In contrast, others are confused or unrealistic. Thus, in Super's system, an additional task of the vocational counselor is that of assessing the client's vocational maturity by having the individual offer a self-appraisal of his or her competence as a worker and by evidence of the individual's level of involvement and expressed satisfaction in different types of work.

A second model of vocational development that assigns a central role to personal identity is the trait-factor theory espoused by Holland (1973). Two ways that Holland's proposal differs from that of Super are (1) in the way in which Holland matches types of personal identity to types of occupations and (2) his rejection of Super's vocational-stage concept. In Holland's theory, six personal-identity types are depicted as points on a hexagon (Figure 7.1). Each type is expected to be best suited to certain kinds of occupations. For example, the type of person labeled *realistic* is inclined to be mechanical, physical, concrete rather than abstract, practical, asocial, and materialistic—characteristics assumed to be appropriate for such occupations as those of machinist, auto-repairman, and engineer. The opposite type of personality, directly across the hexagon, is labeled *social*. It is found in people who are sociable, cooperative, helpful, sensitive, and understanding. Occupations well suited to such traits include those of recreation-club director, teacher, social worker, and counselor. In like manner, the other personal-identity types in Figure 7.1 form opposite pairs across the hexagon—conventional versus artistic, enterprising versus investigative. According to Holland's system,

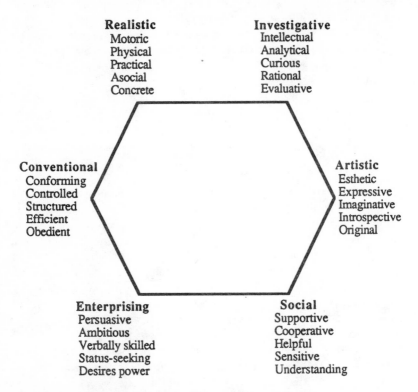

Figure 7.1. Holland's Trait-Factor Theory of Career Choice
SOURCE: Adapted from Holland, 1973; Osipow, 1983, pp. 83-84; Whitbourne & Weinstock, 1986, p. 384.

people whose traits represent a rather pure case of one of the six personality types are usually better able to find an appropriate occupation than are people whose personalities represent a mixture of traits from more than one type. Individuals whose personal identities are comprised of characteristics from neighboring types, such as artistic and investigative, are better equipped to find a compatible vocation than are ones whose characteristics are a combination of directly opposite types or of three or more types. In Holland's opinion, people seek occupations that are congruent with their personalities. When congruence is achieved, individuals experience a high level of satisfaction and success because they are applying their preferred skills and expressing their identity. On the other hand, when their personal identity and their work environment are incompatible, they are unhappy and try to change occupations.

Whereas Super has envisioned four stages of vocational development through which people progress during their adult years, Holland has contended that such a stage concept is of little or no value in vocational counseling. Instead, he believes that the idea of personality-environment congruence is valid at all age levels, not dependent on age, except for the influence that may be exerted on occupational efficiency by decreased abilities that can accompany the passing years.

Empirical tests of Holland's model have provided a measure of support for his theory. However, predictions based on his model have been far from perfect, perhaps because the theory fails to account for variables other than personality types in the effort to explain people's selection of jobs. An additional factor influencing vocational choice is the amount of compensation that the job offers. People may continue in an unpleasant and difficult occupation if the pay is high enough. Employment opportunities constitute another factor. The geographical location of jobs, how much training and experience they require, and the current job market all influence the kinds of employment that are available to the young adult. As a result, people frequently are not free to select a job that best matches their vocational identity.

Thus, while both Super's and Holland's schemes are far from perfect in predicting career choice and stability, research evidence suggests that people's self-concept or vocational identity is still a significant factor in career selection and satisfaction. Hence, the factor of personal identity remains an important consideration in vocational counseling.

INTERACTIONS OF FAMILY-RELATED AND WORK-RELATED IDENTITIES

As mentioned at the beginning of this discussion of identity, Whitbourne's studies of self-concept in adults led her to conclude that the central focus of personal identity in most people's lives derives from their self-perceptions as a family member and as a worker. The potential conflict between these two roles can precipitate problems in the home or on the job that bring clients for counseling. In Whitbourne's analysis of such problems, how the family-related and work-related identities interact depends on the significance that each is given within the person's overall identity.

If an individual regards herself as a worker who wants to achieve career success at all costs, involvements in the family domain will be regarded as prohibiting. Similarly, if an individual regards himself as a "family man," it will be difficult for him to find satisfaction in a time-consuming job. He will regard as an intrusion on his personal life any attempts by his employer to be forced to put in more effort on the job. However, if the person regards both areas of life as important to his or her overall identity, then compensations will be sought across areas to resolve potential conflicts. These compensations may be no more complicated than using one's imagination to think about one area of activity while engaging in the other. The individual's imagination may also be applied with more practical results, by designing creative solutions to potential work-family incompatibilities. (Whitbourne, 1986, p. 211)

These observations suggest that the counseling process in cases of home/work-identity conflicts can center on (1) helping clients to honestly identify how heavily their sense of self depends on family as compared to work, (2) deciding whether a change in the emphasis of such dependence would be acceptable to clients themselves and to others who are important in clients' lives, and (3) generating potential methods that clients might adopt toward resolving the conflict between family and work commitments.

CRITICAL EVENTS AND CLIENTS' PROBLEMS IN EARLY ADULTHOOD

The three illustrative types of counseling cases considered in this section concern (1) conjugal relationships, particularly marriage and divorce, (2) career planning, and (3) financial planning.

Conjugal Relationships—Marriage and Divorce

Although choosing a marriage partner is not an essential task of early adulthood, it is still a typical task, as approximately 97% of Americans do at some time wed (Lidz, 1980, p. 24). However, as mentioned earlier, decisions required in performing this task have multiplied as family structures and conjugal relationships have undergone dramatic change since World War II, progressing from a time of relatively rare divorce to one in which half of marriages will end in divorce and the majority of divorced people will wed a second time, usually within a period of three to five years.

Indeed, in a matter of a few decades, marriage norms have shifted from a standard which once required a couple to remain married even when they retained little or no emotional attachment to one another to one which virtually requires them to relinquish their relationship if they are not deeply emotionally involved. (Furstenburg, 1982, p. 111)

The dissolution of marriages has thus become common during a time when people still generally view divorce and serial marriage as deviations from acceptable conjugal tradition. As a consequence, a large proportion of people who seek counseling in their early adult years are ones who are troubled over their modes of sexual expression and living arrangements—unsatisfactory marriage, divorce, cohabitation without marriage, homosexuality, and the like. These troubles are compounded by the rapidity of social change which finds cohorts of older adults often abiding by values different from those that guide the conjugal relationships of the younger generation. Furthermore, laws governing marriage and sex behavior that were founded on social values of the past remain in effect, while a widening range of options for sexual and habitation relations is practiced throughout the society.

Sociologists have posited a variety of reasons for these changes in conjugal stability. The traditional family pattern that had evolved by the mid-twentieth century was one in which marriage marked the confluence of a series of interconnected events that typically occurred during the early-adult years. These events included "departure from the family of origin, the initiation of sexual activity, entrance into the labor force for men and withdrawal from the labor force for women, the inception of parenthood, and the establishment of independent residence" (Furstenburg, 1982, p. 111). However, following World War II, a range of changes began eroding this singular form of "normal" adult life, so that there was no longer such a convenient coordination of key events. Changes included (1) most individuals' engaging in sexual relations well before they married, (2) more women in the labor force, (3) greater population mobility, so that people moved readily into new social settings where they witnessed alternative lifestyles, (4) more government welfare provisions, so that marital dependency became less necessary for women, (5) the reduction of legal and social barriers to the release of people from unrewarding marriages, and (6) increasing emphasis in American culture on personal fulfillment, so that young people tended to build up expectations of enduring happiness when wed.

The conditions of marriage and family in American society are not identical for all ethnic groups. For example, Glick (1985) has summarized the status of Black families in the following manner, with the added observation that these characteristics may be more indicative of Black families' below-average socioeconomic status than of their ethnic nature:

> Compared with the American average, Black families are more likely to have children present, to be one-parent households, to postpone marriage . . . to separate or divorce, to have fewer intact marriages, and to be less likely to remarry after divorce. In addition, married Black women are more likely to be in the work force than married White women. As with other groups, birthrates vary by education: Poorly educated Black women have higher than average birth rates, and the more highly educated have lower than average birthrates. The rate of intermarriage is increasing and, compared with either all-Black or all-White marriages, such marriages are more likely to end in divorce. (p. 120)

As a result of present-day trends in living arrangements, counselors have been increasingly called upon to help young adults select a marriage partner, adjust to a conjugal agreement (either an official marriage or an informal, live-together arrangement), repair a damaged relationship, cope with child-rearing responsibilities, decide when to dissolve a relationship, obtain a satisfactory separation or divorce, adjust to a condition of divorce, contemplate a second marriage, and more. The following discussion focuses on three of these problems, briefly describing their nature and identifying some ways in which counselors attempt to help young adults manage their conjugal relationships.

TYPICAL PROBLEMS OF MARRIAGE AND DIVORCE

The illustrative issues reviewed below are those of selecting a partner, sustaining a marriage, and adjusting to divorce.

Selecting a Partner

In recent decades, as increasing numbers of young people have cohabited without legally being wed, one of the arguments offered in support of this arrangement as a precursor to official marriage is that it enables the couple to understand what married life really will be like. In effect, cohabitation is viewed as a training period for marriage and thus for mate selection (Trost, 1975; Ridley, Peterman, & Avery, 1978). By this line of logic, if the pair then do decide to wed, their marriage will be of high quality and will last.

However, a growing number of studies indicates that cohabitation either has a negative effect on marital adjustment and communication or, at best, has no influence on the quality of marriage (DeMaris & Leslie, 1984). After Booth and Johnson (1988) analyzed telephone interviews with a national sample of 2,033 respondents, they rejected the idea that cohabitation improves mate selection and marital training. Instead, they found that a couple's living together prior to marriage was associated with a low level of interaction and communication in the marriage and to high levels of disagreement and proneness to divorce. The exact reasons for these relationships were not apparent, but the data did indicate that many of those who engaged in such a premarital arrangement pursued unconventional lifestyles that included drug use, inability to handle money, trouble with the law, unemployment, and personality problems. Hence, cohabitation itself may not be an important cause of marital disorder, but a significant number of people who opt for premarital cohabitation may be ones who would be poor marriage risks under any circumstances.

Two implications that the foregoing observations hold for counselors are that clients who are viewing cohabitation as a constructive arrangement for choosing a marriage partner should (1) be informed that, in general, premarital cohabitation is not a good predictor of successful marriage and (2) be encouraged to analyze their own living habits, ambitions, and personality and to compare these with the living habits, ambitions, and personality of their potential spouse in order to estimate how likely it is that they will be satisfied to spend an enduring marital relationship with a person of that kind.

One item of conventional advice to couples is that they postpone getting married until their period of close friendship, or formal engagement, is long enough for them to identify clearly the expectations and habits that their potential mate would bring to the marriage. Another traditional piece of advice is that they not wed until they are old enough to recognize the responsibilities and restrictions on lifestyle that a lasting marriage involves. Recent data on marriage and divorce suggest that both of these principles are still generally sound. For example, it continues to be true that the highest incidence of divorce occurs among those who marry young, since the rate of divorce for teenager marriages is over twice that for people who first marry in their late twenties (Duvall, 1977, p. 437). As a consequence, when couples seek premarital counseling, the issue of what expectations the potential marriage partners hold can be included as an important topic of discussion.

Even when young adults recognize that their intended partner has convictions or habits that they dislike, they still wed in the hope that "things will work out" or that "I'll be able to change him (or her) once we're married." Such hope may arise either in the romantic flush of young love or, at a later age, in the fear that "this may be my last chance to get married." However, the likelihood that significant improvements in one's spouse can be effected amicably, if at all, is often quite remote, so the decision to accept the intended spouse "as is" becomes a far sounder basis for a lasting marriage. This matter is a useful one for young people to face during premarital counseling.

Sustaining a Marriage

It is clear from present-day divorce statistics that the traditional marriage-ceremony pledge—*for better, for worse, till death do us part*—is, for many couples, no longer a binding commitment. Even when they intend the pledge at the time of the ceremony, they can later change their minds as troubles arise in the relationship. Consequently, young adults who face marital problems often seek the help of friends or professional counselors in an effort to remedy the apparent cause of their discontent—either to save the marriage or to separate.

A variety of factors can contribute to marital distress. Which of these are at fault in a given case is often not obvious from clients' initial description of what has gone wrong with their marriage. Thus, one of the counselor's typical tasks is to discover which aspects of their marital arrangement have gone awry, so that a decision can be reached about what, if anything, might be done to improve the relationship. The following overview illustrates the nature of such factors.

A major source of difficulty is the conflict in expectations that the couple may bring to the relationship. Such expectations can be of many kinds. They may concern the frequency and form of sexual behavior, how much money the wage earner (or earners) should make, who should control the family finances, how money should be spent, the division of labor in the household, religious beliefs and practices, the use of leisure time, the occupational roles that each partner should play, child-raising practices, obligations to parents and parents-in-law, the types of friendships that the couple will develop outside the home, and the amount of time that they will spend together in shared activities as compared to time spent alone in individual pursuits. In addition to these broad areas of potential conflict are the petty daily habits of one partner that grate on the other partner's nerves. Minor irritants can cover a wide range of events, such as differences of opinion about hanging up clothes, leaving dishes in the sink, turning off lights, spitting on the sidewalk, putting one's feet up on the couch, using swear words and bad grammar, grooming, wearing clothes inappropriate to the occasion, and far more. From the viewpoint of marital compatibility, it is not that one partner is right and the other wrong in such matters. Rather, the problem is that they disagree. If both agree that the wife should control the family finances or that the top can be left off the toothpaste tube, then these events do not threaten the stability of the marriage. Therefore, the areas of disagreement are the ones that require particular attention in counselors' efforts to help clients to improve their marriage.

However, even when couples have had a reasonable understanding of their mate's traits and have accepted these at the time of marriage, the relationship can still go wrong. This may result from one or both of the partners, during the years of marriage, changing in ways that render them incompatible. For example, the husband may turn bald and grow very overweight, so that his wife finds him physically offensive. Or, when children are born to the couple, the young parents may newly discover that they disagree on child-rearing methods. In addition, problems can arise from events that could not reasonably have been predicted ahead of time, such as the effect on the marriage of an infirm, cantankerous relative's coming to live in the home. The trouble may also begin when one of the marriage partners responds to stress by habitually turning to alcohol or drugs.

As the above observations imply, a key task in marriage counseling with couples is to help them (1) identify what they expect of their spouse, (2) decide what changes they would require in the spouse in order to sustain the marriage, and (3) decide what changes they themselves are willing to make in their own behavior and in their expectations so as to keep the marriage intact. Thus, for a distressed client who hopes to sustain the marriage, counseling may result either in a change of attitude (accepting the existing reality of the marriage) or in a change of behavior (acting differently in the marriage), or in both.

Adjusting to Divorce

As suggested earlier, the greatest incidence of divorce occurs in the early years of marriage; the likelihood of a couple's separating diminishes with the passing years. The highest rate of divorce is found among young men. Those who marry in their teens can be four times more likely to divorce than ones who marry in their late twenties. Divorce rates are not identical across ethnic groups—the percentage of divorces among Blacks and certain other nonwhite groups in the United States is twice that of whites. Furthermore, the incidence of divorce is higher among people with low incomes than among those who are financially secure (Duvall, 1977, pp. 436, 474).

Reasons that couples give for dissolving their marriage can include any of the sources of conflict cited under *Sustaining a Marriage*, but among the most frequent are physical and verbal abuse, financial problems, and sexual incompatibility.

> Within a conflict-torn marriage alienation proceeds to the point where it cannot easily be stopped. Each additional crisis or conflict redefines the relationship in a way that precipitates it towards even greater alienation. Destructive quarrels, characteristic of marriages that end in divorce, alternate with intervals of peace during which there may be efforts to continue to live together. Then the conflict resumes around another sore point and continues until separation is more bearable than continuing to live together. The process of alienation proceeds through a series of crises that bring the couple to the final break. (Duvall, 1977, p. 442)

Once the marriage ends, the two individuals face the problem of adopting a new lifestyle that typically requires some change in their housing, financial arrangements, division of property, child-care duties, circle of friends, sexual activities, leisure-time pursuits, emotional support, and self-concept. Trials that people suffer in trying to manage this transition often cause them to seek counseling.

APPROACHES TO MARRIAGE COUNSELING

The phrase *marriage counseling*, in its general form, describes the process of offering aid during any of the three relationship situations mentioned above—premarital planning, sustaining a marriage, or adjusting to divorce. This kind of counseling is sometimes also extended to include cohabiting couples, whether heterosexual or homosexual.

There are numerous alternative methods of marriage counseling, with the choice of method in any given case depending on the type of problem that the client presents, on whether one or both marriage partners come for help, and on the particular therapist's talents, training, and theoretical bent. There is no general agreement in the professional literature that one of these counseling approaches is superior to the others. This lack of consensus appears to result from differences among clients and their problems, differences in the skills of therapists, and differences in the evidence gathered by therapists to appraise the success of their efforts.

A convenient way to perceive the variety of popular approaches is in terms of the combinations of people involved and the counseling techniques applied.

Six combinations of client-therapist relationships identified by Cookerly (1976) bear the labels: (1) individual (one spouse is treated in one-to-one counseling sessions), (2) individual-group (one spouse is treated in group sessions), (3) concurrent (both spouses are treated, but in separate individual sessions), (4) concurrent-group (both spouses are treated within the same group), (5) conjoint (both spouses are treated together in the same individual session), and (6) conjoint-group (both spouses are treated together in the same group session). The client-therapist combinations increase even further if more than one counselor participates in a case. For example, two counselors can collaborate in concurrent individual sessions (one therapist is assigned to the wife, the other to the husband) or in any of the group forms of therapy. Additional combinations result if other types of clients also become involved in the marital-counseling process, such as children, the couple's parents, or an ex-spouse when child-custody issues are involved.

The variety of techniques that may be employed in marriage counseling is suggested by the following sample of approaches that bear the titles *communication enhancement, behavioral contracting, interactional therapy, strategic therapy,* and *sex therapy.*

Communication-enhancement methods are founded on educational rather than therapeutic models. They are designed to teach people concrete skills of relating to a spouse and other family members. Such skills include speaking honestly, explaining clearly, listening empathetically, responding assertively, and rephrasing in one's own words what the other person says in order to get into the other's frame of reference. Ways of teaching these skills include description, demonstration, and guided practice (Olson, 1976, pp. 7-8, 42-50).

Behavioral contracting focuses on changing individuals' specific actions which apparently are contributing to marital disorder. An assumption underlying the behavioral model is that an increase in the client's positive acts and a decrease in negative ones will produce positive changes in both the feelings and the beliefs of family members.

Interactional therapy, as derived from the leadership of Gregory Bateson, has some aspects of behavioral therapy, in that it centers chiefly on relieving observed symptoms.

> Our approach is fundamentally pragmatic. We try to base our concep-
> tions and interventions on direct observation in the treatment situa-
> tion of *what* is going on in systems of human interaction, *how* the
> systems continue to function in such ways, and *how* they can be
> altered most effectively. The question of *why* is not relevant and is
> avoided. (Sieburg, 1985, p. 145)

Three of the specific techniques recommended in interactional therapy are those of (1) relabeling or reframing (changing the concep-
tual viewpoints from which a situation is interpreted), (2) homework assignments (directing clients to act in specific ways in their relations with others), and (3) paradoxical prescriptions (instructing clients to do even more of a troublesome symptom, on the expectation that the symptom will become so awkward that it will be dropped) (Sieburg, 1985, pp. 145-147).

The kind of strategic therapy espoused by Jay Haley places the counselor in an active, dominating, directive position rather than a passive, client-centered role. The therapist's task is to identify solva-
ble problems, set goals for the client, create interventions to achieve the goals, change the interventions if they fail to work, and assess the ultimate outcome. Therapy is usually brief rather than long term. Insight on the part of the client is considered unimportant, and there is little concern for unconscious processes. Treatment techniques in Haley's model closely resemble those of interactional therapy (Sieburg, 1985, pp. 149-156).

A couple's sexual relations are very often the source of difficulties that bring one or both partners to a physician or counselor. Even when sexual malfunction—such as male impotence or female orgasmic dysfunction—is not the complaint which the client initially presents to the therapist, sexual maladjustment is frequently associated with, or underlies, the presenting problem. Thus, sex therapy is perhaps the most common variety of counseling that centers on a particular aspect of married life. Many techniques have been employed in sex therapy, including the traditional psychoanalytic interview (free association and dream interpretation), clients' answering and discussing sex-knowledge-and-attitudes questionnaires, therapists' dispelling myths about sexual functions, couples' sharing sexual fantasies and preferences, counselors' offering instruction in lovemaking techniques through the use of still pictures or films, and therapists' guiding a couple's exploring each other's body during a private session of sexual activity (Maddock, 1976, pp. 355-382).

While the above examples touch on only a limited number of the techniques employed in marital counseling, they do demonstrate something of the range of diversity in the field.

Whatever specific techniques family therapists use, they increasingly have come to operate from a systems conception of their task. They are concerned not only with the behavior of their immediate client but also with the patterns of communication, power affection exchanges, and division of labor among all family members. Changing the function of one member of the system will, to some extent, alter the function of the rest. Thus, the counselor's awareness of all family members' roles and relationships becomes important in the effort to aid any one of the members.

Career Planning

With youths in their late teens and twenties, a counselor's typical role in career planning consists of helping the client to recognize the types of occupations available, the training and working conditions that such occupations entail, the client's own characteristics (skills, interests), and how well the occupations' conditions match the client's traits. Counselors also aid young adults in deciding which occupation to enter and how best to get a job in that field. As a result, one type of normative data useful in career counseling is information describing trends in the job market, so that clients can estimate the kinds of opportunities available in the years ahead. A second type identifies popular techniques which counselors use to collect pertinent information about client characteristics. The following discussion focuses on these two matters.

NORMATIVE INFORMATION ABOUT JOB OPPORTUNITIES

Technological advances have caused significant shifts in the kinds of jobs available to young adults. For example, the extremely rapid growth of the electronics industry has brought such products as color television, microcomputers, videotape recorders, and compact-disk players into most American homes, schools, and offices. Furthermore, automation in factories has eliminated thousands of semi-skilled jobs, while robots increasingly take over routine manufacturing operations. As these changes occur, fewer workers are needed in goods production, and more are needed in sales and other services.

A further cause of change in the job market has been a shift in the locations of jobs. For instance, numbers of American steel-production plants, which were major employers in past decades, have been forced to close as the result of competition from foreign nations. Likewise, a growing portion of the American public has been buying foreign-built cars, cameras, and electronics equipment, so that jobs in producing such products have moved to other countries.

Other significant influences on the nation's labor structure are demographic. Each decade produces growing numbers of elderly people who need health services, so, each year, more jobs become available in health care. Furthermore, increasing proportions of Hispanic, Black, and Asian ethnic groups are joining the labor force, thereby changing the ethnic pattern of employees in different occupations.

In view of these changes, it becomes important for vocational counselors and their clients to know what can be expected in the American job market in the future. The following figures illustrate some general job-opportunity trends that can affect career planning over the coming years.

To begin, during the 1990s, the number of different job titles will continue to be very large—an estimated 35,000. Thus, the young adult has a complex array of possibilities to consider. However, there are notable differences in the availability of jobs in different occupational fields. For instance, employment trends suggest that the number of jobs in goods-production between 1986 and 2000 will decline slightly (27.9 million jobs to 27.6 million) while jobs in services will grow by nearly 20 million (75.6 to 96.7 million). Every industry in

Table 7.2 Additional Jobs Available—Years 1986 to 2000

Type of Occupation	New Jobs Expected (in millions)	% Growth of Jobs in the Occupation
Service workers	5.4	31
Sales workers	3.7	30
Professional workers	3.7	27
Executive, administrative, managerial workers	3.0	29
Administrative-support and clerical workers	2.3	11
Precision production, craft, repair workers	1.7	12
Technicians and related support workers	1.4	38
Operators, fabricators, laborers	0.4	3
Agriculture, forestry, fishing workers	(loss) –0.2	(loss) –0.5

SOURCE: Adapted from Abramson, 1987, p. 30.

the service-producing sector will continue to expand, whereas growth in the goods-producing sector can be expected only in the construction division. Among the six categories of the service-producing sector, the greatest increase will be in direct-service occupations (10 million new jobs). Considerably less growth will appear in retail trade (4.9 million); in finance, insurance, and real estate (1.6 million); in wholesale trade (1.6 million); in government (1.6 million); and in transportation, communications, and public utilities (one-half million). (Abramson, 1987).

When occupations are divided into groups representing types of work, the growth in numbers of workers over the 1986-2000 period is estimated as shown in Table 7.2. Thus, there will be ample new job opportunities in service, sales, professional, and administrative positions, whereas jobs in agriculture, forestry, and fishing will continue to diminish.

Analyzing occupations in more specific categories reveals that a relatively small number (fewer than 30) will account for more than one-half of the overall job growth during the 1990s. The following examples illustrate the numbers of new jobs expected in several of these popular fields: retail sales (1.3 million), waiters/waitresses (752,000), registered nurses (612,000), janitors/cleaners (604,000), general managers and top executives (582,000), general office clerks (462,000), secretaries (424,000), guards (383,000), computer programmers (335,000), kindergarten/elementary teachers (299,000), computer systems analysts (251,000), cooks (240,000), gardeners (238,000), stock clerks (226,000), electronics engineers (192,000), and lawyers (191,000). As these figures suggest, the greatest growth will be in somewhat lower-paying service jobs, in nursing and teaching, and in the burgeoning electronics industry (Abramson, 1987, p. 31).

Among the 20 occupations that are expected to record the fastest growth in the 1990s, 12 are in the area of health services, including paralegal personnel, medical assistants, physical therapists, home health aides, data-processing equipment repairers, computer programmers, dental hygienists, and occupational therapists. Changes in technology and increased use of imported goods will bring a decline in job opportunities for electronic assemblers, railroad workers, industrial truck operators, telephone repairers, stenographers, farm workers, directory-assistance operators, and typesetters (Abramson, 1987).

Of particular importance to educational counselors is the fact that jobs in which a large proportion of workers have college training are among the fastest growing occupations (executive, professional, technical, sales, administrative, service, precision-production, and others). In contrast, occupations in which a large percentage of workers have less than four years of high school are among the slowest-growing fields. Also, workers with more education earn more. For example, in 1986 the average income of jobholders with four or more years of college was $33,443; with one to three years of college, $23,154; with four years of high school, $19,844; and with less than four years of high school, $16,605. In addition, the more education workers have, the less likely it is that they will be unemployed (Abramson, 1987, pp. 35-36). Those with less than a high-school education will have more difficulty finding a job in the future, especially one with good pay and chances for advancement (Kutscher, 1988, p. 8).

During the period 1965 through the mid-1980s, the prospects of a good job for every college graduate was somewhat bleak, so that young adults with doctorates in foreign languages could end up driving taxis and those with bachelor's degrees in history or teaching might become house painters or shoe-store clerks. Despite their difficulty finding a suitable job during these years, by 1986 almost three-fourths of the 23.4 million college graduates in the labor force held jobs that usually required at least four years of college education. The outlook for college graduates during the 1990s is far better. Economic projections for 1986 to 2000 suggest that jobs requiring a college degree will increase by more than 40% in professional occupations, by 60% in managerial occupations, by 70% in technician positions, by 75% in marketing and sales, and by 50% in administrative support. As a consequence, it is expected that 10 out of 11 college graduates entering the labor force will be able to get a college-level job (Sargent, 1988).

> The prospect of a continued surplus of college graduates—however small—implies that not all graduates who enter the labor force will be able to enter the occupations of their choice. Those graduates who carefully select their career objectives, acquire the most appropriate academic preparation, and who are most adept at locating job openings and marketing their abilities will enjoy the smoothest transition from school to work. Others will have to scramble for the available jobs, risking brief periods of unemployment, relocating to other areas of the country to find jobs, accepting jobs that do not require their level of education, or jobhopping before finding a satisfying position. Nevertheless, most future graduates are expected to find jobs that are challenging and satisfying. In addition, the noneconomic advantages of a college education remain undisputed—opportunities for learning, personal development, and broadening interests. (p. 8)

What, then, are the overall growth projections for the labor market? Between 1986 and 2000, the total number of people in the labor force is expected to increase by 21 million, or 18%, which is a somewhat slower growth rate than that during the period 1970-1986. Both younger and older workers will become a smaller proportion of the work force. For example, by 2000 the number of jobseekers aged 16 to 24 will decline from the 37 million in 1979 and 34 million in 1986 to 31.5 million. The high rate of young people's entering the job market by the close of the 1970s resulted from the children of the "baby boom" (1946-1964) and a rising percentage of women joining the world of work. However, between 1990 and 2000, the products of the baby boom will already be in the job market, and the growth in women's participation will continue at a slower pace (Kutscher, 1988).

Whereas the national trends illustrated above can aid counselors in sketching a general picture of job opportunities for clients, the trends fail to describe employment possibilities in particular communities or at a particular season of the year. Therefore, to supplement such information as the above (derived from the federal government's *Occupational Outlook Quarterly*), counselors profit from obtaining specific job information from such state and local sources as public employment agencies, city and county vocational-service bureaus, and the school system's vocational-guidance center.

INFORMATION ABOUT CLIENT CHARACTERISTICS

Some writers on vocational guidance divide the counselor's task into two phases—career counseling and job-placement aid. Each phase has its own objectives. Career counseling aims at helping a client to identify a vocational objective that is consistent with the individual's interests and abilities as well as with job-market opportunities. The job-placement phase, coming after a vocational objective has been established, aims at preparing the client to compete successfully in the job market (Chandler, 1985, pp. 354-355).

Career Counseling

One purpose of the career-counseling phase, whether conducted with an individual client or with a group, is to have clients recognize their present interests and life goals and to analyze the apparent sources of those interests and goals. This activity can focus attention on such a variety of issues as clients' relationships with their parents, the vocational ambitions that the parents hold for them, the idols on whom clients wish to model their careers, clients' perceptions of the demands and rewards of different occupations, and more. Both standardized assessment instruments and personal discussions are useful in collecting the information needed during this phase. For example, not only may the *Strong-Campbell Interest Inventory*, the *Kuder Occupational Interest Inventory*, Holland's *Vocational Preference Inventory*, and the *Career Occupational Preference Survey* help people to identify jobs consistent with their interests, but they may also reflect a client's pattern of interests which may suggest topics that can be profitably explored in the counselor's discussions with the client. Sentence-completion devices and other projective techniques, such as the *Thematic Apperception Test*, can also aid in a counselor analyzing people's interests and attitudes.

A second purpose in career counseling is to guide clients' assessment of their talents and skills and to compare this assessment with the training and skills needed for different jobs. A wide variety of tests is available to help with this task. Among these are measures of general intelligence *(Wechsler Adult Intelligence Scale)*, of problem-solving and professional judgment *(Otis-Lennon Mental Abilities Tests, Watson-Glaser Thinking Appraisal)*, and of diverse types of aptitude

	Job Requirements								Work Environment			Occupational Characteristics				
	1. Leadership, presentation	2. Helping/instructing others	3. Problem-solving/creativity	4. Initiative	5. Work as part of a team	6. Frequent public contact	7. Manual dexterity	8. Physical stamina	9. Hazardous	10. Outdoors	11. Confined	12. Geographically limited	13. Earnings	14. Employment growth	15. New jobs 1984-1995 *	16. Entry requirements
Jewelers	Δ	Δ	Δ	Δ	Δ	Δ	Δ				Δ		L	L	3	M
Bookbinders		Δ			Δ		Δ	Δ	Δ		Δ		L	M	14	M
Machinists					Δ		Δ	Δ	Δ		Δ		M	L	37	M
Upholsterers							Δ	Δ			Δ		L	L	6	M
Butchers/meatcutters						Δ	Δ	Δ	Δ		Δ		L	L	–9	M
Printing press operators		Δ	Δ		Δ		Δ	Δ	Δ		Δ		M	M	26	M
Aircraft pilots			Δ	Δ	Δ		Δ				Δ		H	H	18	M
Auditors/accountants		Δ	Δ		Δ	Δ					Δ		H	H	307	H
Truckdrivers				Δ			Δ	Δ			Δ		M	M	428	M
Computer operators			Δ		Δ		Δ				Δ		L	H	143	M
Computer programmers			Δ		Δ						Δ		H	H	245	H
Cashiers		Δ				Δ	Δ				Δ		L	H	566	L
Secretaries				Δ	Δ	Δ	Δ						L	L	268	L
Retail sales workers	Δ	Δ		Δ		Δ							L	M	583	L

* Numbers of new jobs in thousands.

Figure 7.2. Characteristics of Occupations

SOURCE: Figure adapted from Fountain, 1986, pp. 2-12.

(*Differential Aptitude Test, Primary Mental Abilities Test, California Aptitude Survey*, and *Johnson O'Conner Research Foundation Tests*). School records reflecting the level of individuals' success in various subject-matter areas can also be helpful in aptitude assessment.

The activity of matching clients' interests and training with types of occupations can be promoted by the use of charts that depict characteristics of occupations and the likely future for openings in such jobs. Figure 7.2 illustrates a portion of such a chart, adapted from a lengthy series of graphic descriptions issued periodically by such agencies as the U.S. Department of Labor. The *job requirements* listed across the top of the chart enable counselees to estimate how well an occupation might suit their own skills and tastes. For instance, a job calling for initiative will be one in which the employee is expected to determine, without close supervision, what needs to be done. Likewise, the *work environment* items furnish some idea of what the job setting will offer. For example, a confined job requires that the employee stay in a specific place for most of the workday. Under *occupational characteristics*, the column entitled *earnings* shows whether the income from the job is comparatively high (H), medium (M), or low (L). The prospects for future growth of employment opportunities are also rated high, medium, and low. The number of new jobs projected for each occupation on the U.S. labor market are expected to increase by 583,000, whereas opportunities for butchers are expected to decline by 9,000. Entry requirements for occupations are rated L (high school or less), M (post high-school training, such as apprenticeship, junior college, or extensive job experience), and H (four or more years of college usually required). (Fountain, 1986, pp. 3-4)

Job Placement

The counseling tasks during the job-placement phase involve helping clients to locate specific jobs that they would like to enter and preparing them to apply for such jobs and successfully begin work.

Aid with locating suitable jobs includes guiding clients to such sources of information about job openings as want-ads in newspapers, job lists at local employment services, acquaintances who work at such jobs, and telephoned inquiries to companies listed in the yellow pages of the telephone directory.

The counseling task of preparing clients to apply for a job and to begin working successfully includes showing them how to write letters of application and how to create a resume of their educational background, special skills, training, interests, and work experience. Such preparation may also offer clients practice in introducing themselves to an employer, responding to interview questions, negotiating employment terms, and conversing with fellow workers upon first meeting them. Advice can also be offered about how to dress appropriately for different types of job interviews and about the kinds of behavior that employers typically like and dislike.

Financial Planning

The early-adult years are the time when most people are expected to take complete responsibility for their financial fate, both for acquiring income and for determining expenditures. Furthermore, as they become parents, young adults face a second challenge in personal finance—that of guiding their children in how to manage money. Many young people suffer serious difficulties in meeting these obligations, especially in a society which inundates its members with advertising that portrays overindulgent spending and indebtedness as virtues. Nor has the federal government served as a constructive model of financial wisdom. National leaders, like the purveyors of credit cards and charge accounts, have persisted in practicing deficit spending.

The observation that, in recent decades, personal financial planning had become a growing problem in the United States is reflected in statistics on consumer income and indebtedness. By the latter 1980s, over 70% of American families possessed credit cards, with an average of five cards per family. During a typical month, over 80% of cardholders had used their accounts for purchases, with the average amount charged during the month being $150. The total personal debt in the United States, in the form of outstanding consumer credit, grew steadily over the decades of the 1970s and 1980s, with the growth in credit being far more rapid than population increase. For example, while the population increased by an estimated 20% over the 1970-1987 period, outstanding consumer credit grew by 575%. The portion of a family's disposable income represented by consumer debt expanded from 19% to 24%. Total debt (mortgages, consumer credit, and other types) rose by 960%. Reports of people's incomes and expenditures by age stages showed that in the mid-1980s, among youths and young adults under age 25, expenditures exceeded income (before taxes) by 11%. At all age decades from 25 to 65, income (before taxes) exceeded expenditures by around 14% (U.S. Bureau of the Census, 1988).

In effect, difficulties with personal finances are an intimate part of the troubles that many clients suffer in early adulthood. As a consequence, providing aid with financial planning can become a key aspect of counseling young adults. Sometimes clients can pinpoint their difficulties as being strictly financial, so they seek advice from someone whose specialty is financial planning. But, in many cases, money matters are only one part of the distress suffered by young people, since issues of personal finance are linked into a network of other troubles, including their job, marital condition, social life, relations with their parents, and more. Therefore, questions of money management frequently arise in counseling cases that are not limited to financial concerns.

Among the issues often important in such counseling are the three illustrated below: (1) common problems in managing personal finances, (2) the interaction of couples' finances and their personal relationships, and (3) teaching children to manage money.

COMMON PROBLEMS IN MANAGING PERSONAL FINANCES

An impression of the kinds of difficulties that young adults frequently bring to counselors is offered by the following list of money matters featured in magazine articles by personal-finance consultants:

Clients have only a vague idea of where their money goes, since they spend by impulse rather than by allocating portions of their income ahead of time to different aspects of their lives. Such individuals may profit from establishing a budgeting process.

People use credit cards and charge accounts as a way of living beyond their immediate income, deluding themselves into feeling that when the time comes to pay, more money will be available. In doing so, they end up paying 20 or 30% more than the original price for goods and services, since the interest cost for credit accounts is high. Often the cure for this habit is that of paying cash for everything except such large items as a car or a house.

People spend their entire income each month, making no provision for savings. Therefore, when an emergency arises, they must borrow money and pay interest on it or they will suffer other unpleasant consequences, such as being expelled from their apartment house because they have sacrificed their rent money to care for the emergency. Often these people cannot give up immediate pleasures for future security. "I want the best of both worlds. I want to save but not if I can't enjoy myself" (Trunzo, 1987, p. 158).

Young people frequently wish to wear clothes, buy wine, or drive a car that they believe has high prestige value. As a consequence, they pay for products and services which have much of the cost in the fashionable name and not in the quality of the product. Hence, their purchases outstrip their income. Linked to this pattern of prestige spending is the habit of buying goods without shopping around or without waiting for a sale at which the goods could be bought for less.

The growing incidence of divorce has exacerbated the financial difficulties of early adulthood, as a family's separation requires that two households be maintained and that child-support and alimony payments be added to one spouse's routine living expenses.

Clients find themselves in jobs that fail to provide an income which reasonably matches their needs. Counseling such individuals may thus call for a review of their career plans and an identification of opportunities for vocational advancement which they either had not recognized or had been hesitant to pursue.

As the above examples suggest, counseling people who have personal-finance problems is not merely a matter of furnishing them technical information about budgeting, shopping, and job opportunities. Often, more basic foci of attention are the clients' goals, system of values, and self-concept.

FINANCES AND COUPLES' RELATIONSHIPS

A study by Blumstein and Schwartz (1983) of the personal-social adjustment of 5,945 American couples included an investigation of the pairs' conflicts and agreements over handling money. Of the total number of couples, 60% were married, 11% were cohabiting male/female partners, 16% were gay men, and 13% were lesbians. The sample was selected to represent all major regions of the United States, although ethnically the respondents were 95% whites.

Generalizations that the researchers drew from their study included:

(1) Money matters are the most-commonly discussed issue in marriage, and frequently they are the greatest source of conflict between partners, with married couples fighting over money more often than other types of couples.

(2) The belief that the husband should be the major provider continues to be the dominant conviction among both men and women.

(3) Money plays a highly important part in establishing the balance of power in most couples' relationship. The amount of money that a person earns, compared with the partner's income, determines the partners' relative power, except among lesbian pairs. "These patterns have led us to conclude that it is men—who for generations have learned in the work place the equation that money equals power—who have recreated this experience in the home. Wives and cohabiting women fall prey to the logic that money talks. But women seem capable of escaping the ruthless impact of money when no man is present" (Blumstein & Schwartz, 1983, pp. 55-56).

(4) More dissension occurs over how money should be spent than over

how much the couple has. But when partners are disappointed over how much they have, their entire relationship suffers, except among lesbians. Among all four types of couples (married, cohabiting, gay, lesbian), partners who felt that they had equal control over how to spend their money enjoyed a more peaceful relationship than did partners who felt that one of them dominated decisions about expenditures.

(5) Before getting married, many couples are ignorant of their intended spouse's economic history or outlook, so they do not know what to expect in terms of their financial relationship, with the result that subsequent dissension over money matters comes to them as an unpleasant surprise.

For counselors, these findings suggest that finances will very often be embedded in the problems for which couples seek help. Thus, if financial questions are not among the issues that clients present to the counselor, it may be useful for the counselor to direct attention to money matters in order to discover whether this area of the couple's life is contributing to their unsatisfactory relationship. Blumstein and Schwartz (1983, p. 93) concluded that:

> Money management is accomplished with the least conflict when partners have an equal influence over decisions. If either partner is too dominating, conflict occurs. This is especially true when traditional roles are violated. It may be tedious for couples to create budgets together and decide jointly what to spend on everything from groceries to entertainment to clothes and even furniture. And it may not be possible for the two partners to do all their spending separately and not impinge on each other's decisions. [But] when couples *do* take the time to share control over money management, they seem to have happier, calmer relationships.

TEACHING CHILDREN TO MANAGE MONEY

A frequent complaint of parents is that their offspring, whether age 5 or 25, are unwise in their use of money. As a result, when parents seek a counselor's guidance in child rearing, their concern often includes a request about how best to train their children in reasonable, responsible practices of personal finance. The notion that this concern is common among parents is suggested by the frequency with which articles on such issues appear in magazines on family money matters. A typical hope held by those who seek this guidance is that constructive money-management habits established in child-hood will carry over into adult life.

Child psychologists, educators, and financial-services experts who have studied the development of children's attitudes toward money have generated a series of guidelines to help parents train children in responsible financial practices. Two major elements in such advice are that (1) beginning at a relatively young age, children should be provided a weekly allowance and (2) children should be guided toward regularly saving a portion of their income.

Using an Allowance

Estess and Rosenthal (1988) compiled the advice of a variety of experts to produce the following suggestions:

Children should begin to receive a weekly allowance by the time they enter school at age five or six. The allowance should be distributed at a specific time, preferably in mid-week rather than on the weekend. Since most children's money is spent on the weekend, if they receive their funds in mid-week, they are more likely to plan ahead of time how they will use it rather than adopting the habit of getting rid of it thoughtlessly at the time it is received.

The amount that a child receives should, if possible, be comparable to what age peers in their area get. Furthermore, what the allowance is to be used for should be explained clearly. In some homes, an allowance is entirely spending money, with the child being free to decide how it is all dispensed. In others, the allowance can be provided under an allocation system, such as a specified portion for school lunches, another portion for charity, and the remainder to spend with no questions asked.

If the child overspends before the week is past and asks for more—or for an advance on the following week—the parent should refuse, so that the child can learn the consequences of poor planning and so that he or she does not get into the habit of deficit spending. Whenever the young person pleads for an increase in the allowance, it is wise for the parent to listen to the child's reasons and, through negotiation, decide whether an increase would be reasonable.

As members of the family, children should be expected to contribute to the general welfare—do chores—in keeping with each one's stage of development. The allowance should not be payment for the chores, but a right. Different sanctions, other than withholding the allowance, should be imposed for negligence in performing chores.

As children grow older, they become able to take on extra jobs beyond their normal chores. For these jobs, they can receive pay, thereby beginning to learn what it is like to be employed.

Guidelines suggested for supervising paid jobs include: (1) Evaluate children's job performance so that they become accustomed to doing jobs well, (2) pay by the job and not by the hour, so that dawdling is not encouraged, and (3) pay children who work for you, but don't pay them for working for someone else (Estess & Rosenthal, 1988).

Stages of Development in Children's Money Management

From their survey of the opinions of experts on matters of children and personal finance, Estess and Rosenthal (1988, p. 33) have prescribed a hierarchy of six desirable growth stages in children's money management from age 3 through adolescence. For ages 3-5, the authors suggest that children learn number concepts by keeping coins in a piggy bank and being allowed to pay for small items. For ages 6-7, children should receive a weekly allowance and be offered the opportunity to earn more money for special household jobs beyond their regular chores. At ages 8-10, children can open a bank account where they can save a portion of their allowance and of gifts of money. They also can become collectors of such items as stamps or baseball cards or other items which they learn to trade and bargain for among their companions. At the end of elementary school, the allowance of children ages 11-12 can be increased, and they can be taught smart buying by comparison shopping and watching for special sales. At ages 13-14, the period for awarding the allowance may be changed from weekly to monthly or quarterly, and budgeting can be taught. Teenagers can be encouraged to take odd jobs, and a portion of their earnings may be set aside for college or other postsecondary-school use. At age 15 and beyond, youths can be introduced to different ways of investing money. They can file their own tax return if they have been employed, and they may negotiate with parents regarding what part of the expense they will assume for using the family car—such as a portion for gasoline costs.

CONCLUSION

The early adult years have been pictured as a period of life when grown youths first take on such major responsibilities as marriage, parenthood, full-time employment, and mature citizenship. It is also the period during which physical skills and mental abilities usually rise to their peak efficiency and subsequently begin a slow decline. The substantial difficulties that people often experience when confronted with these developmental tasks bring many of them to professional counselors for help.

8

The Mid-Life Years: Ages 40 to 60

An assortment of terms commonly applied to middle age—*mid-life crisis, the empty nest, the declining years*—imply that this time in the life span can be a stressful period of readjustment. However, several conditions of middle age complicate the efforts of counselors to use normative data in estimating significant ways in which their clients in the 40-to-60 age range will be alike in abilities and in personal/social adjustment.

One such condition is the patterning of ways in which physical strength, stamina, and reaction-time diminish in the general population from the outset of early adulthood into old age. This decrease can reduce middle-aged adults' ability to perform physical tasks as adeptly as they did in earlier years.

A second condition, which may compensate for the first, is the experience that the middle-aged adult has accumulated over past decades, experience which can result in greater wisdom and expertise during the mid-life years, thereby partially counteracting the reduction in physical strength and agility that has occurred. As a consequence of experience, people in their middle years may be as effective in their occupational and social activities as they were during early adulthood, or even more so.

A third significant condition is the individual's style of life. As a result of both personal choice and *fate* or *luck* (meaning events outside one's control), different people pursue different patterns of daily living that influence their ability to satisfy their desires and to cope with the demands of their environment. From the standpoint of personal/social adjustment, the lifestyle of a chronic alcoholic differs from that of a health enthusiast who follows a consistent regimen of diet and exercise. The lifestyle of a high-school dropout who is a single mother of three teenagers is different from that of a compatibly married, childless couple who both work in executive positions.

A fourth factor is the person's biological inheritance, which is responsible for the genetically controlled timing mechanism that influences when during the life cycle different internal events will occur, including such events of mid-life and old age as the reduction of physical strength and agility, the reduction of ability to manage stress, the reduction of resistance to disease, the reduction of sexual desire and prowess, and the reduction of mental skills. People's genetic endowment partially accounts for the marked differences among individuals of the same chronological age in the time of life when these changes take place. A woman age 60 may look and function more like a typical 40-year old, whereas one who is age 40 may be more like a typical 60-year old. As a consequence, some experts in the field of life-span development have suggested that the concept of *functional age* is more useful than *chronological age* for judging how well people in their middle and late years can manage their affairs. Functional age does not mean how many years a person has lived but, rather, refers to the individual's ability to perform the tasks of daily life. Although attempts have been made to devise evaluation techniques for estimating an individual's functional age, such techniques are not in widespread use (Salthouse, 1982, pp. 14-16). One problem with these attempts has been that of determining which factors in a person's life should be assessed or, indeed, can be assessed accurately. A further problem arises from the fact that people's abilities do not all diminish at the same rate. This means that a single functional age cannot properly be assigned to represent an individual's overall life performance. Instead, different functional ages need to be determined for different abilities so as to reflect the patterning of a person's capabilities. In any event, the concept of functional age is useful to counselors, since it may alert them to the shortcomings of chronological age for estimating the physical, mental, social, and emotional characteristics of mid-life clients. Although normative data can suggest general trends for the mid-life years, a counselor needs to assess each client's status in various aspects of life in order to select treatment procedures that are likely to succeed.

In brief, chronological age is less reliable during mid-life for estimating clients' physical and mental abilities than it is during the first and last decades of the life span. However, even with the extensive individual differences among the middle aged, there are also general developmental trends that are useful for counselors to recognize. Furthermore, there are life-adjustment problems frequently faced during these years. Such trends and problems form the subject matter of this chapter.

The following are prominent kinds of problems brought to counselors by middle-aged clients:

—Mothers whose lives were dedicated to homemaking and child rearing for two decades or more but who now are without meaningful occupation as their children have grown up and left home.

—People who face career changes, either because their skills no longer fit the needs of a changing job market or because their ability to cope with the demands of their job has diminished with advancing age.

—Those who are suffering stress on the job and are seeking ways to resolve the conflict between their job responsibilities, family commitments, and their own diminishing energies.

—Women distressed by the approach and occurrence of menopause—that event signaling the end of their capacity to bear children.

—Both sexes—but more often women—sufficiently concerned about mid-life changes in physical appearance that they seek counseling. The counseling is intended either to guide them toward retrieving what they conceive to be their "lost looks" (such as by losing weight) or to help them adopt constructive attitudes toward the inevitable physical changes (such as wrinkles or advancing baldness).

—Men and women distraught by their diminishing sexual desire and their decreased ability to engage in sexual intercourse.

—People disturbed by the death of a child, parent, spouse, or close friend, so they seek help in managing their grief.

In keeping with the approach in previous chapters, this chapter is divided into two major sections. The first reviews general mid-life development trends that carry implications for counseling. The second offers normative information about four kinds of counseling problems with which middle-aged clients often seek aid—weight control, grief over the death of a loved one, reproductive changes (menopause), and career decisions.

PATTERNS OF MID-LIFE DEVELOPMENT

In earlier chapters, we focused on the increase in physical and mental abilities with advancing age. But, by mid-life, people can no longer expect continuing improvement in their fitness and skills. At least some abilities are bound to decline, with resultant consequences for personal/social adjustment. Furthermore, during mid-life, changes occur in family patterns and social relationships, as well as in job performance. The following discussion centers on typical characteristics of such changes. As a result, questions of significance for counseling people in the 40-to-60-year age range include: "In what aspects of life do a middle-aged person's abilities decline, and at what rate?" "In what aspects is there little or no decline?" "What mid-life trends often appear in family life and other social relationships?" "What are common problems arising in careers and work performance?" "How may people's self-concepts alter in middle age?" And "What are the consequences of all these trends for the conduct of counseling?"

Changes in Physical and Psychophysical Abilities

As in Chapter 7, the term *physical* is used throughout the following discussion in reference to gross bodily functions, such as strength and stamina. *Psychophysical* is used to mean observable behaviors that require combining perceptual skills—sight, hearing, touch—with physical movements, as in acts of eye-hand or ear-foot coordination.

Following early adulthood, the physical functions of the body progressively decline in their efficiency. The heart does not pump as well, sugar in the blood does not metabolize as effectively, the lungs do not breathe as deeply, muscles do not readily increase in strength, and kidneys do not filter waste products as efficiently. For people who take relatively good care of their health, these changes do not significantly affect their leading normal lives during the middle years, since body functions always have a reserve capacity. However, when an emergency occurs that places unusual stress on the body, middle-aged people may lack the capacity to respond satisfactorily. Physical performances particularly susceptible to the onslaught of the passing years are ones requiring unusual strength, endurance, and precision of eye-hand or eye-foot coordination. It is often difficult for middle-aged adults to recognize and admit that their physical abilities are on the decline. As a consequence, they continue to engage in physically and emotionally demanding activities for which they are no longer equipped. In their work and play, middle-aged adults may press themselves to a point of exhaustion or may ignore their increasing susceptibility to infection, extremes of heat and cold, time changes involved in long-distance air travel, and emotionally stressful events.

When a crisis occurs, they are astonished and distraught by their failure to respond as they had in earlier years. The crisis may be an injury, a fainting spell, a heart attack, failure to complete a task, defeat in a contest, costly errors on the job, or a distressing argument. The crisis may then bring them for counseling, either voluntarily or at the urging of a relative, friend, or employer. The task of the counselor becomes one of helping clients to accept the reality of their physical condition and, in light of this acceptance, to reorder their ambitions and lifestyle to suit this reality. Counseling techniques appropriate for this assignment can include:

(1) Providing information about physical development and health practices in mid-life and about ways to reorganize one's goals and activities in keeping with the changes of middle age. Constructive health practices can include (a) establishing a routine of exercise at least three times a week, (b) stopping smoking, (c) limiting alcohol consumption, (d) having regular physical examinations that include a check on blood pressure, cholesterol, and triglyceride levels, (e) adopting eating habits that maintain proper weight and health, and (f) avoiding unnecessary tension.

(2) Offering opportunities for emotional catharsis, so that clients can express their disappointment and fears in the presence of an accepting confidant.

(3) Establishing a schedule of behavioral changes that can effect a transition to a lifestyle appropriate to the clients' physical status.

(4) Assisting clients in facing the truth about their physical condition and about their life goals by means of such counseling approaches as reality therapy, gestalt therapy, rational-emotive therapy, or the like.

Stability and Decline in Mental Abilities

In the early decades of the twentieth century, as psychologists developed tests of mental skills, debate ensued over the nature of intelligence. Was intelligence a single power that determined a person's level of success equally in all phases of intellectual activity? Or was intelligence composed of different types of abilities, so that an individual could be higher on one type than on another, with the result that the efficiency of the different abilities could decline at different rates with the passing years? As suggested in Chapter 7, research over recent decades has demonstrated that the second of these possibilities is the more valid. Thus, it is more accurate to speak of *types of intelligence* or of *cognitive abilities* than to refer to mental functioning simply as overall *intelligence* or *cognitive ability*. Horn and his colleagues (1967, 1976, 1980) have proposed that trends in mental development be conceived in terms of two major types of intelligence.

> One type, called fluid intelligence, is expected to decrease with increased age in adulthood. It is assumed to be reflected in tests of figural relations, memory span, induction, and most processes involved in acquiring new information. The second type, ... called crystallized intelligence, is assumed to be the cumulative end product of information acquired by the activity of fluid intelligence processes. It is thus the sum total of the culturally dependent information stored by the individual as a result of his or her interactions with the environment. Crystallized intelligence is presumed to be measured by such tests as vocabulary, general information, comprehension, arithmetic, and reasoning with familiar material. (Salthouse, 1982, pp. 69-70)

The proposed distinction between fluid and crystallized types of intelligence is not entirely precise, nor are the theoretical underpinnings clear. The distinction, however, does reflect the results of a variety of empirical investigations and, as such, is of practical use to counselors in their expectations about the problems of clients in mid-life and later. Salthouse (1982, p. 69) has summarized these apparent trends in the form displayed in Table 8.1.

Thus, in general, it is expected that during middle age, most people will have more difficulty adopting new viewpoints and new abstractions (less intellectual flexibility) as well as learning new material (processing new information) than they did during adolescence and early adulthood. However, the special skills and wisdom that middle-aged people have gained from experience, and their ability to apply such knowledge in solving familiar types of problems, will likely remain essentially intact. This observation is drawn from a growing body of evidence which suggests that there are two general ways in which people process information, *automatic* and *effortful* (*effortful* meaning *controlled*). Older adults "frequently show no noticeable deficits in performing well-practiced [automatic processing] skills, even though there may be a decline in performing novel tasks or in acquiring and processing new information [effortful processing]" (Rybash, Hoyer, & Roodin, 1986, p. 91). Such an understanding of intellectual functioning in middle age is of particular use in counseling clients who face mid-life changes in their careers. These clients

Table 8.1 Types of Stable and Declining Mental Abilities

Age-Stable Abilities	Age-Decline Abilities
Accumulative effects of differential experience	Native capacity or "sheer modifiability"
Language functions	Nonlanguage functions
Recall of acquired information	Understanding and adopting new methods of thinking
Familiar materials	Abstract materials
Accumulation of verbal or factual information	Flexible use of mental resources
Verbal abilities	Performance (physical) abilities
Stored information	Immediate adaptive ability
Static intelligence	Flexible intelligence
Specialized abilities	Unspecialized abilities
Structure	Process
Utilization of stored information	Processing and integrating new information

SOURCE: Adapted from Salthouse, 1982, p. 69.

probably will be more successful in areas related to their past experience than in ones demanding perceptions and learnings significantly different from those that they faced in the past. For instance, young people's apparent greater facility in adapting to a computerized world, as compared to their middle-aged parents' lesser facility, would appear to illustrate this point.

However, applying normative trends to individual cases requires a strong measure of caution, for there are marked differences between individuals in both the level of abilities that they bring to middle age and the rate at which their intellectual skills decline. Consequently, for the individual client, information needs to be collected by means of interviews, tests, and records of job performance to determine how that person's intellectual talents are patterned and how stable they appear to be.

The Quality of Family Life

General mid-life trends in the quantity and quality of interpersonal relationships have been observed within the family structure, whether the family is of a traditional type or is one of the living arrangements that have become more common in recent decades, such as stepfamilies and cohabitation among the unwed (either heterosexual or homosexual). The two types of relationships considered in the following paragraphs are ones often involved in the problems brought by clients to the counselor's office. These are relationships (1) between spouses and (2) between parents and their grown children.

SPOUSE RELATIONSHIPS

In families with children, parents' mid-life years are a time when their children progress from adolescence to young adulthood and leave home to establish households of their own. The parents, whose lives for two decades or more have been dedicated heavily to child rearing, are now obliged to readjust their own relationship as a couple alone. In the 1950s and 1960s, assorted studies suggested that marital happiness was lower in mid-life than it had been in the earlier years of marriage. However, a number of surveys in the 1970s indicated that marital satisfaction for a majority of middle-aged couples often approached the level of contentment remembered from the initial years of married life (Duvall, 1977, p. 373).

The degree of marital happiness in middle age can be influenced by a variety of factors. One is the couple's sexual compatibility. In a survey of 100,000 women, sexual satisfaction was closely associated with communication with their husbands and happiness in marriage; over two-thirds of the respondents judged their sex life to be either good or very good, no matter how many years they had been wed (Levin & Levin, 1975, pp. 54-57). Masters and Johnson (1968, pp. 271-275) reported that wives who enjoyed well-adjusted, stimulating marriages found little or no disruption of their sexual interest and activity in mid-life and into old age. The extent of sexual compatibility depended significantly on the two partners' mutual communication and personality evaluations of each other. Lower sexual satisfaction was experienced when either one or both of the partners believed that they were misunderstood and undervalued or that they were perceived by their mate as boring, unattractive, unintelligent, or undependable.

Among middle-aged men, sexual adequacy can diminish for a variety of reasons, including mental or physical fatigue, boredom with their mate as a sex partner, infirmity (their own or their partner's), preoccupation with their job or other concerns, and fear that their sexual performance will be inadequate (Masters & Johnson, 1966, p. 264). Duvall (1977, pp. 375-376), after reviewing a range of research on men's sex lives in middle age, concluded that anxiety over declining virility and a loss of personal attractiveness can cause some men to seek reassurance and variety through extramarital sexual encounters.

> Among postparental husbands, one-half expressed a desire for and one-fourth have been involved in extramarital affairs.... Poor marital adjustment and satisfaction are significantly related to husbands' (but not to wives') extramarital involvements.... About one-third of all wives in the *Redbook* study [of 100,000 women] reported having had lovers outside of marriage. The longer a woman had been married, and the greater her opportunities for extramarital affairs, the more likely she was to have them. (Duvall, 1977, pp. 375-376)

PARENT-CHILD RELATIONSHIPS

The process of middle-aged parents' launching their daughters and sons into adult life is frequently a painful one for both generations. For a variety of reasons, parents are typically reluctant to set their children entirely free to make their own way in the world. Parents often feel a responsibility to protect their offspring by preventing them from making errors in the choice of a career, a mate, the use of money, and a lifestyle. Another reason for the reluctance is that much of the meaning of life for parents—particularly the mother—has resided in the role of child rearing. When the adolescent becomes a young adult, it is then often difficult for parents to loosen their ties with the youth and thereby diminish their own sense of importance. A third reason is that adult children themselves are frequently unsure of how much independence they want. Not only do they usually have a strong need for the continuing emotional support of a mother and a father, but they often must turn to their parents at times of financial difficulty, times of deciding on a career and on marriage, and times of negotiating with such agencies as the income-tax service, a college, an insurance company, or the courts. Professional counseling may be sought in the family members' efforts to achieve a successful transition in such parent-child relations.

Middle-age parents' troubles with their sons-in-law and daughters-in-law are common causes of strained relations between parents and their grown children. The most frequent source of this disharmony is a lack of mutual acceptance and respect between the in-laws, a difficulty frequently resulting from parents' reluctance to let their grown offspring make their own decisions. This can occur when parents continue to advise and criticize their sons and daughters, with the criticism often focusing on the young person's choice of a mate and companions. The emotional distress occasioned by the resulting simultaneous feelings of resentment and of attachment between a parent and a child may bring one or both of these parties to the counselor's office.

Career Patterns and Work Performance

Studies of occupational performance cite a number of work-related conditions that frequently affect personal/social adjustment during the mid-life years. The five sources of work stress for the middle-aged identified by Cooper in a review of research on occupational efficiency are: work load, work-role ambiguity and conflict, interpersonal relations, career prospects, and home-work interface difficulties (Cooper, 1981, pp. 94-99).

Work-load pressures can be quantitative (too much to do) or qualitative (assignments too difficult). Investigations have shown that quantitative overload is strongly linked to increased cigarette smoking (a risk factor in coronary heart disease). Heart attacks in middle age are more common among people holding two jobs and among ones working at a single job more than 60 hours a week. Work overload is also related to such indicators of stress as escapist drinking, job dissatisfaction, feelings of threat and embarrassment, work absenteeism, low self-esteem, low work motivation, high cholesterol levels, and increased heart rate. At mid-life, two variables that can contribute to work stress are (1) the increased expectations for performance that accrue with the individual's rise to more demanding positions in the occupational hierarchy and (2) the middle-aged worker's inability to perform at peak efficiency as a result of declining abilities and energy.

The factor of work-role ambiguity comes into play when people are unsure about colleagues' expectations and about the exact responsibilities and extent of decision-making power that their job entails. For example, finding themselves assigned tasks which they feel are not reasonably part of their job adds to workers' dissatisfaction. Role conflict is particularly prominent among people in management and supervisory positions to which they have advanced by the time of middle age. Symptoms of stress identified in such workers include increased heart rate and blood pressure, life dissatisfaction, low self-concept, decreased motivation, and a desire to quit the job. Closely allied with work-role conflict is the factor of interpersonal relations, particularly a pattern of abrasive interaction between workers at different levels of the administrative system—between senior and junior managers, foremen and laborers, bosses and secretaries. Job stress is heightened by inconsiderate and insulting styles of giving assignments, assessing workers' performance, and reacting to workers' concerns and problems.

Young workers—those still in their twenties and thirties—can expect to progress regularly up the lower rungs of their occupation's ladder and can change companies or even vocations without seriously damaging their future career chances. However, by middle age, career advancement becomes more problematic:

> ...most workers find their progress slowed, if not actually stopped. Job opportunities become fewer, those jobs that are available take longer to master, past (mistaken?) decisions cannot be revoked, old knowledge and methods become obsolete, energies may be flagging or demanded by the family, and there is the press of fresh young recruits to face in competition.... The fear of demotion or obsolescence can be strong for those who know they have reached their "career ceiling"—and most will inevitably suffer some erosion of status before they finally retire. (Cooper, 1981, pp. 96-97)

Finally, stress in middle age frequently derives from a conflict between conditions at work and conditions at home. In the period of life when the individual is seeking to cope with on-the-job stressors, there are often conflicting demands from the family. To succeed vocationally, the wage-earner depends on the support and understanding of those at home. Because much of what is significant in the worker's life is found in the job—doing well, gaining status and self-satisfaction by rising in the occupational structure—the job's demands can often take priority over attention to family members. Furthermore, the children of middle-aged couples are typically in their teens or early adult years, which can be a trying time for parents, especially in a youth culture that fosters a hedonistic attitude toward illicit drugs, sexual behavior, and personal finance. Tensions between job and home mount even higher when both husband and wife are employed, which now has become the dominant pattern in American families. Job-home conflict also increases in the one-parent family, a type of household still on the increase in American society. As a consequence, the potentials for work-home conflict appear greater today than they were in past decades.

Because of such conditions as the above, the problems that middle-aged clients bring to counselors often involve career adjustments.

Mid-Life Self-Concept

Whitbourne's (1986) study of adults in mid-life led her to conclude that:

> Adult identity does not undergo regular, predictable shifts in its structure and content according to a timetable set by the individual's chronological age, nor does it remain invariant over the adult years. Instead . . . the individual's identity can change in adulthood when there is the right combination of circumstances and readiness or need on the part of the individual. If neither of these conditions are met, the adult's identity may never change. If change is necessary for the individual's sense of well-being and the opportunity for change is present, then adult identity may take on a new form at that point. (p. 7)

The stimulus for a revision of identity during middle age can be either a predictable event, for which a person can prepare, or an unpredictable one that comes as a sudden jolt. Which of these sources of stimulus is involved can influence the mode of counseling with clients who come for aid with mid-life identity problems.

Predictable stimuli are ones related to the normal life cycle, such as children's growing up and leaving home, the wife's going through menopause, or the husband's strength and energy gradually diminishing. Unpredictable stimuli can be such events as the death of a spouse, the dissolution of a marriage, the loss of a job, the onset of a serious disease, or the occasion of a crippling injury.

Predictable changes are ones which many of the mid-life individual's age-peers are experiencing, so that frequent samples of how people react to such changes are readily observed. In addition, magazine articles and television programs that focus on problems of adjustment at different stages of life often provide information about predictable events that is of use to the interested middle-aged adult. The fact that most of these events come on gradually and are universal allows a person not only to prepare for them but also to gain some measure of comfort in knowing that they are *normal* for their age stage. As a consequence, counseling individuals who are entering the early phases of predictable changes allows more time for gradually inducing the alterations in their attitudes and behavior that are needed for coping with this new reality.

In contrast, unpredictable changes usually confront clients with the shock of sudden emergency, as the unexpected event finds them ill-equipped to cope with what has occurred. Consequently, unpredictable incidents are more likely to call for counseling that includes interventions suited to crisis situations—a telephone hot-line, the immediate availability of counseling, or the short-term administration of tranquilizers.

However, whether the events are expected or unexpected, the task of effecting a shift in personal-identity in response to the events is likely to require an extended series of counseling sessions because people's self-perceptions by the time of middle age are usually firmly set and resistant to change.

MID-LIFE EVENTS AND CLIENTS' PROBLEMS

The four types of mid-life counseling cases inspected in some detail in the following pages concern weight control, bereavement at the death of a loved one, changes in reproductive capability (particularly the matter of women's menopause), and career decisions.

Weight Control

There is some confusion in the area of weight control caused by differences in what people mean by the words *overweight, fat*, and *obese*. In writing about such matters, Bennett and Gurin (1982) suggest that the term *fat* be used to identify people "who carry more adipose tissue on the body than the average person of their age, height, and skeletal structure. In this sense, *fat* is not a shameful condition ... [it may] of itself have little consequence for health, and there is no evidence that fat people consistently eat more than the lean" (Bennett & Gurin, 1982, pp. xiii-xiv). The authors use *overweight* to describe persons whose weight is greater than some explicit standard of desirable or ideal weight. The word *obese* is applied to those who are so fat that their health is threatened or impaired. Throughout the following discussion, the terms *fat, overweight*, and *obese* will be used with these meanings.

As implied by the description of anorexia nervosa in Chapter 6, worry over body weight is not limited to one stage of life. From late childhood into old age, people's weight—particularly greater weight—is a concern for which they often seek professional help. However, several conditions of the mid-life years make the issue of weight control especially prominent in middle age, thus warranting its special attention in the present chapter.

One condition is the more sedentary lifestyle that many middle-agers adopt. They tend to exercise less, yet continue to eat the same amount as before, so their weight increases as the body's demand for calories declines with the advancing decades. The combination of less exercise and more weight places extra strain on the cardiovascular system and the muscles, particularly when an emergency occurs that produces unusual physical and psychological stress. A cyclical relationship obtains between weight and exercise. The less the exercise, the more the weight. The greater the weight, the more difficult it is to generate the motivation to exercise. Avoiding exercise (such as failing to take a brisk walk each day or so) can contribute to a variety of mid-life physical disorders—weak bones (osteoporosis) in older women, the type of diabetes common in middle age, posture problems, and the accumulation of the type of cholesterol that blocks blood vessels.

Another condition that makes fatness a problem for the middle-aged is the effect of excess weight on people's self-concept. Since a sense of adequacy and attractiveness is usually linked at least partially to physical appearance, in middle age a variety of typical physical changes can threaten one's self-perception. Hair begins to thin and turn grey, and bald spots appear. The elasticity of the skin declines, so that jowls sag, bags develop under the eyes, and slack neck-folds or a double-chin appears. Although it is true that gaining weight serves to fill out some of the wrinkles and sags, the added weight itself is considered unattractive by popular social standards. Women pictured on television as models of attractiveness are usually slender, so that plump is not an ideal to be pursued. The model man is lean or muscular without being fat. People with protruding stomachs are laughed at, not admired. Therefore, much of the concern of those who come for weight-control counseling is over the discrepancy between how they want to look and how they think they do look. This means that the counseling process will involve attention to supporting or reconstructing the mid-life client's personal identity as it relates to weight and appearance.

TREATING PROBLEMS OF EXCESS WEIGHT

When someone asks a physician, nutritionist, or psychological counselor for help with a problem of fatness, it is important for the therapist to learn why the client considers his or her weight excessive.

Is the weight a health hazard? Does it limit the individual's activities, such as participation in sports? Does the person "feel fat and unattractive?" Do others—such as a husband or wife—complain about the weight?

It is also useful to learn what outcome the client is seeking. Usually the desired outcome is to lose weight. However, in some cases the goal is not to become leaner but, rather, to "accept the way I am without feeling ashamed." This means fitting the weight condition more comfortably into the client's self-concept, style of life, and social relationships. The individual may also come to the therapist with one of these two goals in mind but change during the counseling process, perhaps deciding on a combination of losing some weight but also accepting a "somewhat plump" appearance as being quite satisfactory.

A treatment program, in effect, should suit both the reasons why the client regards his or her weight as a problem and the outcomes which the client hopes to achieve. Goals and methods of treatment should also accommodate for the condition of the client's metabolic system and for his or her lifestyle. What will work for an individual whose immoderate eating and drinking habits are chiefly responsible for excessive weight will usually differ from what will work for a person whose metabolic system has produced weight gain on even a small intake of food. A malfunctioning thyroid gland requires medical attention, not simply willpower and a change of diet.

A great quantity of both scholarly and popular writing is available on weight control. An analysis of the literature generally favors behavioral techniques over other approaches for treating weight problems where medical disorders are not involved. Most behavioral programs include one or more of the following components: (1) self-monitoring of body weight and/or food intake, (2) changes in diet, (3) goal setting, (4) counseling that focuses on exercise, nutrition, and other health practices, (5) tangible consequences devised either by the counselor or client for abiding by (rewards) or deviating from (punishments) a planned program of nutrition and exercise, and (6) stimulus-control procedures.

A typical behavioral-treatment pattern as outlined by Gutsch and Daniels (1985, pp. 43-44) consists of such steps as:

(1) Setting up a self-monitoring program in which the client keeps a log of the food eaten daily (including the number of calories consumed) and of the client's weight as measured at the same time each week.

(2) Instituting an exercise plan that includes graded increments of energy requirements.
(3) Establishing stimulus-control measures. For example:
    (3.1) Separating eating from all other activities, such as viewing television or reading.
    (3.2) Making sure that high calorie foods are not available in the house.
    (3.3) Reducing food portions by using small plates and storing surplus food before eating.
    (3.4) Eating slowly, completely chewing and swallowing each bite before taking another bite; putting down eating utensils while chewing.
    (3.5) Avoiding eating food in an effort to keep from "wasting" it (just because it was purchased).

In Western societies during recent decades, the intense interest in reducing weight has spawned scores of diets and exercise plans, nearly all of them advertised as the universal solution to fatness. Each kind has been lauded by adherents who found it successful and criticized by those people disappointed with its outcome. Such varied results support the observation that the substantial differences among individuals in their physical constitutions, food preferences, self-discipline, work habits, recreational pursuits, and family-life patterns make it unreasonable to expect that a single kind of weight-control treatment will suit everyone. Thus, the process of counseling usually involves exploring multiple facets of a client's life in order to discover what combination of sympathetic listening, confronting reality, personal-history retrospection, behavioral programming, and the like will best suit the needs of that particular client. When one treatment program has not succeeded as hoped, counseling can involve a reevaluation of the individual's attitudes, goals, and life patterns to identify another approach that appears potentially more effective.

Bereavement and Acute Grief

Not everyone defines the words *bereavement, grief,* and *mourning* in the same way. So, to provide a common foundation for the discussion of such matters, I am adopting the following meanings: *Bereavement* is the fact of loss through death, and *bereavement reactions* are "any psychological, physiologic, or behavioral response" to bereavement. *Grief* is a psychological condition of "anxiety or mental anguish" that "follows or anticipates bereavement." And *mourning* is the social expression of grief, including rituals (Osterweis, Solomon, & Green, 1984, pp. 9-10; Pine, 1976, p. 106).

Acute grief can be occasioned by various events—the death of a loved one, divorce, a serious financial setback, personal injury, the loss of a pet, the destruction of one's home by fire, the loss of valued documents or mementos, and more. However, grief following a death is perhaps the most frequent and serious type for which people seek counseling aid, so the following discussion is limited to grief related to death. In the early 1980s, about 5% of the population each year faced the death of an immediate member of the family. A far greater number faced the death of a friend. Around 400,000 of the deaths were of children and youths under age 25, but the larger number were adults, particularly the elderly (Osterweis, Solomon, & Green, 1984, pp. 4, 17). Holmes and Rahe (1967) developed a scale for quantifying the relative stress imposed by different kinds of life incidents, and they concluded that the death of a spouse was the most severe distressing event during adulthood. Over the twentieth century, the age levels at which death most often occurs have changed. In 1900, 53% of the deaths were of children under age 15, while by 1970, over two-thirds of those dying were over 65 (Pine, 1976, p. 109).

Although grief caused by the death of a friend or relative can occur at any time in one's life, it is apparently faced most often by people in their middle adult years, since they are the ones who are most apt to lose parents, their own children, siblings, and close friends. For this reason, I have placed the issue of bereavement and grief in this chapter about mid-life problems.

CONCOMITANTS OF BEREAVEMENT

The extent of distress at the death of someone close varies markedly from one person to another. Acute forms of grief that may call for professional attention are usually shown by observable symptoms that follow a crisis. Lindemann (1944) identified five conditions typically displayed in such cases: (1) somatic distress, such as gastrointestinal disorders, (2) a preoccupation with the image of the deceased, (3) a pervading sense of guilt, (4) hostility, and (5) a disordered way of conducting one's life. Other common symptoms can include crying sessions, extended sorrow, anxiety and agitation, sleeplessness, lack of interest in things that would normally attract the person's attention, and loss of appetite (Osterweis, Solomon, & Green, 1984, p. 18). Parkes (1972) adds such indicators as deep sighing, obsessive concentration on the loss, and restless but aimless hyperactivity.

Although the death of a loved one may occur more often for the middle-aged, research suggests that grief is more intense and its consequences are more lasting for children, adolescents, and young adults than for older adults. All studies "document increases in alcohol consumption and smoking and greater use of tranquilizers or hypnotic medication among the bereaved.... Risk factors for poor outcome include poor previous physical and mental health, alcoholism and substance abuse, and the perceived lack of social supports. It is unclear whether sudden death or lingering illness produces more disturbing outcomes" (Osterweis, Solomon, & Green, 1984, p. 40).

ASSISTING THE BEREAVED

Because there is great variation among individuals in their response to death and in their reactions to types of aid or therapy, it is not possible to cite any one counseling approach likely to be effective with everyone. The best that survey data and clinical experience can offer is an array of techniques that have been effective in certain cases, along with a suggestion of the conditions under which one technique is likely to work better than another.

Consolation or counseling at times of bereavement is most often provided by members of the family, friends, a pastor or priest, a physician, or a funeral director. However, because of the increased mobility of present-day populations, cases of acute grief appear before counseling psychologists more often today than they did in the past. In present-day America, over a five-year period, one-quarter of the population moves to a different location, thereby limiting face-to-face communication among members of the extended family. "This places great demands on the nuclear family for ongoing emotional social support when a member of such a family dies, both because other family members may live far away and because bereaved persons who are new to a community lack strong links to other people or institutions that could assist them" (Osterweis, Solomon, & Green, 1984, p. 5). When grief is prolonged and profound or family and friends are not at hand, therapists can be called upon to offer aid. The service of a therapist may also be sought by family members or friends who are trying to help the bereaved individual but are unsure of the best way to go about it. As a consequence, a counselor's client may be either the bereaved person himself or herself or a friend who is seeking guidance on how best to fulfill the role of confidant and supporter to the bereaved.

Typical of counseling methods recommended in the literature on bereavement is that proposed by Raphael. To assess the psychological condition of the bereaved at the outset of the counseling encounter, Raphael (1983, pp. 362-367) suggests four questions to ask. The first is intended to show the bereaved that the counselor is a caring person, willing to talk about the death as a natural and appropriate area for discussion. "Can you tell me a little about the death? What happened? What happened that day?" The answers not only reveal the bereaved's version of the conditions of the death, but they also show the individual's capacity to talk about the event and they reflect the bereaved's emotional response—anger, helplessness, fear of vulnerability, denial, or avoidance.

The second question is designed to elicit a history of the lost relationship—expectations, hopes, fulfillment, disappointment, ambivalence, dependence, yearning, good times and bad times. "Can you tell me about him (her), about your relationship from the beginning?"

The third query centers on how the person has responded since the death, what use the bereaved sees in family or social-network support, how the individual is managing daily affairs, and what emotional or social blocks may stand in the way of a resolution of the grief. "What has been happening since the death? How have things been with you and your family and friends?"

The last question is intended to reveal evidence of prior crises or stressors and their possible influence on the individual's achieving a satisfactory recovery from the event. "Have you been through any other bad times like this recently or when you were young?"

On the basis of answers to these questions, the counselor plans interventions intended to facilitate resolving the bereavement. The method recommended by Raphael is labeled "short-term focal psychotherapy":

> with focus in this instance on the recent loss crisis and the particular parameters of risk. It is carried out over one to six or even eight sessions, usually in the bereaved's own home. Sessions are often one and a half to two hours in duration, since this time seems to fit with the bereaved's needs in the crisis period. . . . The goals of the intervention are generally to encourage the expression of grieving affects and promote the mourning process. Particular goals are defined for each individual as well and reflect his risk profile. Thus they may include the working through of

traumatic-stress-syndrome effects related to the circumstances of the death.... Or it may be that the angry sense of desertion with the death of a partner in a very dependent relationship may have to be dealt with. (Raphael, 1983, p. 368)

Counseling techniques are adjusted to the state of the bereaved at the particular moment. They include encouraging the expression of yearning for the lost person and of anger at the loss. But when the anger is displaced onto others, the counselor attempts to help the bereaved face the origin of the anger at the deceased. The counselor also fashions sympathetic and realistic responses to the client's expressions of sadness, relief, regret, and guilt.

Parkes and Weiss (1983), in their report of the Harvard Bereavement Study of widows and widowers, identified issues to which counselors should attend when providing help to the bereaved or to those who seek to aid the bereaved. The issues include: normal versus abnormal grief, counseling before and after bereavement, cases of unexpected death, ambivalent relationships, and matters of dependency.

Normal Versus Abnormal Grief

Grieving is the common—and thus "normal"—reaction to be-reavement by those most affected by the loss. During the period immediately following the loss, the distressed are unable to conduct their lives as they did before, and they need sympathetic care and protection. It is also "normal" for their grief gradually to abate, permitting them to reorganize their lives and "achieve a new and independent level of functioning. If, for any reason, this 'recovery' fails to take place, we might say the reaction is 'abnormal' ... [resulting in] long-lasting distortions of the individuals' abilities to function. Here it might be appropriate to invoke the concept of 'illness,' although it may not always be necessary or useful" (Parkes & Weiss, 1983, pp. 5-6). The assistance of a professional therapist is more crucial in cases of "abnormal" grief than in instances of "normal" grief that often can be managed adequately with the support of family and friends.

Counseling Before and After Bereavement

The loss of a loved one can be either expected or unexpected. Long-term cancer is a typical precursor of expected loss. In contrast, death from an auto accident or fatal heart attack are instances of unexpected loss. In cases of expected loss, the task of treating bereavement begins before the death of the ill person, then continues after the death. In cases of unexpected loss, the need for bereavement counseling obviously cannot be recognized until after the death has occurred, thereby making the counseling conditions somewhat different for the two situations.

Parkes and Weiss (1983, pp. 229-233) have offered the following observations on which physicians, psychiatric social workers, and counseling psychologists might base their approach to family members of patients who are suffering a terminal illness: When first informing the family of the patient's fatal condition, it is well to begin by learning what family members already understand about the patient's illness and its prognosis. Then, in view of what they believe and hope, the counselor can formulate an explanation of the case that accommodates for the family's misconceptions and fears rather than bluntly shocking them with news of the patient's likely fate.

> People absorb information most effectively when the information fits with their existing views. Information that requires radical reorientation and is, in addition, highly unpleasant, is apt to be distorted, suppressed, or exaggerated. It is therefore most important for those providing information to find out if they are being understood. What does the family make of what they have heard? ... Insofar as it is possible, patients and their families should share information rather than deal with the information in mutual isolation. Unfortunately, professionals sometimes encourage families to withhold information from patients, on the grounds that patients would otherwise become painfully anxious; at the same time, patients often withhold from their families their actual awareness of events. It may be that some families manage best with this kind of mutual pretense, but most families will do better if there is opportunity for mutual support based on open communication. (Parkes & Weiss, 1983, p. 232)

In cases of unexpected loss, the bereaved are in immediate need of support, of an opportunity to express their emotions and to talk through the changes that the loss will likely bring in their lives. Thus, a counselor, as a sympathetic listener, can first serve as a catalyst for catharsis while the bereaved ones release their fear, confusion, guilt, and anger at the unfair turn of fate which they have suffered. The traditional mourning rituals of a wake or a funeral may assist them in accepting the reality of the loss. The counselor may also be called upon to help the bereaved decide how to put immediate affairs in order. Subsequently, the counselor may aid family members in reordering their lives for the future, a process that can require a series of sessions in which the therapist provides information and guides clients in generating and assessing alternate plans for the months ahead.

Ambivalent Relationships

Studies of bereavement suggest that grief responses of people who had an unambiguous relationship with the deceased often differ from those of people whose relationship had been ambivalent—that is, had been a mixture of affection and resentment, attachment and dislike. An attitude of ambivalence appears to contribute to the avoidance or delay of grief, with the individual suffering combined feelings of relief, guilt, and a continuing need for attachment (however imperfect that attachment may have been) which is now going unfulfilled. Ambivalent individuals appear not to achieve the recovery from their distress as readily as those whose relationships were unambiguous. At least a portion of those who do not spontaneously express grief after the death can be aided by a counselor who encourages them to mourn and to pour forth the thoughts and feelings precipitated by the loss. Parkes and Weiss (1983, p. 243) speculate that by facilitating mourning, the counselor may help ambivalent clients to (1) face the reality of their loss, (2) begin to reassess their new status, (3) obtain from the counselor the emotional support no longer available from the lost attachment figure, and (4) "mitigate feelings of guilt and reduce self-punitive tendencies by combining the functions of confession and ordeal."

Severing a Dependency Relationship

An unexpected and untimely death is particularly distressing to those who depended heavily on the person who has died because the loss frightens the child, spouse, sibling, or parent who has always counted on the material and emotional support of the loved one who is now gone. The shock of being left alone can thus produce a debilitating sense of helplessness.

A counseling tack recommended by Parkes for such cases consists of a two-stage sequence pursued over a period of time. The first stage involves the therapist's serving as a sympathetic, wholehearted supporter. The client is not discouraged from becoming emotionally attached to the therapist. However, to avoid the danger of continuing dependency, the therapist makes clear that the support will be gradually removed as the client gains strength and skills to operate independently. In other words, an optimistic view of the future, when clients can manage affairs on their own, is held up as the goal. During this first stage, wholehearted support is provided by the counselor, who listens understandingly to the client's expressions of fear, loneliness, sadness, anger, and self-reproach, with these expressions of grief neither encouraged nor discouraged but simply accepted as normal. "The very act of giving unqualified attention to another person goes some way in convincing that person that he or she is worthy of the attention" (Parkes & Weiss, 1983, p. 249).

When trust in the counselor has been well established, the emphasis is gradually shifted from support to encouragement. In this second stage, the counselor proposes specific, small steps that the client can take toward independent action, steps involving tasks at which the client can succeed. The counselor expresses admiration and pleasure with the client's success at the tasks, so that the client is emboldened to accept increasingly more demanding responsibilities. "The therapist's confidence in the ability of the bereaved to grow and to begin to rebuild his or her life can be conveyed directly by exhortation and indirectly by a tacit assumption that the need for support is diminishing over time" (Parkes & Weiss, 1983, pp. 247-248).

Varieties of Aid to the Bereaved

One-to-one therapy is not the only form of counseling for helping the bereaved. Group therapy is also used extensively, particularly with members of a grieving family. Not only does the group setting provide an opportunity for the bereaved to witness others in the same situation, but it also enables them to gain a feeling of self-worth that can come with moving beyond their own grief into offering consolation and support to others. The group-therapy configuration also economizes on the therapist's time. The contact between counselor and client need not always be face-to-face. Periodic telephone conversations are frequently useful in counselors' offering support to grieving clients. Furthermore, bibliotherapy can help the bereaved gain consolation and guidance from the published experiences of other who have faced the death of a loved one.

The desirability of using of drugs to relieve the symptoms of grief is a matter of some controversy. Raphael (1983, p. 384) has noted that while the prescription of antidepressants is inappropriate for normal grief, it can be desirable for marked depression that is associated with bereavement.

Conclusion

Although the elaborate, extended displays of mourning observed in Western societies of the past have markedly diminished, grief is still the typical immediate reaction of people who have lost a relative or friend through death. In a state of bereavement, people commonly are distraught, depressed, and unable to manage daily affairs the way they did prior to the loss. During this period they profit from the sympathy, material support, and consolation of family, friends, and such professionals as counselors, pastors, and physicians. Most bereaved persons gradually come to accept the reality of the loss, conquer their sorrow, and shoulder the normal responsibilities of daily living. Counselors can aid in this process by providing information, instruction, and encouragement toward independence in problem solving. As a result, within a period of a few weeks or few months, most people will have overcome their grief. Some, however, continue to act unremittingly distraught, angry, guilty, helpless, or dependent. In these cases, long-term therapy is required.

Reproductive Changes—Menopause

The term *climacteric* or *change of life* identifies the marked decrease in reproductive capacity in women and men that culminates in the menopause in women. Whereas the word *menopause* originally designated the cessation of menstrual periods, it is now more commonly used to describe the years just before and after the end of menstrual activity, so that its meaning has become equated with that of *climacteric*. The average time for the end of menstruation is around age 50 in industrial societies, but the event can appear as early as the late 30s or as late as the middle or late 50s (Notman, 1980, p. 96).

In modern times preparations of the hormone *estrogen* have been introduced as a treatment for the drop in the normal production of that hormone that occurs over the post-menopausal years.

> To some extent this has resulted in neglect of other factors which may be more relevant, and the "change" has become the scapegoat for a multitude of complaints . . . attributed to the menopause. This approach has great attractions, since attitudes toward "psychological" symptoms and "psychological" treatment still tend to be negative, while "menopausal" symptoms and "hormone" treatment are very much more acceptable. (Ballinger, 1981, p. 279)

Until the past two or three decades, a widespread conviction in the psychiatric community was that the climacteric, particularly in women, often precipitated a form of psychotic depression referred to as *involutional melancholia*. Thus, members of both the medical profession and the general public came to expect some degree of depression and disturbed behavior to accompany the "change of life." As a consequence, many women anticipated menopause with great apprehension. However, more recent investigations have suggested that "there is no evidence of any increase in affective disorder or mental hospital admissions in general at the time of the menopause, other than as part of the gradual increase seen with increasing age in both sexes" (Ballinger, 1981, p. 283). This does not mean that the notion of both physical and psychological problems' occurring during the climacteric period was simply an illusion. Rather, it means that the types, sources, and treatment of problems at this stage of life are more complex than a chemical-change interpretation of menopause would imply.

CORRELATES OF MENOPAUSE

A set of characteristics traditionally associated with "the change of life" comprise what has been called *the menopause syndrome*. Physical conditions within the syndrome include hot flushes, night sweats, and accelerated loss of calcium from the bones (osteoporosis). Some women also report painful coitus (dyspareunia) resulting from the vagina becoming shorter and narrower, accompanied by a decline in the vagina's ability to lubricate and expand. All of these symptoms appear related to reduced activity of the ovaries and to diminishing estrogen levels. In other words, the evidence suggests that such conditions are directly caused by alterations in body chemistry that occur with the cessation of menstruation.

A psychophysical effect usually included in the syndrome is insomnia. Although complaints of sleep disorders commonly increase with age, the rather sharp rise in sleep disturbance reported by women around age 50 is not reported by men. Studies of the administration of estrogen to women suffering from sleeplessness "support the view that insomnia may be related to hormonal changes at the time of the menopause. The use of estrogen preparation rather than cerebral depressants as hypnotics at this time is clearly worthy of further investigation" (Ballinger, 1981, p. 289).

A psychological symptom often attributed to menopausal change is a reduction in libido—that is, a decrease in sexual desire and enjoyment. However, Belsky (1984), in summarizing Masters' and Johnson's research on sexual behavior over the life span, concluded that there are:

> only minor changes in responses most clearly indicative of female sexual performance and pleasure. For example, the clitoral response to sexual stimulation was virtually unchanged. . . . Also, the older women were just as capable of orgasms as the younger group. On the average, though, they did have fewer orgasmic contractions and less prolonged orgasms than the young. . . . The investigators concluded with a brief but important statement: "There is no time limit drawn by advancing years to female sexuality." (p. 168)

Duke University researchers have identified a continuity of sexual interest and pleasure over the decades. Respondents who reported being highly sexually involved when young continued to report a similar level of involvement during middle age (Pfeiffer, Verwoerdt, & Davis, 1972).

(In passing, it may be noted that significant differences have been observed between women and men in their sexual capabilities during the climacteric. Compared with younger men, most older males take longer to achieve an erection, their erections never reach the maximum levels of their younger counterparts, and their erections are slower to rebound after a partial loss. However, older men can generally maintain an erection longer without ejaculating [Belsky, 1984, p. 168]).

Several other conditions for which menopause was traditionally blamed—weight gain, depression, crying spells, feelings of inadequacy—have subsequently been judged no more frequent among menopausal women than among ones of the same age and general health status who are not going through menopause (Nathanson & Lorenz, 1982). While menopause may be interpreted by a woman as the loss of a crucial element of her female identity, it is this interpretation rather than the biochemical change itself that appears to cause the undesired psychological symptoms often attributed to the climacteric.

A final issue associated with women's loss of reproductive capacity is the question of what influence hysterectomy has on female sexual behavior and mental health. In recent years, hysterectomy has become the most frequent form of major surgery performed in the United States. The operation consists in the removal of at least the woman's uterus and cervix and commonly the ovaries and fallopian tubes as well, resulting in menopause for women who had still been menstruating. The rapidly rising number of hysterectomies has occasioned a great amount of controversy about whether so many are really warranted. Whereas the danger of physical complications is rather minor, critics propose that psychological damage far too frequently results from the event. Studies suggest that the psychological outcomes of hysterectomy, like those of natural menopause, may be in large part due to the expectations that women hold for the event. After Belsky (1984) reviewed the limited amount of evidence on this issue, she observed that, as with normal menopause, "replacement estrogen administration after the surgery had no effect on sexuality. In contrast, how a woman had felt about the procedure clearly did. Women who said they had felt before the operation that it would alter their sexuality were those who were most likely to experience actual declines. . . . [Thus,] it does seem that if a woman expects a negative outcome from the procedure, then she is likely to get that result" (p. 172).

COUNSELING DURING THE CLIMACTERIC

As the foregoing review of typical characteristics of menopause suggests, the treatment of women clients during this time of life can properly consist of both medical and psychological approaches. The most common medical treatment is the administration of estrogen in order to readjust the hormonal imbalance that frequently occurs with the cessation of menses in women. (No such hormonal treatment is called for during the gradual diminution of sexual potency in men.) The surgical procedure of removing women's reproductive organs is also common, although, as noted above, the appropriateness of this procedure in all the cases in which it has been performed in recent times is debatable.

Whereas a physician's providing estrogen can often reduce such physical symptoms as hot flashes, night sweats, and perhaps insomnia, such symptoms as weight gain and feelings of worthlessness and sexual inadequacy call for psychotherapeutic approaches. Whether or not people are actually in the climacteric period, the mid-life years confront them with the facts of advancing age. Menopause simply serves as a dramatic signal that a major segment of life has passed. As noted earlier, middle age means changes in physical appearance and a decline in strength, agility, and endurance. Psychologically, mid-life can bring a diminishing ability to grasp new ideas and a decrease in certain forms of memory. Sexually, it means decreased attractiveness and, perhaps, reduced sexual drive. Vocationally, it means that dreams of occupational advancement of earlier years may now never be realized. As for family life, children have grown and left home. Thus, counseling during the climacteric is intended to help clients cope with these typical changes of mid-life. Psychotherapy, therefore, consists of the counselor's (1) examining the client's complaints and symptoms, (2) estimating the kinds of changes in the client's perceptions of self and others—as well as in the client's goals, habits, activities, and social setting—that might result in a more satisfying life, and (3) applying a therapeutic approach that seems best suited to effecting these changes. What that approach will be depends on both the nature of the client's symptoms and the counselor's psychotherapeutic preferences (such as a behavioral versus a psychoanalytic approach or client-centered counseling versus rational-emotive therapy).

Career Decisions

Recent decades have witnessed an increase in the number of people who change careers in mid-life. One cause of the increase is a growing number of women who, after dedicating their early adult years to child rearing, now have no children at home and thus feel free to join the labor force. Another cause is the accelerating pace of technological innovation in the job market. When an industry changes from skilled or unskilled hand-labor to computers and robots, middle-aged employees are displaced from their traditional jobs, and they must either equip themselves for other occupations or move to locations where the older manufacturing techniques are still in use. Mid-life job changes are also common for men and women in the armed forces who have completed 20 or 30 years of military service and now, in their forties or fifties, draw retirement income but also wish to start a second career. In addition, there are people who simply tire of what they have been doing in the past, or else their mid-life physical or psychological condition renders them poorly suited to their old job, so they face the need to find a more appropriate occupation.

The process of vocational counseling for the middle-aged is much the same as that described in Chapter 7 for young adults, except that most mid-life clients already have had some employment experience, their physical endurance and ability to acquire new skills may have declined, and their vocational preferences may be more precise than those of young adults.

The types of guidance provided to adults who are making mid-life career changes can include such planning schemes as the step-by-step process recommended by Rose (quoted by Goldschmidt, 1988, p. 20). First, job hunters are asked to list all paid and unpaid work experience that they have had to date, including any part-time work, such as during college. In the list, they mark those experiences that were most enjoyable, indicating which aspects of each job were most satisfying. Second, clients are advised to talk with friends and acquaintances for ideas about what kinds of jobs that would have features similar to those in their list, especially jobs with the characteristics found to be most satisfying in the past. Third, they collect information about new, additional fields of interest through consulting a library of publications on careers (the career-guidance division of the local high school, the public library, or an employment bureau). Fourth, if the desired job is of a type entirely new to them, they can profit from gaining direct experience in that type of employment, perhaps by doing volunteer work for an organization (helping with publicity for a philanthropic organization as preparation for a career in public relations), by taking up a hobby (making stuffed toys as preparation for a job in toy design), or by enrolling for training (taking courses in electronics as preparation for work in television or computer repair). Fifth, clients begin job interviews, well prepared ahead of time with the types of answers that they intend to give during the interviews. In addition, Rose suggests to mid-life clients, "because you have no track record in the field, employers often judge career changers' capabilities by the quality and content of questions they ask" (p. 20).

CONCLUSION

In this chapter, the middle years have been pictured as a period of life in which people can be highly productive in their occupations, although their ability to adjust to new situations readily is likely waning. Advancing through middle age usually brings a gradual decline in physical agility, strength, and stamina, so the mid-life adult needs to adjust physical activities to the realities of this decline or else suffer a growing incidence of muscle aches, strained ligaments, and heart attacks. As their former youthful physical appearance fades, they may try to recapture their looks by exercise, diet, and cosmetic repair. If they have children, their problems in child rearing typically require coping with adolescents and young adults who are seeking independence yet are still dependent on parents for emotional and financial support. A mid-life married couple's relationship may have changed over the past two or three decades in ways that render them less compatible; and, as they foresee that the active years left in their life span are limited, they may reevaluate their commitment to their marriage partner. Furthermore, tragedies in their lives, such as the death of loved ones, failing health, or the loss of a job, can require marked adjustments in their customary style of life. To cope with any of these events, mid-life adults may seek professional counseling.

9

The Final Decades: Age 60 and Beyond

At the outset, it should be recognized that using age 60 as the point identifying the advent of old age is rather arbitrary, since there is no obvious break between the mid-life years and the time that people qualify as elderly. The task of determining when old age begins is confounded both by differences in individual people's growth patterns and by successive phases of aging during the final decades of life. Not only may individuals who are the same chronological age display different degrees of decline, but the elderly as a whole can also be categorized into several subgroups. For example, Botwinick (1984) has proposed four phases of old age representing different degrees of health, ability, and the survival ratio of women to men—the young-old (55-64), middle-old (65-74), old-old (75-84), and very old (85 and over). In regard to gender differences, during the past decade, there were slightly more males than females at all ages under 25, but at all ages past 25, the proportion of women was progressively higher. By age 60, there were 115 women to 100 men; by age 75, more than 150 women to 100 men; and by age 85, over two women for each man. In the late 1970s, life expectancy for men in the United States had reached 72 years, while, for women, it was five years longer. This increasing ability of people to survive to advanced age portends an expanding future of older people's needing counseling aid, as the numbers beyond age 65 are expected to double over the next four decades (Siegel, 1980).

The types of aged clients that counselors meet include ones who:

—Despair of the future because they recognize that they face certain death, their lifelong friends are either gone or suffer poor health, and they see no purpose to their own lives. They may consider doing away with themselves, since they see nothing to live for.

—Have retired—or been forcibly retired—from an occupation, and they lack the inner resources, interest, and initiative to find a meaningful avocation to pursue.

—Are in poor health. Their mobility is diminished, their reaction time is reduced, and they are frequently in pain. Thus, they dwell on their infirmities, complain about their lot in life, and become a tiresome burden on others, such as their children and grandchildren.

—Lose their sexual potency, a condition that may estrange them from a life partner who has maintained interest in sexual activity. Some come to feel that sexual activity is a nuisance rather than a pleasure, and they are thus irritated with their partner if the partner attempts overtures.

—Worry about money as economic inflation increases and their own limited retirement income diminishes in value. In contrast to the economic condition of younger adults, the elderly rarely have the ability to generate new income to cover rising costs.

—Are distressed over their diminishing mental abilities. They forget where they have put things, are unable to calculate their income tax or to keep their checkbook balanced, become confused about appointments that they are to keep, and repeat over and over the same stories or comments that they uttered the day before or last week.

—Are lonely and feel rejected. Without an occupation, without nearby friends and relatives, without the energy or initiative to pursue a hobby, without the strength or persistence to concentrate on reading or an avocation—they sit or lie around depressed as the days drag by.

In keeping with the pattern of previous chapters, the following analysis is divided into two major sections. The first offers general normative information that may help counselors to understand characteristics of old people as a group. The second section directs attention at two types of older clients frequently met in counseling practice: (1) those who are depressed, lonely, and lack incentive to live and (2) those whose deteriorating abilities render them unfit to manage their affairs.

GENERAL CHARACTERISTICS OF THE ELDERLY

The topics reviewed in the following pages include the physical and mental abilities of the aged, their self-perceptions, ways that other people's perceptions may influence an elderly person's well-being, characteristics of the elderly's living conditions, and coping strategies common among older adults.

The Physical Condition of the Aged

Perhaps the most obvious characteristics of advanced age is a decline in physical appearance, strength, stamina, and agility. One of the prominent fears among the elderly centers on this decline. The aged are apprehensive that their debilities will increase, thus reducing their self-control and independence, causing them frequent pain, diminishing their sphere of activity, and making them a burden on friends and family. Indeed, there is good reason for this fear, since the human machine, even under the most favorable circumstances, eventually breaks down. Despite the advances in medical science that have raised the average life expectancy, the genetics of human growth place limits on how long the human mechanism can last. Scientists continue to debate the question of what people's most ultimate age might be, possibly 110 or 120 years, or perhaps a bit longer. But, sooner or later, aged bodies give out and death occurs.

Although the immediate cause of death in the elderly is usually listed as heart failure, cancer, or the like, the more basic cause is the failure of the immune system to protect the individual as it did in earlier years. In old age, the body's protective equipment deteriorates, leaving the elderly particularly vulnerable to bacteria and viruses. Furthermore, the natural biological mechanisms for repairing damaged parts—a broken hip, malfunctioning kidneys, torn muscles—also degenerate, so that recovery from ailments becomes slowed or impossible. The body's system for controlling cellular growth can also go awry. Cancer, the number two killer of the aged in modern industrial societies, is the prime example of cell-control malfunction. A second example is prostate disorder in men. The prostate gland, located at the root of the penis in the male, produces fluid to convey spermatozoa out through the penis during sexual intercourse. Because the tube for carrying urine from the bladder to the penis also passes through the prostate, that gland shuts off the possible flow of urine from the bladder during intercourse. In mid-life and later, prostate cells tend to increase excessively, so that the channel for passing urine is gradually squeezed closed. If the urinary tract becomes completely blocked, the body is poisoned by its liquid wastes, and death can ensue. The typical treatment for uncontrolled prostate growth is an operation to expand the passage or to remove the gland entirely. Annually, an estimated 350,000 to 375,000 American men undergo prostate surgery. By age 80 or so, nearly all men experience some degree of prostate difficulty.

A host of physical ailments bring pain and interfere with the activities that the elderly wish to pursue. Visual acuity diminishes as the crystalline lens in the eye loses its elasticity, as cataracts cloud the pathway for light to enter the eye, and as the valve system for maintaining balanced pressure within the eyeball fails to operate properly, producing glaucoma (increased pressure that shuts off blood nutrients to the nerves in the retina) that can result in both fierce headaches and blindness. Auditory acuity also diminishes as infections from the throat may damage the middle or inner ear, and as the sensitivity of the ear drum and the delicate bones that convey sound to the ear's receptor nerves deteriorates. The segments of cartilage that, in earlier years, served as shock absorbers between the bones of the spine become depressed, reducing the flexibility of the spine so that back pains become more common. Joints of the limbs suffer changes that bring the pain of arthritis and bursitis. The proportion of muscle to other body tissues diminishes, so that the aged person's strength declines.

Such disorders cause the elderly to be frequent visitors to the physician's office and the hospital. Data on the number of patients on short-term stays in nongovernment hospitals in the United States in 1986 indicate that 31% of those over age 65 were treated for heart disease or cerebrovascular (blood circulation in the brain) conditions, 12% for digestive problems, 11% for diseases of the respiratory system, 10% for cancerous conditions (malignant neoplasms), 8% for injury or poisoning, and smaller percentages for disturbances of the urinary, skeletal, sensory, and metabolic systems (Public Health Service, 1987:6).

Consider next the frequency of fatal physical disorders that end the lives of the aged. Table 9.1 displays the seven most common causes of death among U.S. Americans over age 65 in the latter 1970s.

As these figures indicate, the greatest number of deaths are caused by the failure of the blood-supply system to provide nutrients to the brain and other body organs. In effect, heart disease, cerebrovascular disease, and arteriosclerosis (hardening of blood vessels) account for over half the deaths of people beyond age 65. Thus, adopting habits in mid-life and thereafter which help sustain the health of the cardiovascular system may, for a significant number of the aged, prolong life and enhance the maintenance of both mental and physical abili-

Table 9.1 Leading Causes of Death for Ages 65 and Over

Cause of Death by Rank	65 to 74 Years	75 to 84 Years	85 Years and Over
	Percent Death Rate		
Diseases of the heart	41	44	48
Malignant neoplasms (such as cancer)	25	17	9
Cerebrovascular diseases (such as strokes)	9	14	17
Influenza and pneumonia	2	4	6
Arteriosclerosis	1	2	5
Diabetes mellitus	2	2	1
Accidents	2	2	2

SOURCE: Data adapted from Botwinick, 1984, p. 45.

ties. Progress toward this goal can be fostered by attention to such practices as avoiding excess body weight, engaging in moderate exercise, maintaining a balance of protein and carbohydrates in the diet, reducing the intake of saturated fats, taking vitamin and mineral supplements, avoiding the use of tobacco, and limiting alcohol consumption.

As information about diet and exercise illustrate, the physical decline of the elderly is effected not only by the individual's genetic time table but also by present and past lifestyles—smoking a pipe, eating quantities of chocolates, drinking alcohol, avoiding physical exercise, staying up late at night to watch television, and the like. Conventional wisdom would suggest that altering these habits might well extend the life span, even though the task of getting people to change such patterns in late life is usually quite difficult. However, counselors often must decide how much effort, if any, they should spend trying to get aged clients to change habits that seem to decrease physical well-being and longevity. Old folks await two inevitable conditions—decline in abilities and death. By the time they reach old age, people usually recognize that their earlier dreams of future accomplishment and pleasure are no longer tenable. When they pass age 70, 80, or 90, their few remaining pleasures may rest in habits that do not promote health and long life. Thus, in seeking to help the aged, counselors need to weigh the value of slightly pro- longing life against the pleasures of "bad habits" that the aged cling to. In some cases at least, the decision may be to encourage an old person to continue indulging these pleasures without feeling guilty. In other cases, the decision may be to encourage the elderly to alter such habits, since doing so could substantially enhance their well-being in the years ahead.

Mental Characteristics of Old Age

There is an extensive body of normative evidence about the sorts of decline found in the mental abilities of the aged as a group. It is clear, however, that there are also substantial differences among elderly people of the same age in how well they have maintained their earlier intellectual and psychomotor skills. Such information can influence the counselor both in understanding clients' potential self-perceptions and in selecting treatment approaches. In regard to self-perceptions, the elderly are often distressed and disgusted with themselves as they recognize that their intellectual agility and their memory for details, which served them so well in earlier times, are now slipping away. In regard to selecting a treatment approach, the counselor's assessment of the current state of elderly clients' intellectual abilities can affect the therapist's estimate of how much responsibility clients can assume for solving their own problems and how much responsibility other people must assume for them.

Patterns of change in cognitive skills with advancing age have been traced through experiments on reasoning and decision making, memory, spatial abilities, perceptual-motor and cognitive speed, and sensory acuity. In each of these realms, the elderly generally do less well than younger adults. It is also apparent that, in all of the realms, as the complexity of tasks increases, the performance of the aged declines (Salthouse, 1982, pp. 200-201). For counselors, one implication of these results is that the elderly cannot be expected to engage successfully in as complex vocational, avocational, and daily-living problem solving as they did in earlier years. The aged will manage their affairs more adequately if complex situations are broken down into simpler subtasks.

Some specific types of skills studied in laboratory experiments are those involving creativity (finding novel solutions to problems), flexibility (willingness to change the approach to a problem or see new implications as additional elements are added to the problem situation), organizational skills (grouping the factors in a situation in a manner that promotes an efficient solution to a problem), ability to derive logical deductions, ability to discriminate relevant from irrelevant information, and skill in abstracting information from situations. In laboratory tests of all these traits, younger adults have surpassed older adults, with the decrement in performance being greatest after age 70. The ability to comprehend new information and explanations also suffers loss with the advancing years (Salthouse, 1982).

When perceptual-motor abilities (as measured by identifying routes through a maze, recognizing designs, performing finger-dexterity tasks, and the like) are compared with more distinctly cognitive abilities (verbal analogies, logical deduction, and others), the decline in the perceptual-motor skills comes earlier than does the decline in mental tasks (Belsky, 1984, p. 124).

Studies of memory suggest that elderly people are deficient both in ability to encode new information for purposes of storing it and in ability to retrieve what has been stored (Belsky, 1984, p. 148). Thus, to help the aged counteract this trend, counselors can offer them training in associating items to be remembered with objects in their environment or with rhymes, and clients can be encouraged to spend more time reviewing what they have learned than would have been necessary during earlier periods of their lives. Furthermore, when the elderly are asked to recall information, giving them extra time to answer will often result in success, since the problem is that their recall time has been slowed, not that the information has been irretrievably lost.

An important caution issued by researchers in this field is that the foregoing conclusions have been drawn chiefly from laboratory experiments utilizing the sorts of verbal analogies, puzzles, and logic problems found on mental tests. Far fewer studies have been conducted in real-life situations, so that the exact relationship is not clear between those mental abilities exhibited in laboratory tests and people's skill at managing daily-life problems. As noted in Chapter 8, a substantial amount of experience that an aging adult has had in a given field of endeavor can often compensate for a decline in the ability to adapt to novel situations. Therefore, in counseling the elderly, a therapist can recognize that older people's skills in managing their problems will often depend on how familiar they have been in the past with similar problems rather than on their intellectual creativity, cognitive flexibility, storage of new information, or rapid recall of names, places, and ways of performing a relatively new task.

In addition to tracing the course of cognitive change in the aged, researchers have studied correlates of mental health in older adults, with *mental health* defined in terms of people's self-reported well-being and their observed successful aging. The chief purpose of such studies has been to identify conditions in aged people's lives that may contribute to poor mental health, so that altering the conditions might enhance their life satisfaction and adjustment. In a summary of investigations of such correlates, Gerson, Jarjoura, and McCord (1987, pp. 368-370) concluded that regardless of how mental health is measured (self-report, observer's rating scale, interview), people with better mental health tend to be in better physical health, have higher education, are able to engage in more daily-living activities, and have more adequate social and economic resources than do people with poorer mental health. Married men showed better mental health than those who were not married, and social resources were strongly associated with mental health for women, but less so for men. Although such correlational studies do not demonstrate how much, if at all, the related variables help to cause better mental health, the results do suggest to the counselor that efforts to improve a client's status on any of the variables might serve as a positive step toward improving the counselee's mental well-being.

Self-Perceptions and Others' Perceptions of the Elderly

An important interaction takes place between the way others view the aged and the way the aged view themselves. Oftentimes, others' perceptions—either openly expressed or implied—help to determine the elderly person's self-concept and resultant behavior. For counselors, there are at least three implications that derive from the nature of popular stereotypes of the elderly. First, the general public's stereotypical notions can influence the way in which the public treats old people. Second, if the elderly themselves accept popular stereotypes as valid, they may behave in ways that are not in their own best interests. Third, the approaches that counselors adopt with the aged can be affected by how counselors interpret the public's perceptions. In the following paragraphs, we first inspect popular notions about the nature of old age before considering in more detail the implications for counseling.

The many studies conducted of others' conceptions of the aged have taken one of two main forms. They have focused on either (1) beliefs about the elderly in general (old people in the abstract), as gathered by means of questionnaire and interview surveys, or (2) beliefs about specific elderly people, as found in respondents' reactions to personality descriptions of individuals. The results of most surveys have pictured the elderly in a negative light—as unattractive in appearance and manner, feeble, forgetful, lacking good judgment, boring, and less than competent in occupations. Young people more often than older ones have expressed such negative views. But negative stereotypes of the abstract *old person* are often shared as well by the elderly themselves, even when they are personally acquainted with numbers of their peers who do not fit those stereotypes (Botwinick, 1984, pp. 17-37). In contrast, studies of belief about specific elderly people described in biographical sketches more often indicate that conceptions of the aged are not so stereotypical when individual old people are being judged. Elements other than age sometimes influence people's appraisals of individuals described in personality sketches—such elements as occupation, socioeconomic status, and past accomplishments. However, negative stereotypes were still found in a study of college students' comparisons of specific younger, middle-aged, and older adults as job applicants. The majority of students in three separate universities proposed that older applicants would be inferior to younger ones in health, energy, competence, intelligence, attractiveness, memory, social involvement, and reliability (Levin, 1988).

The significance of the interaction between others' views of the aged and the behavior of old people has been emphasized in recent years in investigations of the relationship between aging and one's sense of control (Baltes & Baltes, 1986). In one version of this relationship, the ecology of the individual's physical and social setting is seen as contributing significantly to the elderly person's sense of well-being, selection of activities, and longevity. This is not to say that biological changes are unimportant in determining the condition of the aged. However, within the limits that genetics and biological factors establish for old age, there is a wide range of responses that the elderly can make to their condition, and the way in which others treat old people is important in fashioning which of these responses will be adopted. Recent theory has focused particularly on two questions relating to who the elderly think influence their fate: (1) "Who is responsible for causing the person's problems?" (the issue of blame) and (2) "Who is responsible for solving the problems?" (the issue of control) (Karuza, Rabinowitz, & Zevon, 1986, p. 374). Proponents of such theory argue that much of the physical and psychological deterioration associated with advanced age is due to reduced personal control that comes with being old. Also, the kinds of help offered to the aged (including the kinds of counseling approaches) reflect the helpers' particular perceptions of aging, with the nature of these perceptions either enhancing or diminishing the elderly individual's sense of control.

To illustrate the importance of helpers' perceptions, Brickman et al. (1982) analyzed four models of helping and coping. The four alternatives were distinguished in terms of how they attributed the blame for causing problems and the responsibility for solving them. First is the *moral model*, which proposes that old people are responsible both for causing their problems and for finding solutions. The elderly are seen by others and by themselves as being lazy, capable of providing solutions but not sufficiently motivated to get the job done. The kind of outside help needed is the urging and encouragement of others to build the individuals' confidence in their ability to manage their own affairs. Popular self-help programs, such as EST, are founded on these assumptions.

Second is the *enlightenment model*, which blames people for causing their own difficulties but does not expect them to find solutions. The outside help that they need consists of:

> "enlightening" individuals about the true nature of their problem and the difficult course of action that will be needed to deal with it. Individuals see themselves or are seen by others as guilty, or at least responsible by their past behavior, for their current suffering or misfortune. It is their impulses—to drink, become self-destructive, feel sorry for themselves—that are out of their control, impulses that can be reined in with the help of others. Helpers are sympathetic individuals who know what the individual is suffering yet are willing to give the individual necessary guidance, emotional support, and perhaps even discipline. (Karuza, Rabinowitz, & Zevon, 1986, p. 379)

Halfway houses and support programs for released prison inmates or former drug and alcohol addicts often reflect the enlightenment model in their practices.

Third is the *compensatory model*. People are not blamed for causing their difficulties, but they are held responsible for finding solutions. Such individuals are considered by others to be victims of deprivation, maltreatment, or misfortune. The help that they are offered is comprised of services that compensate for their past ill fate or that solve their problem—advice, tutoring, special training programs, supplies and equipment (books, a car, tools, computers), rehabilitation therapy.

The fourth variety is the *medical model*, which pictures individuals as neither the cause of their problems nor the source of the solutions. Such people are viewed by others, as well as by themselves, as sick, helplessly handicapped, inept, or powerless. They are the passive recipients of medical and psychological treatment administered by experts. The control of their lives is completely in the hands of others.

The task of the counselor, in respect to the models, is to estimate which of them most accurately matches the reality of a given client's life and then to adopt the helping approach that best fits this reality. Applying the wrong model either can fail to enhance the elderly person's control or it can heap responsibilities on the individual which he or she is ill equipped to bear. For example, studies of learned helplessness have suggested that applying the medical model to clients whose life conditions better match a moral or enlightenment model can serve to turn a potentially independent individual into one who accepts helplessness as a proper state of existence (Abramson, Seligman, & Teasdale, 1978). On the other hand, exhorting the elderly to "forget the self-pity and join in the activities," when the client actually suffers organic disorders, serves only to increase the client's misery and feelings of guilt, and it can hasten the end of life.

Elderly People's Living Conditions and Personal Relations

Living arrangements are important for older adults' personal/social adjustment, since the arrangements influence their sense of control, of emotional and material support, and of the availability of help when it is needed. Demographic data can aid counselors in estimating the way in which living conditions may be affecting the lives of elderly clients whom they encounter. The following examples illustrate such information.

By the mid-1980s, people age 65 and over comprised about 12% (around 28 million people) of the U.S. population of 237 million. Among those over 65, an estimated 94% lived in the community— that is, they lived outside of nursing homes or other institutions. A census study focusing on the problems of elderly people living alone showed that of the 26.3 million older adults living in the community, nearly one-third (8 million, or 31%) lived alone, while just over two-thirds lived with others. Those living alone were slightly older (75.2 years) than the ones living with others (73.4 years). Eighty percent of the ones living with others were women. Although past research has suggested that the elderly who live alone are at high risk of need for long-term care and institutionalization, many of those in the survey were not disabled, in poor health, or lacking in medical attention or companionship. Most had family members nearby, with whom they enjoyed frequent contact, particularly by telephone. Only 11% lived in retirement communities. The majority (62%) had lived in the same residence for more than 10 years. Only one-quarter had moved to their present location within the past five years (Kovar, 1986).

The potential for feeling isolated and lonely increases for the aged who live by themselves and have no children. Of those surveyed in the mid-1980s, over one-quarter (29%) had no children, but most of the remaining 71% had frequent contact with one or more of their children. Only 11% of the 8 million who lived alone had neither a living child nor a sibling. Within the two weeks prior to the interviewers' survey, 73% of the elderly had gotten together with relatives, 84% had talked with relatives on the telephone, and only 12% had done neither (Kovar, 1986).

> Although the people in this study who were living alone were no different from those living with others in the frequency of their use of health services or the number of days they had spent in bed during the year despite their being older, their perception of their health, whether measured on a scale of excellent to poor or by limitation of activity, was better . . . many of these older people who were living alone may *not* be at unusually high risk of death. They may not even be at unusually high risk of institutionalization. They had frequent contact with family and neighbors. They had lived in the same place for many years. Those who had children lived near them and saw them frequently. Almost all had telephones and used them to stay in touch with family and neighbors. (Kovar, 1986, p. 5)

In recent years, researchers have focused increased attention on older adults' social networks and social support. The term *social network*, as used here, refers to the numbers and types of people with whom the older adult interacts, as well as the kinds of relationships among these people. The phrase *social support* is defined as the degree to which an older adult's essential social needs are gratified through interaction with members of that individual's social network. Social support can include expressions of emotional concern, instrumental aid (goods and services), information, and appraisals of the elderly person's situation. Social support can be either formal (social-service agencies, nursing-home care, mental-health clinics, hospitals) or informal (family, friends, neighbors, companions in recreational settings, fellow employees).

An understanding of social-support systems in the aged can assist counselors in proposing social-network changes that may enhance the mental and physical health of elderly clients. Although the operation of networks among older adults is far from completely understood, recent studies have identified several conditions that appear to contribute significantly to the well-being of the elderly. Therapists can seek to arrange such conditions in their efforts to improve aged clients' welfare. For example, Revicki and Mitchell (1986), in a study of 210 people in a predominantly rural area of the Southeastern U.S., discovered that the telephone represented "an independent and distinct dimension of social support.... Social contacts using the telephone were associated with greater life satisfaction, self-esteem, and reduced mental health problems. Individuals providing services to the elderly may assist by maintaining telephone contact and encouraging this kind of contact among the otherwise isolated elderly" (p. 245).

An investigation of 394 noninstitutionalized elderly in the Midwest revealed that those older adults who had no nearby family had used hospital emergency rooms 7 to 30 times more often than elderly persons with family in the area. The researchers concluded that elderly people without family support often make inappropriate use of emergency rooms as a "lay referral system" rather than for true emergencies. "This ... suggests that even relatively healthy elderly persons without family networks (as well as the frail elderly) ought to be included in community-based, integrated systems of health and social services" (Coe, Wolinsky, Miller, & Prendergast, 1985, 621).

A wide range of studies shows that the vast majority of personal-care services received by the dependent elderly in the community are provided by the informal support network composed of family, friends, and neighbors. The family is particularly well adapted to meeting the labor-intensive, nontechnical care needs of the chronically ill. A national survey in the U.S. showed that spouses, compared to adult children, tolerate for a longer time the growing difficulties of caring for a chronically disabled relative before they call on formal home-care services, such as nursing aid. Formal home-care services are solicited even sooner for the chronically ill living alone or with nonrelatives. Advice that counselors may offer regarding home care for the chronically disabled can be based on a recognition that, in general, "services provided by friends and relatives are usually pre-ferred to services delivered by formal suppliers (either in the com-munity or the nursing home) [so that] informal care services are probably judged to be 'superior goods' from the perspective of the dependent elderly" (Soldo, 1985, p. 302).

The patterns that social support may assume have been investi-gated with increasing frequency, as researchers seek to discover principles that govern social networks. Types of principles generated from investigations in recent years can be illustrated with the work of Peters, Hoyt, Babchuk, Kaiser, & Iijima (1987) on primary-group support systems among aged persons in a small Midwestern college town. One issue that the research team studied was the question of whether the elderly sought the aid of particular people for each kind of problem or whether they went to the same consultants no matter what the problem might be. For this sample of Midwesterners, the team learned that, whether the elderly needed a specific sort of help or wanted emotional support, their first choice was their spouse, followed by adult children, friends, siblings, and other relatives, in that order. When soliciting the aid of adult children, they most often looked to a child residing nearby, usually a daughter. Proximity was also an important factor in their seeking the aid of friends, siblings, and other relatives. Frequently, the elderly used several such sources.

> multiple helpers and confidants were used despite a strong tendency to turn more often to spouse or an adult child. Circumstances, conven-ience, or personal preference may lead to the selection of other helpers. Confidants other than spouse or child can add perspective to a prob-lem or concern, as well as confirmation, reinforcement, and reassur-ance. . . . (p. 410)

Another facet of social networks receiving attention is that of the relationship between the emotional well-being of the elderly and their social interactions. The issue here is not simply the question of where the aged go for help but, more broadly, the matter of which social relationships they find most satisfying. The term *emotional well-being* refers to "a state of mind inclusive of feelings of happiness, contentment, and satisfaction with the conditions of one's life; the concept is often used interchangeably with terms such as *morale* and *life satisfaction*" (Lee & Ishii-Kuntz, 1987, p. 459). In a study of 2,872 respondents aged 55 and over in the Northwestern U.S. (supple-mented by an extensive review of the research literature), Lee and

Ishii-Kuntz learned that increased social interaction with friends served to decrease loneliness and increase morale, while interaction with family members had essentially no influence. In contrast to a simplistic version of activity theory (that the more activity and social interaction, the higher the morale), the Lee and Ishii-Kuntz results suggest that positive morale is fostered by friends whom the elderly have purposely chosen but is not necessarily affected by relatives to whom the aged are bound by custom.

> This does not necessarily mean that older people do not wish to interact with their children, or vice versa. The symbolic meanings of this interaction to the participants, however, may be different than those that attach to interaction with friends in ways that affect the psychological rewards derived from the two types of relationships. . . . The fact of being chosen as a friend by another individual is . . . psychologically rewarding, but because individuals are not "chosen" as kin, kinship relations do not have these consequences. (p. 477)

To summarize, normative information reflected in the foregoing types of studies can aid counselors in estimating both (1) the attitudes and patterns of life of elderly clients whom they newly meet and (2) the outcomes likely to result from different treatment techniques. For example, the elderly as a group may be expected to turn first for help to close relatives (spouse, adult child), but, in their daily living, their morale will more often be enhanced by interaction with friends than with relatives. While these appear to be the general trends, such may not be the case for a particular client. Hence, during the counseling encounter, the therapist can pose questions designed to reveal whether the client at hand is typical of those described in the research reviewed above.

Coping with Advanced Age

Even in the face of declining health and ofttimes decreased economic and social resources, many older adults still have fewer mental disorders and express greater satisfaction with life than do younger populations (Koenig, George, & Siegler, 1988, p. 303). To learn why this is so, researchers, have studied elderly people's coping mechanisms, with the term *coping* meaning "efforts, both action-oriented and intrapsychic, to manage (that is, master, tolerate, reduce, minimize) environmental and internal demands, and conflicts among them, which tax or exceed a person's resources" (Lazarus & Launier, 1978).

Coping strategies are of two major types, instrumental and palliative. Instrumental strategies, such as making a phone call or taking up a hobby, are action-oriented steps directed at resolving a problem. Palliative strategies are intrapsychic—assuming an attitude that permits one to tolerate a problem situation. Hence, whereas instrumental techniques are designed to change environmental circumstances, palliative techniques involve adopting a perspective that accepts those circumstances.

> Although action-oriented behaviors such as information-seeking and problem-solving activities (instrumental) have traditionally been heralded as the more effective type of coping strategy, more recently it has been observed that effectiveness of a coping behavior is greatly dependent on the possibilities (or lack of possibilities) for action in a specific situation.... By this reasoning, effective coping in an unchangeable situation would more likely involve emotion-regulating behaviors, rather than problem focused ones. Folkman et al. (1987) have recently demonstrated that older persons tend to use more passive, emotion-focused coping behaviors than do younger individuals. They also reported that older persons were more likely than younger persons to appraise stressful situations as unchangeable. (Koenig, George, & Siegler, 1988, p. 303)

Illustrations of instrumental coping techniques are those of going to a doctor or counselor, seeking information about the problem, praying, resting, or joining a social group. Palliative techniques include the individual's thinking of religion, recognizing that he or she is better off than many other people, vowing to manage despite the difficulties, and realizing that things are not as bad as they seemed at first. In a review of research on older adults, Koenig, George, & Siegler (1988) noted that religious attitudes and activities were the most frequent coping behaviors reported by the elderly. In one study, the most common types of religion-related responses that helped the aged regulate their emotions when facing stressful experiences were: trust in God, prayer, the aid of church friends, engaging in church activities, receiving the minister's help, and reading the bible. Second in importance after religious activities were behaviors that distracted attention from stressful problems by engaging the person in pleasant or productive interests—funneling energies into work, indulging in recreation, participating in social functions, caring for children, watching television, pursuing a hobby, and reading. During stressful times, family and friends played an important part in helping the aged to manage their difficulties.

Several implications for counselors can be drawn from such research on coping strategies. First, the great diversity of strategies found among the elderly suggests that a coping technique suitable for one person may not be appropriate for others. If coping options are to be successful, they need to match significant conditions of the particular client's life. Hence, counselors are most likely to be helpful if they: (1) know a wide range of coping techniques that others have tried, (2) are able to estimate which of these approaches might be well suited to the conditions of the present client's life, and (3) can present the promising options to the client in a way that encourages that person seriously to consider trying them. In estimating the suitability of a potential technique, counselors can attend to such factors as the client's physical abilities, health status, mental agility, energy level, living environment, financial condition, social skills, expressed interests, and past patterns of living. There are several useful ways to introduce options—engage in an activity along with the client (play bridge, go shopping, attend a musical or dramatic event), help the client enroll (in a lawn-bowling club, in a bingo club, in a sewing group), enlist a friend or relative who will accompany the client (attend church, go swimming, take walks), relate anecdotes of people who have used the technique (ways in which others have borne adversity), and show pictures or videotapes of older adults participating in such events.

COMMON TYPES OF COUNSELING CASES
AMONG THE ELDERLY

Very often, the problem of an elderly person that calls for counseling intervention is complex, involving multiple causes and effects. Poor physical health frequently goes hand in hand with cognitive deterioration, resulting in reduced social intercourse, loneliness, the incapacity to make decisions about medical treatment or financial matters, fear of death, and the lack of incentive to live. In other instances, the individual's difficulties are more circumscribed, with an ailing heart and limitations of mobility being the principal disorders, while cognitive abilities remain basically intact. In such cases, a hobby and social relationships can provide a purpose in life. Even though the difficulties of the aged are frequently a mixed bag of causes and results, for purposes of discussion, it is useful to separate them into limited types because not everything can be analyzed simultaneously. Thus, for reasons of convenience, I have divided the second half of this chapter into two common types of problems, recognizing all the while that the two may be interlinked in a given elderly person's life. The problems are (1) depression, loneliness, and a lack of incentive to live and (2) an intellectual incapacity to manage one's own affairs.

Depression, Loneliness, and Lack of Incentive to Live

The term *depression* does not identify either a consistent cluster of symptoms or a single type of cause. Instead, the term is a label applied to symptoms that may be only roughly similar in different clients, and the causes can be varied and complex. The most obvious emotional signs are a gloomy, brooding response to all aspects of life, constant frowning, lack of expression of joy or optimism, and spells of weeping. Thoughts that often accompany this dour appearance include the elderly persons' unrealistic beliefs that they are unworthy, useless, unappreciated, guilty of mistreating others or of wasting their own lives, facing a future of no significance, and bound to die soon without having accomplished anything of value. In behavior, the depressed person is often listless, sleeps a lot, stays alone, and complains to others of aches, of being neglected, and of the futility of existence. In extreme cases, the depressed state can include obsessions (constant worries that interfere with the conduct of daily life), delusions (unrealistic beliefs, such as guilt for imagined sins), or hallucinations (imaginary sights and sounds).

In their condition of depression, the aged may become suicidal. During the lifespan, the highest incidence of suicide among males in the United States comes after age 65, with the rate increasing as age advances. In contrast, the highest incidence among females comes around age 45, with the rate decreasing thereafter. In short, elderly men commit suicide far more frequently than do elderly women. Furthermore, the highest rate of suicide at all age levels is among white males, while the rate among Black males is only half as large and that among both Black and white females is less than one-quarter as large (Centers for Disease Control, 1986, pp. 114-115).

Characteristics of depression can vary markedly from one person to another. Some people display only a few symptoms, while others display many. The depressed state may occur briefly, then pass away, or it can be periodic and chronic. The level of depression may be slight, or it may be deep and abiding. Because of the diversity of forms that depression assumes, the exact proportion of old people who are significantly depressed is unknown. However, it is clear that the incidence of depression is rather high, certainly higher than it is among younger adults. In one longitudinal study of normally aging volunteers in the Southeastern United States, between 20 and 25% of the elderly were judged at any one time to suffer from depression. Over a period of months that involved 10 diagnostic visits, 60% of the group were judged as having been depressed on at least one occasion (Gianturco & Busse, 1978).

CORRELATES AND CAUSES OF DEPRESSION

Just as the signs of depression can be diverse, so also can the apparent causes, with both biological and social-psychological factors cited as likely sources of depression.

As for biological conditions, studies of the operation of the brain suggest that various electrochemical conditions of the neural system might precipitate depression in certain people. One factor, in some cases, appears to be an imbalance of chemical substances (neurotransmitters) that carry electrical impulses from one nerve cell to the next. At least one of these substances (norepinephrine), when present in the brain in subnormal amounts, can result in a depressed state, with subnormal quantities being perhaps more frequent among the elderly than among younger people. This kind of depression can often be reduced by the administration of drugs that increase norepinephrine (Greist & Greist, 1979). Despite the identification of such likely physiological bases of depressed states, the biology of depression is far from understood.

Among social-psychological factors in the lives of the aged, researchers have recognized an array of events that frequently precede depression, events thus cited as contributing causes. The most prominent of these appears to be poor health, which more often accompanies depression in men than it does in women. In a smaller number of cases, retirement from a vocation or the death of a spouse can precipitate the disorder. Financial insecurity may also be the focus of depression, especially among women (Belsky, 1984, p. 242). Thus, various kinds of loss, with resultant feelings of helplessness and lack of control over their lives, are often linked to depression in the aged.

The ultimate damage wrought by depression can be suicide. While the rate of suicide among adolescents and young adults has doubled over the past decade, the geriatric rate continues to be about twice that of adolescents, and thus is a serious problem (Neshkes & Jarvik, 1986, p. 54). According to Osgood (1985, p. 12), the highest incidence of older adults' taking their own lives is found among urban, white, Protestant males who are widowed or divorced and who are now retired or unemployed. Blue-collar workers and ones whose careers have suffered ups and downs are suicidal more often than are white-collar and professional people whose careers have been orderly. In terms of personal/social characteristics, suicide is more frequent among people who had hypercritical, rejecting parents, whose inter-personal relationships have been unsatisfactory, whose work record and marital history have been poor, and who have had previous periods of depression.

Depression deep enough to put the elderly at risk of suicide can often be inferred from a combination of three conditions: (1) loss of vital resources (health, finances, social-emotional relationships, men-tal abilities), (2) stressful events that reduce individuals' control over their fate (death of loved ones, dismissal from a job, a move to a strange environment, traumatic conflict with a relative or trusted friend), and (3) signs of despair (loneliness, hopelessness, lowered self-esteem, alcoholism, drug abuse) (Osgood, 1985, pp. 108-111).

COUNSELING DEPRESSED CLIENTS

It may be apparent that there is no single counseling mode appropriate for all depressed older adults. The mode of counseling that will succeed best in a given case depends upon several signifi-cant conditions in the client's life. Such conditions include the state of the client's health and mobility, mental abilities, financial condition, friendship and social-support patterns, talents, and potential inter-ests. Hence, it is important in the diagnostic phase of each case for the therapist to estimate the nature of these conditions and then fashion a treatment approach that accommodates for the conditions. The following cases illustrate this point in relation to three different counseling techniques.

Case 1

The client is an 88-year-old woman in a retirement facility that provides each person an apartment, medical attention, and food service in a central dining hall. During her active adult life, she had been a part-time travel agent. Her husband, the owner of a hardware store, died 20 years ago. The widow is financially secure and mentally alert but depressed over her lack of mobility, since a series of mild strokes have made walking difficult. When standing, the client tires easily and tends to lose her balance. She says that she is soon to die and complains of not being able to drive a car, so she must depend on friends and relatives for transportation.

When a counselor visited her, the elderly widow was polite but spoke in a despairing manner about her current life until the counselor asked about her days as a travel agent. At the mention of this subject, the widow's manner changed. Her speaking tone brightened as she related a series of amusing experiences from earlier periods of her life—experiences which cast her in the role of a clever, well-liked business woman. When the session ended, she appeared quite cheerful. The counselor, after promising to return and chat again, suggested to those who administered the retirement facility that anyone, such as relatives or volunteer aides, could use this same technique of encouraging the 88-year old to engage in periodic *retrospective biographical recall* as a way of relieving her spells of depression. In effect, what the widow appeared to need was an opportunity vicariously to relive events from a happier time of life when she had been healthy, energetic, productive, and apparently sought out and esteemed by others.

Case 2

The clients are a husband and wife, ages 71 and 69, who have newly moved from Minnesota to a retirement community in Arizona. During their early weeks in the community, they have stayed by themselves and, when speaking with others, have openly regretted leaving their longtime home in the North. A counselor, in the role of recreation consultant to the community, meets with the couple to explain the activities available in the area. She learns that both the husband and wife are in good health, so she proposes that they consider attending such events as the weekly square dance, lawn bowling, and swimming in the community's pool. She also invites them to an upcoming holiday barbecue. When the couple display somewhat hesitant interest in these activities, the counselor asks two other couples who are long-term, active residents of the retirement facility to call on the new couple and encourage them to join the square-dance and lawn-bowling groups. Stimulated by the friendly overtures, the new couple do become actively engaged, and their symptoms of depression and loneliness are dispelled. Thus, the counselor's efforts have helped the couple to achieve a satisfactory transition from the lifestyle they left in Minnesota to a new lifestyle and circle of friends in the retirement setting. The two-pronged counseling approach has been that of (1) informing the clients of potentially interesting pastimes in the company of a new set of compatible companions and (2) enlisting the aid of friendly couples of similar age and interests to welcome the newcomers into the community's social life.

Case 3

A 78-year-old man in a publicly supported nursing home appears despondent over his financial insecurity, failing health (including arthritis, high blood pressure, and a weak heart), lack of companionship, and disappointment with both his past life and an unpromising future. On several occasions, he has spoken of ending his own life. The physician attending the patient has sought to ameliorate the patient's depressed state by administering drugs to increase the neural system's norepinephrine. At the same time, a counseling psychologist has attempted to distract the patient from his ailments by appealing to his longtime interest in baseball and by encouraging a friendship with another male patient in the home. The treatment effort has involved the psychologist's (1) learning of the patient's interest in baseball during three conversations about a wide variety of topics, (2) arranging to have a television receiver installed in the patient's room so that he can view baseball games and other programs, (3) furnishing the patient copies of a baseball magazine, (4) suggesting to the patient's adult son that the son visit his father at a time when a baseball game is being broadcast, so that the two might watch together and thus have something to talk about other than the father's complaints, and (5) inviting an elderly man from another wing in the nursing home to visit the patient in the company of the psychologist so that the two aged residents might become acquainted and perhaps watch televised sporting events together.

In addition to working directly with depressed clients, counselors frequently are called upon as well to help with the problems of the aged's caregivers, particularly the problems of family and friends.

Sometimes staff members of nursing facilities also require counseling support.

Lack of Intellectual Capacity to Manage One's Own Affairs

There is obviously no set standard of intellectual ability that individuals must have to manage their own affairs. At all stages of life, society has arrangements for matching life's tasks to different people's cognitive abilities. A mentally retarded young man is assigned simpler tasks to accomplish for himself; then other people help him to solve the more difficult problems that he encounters. In contrast, a gifted scientific thinker or skilled political leader is offered opportunities to grapple with very complex issues, then is rewarded with fame and fortune for succeeding in these activities.

From adolescence into mid-life, most people learn to accept—though perhaps reluctantly—the status to which they are relegated on the basis of their intellectual capacities. Most come to recognize the reality of what they can accomplish intellectually, and they become accustomed to operating on that level. But old age changes this. Declining cognitive abilities in the elderly forcibly demote them from the position of control and self-sufficiency that they have enjoyed in the past. In old age, they make embarrassing and costly errors, they become confused and hesitant, their pride is injured, and their independence is diminished as they must now depend increasingly on others to do their thinking. Therapists may then be called upon to help those who suffer such difficulties. In pursuing this assignment, counselors can profit from recognizing common varieties of cognitive decline, methods of treatment, and the likely outcome of different treatments.

For convenience of analysis, it is useful to divide kinds of intellectual deterioration into two groups—organic and functional—on the basis of their apparent causes. In organic disorders, the physiological causes are known. Functional disorders, on the other hand, are emotional disturbances for which a physiological source has not been identified. Judging whether the cause is organic or functional or some mixture of both is important to a therapist in deciding what treatment is most reasonable and what outcomes may be expected.

The following review focuses on the three most common types of organic mental disturbances in the aged. Two of the types are varieties of dementia (senile dementia and multi-infarct dementia). The third is delirium. The term *dementia* identifies a set of cognitive disorders which are marked by the progressive deterioration of mental functions, often initially displayed in difficulty to recall recent events. An estimated 5 to 8% of people over age 65 and not in nursing homes suffer moderate or serious dementia (Kay & Bergmann, 1980). Inside nursing homes and other care units, up to 70% of the inmates are estimated to be dementia patients (Blazer, 1980). The term *delirium* identifies an acute mental disorientation which might be mistaken for dementia, except that it occurs rather suddenly, clouds the person's memory for both recent and past events, may include visual hallucinations, and may occasionally pass away with no evidence of memory loss (Sloane, 1980).

In modern times, as people tend to live longer, with each passing decade the population includes increasing numbers of the aged and, consequently, larger numbers of those with dementia and delirium, so that counselors can look forward to more and more clients of these types.

SENILE DEMENTIA

What in the past was called *senile dementia* has become known more recently by two other terms as well—*Alzheimer's disease* and *primary degenerative dementia*. The designation *Alzheimer's disease* has typically been used for cases in which the observable onset of cognitive deterioration occurs before age 65. It now appears, however, that both the behavioral symptoms and the organic damage in Alzheimer's disease and senile dementia are essentially the same, so that the two may be regarded as the same disease. The disorder is caused by anatomical changes in the brain (atrophied brain cells, abnormal structures called *senile plaques* and *neurofibrillary tangles*) which diminish the quantity of operating neurons and their interconnections, thereby reducing the individual's cognitive abilities. Around 50% of the aged who suffer dementias are victims of this disease, making it the most common major mental disorder of old age. More women than men suffer from it. Although the disorder may occur at any age after around 40 or 45, the height of its onset comes around age 80, when one out of every 20 people contracts it (Gruenberg, 1979).

> What looks like a dementia often temporarily appears after an older person experiences a change in his or her environment because the amount of new information that needs to be immediately assimilated creates a kind of sensory and memory overload. In addition, the

stress of a change may cause or exacerbate intellectual impairments because of the disruptive impact of anxiety.... However, although senile dementia is often exacerbated by environmental change or other external factors, it does have a primarily organic basis. (Belsky, 1984, p. 233)

The chief observable symptoms of senile dementia are loss of memory, a decreasing orientation to time and place, inability to make decisions, and a wandering thought pattern. The memory impairment includes one or more of four areas: cognition, speech and language, visuospatial skills, or personality. Patients with isolated disturbances in a single function are typically labeled with more specific terms than dementia, such as aphasia for an isolated disturbance of speech and language (Robinson, 1986, p. 75). As an aid in diagnosis, Reisberg (1986) identified behavioral markers distinguishing seven stages of Alzheimer's disease, extending from normal mental functioning (stage 1) to severe physical and mental deterioration (stage 7). At stage 2, the individual manifests only the minor difficulties in recalling words that are common in normal aged adults. At stage 3, deficits are noted in demanding employment settings. At stage 4, the person has trouble with such complex tasks as managing financing or planning a dinner party. In stage 5, the patient needs assistance in choosing proper attire, and in stage 6, he or she needs help dressing, bathing, and controlling urinary and bowel functions. At stage 7, speech is limited to around a half-dozen intelligible words; then by gradual steps, the patient loses all intelligible speech and the abilities to walk, sit up, smile, and finally, to hold the head up.

A variety of diagnostic checklists have been devised to aid practitioners in estimating whether a patient suffers from dementia (Robinson, 1986). Typical questions or requests posed to the patient include: "What is today's date?" "What day of the week is it?" "What season of the year is it?" "What is your telephone number?" "How old are you?" "Who is president of the United States?" "Name these things as I point to them (watch, pen)." "Repeat these words: 'no ifs, ands, or buts'." "Subtract 3 from 20, then keep subtracting 3 from each new number." "Copy this drawing (two intersecting pentagons)."

In order to clearly distinguish true dementia from depression (pseudodementia), it is necessary to chart the disorder over a period of months. "Pseudodementia is characterized by short duration (a few months) and rapid progression of symptoms. Marked awareness of the impairment is reported by the patient and family. Performance on mental status examination is marked by variability in performance, poor effort 'don't know' answers, and a depressed affect" (Robinson, 1986, p. 77).

As yet, the medical profession has found no way either to cure senile dementia or to halt its advance. Only in a few cases can the symptoms be arrested or reduced for a time. "Recent information suggests that, despite appropriate treatment, the probability of complete recovery from cognitive impairment in a community population of impaired elderly is a very low 1 to 3%" (Robinson, 1986, p. 81). As a consequence, the aged suffering from senile dementia require progressive amounts of custodial care. The type of care that is given may ameliorate somewhat the effects of the disease on both the patient and the caregivers. The role of the counselor relates to this care, with the clients often being of two varieties—the patient who suffers the disease and the people charged with the patient's care.

The counselor's direct work with the dementia patient is typically of greatest use in the early stages of the disease, when the patient has some recognition that memory and judgment are decreasing. The counselor's help at this time can take the form of guiding the older adult's practice in memory devices and of assuaging the patient's feelings of guilt and frustration at forgetting and having trouble making decisions. The memory practice can include learning word associations for new names or places that the patient wishes to recall, devising rhymes as mnemonic devices, writing down items to be recalled, and frequently repeating (drilling) on things to be remembered. The treatment of guilt and frustration can consist of reassuring the client that everyone experiences slips of memory and of suggesting that the client seek the opinions of others in the process of arriving at a decision.

Although therapists do work directly with the demented elderly, the greater part of their efforts is often directed toward helping those people who are responsible for the day-by-day welfare of the aged patients. Such people are either relatives, close friends, or staff members of nursing and retirement facilities. Family members who care for a demented relative in the home typically find the responsibility quite stressful. In a study of 58 families of Alzheimer's-disease patients, Quayhagen and Quayhagen (1988, p. 394) learned that the characteristics of the demented patients which most often upset the caretakers were the following: repetitive questions (81% of caretakers), difficulty handling money (69%), embarrassing behavior (primarily sexual, in the cases of men) (67%), difficulty bathing (67%), difficulty cooking (in the cases of women) (62%), difficulty staying alone (62%), dangerous behavior (59%), and incontinent behavior (57%). The techniques that caregivers most often used to cope with the stress of their task were those of seeking help from others (77%), problem solving (52%), existential growth (41%), and self-blame and fantasy (40%). Of these techniques, the ones that appeared most successful in reducing the caregivers' stress were existential growth (developing positive attitudes toward themselves and their lives), problem solving (systematically working out ways of coping with problems), and seeking aid from others. In contrast, fantasizing and blaming themselves usually did not reduce stress.

In the Quayhagen and Quayhagen study, the methods most often used to provide cognitive stimulation for the demented elderly were those of encouraging physical exercise and social/environmental stimulation. Social stimulation activities included dining out, television viewing and radio listening, church attendance, and directed conversations on family concerns and past experiences.

From such studies as the above, therapists can derive suggestions about how to aid caregivers of dementia patients. For example, during counseling interviews, therapists can:

(1) Discover the caregiver's perceptions of the elderly patient's condition: "What kinds of problems does your mother have?" "How long has this been going on?" "What do you think has caused this?" "What do you think might help her?"

(2) Learn the client's attitude toward the role of caregiver: "Is the job of taking care of your mother pretty difficult?" "If you did not have to do these things for her, how would you like to be spending your time?" "Is there anyone else you think of who should be helping to take care of your mother?" "What are the things your mother does that upset you or that upset other people who come around?"

(3) Learn what techniques the caregiver believes can help to slow the pace of the patient's cognitive deterioration: "Is there anything you try in order to help her remember things or to help her avoid making mistakes?"

(4) Discover the client's ways of trying to relieve the stress of the caregiving duties: "What do you do to keep from feeling too bad about the problem of taking care of your mother?"

From such inquiries as the above, counselors can estimate the kinds of help that may be most useful in the particular case. For instance, if the replies about the patient's condition suggest that the caregiver does not understand the nature of senile dementia, then the therapist can furnish information about the symptoms, terminology (such as *Alzheimer's disease* and *brain damage*), and expected course of the disease. Such information can be in the form of oral explanation or a pamphlet, or both. If replies to the questions about the caregiver's attitudes about the role suggest that he or she feels both guilty and resentful about his or her plight, then the therapist may choose to encourage catharsis, to help assuage the guilt feelings, and to propose ways of reacting to the patient's mental shortcomings that are more constructive than those which the client is now using. For example, if the client indicates that he or she scolds the mother for making mistakes in order to make the elderly woman "pay better attention next time," the therapist may suggest replacing the scolding with methods that do not hurt the old lady's feelings and do not cause the caretaker to feel guilty and resentful later on. These more constructive ways of responding can include letting the dementia patient's mistakes pass without comment, rearranging the environment so that the mother does not again face so many situations in which she makes mistakes, and reassuring the elderly woman that "anybody could do that—don't worry about it." To assist the client in adopting such responses, the therapist may initiate brief role-play sessions in which the counselor takes the part of the elderly mother so that the client can practice constructive responses to the elderly woman's mistakes.

If the counselee's answers to the diagnostic questions indicate that he or she has not been adopting profitable cognitive-stimulation activities with the mother, the therapist can suggest such activities and have the client select which of them appear practical in his or her situation and he or she could apply these activities in the future. Likewise, if the client has been unable to achieve relief from the stress of his or her caretaking duties, the counselor can propose options for gaining relief, and the client can decide which of the options might be suitable in his or her case. The selection of options could also lead to further counseling sessions that provide opportunities for the caregiver to achieve existential growth by means of psychoanalytic, gestalt, or rational-emotive therapy.

MULTI-INFARCT DEMENTIA

The second most frequent form of major cognitive decline is multi-infarct dementia, caused by many small blockages or breakages (strokes or infarcts) in blood vessels to the brain so that oxygen to brain cells is cutoff and the brain cells die. Because the timing of the small strokes is usually random, the mental deterioration caused by such infarcts is typically irregular, although progressive. The elderly person's behavior may be stable for a period then take a turn for the worse, with the individual's memory and orientation to the world becoming rather suddenly diminished (Sloane, 1980).

The incidence of multi-infarct dementia is less than was thought in the past, when it was considered the most common organic brain disorder. Current estimates are that this disease is the cause of between 15 and 20% of the cases of dementia in the aged (Terry & Wisniewski, 1977), and it is more common among men than among women.

As with senile dementia, symptoms of multi-infarct dementia include memory loss, decreased orientation to time and place, difficulty in maintaining a consistent line of thought, and problems in making decisions. But, unlike senile dementia, multi-infarct dementia may also be accompanied by other evidence of infarcts—hearing and sight difficulties, problems controlling the arms or legs, trouble maintaining balance.

Because the symptoms of senile and multi-infarct dementia are so often similar, it is impossible in many cases to estimate, without a post-mortem autopsy, the exact nature of the organic deterioration that caused an individual's cognitive decline. This diagnostic task is further complicated by the fact that an estimated one-quarter of multi-infarct patients also display the organic changes that typify senile dementia.

Because such physiological conditions as high blood pressure can contribute to the frequency of strokes, medication and changes in diet that reduce blood pressure may diminish the rate at which infarcts occur and thereby may slow the progress of the disease. However, no cure has been found for the loss of brain cells, so the disorder typically advances as increasing areas of the brain are destroyed.

The counseling techniques suggested for cases of senile dementia are applicable as well in cases of multi-infarct dementia.

DELIRIUM

The mental disorientation symptomatic of delirium is caused by a sudden disturbance of brain chemistry. Although spells of delirium can occur at any time during the life span, old people are particularly prone to experience them because the elderly are so often on medication and because the ability of the aging brain to withstand physical and psychological trauma is diminished. The chemical disturbance can be set off by a wide variety of events, including improper medication, a diet deficient in vitamins and protein, accidents, a stroke, fever, constipation, the aftereffects of surgery, preexisting brain damage, drug or alcohol dependence, or emotional shock occasioned by the death of a loved one or a move to a new place of residence. Being hospitalized for a physical disorder is highly stressful to the aged, so that many hospitalized elderly people suffer periods of delirium (Belsky, 1984, p. 238).

The core symptom of delirium is "reduced awareness and attentiveness to the environment, resulting in a clouded state of consciousness. The delirious person has a decreased capacity to attend to environmental stimuli. As a result, the delirious patient is a victim of transient shifts of attention and is easily distracted by irrelevant stimuli. This impaired attentional ability is reflected by disorientation to time, occasionally to place, and—in extreme cases only—to person" (Zisook & Braff, 1986, p. 67). These individuals' perceptual problems may include illusions and hallucinations, more often visual than auditory and more often when they are falling asleep or wakening. Their sleep/wake cycle may be reversed, and, while sleeping, the patient may suffer nightmares. Delirious persons sometimes become hyperactive near dusk and at night but remain lethargic during the day. Their disorganized thought processes can be manifest in fragmented speech, memory loss, and an impairment in problem-solving ability. Their emotions may alternate between euphoria and depression or fear and antagonism. As this recital of symptoms suggests, a prime feature of delirium is its fluctuating character, with symptoms appearing suddenly, then sometimes abating within a few days or weeks.

Prompt diagnosis and treatment of delirious states can usually result in a complete reversal of the disorder. However, if the apparent underlying organic source of the delirium—such as myocardial infarction (loss of blood supply to the heart muscle) or pneumonia—

is not quickly identified and its course reversed, a chronic organic brain syndrome or death may occur (Zisook & Braff, 1986, p. 77). Thus, emergency medical treatment is typically called for.

A counselor working with the delirious patient's friends or family members can assist them by suggesting ways in which they can be of aid. If the elderly person is hospitalized and the family cannot afford a private-duty nurse, it is often helpful if a family member sits with the patient to offer emotional support and reassurance.

> When the patient is not sleeping, night-lights, TV, and radio should be left on to help with orientation. It may also be helpful to have a room with a window and a calendar so that the patient can maintain a sense of time. On occasion, it is also beneficial to have special, meaningful belongings from home, such as family pictures, brought to the bedside. Physician, staff, and family members should take advantage of the patient's lucid intervals to explain in simple terms where the patient is and what is happening. With surveillance and consistent efforts to orient the patient, restraints are seldom necessary. (Zisook & Braff, 1986, p. 77)

Counselors may also find it desirable to warn the elderly person's caretakers about the danger of continuing the administration of certain drugs that the patient had been taking, such as hypnotics, minor tranquilizers, antidepressants, and antipsychotic drugs, since these can perpetuate or intensify delirium. A physician, however, may deem it advisable to prescribe other drugs that may help to calm an agitated patient (low doses of high-potency neuroleptics) or to counteract a serious state of insomnia (low doses of short-acting benzodiazepines) (Zisook & Braff, 1986, p. 77).

In addition to working with family members, the counselor can directly serve delirium patients in two ways. The first is to help assess the individual's psychological condition. The second is to enhance the patient's orientation to time, place, and event. Both of these goals can be pursued in the form of a conversation. Topics that the counselor can use for initiating the chat are ones focusing on the aged person's family, current and former occupations, hobbies, and favorite television programs, magazines, and books. The patient can also be asked about recent news events. One diagnostic purpose of employing such topics is to provide the therapist with evidence about how well the client perceives his or her current condition— what day it is, where the client is now and why, and events of the recent and distant past. A second purpose is to assess the client's ability to think logically—to stick to a topic, to arrange words in a comprehensible sequence, and to follow what others are talking about. Beyond carrying on a conversation, the therapist may also ask the patient to perform simple tasks that provide further evidence of the extent of the delirium. For example, the elderly client can be asked to spell his or her name forward and backward, repeat six digits forward and backward, and copy a geometric design. Administering standardized verbal and performance tests, if practical in the situation, can help in estimating the extent of cognitive dysfunction. The use of such techniques on several occasions is useful for tracing the progress of the client's disorder.

CONCLUSION

This final chapter in our overview of life-span stages has focused attention on general characteristics of the elderly as well as two varieties of disorder that often call for the attention of counselors—marked depression and the deterioration of cognitive skills as a result of organic changes in the brain. Although the chapter has featured typical traits of old age, it is important to recognize that at this stage of life there are very marked individual differences in cognitive skills, attitudes toward life, emotional responses, and environmental conditions of people the same age. Two important tasks of counselors are those of (1) discovering the extent to which typical characteristics of the elderly are true in the case of each new older adult that the counselor faces and (2) adopting those counseling interventions that will be most suitable for this case.

PART 3

Postscript

10

The Search for More Answers

As explained in Chapter 1, the purpose of this book is to offer normative information about different stages of the life span that can be of aid to counselors in understanding the clients whom they encounter. While the contents in Chapters 1 through 9 should be useful to professionals engaged in counseling and psychotherapy, the amount of available normative information of that type is far too large to cover in a single volume. Therefore, it is apparent that the first nine chapters necessarily fall short of meeting counselors' needs for such information. They fall short in at least three ways.

First, the topics selected for inclusion fail to cover many additional normative issues that are of concern to counselors. Only a very limited portion of the professional literature on life-span development, on the nature of societal settings, on types of clients and their problems, and on counseling techniques has been included in this book.

Second, the empirical studies, statistics, and counseling methods described in the volume have focused chiefly on North America. The purpose of this limited focus has been to provide data specific enough to be of greater help to likely users of the book (chiefly therapists and counselors in North America) than would be true if broader, less precise, and less supportable generalizations had been proposed as applying equally well to all of the world's cultural areas.

A third shortcoming is produced by the passage of time. Although I have sought to include the most recent data about societal characteristics as well as recent reviews of practices in life-span development and counseling, the passing years bring rapid changes in technology, socioeconomic conditions, medical discoveries, styles of life, and the like. As a consequence, new information about these matters is continually needed by counselors if they are to keep up-to-date.

As an attempt to remedy the foregoing limitations, in this final chapter I list further sources of normative information which can supplement the contents of the present volume. The sources are organized under four categories: (1) characteristics of groups and societies, (2) stages of the life span, (3) types of problems over the life span, and (4) forms of counseling and psychotherapy.

The sources are of two types—books and periodicals. Items designated as *Useful Periodicals* are principally professional journals and government reports. In the periodical lists, publications of the U.S. government are followed by the letter G in parentheses, such as (G).

CHARACTERISTICS OF GROUPS AND SOCIETIES

U.S. Bureau of the Census. (annual). *Statistical Abstract of the United States.* Washington, D.C.: U.S. Government Printing Office. (Statistics on the U.S.—as a nation and often by state—including birth rates, death rates and causes, marriages/divorces, health expenditures, reported AIDS cases, food/nutrition, drug use [including alcohol and cigarettes], personal health practices, schooling, crime rates, child abuse, juveniles in custody, prison inmates, social insurance and human services, labor force, employment earnings, occupational injury rates, personal income and expenditures, family income, family assets, poverty status).

Useful Periodicals: *Aid to Families of Dependent Children, American Journal of Social Psychiatry, Education and Urban Society, Journal of Children in Contemporary Society, Journal of Social Issues, Journal of Sociology and Social Welfare, Law and Society Review, Social Casework, Social Justice, Social Trends* (G).

STAGES OF THE LIFE SPAN

Sources focusing on the life span are listed under the following topics: life-span patterns and generalizations; genetic, prenatal and perinatal influences; childhood and adolescence; early to late adulthood; and middle age and old age.

Life-Span Patterns and Generalizations

Bigner, J. J. (1983). *Human development: A life-span approach.* New York: Macmillan.

Bloom, M. (1984). *Configurations of human behavior: Life-span development in social environments.* New York: Macmillan.

Callahan, E. J., & McCluskey, K. E. (1983). *Life-span developmental psychology—Nonnormative life events.* New York: Academic Press.

Datan, N., & Ginsberg, L. H. (1985). *Life-span developmental psychology— Normative life crises.* New York: Academic Press.

Forman, G. E., & Sigel, I. E. (1979). *Cognitive development: A life-span view.* Monterey, CA: Brooks/Cole.

Freiburg, K. L. (1987). *Human development: A life-span approach* (3rd ed.). Boston: Jones & Bartlett.

Goldhaber, D. (1986). *Life-span development.* New York: Harcourt Brace Jovanovich.

Haywood, K. (1986). *Life-span motor development.* Champaign, IL: Human Kinetics.

Hetherington, E. M., Lerner, R. M., & Perlmutter, M. (Eds.). (1988). *Child development in life-span perspective.* Hillsdale, NJ: Erlbaum.

Kaplan, P. S. (1988). *The human odyssey: Life-span development.* St. Paul, MN: West.

Lerner, R. M., & Busch-Rossnagel, N. A. (Eds.). (1981). *Individuals as producers of their own development.* New York: Academic Press.

Miller, P. H. (1983). *Theories of developmental psychology.* San Francisco: Freeman.

Newman, R. M., & Newman, P. R. (1980). *Personality development through the life span.* Monterey, CA: Brooks/Cole.

Rebok, G. W. (1987). *Life-span cognitive development.* New York: Holt, Rinehart & Winston.

Ripple, R. E., Biehler, R. F., & Jaquish, G. A. (1982). *Human development.* Boston: Houghton Mifflin.

Sugarman, L. (1986). *Life-span development: Concepts, theories, and interventions.* New York: Methuen.

Useful Periodicals: *Human Development, Journal of Humanistic Education and Development, Life-Span Development and Behavior.*

Genetic, Prenatal and Perinatal Influences

Annis, L. F. (1978). *The child before birth.* Ithaca, NY: Cornell University Press.

Cattell, R. B. (1981). *The inheritance of personality and ability.* New York: Academic. (Research methods and results regarding the inheritance of abilities and personality, normal and abnormal. The book links genetics with learning theory.)

Fabro, S., & Scialli, A. R. (Eds.). (1986). *Drug and chemical action in pregnancy: Pharmacologic and toxicologic principles.* New York: Dekker.

Fedor-Freybergh, P., & Vogel, M. L. V. (Eds.). (1988). *Prenatal and perinatal psychology and medicine: Comprehensive survey of research and practice.* Park Ridge, NJ: Parthenon.

Lipsett, L. P., & Field, T. M. (Eds.). (1982). *Infant behavior and development: Perinatal and newborn behavior.* Norwood, NJ: Ablex.

Stevenson, R. E. (1977). *The fetus and newly born infant: Influences of the prenatal environment* (2nd ed.). St. Louis: Mosby.

Verny, T. R. (1981). *The secret life of the unborn child.* New York: Dell.

Useful Periodical: *Journal of Infant Behavior and Development.*

Childhood and Adolescence

Cole, M., & Cole, S. R. (1989). *The development of children.* New York: Freeman (Strong scientific, multicultural approach).

Lerner, R. M., & Spanier, G. B. (1980). *Adolescent development: A life-span perspective.* New York: McGraw-Hill.

Pravder, M., & Komen, S. (Eds.). (1985). *Adolescents and family therapy.* New York: Gardner.

Santrock, J. W., & Yussen, S. R. (1987). *Child development* (3rd ed.). Dubuque, IA: William C. Brown.

Thomas, R. M. (1985). *Comparing theories of child development* (2nd ed.). Belmont, CA: Wadsworth (Describes and assesses more than a dozen present-day Western theories).

Webb, P. K. (1989). *The emerging child—Development through age 12.* New York: Macmillan.

Useful Periodicals: *Adolescence; Advances in Child Development and Behavior; Annual Progress in Child Psychiatry and Development; Child Care-Health-&-Development; Child Development; Child Development Mono-*

graphs; *Child Psychiatry and Human Development*; *Child Welfare*; *Children Today* (G); *Cognitive Development*; *Journal of the American Academy of Child and Adolescent Psychiatry*; *Journal of Youth and Adolescence*; *Status of Children, Youth, and Families* (G); *Youth and Society* (G).

Early to Late Adulthood

Hultsch, D. F., & Deutsch, F. (1981). *Adult development and aging: A lifespan perspective.* New York: McGraw-Hill.

McKaughan, M. (1987). *The biological clock: Reconciling careers and motherhood in the 1980s.* New York: Doubleday.

Schlossberg, N. K. (1984). *Counseling adults in transition—Linking practice with theory.* New York: Springer (Overview of adult development theories "which illustrates the necessity of connecting knowledge of adult development with helping skills").

Useful Periodical: *Adult Education Quarterly.*

Middle Age and Old Age

Anderson, K. (1987). *Symptoms after 40.* New York: Arbor House (Health and hygiene).

Brammer, L. M., Nolan, P. A., & Pratt, M. F. (1982). *Joys and challenges of middle age.* Chicago: Nelson-Hall.

Butler, R. N., & Lewis, M. I. (1986). *Love and sex after 40.* New York: Harper & Row.

Clay, V. S. (1977). *Women, menopause, and middle age.* Pittsburgh, PA: Know.

Cooper, J. C. (1973). *Religion after forty.* Philadelphia, PA: United Church Press.

Hepworth, M., & Featherstone, M. (1982). *Surviving middle age.* Oxford: Basil Blackwell.

Holmes, D. (1983). *Other cultures, elder years: An introduction to cultural gerontology.* Minneapolis, MN: Burgess.

Hunt, B. K., & Hunt, M. (1974). *Prime time: A guide to the pleasures and opportunities of the new middle age.* New York: Stein & Day.

Huyck, M. H. (1974). *Growing older: What you need to know about aging.* Englewood Cliffs, NJ: Prentice-Hall.

Kitzinger, S. (1985). *Birth over thirty.* New York: Penguin (Pregnancy in middle age).

McConnell, A., & Anderson, B. (1978). *Single after fifty: How to have the time of your life.* New York: McGraw-Hill.

McMorrow, F. (1974). *Midolescence: The dangerous years.* New York: Quadrangle/Times Books (Climacteric in middle-aged men).

Nemiroff, R. A., & Colarusso, C. A. (1985). *The race against time— Psychotherapy and psychoanalysis in the second half of life.* New York: Plenum.

Norman, W. H., & Scaramella, T. J. (Eds.). (1980). *Mid-life: Developmental and clinical issues.* New York: Brunner/Mazel (Intended to "alert the reader to those developmental challenges, options, and potential problematic areas that have important implications in the clinical setting").

Sandford, C. E. (1983). *Enjoy sex in the middle years.* New York: Arco.

Sargent, S. S. (Ed.). (1988). *Nontraditional therapy and counseling with the aging.* New York: Springer.

Sherman, E. A. (1987). *Meanings in mid-life transitions.* Albany: State University of New York Press (Written from experience in a center for psychotherapy where individual, family and group treatment were provided by practitioners of psychiatry, social work, and psychology).

Storandt, M. (1983). *Counseling and therapy with older adults.* Boston: Little, Brown.

Van Hoose, W. H. (1985). *Midlife myths and realities.* Atlanta, GA: Humanics.

Useful Periodicals: *Geriatrics, The Gerontologist, Journal of the American Geriatrics Society, Journal of Geriatric Psychiatry.*

TYPES OF PROBLEMS OVER THE LIFE SPAN

The topics in the following list include AIDS, aging, alcohol abuse, child abuse and neglect, childhood disease and handicap, crime and delinquency, death and grief, drug abuse, eating disorders, marriage and divorce, school problems, self-esteem difficulties, sexual behavior, violence, and vocational planning.

AIDS—Acquired Immune Deficiency Syndrome

Armstrong, D., & Ma, P. (Eds.). (1984). *The acquired immune deficiency syndrome and infections of homosexual men.* New York: Yorke Medical Books.

Cooney, T. G., & Ward, T. G. (Eds.). (1986). *AIDS and other medical problems in the male homosexual.* Philadelphia: Saunders.

Des Jarlais, D. (1988). *AIDS and intravenous drug use.* Washington, D.C.: U.S. Department of Justice.

Patton, C. (1986). *Sex and germs: The politics of AIDS.* Buffalo, NY: Black Rose.

Pierce, C., & Van DeVeer, D. (1988). *AIDS: Ethics and public policy.* Belmont, CA: Wadsworth.

Aging

Avery, A. G. (1987). *Successful aging: A sourcebook for older people and their families.* New York: Ballantine Books.

Birren, J. E., & Livingston, J. (Eds.). (1985). *Cognition, stress, and aging.* Englewood Cliffs, NJ: Prentice-Hall.

Birren, J. E., & Schaie, K. W. (Eds.). (1985). *Handbook of the psychology of aging.* New York: Van Nostrand Reinhold.

Butler, R. N., & Bearn, A. G. (Eds.). (1985). *The aging process: Therapeutic implications.* New York: Raven.

Charness, N. (Ed.). (1985). *Aging and human performance.* New York: John Wiley.

Craik, F. I. M., & Trehub, S. (Eds.). (1982). *Aging and cognitive processes.* New York: Plenum.

Ernst, M. (1977). *Sensitizing people to the process of aging: The inservice educator's guide.* Denton: North Texas State University.

Eyde, D. R., & Rich, J. A. (1983). *Psychological distress in aging: A family management model.* Rockville, MD: Aspen.

Janicki, M. P., & Wisniewski, H. M. (Eds.). (1985). *Aging and developmental disabilities: Issues and approaches.* Baltimore: Brookes.

Keith, J. (1982). *Old people as people: Social and cultural influences on aging and old age.* Boston: Little, Brown.

Sherman, E. A. (1981). *Counseling the aging: An integrative approach.* New York: Free Press.

Usdin, G., & Hofling, C. K. (Eds.). (1978). *Aging: The process and the people.* New York: Brunner/Mazel.

Useful Periodicals: *Psychology and Aging, Research on Aging.*

Alcohol Abuse

Barnard, C. P. (1981). *Families, alcoholism, and therapy.* Springfield, IL: Thomas.

Bepko, C. (1985). *The responsibility trap: A blueprint for treating the alcoholic family*. New York: Free Press.

Davis, D. I. (1987). *Alcoholism treatment: An integrative family and individual approach*. New York: Gardner.

Elkin, M. (1984). *Families under influence: Changing alcoholic patterns*. New York: Norton.

Steinglass, P. (1987). *The alcoholic family*. New York: Basic Books.

Useful Periodicals: *Advances in Alcohol and Substance Abuse, Alcohol Abuse Trend Report, Alcohol and Alcoholism, American Journal of Drug and Alcohol Abuse, Demographic Characteristics and Patterns of Drug Use of Clients Admitted to Drug Abuse Treatment Programs in Selected States* (G), *Drug Dependence* (G), *Drug Enforcement* (G), *Drug Utilization in the U.S.* (G), *Journal of Alcohol and Drug Education, Journal of Drug and Alcohol Abuse*.

Child Abuse and Neglect

American Bar Association. Section on Criminal Justice (1985). *Guidelines for the fair treatment of child witnesses in cases where child abuse is alleged*. Washington, D.C.: Author.

Barnard, G. W. (1989). *The child molester: An integrated approach to evaluation and treatment*. New York: Brunner/Mazel.

Brassard, M. R., Germain, R., & Hart, S. N. (Eds.). (1987). *Psychological maltreatment of children and youth*. New York: Pergamon.

Ebeling, N. B., & Hill, D. A. (Ed.). (1983). *Child abuse and neglect: A guide with case studies for treating the child and family*. Boston: Wright-PSG.

Faller, K. C. (1988). *Child sexual abuse: An interdisciplinary manual for diagnosis, case management and treatment*. New York: Columbia University Press.

Fisher, B. (1980). *Adolescent abuse and neglect: Intervention strategies*. Washington, D.C.: U.S. Government Printing Office.

Maher, P. (Ed.). (1987). *Child abuse: The educational perspective*. Oxford: Basil Blackwell.

Peter, D. (1980). *Dangerous families: Assessment and treatment of child abuse*. London: Tavistock.

U.S. Government Printing Office. (1987). *Abused children in America: Victims of official neglect*. Washington, D.C.: Author.

Walker, C. E., Bonner, B. L., & Kaufman, K. L. (1988). *The physically and sexually abused child: Evaluation and treatment*. New York: Pergamon.

Useful Periodical: *Child Abuse and Neglect.*

Childhood and Adolescent Disease and Illness

Blum, R. W. (Ed.). (1984). *Chronic illness and disabilities in childhood and adolescence.* Orlando, FL: Grune and Stratton.

Burton, L. (1975). *The family life of sick children: A study of families coping with chronic childhood disease.* Boston: Routledge & Kegan Paul.

Copeland, D. R., Pfefferbaum, B., & Stovall, A. J. (Eds.). (1983). *The mind of the child who is said to be sick.* Springfield, IL: Thomas.

Creer, T. L., & Christian, W. P. (1976). *Chronically ill and handicapped children, their management and rehabilitation.* Champaign, IL: Research Press.

Ellis, R. W. B. (1973). *Disease in infancy and childhood* (7th ed.). Baltimore: Williams & Wilkins.

Hobbs, N., Perrin, J. M., & Ireys, H. T. (1985). *Chronically ill children and their families.* San Francisco: Jossey-Bass.

O'Doughterty, M. M. (1983). *Counseling the chronically ill child: Psychological impact and intervention.* Lexington, MA: Lewis.

O'Quinn, A. N. (Ed.). (1985). *Management of chronic disorders of childhood.* Boston: G. K. Hall.

Waddell, C. (1983). *Faith, hope, and luck: A sociological study of children growing up with a life-threatening illness.* Washington, D.C.: University Press of America.

Useful Periodical: *American Journal of Diseases of Children, Pediatrics.*

Childhood and Adolescent Handicaps

Anderson, E. M., & Clarke, L. (1982). *Disability in adolescence.* London: Methuen.

Anderson, K., & Milliren, A. (1983). *Structured experiences for integration of handicapped children.* Rockville, MD: Aspen.

Avenshine, C. D., Russell, A., & Noffsinger, L. (1984). *Counseling: An introduction for the health and human services.* Baltimore, MD: University Park Press.

Baca, L. M., & Cervantes, H. T. (1984). *The bilingual special education interface.* St. Louis, MO: Times Mirror/Mosby College.

Batshaw, M. L., & Perret, Y. M. (1986). *Children with handicaps: A medical primer.* Baltimore, MD: P. H. Brookes.

Bender, M., & Valletutti, P. J. (1985). *Teaching the moderately and severely handicapped* (2nd ed.). Austin, TX: Pro-Ed.

Daniels, P. R. (1983). *Teaching the gifted/learning disabled child.* Rockville, MD: Aspen.

Del Polito, C. M., & Barresi, J. G. (Eds.). (1983). *Alliances in health and education: Serving youngsters with special needs.* Washington, D.C.: American Society of Allied Health Professions.

Garguilo, R. M. (1985). *Working with parents of exceptional children: A guide for professionals.* Boston: Houghton Mifflin.

Gordon, J. B., (Ed.). (1977). *Early childhood education for exceptional children: A handbook of ideas and exemplary practices.* Reston, VA: Council for Exceptional Children.

Haring, N. G., & McCormick, L. (1986). *Exceptional children and youth* (4th ed.). Columbus, OH: Merrill.

Simpton, R. L. (1982). *Conferencing parents of exceptional children.* Rockville, MD: Aspen.

Stewart, J. C. (1986). *Counseling parents of exceptional children.* Columbus, OH: Merrill.

Witt, J. C. (1988). *Assessment of special children: Tests and problem solving process.* Glenview IL: Scott Foresman.

Useful Periodicals: *Adolescent Psychiatry, American Journal of Mental Deficiency, Annual Report to Congress on the Implementation of the Education of the Handicapped Act* (G), *Directory of Special Education Programs for Handicapped Children* (G), *Exceptional Child Education Sources, Exceptional Children, Journal of Autism and Developmental Disorders, Journal of Exceptional Children.*

Crime and Delinquency

Arnold, W. R., & Brungardt, T. M. (1983). *Juvenile misconduct and delinquency.* Boston: Houghton Mifflin.

Bartollas, C., & Miller, S. J. (1978). *The juvenile offender: Control, correction, and treatment.* Boston: Holbrook.

Belkin, A. M. (Ed.). (1978). *The criminal child.* Dubuque, IA: Hunt.

Brandt, D. E., & Zlotnick, S. J. (1988). *The psychology and treatment of the youthful offender.* Springfield, IL: Thomas.

Carey, J. T., & McAnany, P. D. (1984). *Introduction to juvenile delinquency: Youth and the law.* Englewood Cliffs, NJ: Prentice-Hall.

Cull, J. G., & Hardy, R. F. (1973). *Law enforcement and correctional rehabilitation.* Springfield, IL: Thomas.

Dutile, F. N., Foust, C. H., & Webster, D. R. (Eds.). (1982). *Early childhood intervention and juvenile delinquency.* Lexington, MA: Lexington Books.

Henggeler, S. (Ed.). (1982). *Delinquency and adolescent psychopathology: A family-ecological systems approach.* Boston: Wright-PSG.

Kelly, D. H. (Ed.). (1978). *Delinquent behavior, interactional, and motivational aspects.* Belmont, CA: Dickinson.

National Institute for Juvenile Justice and Delinquency Prevention. (1982). *Assessing the relationship of adult criminal careers to juvenile careers: A summary.* Washington, D.C.: Author.

Wenk, E. A. (Ed.). (1976). *Delinquency prevention and the schools.* Beverly Hills, CA: Sage.

Useful Periodicals: *Annual Report on the Runaway Youth Act* (G), *Crime and Arrest Report* (G), *Crime and Delinquency, Criminal Justice and Behavior, Delinquency in the United States* (G), *Federal Probation, Journal of Criminal Justice, Journal of Criminal Law and Crimonology, Journal of Correctional Education, National Crime Survey Report: Teenage Victims* (G).

Death and Grief

Doyle, P. (1980). *Grief counseling and sudden death: A manual and guide.* Springfield, IL: Thomas.

Hansen, J. C. (Ed.). (1984). *Death and grief in the family.* Rockville, MD: Aspen.

Kalish, R. A. (1985). *Death, grief, and caring relationships* (2nd ed.). Monterey, CA: Brooks/Cole.

Rando, T. A. (1984). *Grief, dying, and death: Clinical interventions for caregivers.* Champaign, IL: Research Press.

Schucter, S. R. (1986). *Dimensions of grief: Adjusting to the death of a spouse.* San Francisco: Jossey-Bass.

Springhouse Corp. (1984). *Dealing with death and dying* (2nd ed.) Springhouse, PA: Author.

Drug Abuse

Abel, E. L. (1984). *A dictionary of drug abuse terms and terminology.* Westport, CT: Greenwood.

Bryson, P. D. (1986). *Comprehensive review in toxicology.* Rockville, MD: Aspen.

Cohen, M. (1985). *Marijuana, its effect on mind and body.* New York: Chelsea House.

Coleman, V. (1985). *Addicts and addictions.* London: Piatkus.

Cox, T. C. (1983). *Drugs and drug abuse: A reference text.* Toronto: Additional Research Foundation.

DeLeon, G. (1984). *The therapeutic community: Study of effectiveness.* Washington, D.C.: U.S. Government Printing Office.

Edelson, E. (1987). *Drugs and the brain.* New York: Chelsea House.

Glynn, T. J. (Ed.). (1981). *Drugs and the family.* Washington, D.C.: U.S. Government Printing Office.

Rahdert, E. R., & Grabowski, J., (1988). *Adolescent drug abuse: Analyses of treatment research.* Rockville, MD: National Institute on Drug Abuse.

Weisman, T. (1974). *Drug abuse and drug counseling: A case approach.* New York: J. Aronson.

Useful Periodical: *Journal of Drug Education* (see also Alcohol Abuse).

Eating Disorders

Abraham, S., & Llewellyn-Jones, D. (1987). *Eating disorders: The facts.* New York: Oxford University Press.

Anderson, L., Dibble, M. V., Turkki, P. R., Mitchell, H. S., & Rynbergen, H. S. (1982). *Nutrition in health and disease* (17th ed.). Philadelphia: Lippincott (Detailed principles of nutrition, nutritional counseling, cultural food patterns, nutrition in the life-span, diet in treating disease; eighty pages of statistics on the nutritive value of 730 common foods; height-weight charts).

Bauer, B. G., Anderson, W. P., & Hyatt, R. A. (1986). *Bulimia: Book for client and therapist.* Muncie, IN: Accelerated Development.

Chernin, K. (1985). *The hungry self: Women, eating, and identity.* New York: Times Books.

Eagles, D. A. (1987). *Nutritional diseases.* New York: F. Watts.

Field, H. L., & Domangue, B. B. (Eds.). (1987). *Eating disorders throughout the life span.* New York: Praeger.

Harkaway, J. E. (Ed.). (1987). *Eating disorders.* Rockville, MD: Aspen.

Krause, M. V., & Mahan, L. K. (1979). *Food, nutrition, and diet therapy.* Philadelphia: Saunders (Health of individuals and populations; nutrients in foods; nutrition in the life cycle; cultural dietary variations; nutrition and health disorders).

Larocca, F. E. F. (Ed.). (1986). *Eating disorders.* San Francisco: Jossey-Bass.

Stunkard, A. J., & Stellar, E. (Eds.). (1984). *Eating and its disorders.* New York: Raven.

Winick, M. (Ed.). (1988). *Control of appetite.* New York: John Wiley.

Wurtman, R. J., & Wurtman, J. J. (Eds.). (1986). *Food constituents affecting normal and abnormal behaviors.* New York: Raven.

Marriage and Divorce

Ables, B. S. (1977). *Therapy for couples.* San Francisco, CA: Jossey-Bass.

Bass, H. L., & Rein, M. L. (1976). *Divorce or marriage: A legal guide.* Englewood Cliffs, NJ: Prentice-Hall.

Emery, R. E. (1988). *Marriage, divorce, and children's adjustment.* Newbury Park, CA: Sage.

Gathorne-Hardy, J. (1981). *Marriage, love, sex, and divorce.* New York: Summit Books.

Sack, S. M. (1987). *The complete legal guide to marriage, divorce, custody, and living together.* New York: McGraw-Hill.

Thomas, L. S. (1986). *Tax consequences of marriage, separation, and divorce.* Philadelphia: American Law Institute/American Bar Association Commission on Continuing Professional Education.

Useful Periodical: *Journal of Marriage and the Family.*

School Problems

Bond, G. L., Tinker, M. A., Wasson, B. B., & Wasson, J. G. (1984). *Reading difficulties: Their diagnosis and correction* (5th ed.). Englewood Cliffs, NJ: Prentice-Hall.

Hansen, J. C. (Ed.). (1984). *Family therapy with school related problems.* Rockville, MD: Aspen.

Kinsbourne, M., & Caplan, P. J. (1979). *Children's learning and attention problems.* Boston: Little, Brown. (Diagnosis and treatment of cognitive-power disorders and cognitive-style disorders.)

Torgesen, J. K., & Wong, B. Y. L. (Eds.). (1986). *Psychological and educational perspectives on learning disabilities.* New York: Harcourt Brace Jovanovich. (Ways of classifying learning disabilities; treatments involving drugs, behavior modification, phonemic analysis in reading and computer-assisted instruction.)

Zintz, M. V., & Maggart, Z. R. (1986). *Corrective reading* (5th ed.). Dubuque, IA: William C. Brown.

Useful Periodical: *School Psychology Review.*

Self-Concept, Self-Esteem

Baumeister, R. F. (1986). *Identity: Cultural change and the struggle for self.* New York: Oxford University Press.

Breytspraak, L. M. (1984). *The development of self in later life.* Boston: Little, Brown.

Druckman, D., & Swets J. A. (Eds.). (1988). *Enhancing human performance: Issues, theories, and techniques.* Washington, D.C.: National Academy Press.

Gernsbacher, L. M. (1985). *The suicide syndrome: Origins, manifestations, and alleviation of human self-destructiveness.* New York: Human Sciences Press.

Honess, T., & Yardley, K. (Eds.). (1987). *Self and identity: Perspectives across the life span.* New York: Routledge & Kegan Paul.

Leahy, R. L. (Ed.). (1985). *The development of the self.* Orlando, FL: Academic.

Lee, B., & Noam, G. G. (Eds.). (1983). *Developmental approaches to the self.* New York: Plenum.

Mack, J. E., & Ablon, S. L. (Eds.). (1983). *The development and sustenance of self-esteem in childhood.* New York: International Universities Press.

Sexual Behavior

Aardweg, G. J. M. van den (1986). *On the origins and treatment of homosexuality: A psychoanalytic reinterpretation.* New York: Praeger.

Barnett, W. (1979). *Homosexuality and the Bible: An interpretation.* Wallingford, PA: Pendle Hill.

Bayer, R. (1987). *Homosexuality and psychiatry: The politics of diagnosis.* Princeton, NJ: Princeton University Press.

Bell, A. P., Weinberg, M. S., & Hammersmith, S. K. (1981). *Sexual preference, its development in men and women.* Bloomington, IN: Indiana University Press.

Blackwood, E. (Ed.). (1986). *Anthropology and homosexual behavior.* New York: Haworth.

Diamont, L. (Ed.). (1987). *Male and female homosexuality: Psychological approaches.* New York: Columbia University Press.

Koertge, N. (Ed.). (1981). *The nature and causes of homosexuality: A philosophic and scientific inquiry.* New York: Haworth.

Mohr, R. D. (1988). *Gays/justice: A study of ethics, society, and law.* New York: Columbia University Press.

Money, J. (1988). *Gay, straight, and in-between: The sexuality of erotic orientation.* New York: Oxford University Press.

Violence

Baxter, A. (1987). *Techniques for dealing with family violence.* Springfield, IL: Thomas.

Prentky, R. A., & Quinsey, V. L. (1988). *Human sexual aggression: Current perspectives.* New York: New York Academy of Science.

Useful Periodical: *Journal of Family Violence.*

Vocational Planning

Goodman, L. H. (1982). *Alternative careers for teacher, librarians, and counselors.* New York: Monarch.

Mortimer, J. T., & Borman, K. M. (Eds.). (1988). *Work experience and psychological development through the life span.* Boulder, CO: Westview.

Schlossberg, N. K., and Birk, J. M. (Eds.). (1977). *Freeing sex roles for new careers.* Washington, D.C.: American Council on Education.

Vondracek, F. W. (1986). *Career development: A life-span developmental approach.* Hillsdale, NJ: Erlbaum.

Useful Periodicals: *Occupational Outlook Quarterly, Personnel Journal, Training and Development Journal, Vocational Educator.*

FORMS OF COUNSELING AND PSYCHOTHERAPY

This section lists resources on the following topic: general descriptions of counseling types, cognitive-behavioral counseling, cross-cultural and multicultural counseling, family therapy, group counseling, and parent-child counseling.

General Descriptions of Counseling Types

Belkin, G. S. (1984). *Introduction to counseling* (2nd ed.). Dubuque, IA: William C. Brown. (Purposes, theories [psychodynamic, humanistic, rational, behavior] and situations [life-span, family, group, health, crisis, rehabilitation, school, career, cross-cultural]).

Husen, T., & Postlethwaite, T. N. (Eds.). (1985). *International encyclopedia of education,* (10 vols.). Oxford: Pergamon. (Brief articles about 25 theories of human development and 65 articles about counseling theories and methods).

Sylvia, J. A., & Leiderman, P. H. (1986). The life-span approach to individual therapy: An overview with case presentation. In P. B. Baltes, D. L. Featherman & R. M. Lerner (Eds.). *Life-span development and behavior* (pp. 113-134). Hillsdale, NJ: Erlbaum.

Useful Periodicals: *American Journal of Psychiatry, British Journal of Clinical Psychology, Canadian Journal of Counseling, Clinical Psychology Review, Counseling and Human Development, Counseling and Values, Counseling Psychologist, Elementary School Guidance and Counseling, Journal of Clinical Psychiatry, Journal of Clinical Psychology, Journal of Counseling and Development, Journal of Counseling Psychology, Journal of Mental Health Counseling, Review of Existential Psychology and Psychiatry.*

Cognitive-Behavioral Counseling

Epstein, N., Schlesinger, S. E., & Dryden, W. (Eds.). (1988). *Cognitive-behavioral therapy with families.* New York: Brunner/Mazel.

Morris, E. K., & Braukmann (Eds.). (1987). *Behavioral approaches to crime and delinquency: A handbook of application, research, and concepts.* New York: Plenum.

Useful Periodicals: *Advances in Behavioral Assessment of Children and Families, Journal of Behavior Therapy and Experimental Psychiatry, Journal of Cognitive Psychotherapy, Psychotherapy and Behavior Change.*

Cross-Cultural and Multicultural Counseling

Hansen, J. C., & Falicov, C. J. (Eds.). (1983). *Cultural perspectives in family therapy.* Rockville, MD: Aspen.

McGolderick, M., Pearce, J. K., & Giordano, J. (Eds.). (1982). *Ethnicity and family therapy.* New York: Guilford.

Pedersen, P. (Ed.). (1985). *Handbook of cross-cultural counseling and therapy.* Westport, CT: Greenwood.

Useful Periodicals: *Culture, Medicine, and Psychiatry; Journal of Multicultural Counseling and Behavior; Journal of Multicultural Counseling and Development; Journal of Multilingual and Multicultural Development.*

Family Therapy

Ackerman, N. J. (1984). *A theory of family systems.* New York: Gardner.

Allen, D. M. (1988). *Unifying individual and family therapies.* San Francisco: Jossey-Bass.

Berger, M. (Ed.). (1978). *Beyond the double bind: Communication and Family systems, theories, and techniques with schizophrenics.* New York: Brunner/Mazel.

Berger, M., & Jurkovic, G. J. (1984). *Practicing family therapy in diverse settings.* San Francisco: Jossey-Bass.

Brown, J. H. (1986). *Family therapy: Theory and practice.* Monterey, CA: Brooks/Cole.

Clarkin, J. F., Haas, G. L., & Glick, I. D. (Eds.). (1988). *Affective disorders and the family: Assessment and treatment.* New York: Guilford.

De Shazer, S. (1982). *Patterns of brief family therapy: An ecosystemic approach.* New York: Guilford.

Useful Periodicals: *American Journal of Family Therapy, Family Relations, Journal of Family Issues.*

Group Counseling

Vander Kolk, C. J. (1985). *Introduction to group counseling and psychotherapy.* Columbus, OH: Charles E. Merrill (Types of group approaches [psychodynamic, transactional, Gestalt, Rogerian, rational-emotive, behavioral] and types of clients [disabled, disadvantaged, children, adolescents, families, married couples, vocational, skill-training]).

Useful Periodical: *International Journal of Group Psychotherapy.*

Parent-Child Counseling

Adams, D. W. (1979). *Childhood malignancy: The psychosocial care of the child and his family.* Springfield, IL: Thomas.

Arnold, L. E., & Estreicher, D. (1985). *Parent-child group therapy: Building self-esteem in a cognitive-behavioral group.* Lexington, MA: Lexington Books.

References

Abramson, E. (1987). Projections 2000. *Occupational Outlook Quarterly, 31*(3), 2-36.

Abramson, L. Y., Seligman, M. P., & Teasdale, J. D. (1978). Learned helplessness in humans: Critique and reformulation. *Journal of Abnormal Psychology, 87*, 49-74.

Allen, F. H. (1942). *Psychotherapy with children.* New York: Norton.

Allen, R., & Wasserman, G. A. (1985). Origins of language delay in abused infants. *Child Abuse and Neglect, 9*(3), 335-340.

American Psychiatric Association. (1980). Diagnostic and statistical manual of mental disorders (3rd ed.—DSM-III). Washington, DC: Author.

Anderson, A. E. (1985). *Practical comprehensive treatment of anorexia nervosa and bulimia.* Baltimore, MD: Johns Hopkins University Press.

Ayers, R. R., Cooley, E. J., & Severson, H. H. (1988). Educational translation of the Kaufman Assessment Battery for Children: A construct validity study. *School Psychology Review, 17*(1), 113-124.

Baker, H. J. (1959). *Introduction to exceptional children.* New York: Macmillan.

Baller, W. R. (1975). *Bed-wetting: Origins and treatment.* New York: Pergamon.

Ballinger, C. B. (1981). The menopause and its syndromes. In J. G. Howells (Ed.), *Modern perspectives in the psychiatry of middle age* (pp. 279-303). New York: Brunner/Mazel.

Baltes, M. M., & Baltes, P. B. (1986). *The psychology of control and aging.* Hillsdale, NJ: Erlbaum.

Bandura, A. (1977). *Social learning theory.* Englewood Cliffs, NJ: Prentice-Hall.

Batshaw, M. L., & Perret, Y. M. (1986). *Children with handicaps, a medical primer* (2nd ed.). Baltimore, MD: Brookes.

Bee, H. L. (1981). *The developing child.* New York: Harper & Row.

Bee, H. L., & Mitchell, S. K. (1984). *The developing person: A life-span approach* (2nd ed.). New York: Harper & Row.

Belsky, J. K. (1984). *The psychology of aging.* Monterey, CA: Brooks/Cole.

Bennett, W., & Gurin, J. (1982). *The dieter's dilemma.* New York: Basic Books.

Blackman, J. A. (1983). Prenatal injury. In J. A. Blackman (Ed.), *Medical aspects of developmental disabilities in children birth to three* (pp. 187-193). Iowa City: University of Iowa Press.

Blatner, H. A. (1973). *Acting-in: Practical applications of psychodramatic methods.* New York: Springer.

Blazer, D. (1980). The epidemiology of mental illness in late life. In E. W. Busse & D. G. Blazer (Eds.), *Handbook of geriatric psychiatry* (pp. 249-271). New York: Van Nostrand Reinhold.

Bloom, B. S. (1964). *Stability and change in human characteristics.* New York: John Wiley.

Blumstein, P., & Schwartz, P. (1983). *American couples.* New York: William Morrow.

Boder, E. (1973). Developmental dyslexia: A diagnostic approach based on three typical reading-spelling patterns. *Developmental Medicine and Child Neurology, 15,* 663-687.

Boer, S. E., & Lycan, W. G. (1986). *Knowing who.* Cambridge, MA: MIT Press.

Booth, A., & Johnson, D. (1988) Premarital cohabitation and marital success. *Journal of Family Issues, 9(2),* 255-272.

Botwinick, J. (1984). *Aging and behavior* (3rd ed.). New York: Springer.

Bowles, R. T. (1980). Prologue. In J. V. Cook & R. T. Bowles (Eds.), *Child abuse: Commission and omission* (pp. 1-7). Toronto: Butterworths.

Brazelton, T. B. (1986). Development of newborn behavior. In F. Falkner & J. M. Tanner (Eds.), *Human growth: A comprehensive treatise: Vol. 2 Postnatal growth neurobiology* (pp. 519-540). New York: Plenum.

Brazelton, T. B. (1970). Effect of prenatal drugs on the behavior of the neonate. *American Journal of Psychiatry, 126,* 1261-1266.

Brenner, C. (1955). *An elementary textbook of psychoanalysis.* New York: International Universities Press.

Bricker, D. D. (1986). *Early education of at-risk and handicapped infants, toddlers, and preschool children.* Glenview, IL: Scott, Foresman.

Brickman, P., Rabinowitz, V. C., Karuza, J. Jr., Coates, D., Cohn, E., & Kidder, L. (1982). Models of helping and coping. *American Psychologist, 37,* 368-384.

Broderick, C. B. (1966). Sexual behavior among preadolescents. *Journal of Social Issues, 22(2),* 6-21.

Brody, B. A. (1980). *Identity and essence.* Princeton, NJ: Princeton University Press.

Brown, G. I. (1985). Gestalt therapy. In T. Husen & T. N. Postlethwaite (Eds.). *International encyclopedia of education* (Vol. 5, pp. 2040-2041). Oxford: Pergamon.

Brown, R. (1973). *A first language: The early stages.* Cambridge, MA: Harvard University Press.

Bullen, B. A., Skrinar, G. S., Beitins, I. Z., von Mering, G., Turnbull, B. A., & McArthur, J. W. (1985). Induction of menstrual disorders by strenuous exercise in untrained women. *New England Journal of Medicine, 312,* 1349-1353.

Bullough, V. L. (1981). Age at menarche: A misunderstanding. *Science, 213,* 365-366.

Burden, D. S. (1986). Single parents and the work setting: The impact of multiple job and homelife responsibilities. *Family Relations, 35,* 37-43.

Burgemeister, B. B., Blum, L. H., & Lorge, I. (1972). *The Columbia Mental Maturity Scale.* New York: The Psychological Corporation.

Cappleman, M. W., Thompson, R. J., DeRemer-Sullivan, P. A., King, A. A., & Sturm, J. M. (1982). Effectiveness of a home based early intervention program with infants of adolescent mothers. *Child Psychiatry and Human Development, 13(1),* 55-65.

Capron, A. M., Lappe, M., Murray, R. F., Powledge, T. M., Twiss, S. B., & Bergsma, D. (1979). *Genetic counseling: Facts, values, and norms.* New York: Liss.

Cartwright, G. P., Cartwright, C. A., & Ward, M. E. (1984). *Educating special learners* (2nd ed.). Belmont, CA: Wadsworth.

Castillo, G. (1971). Eight months in the first grade. In G. I. Brown, *Human teaching for human learning* (pp. 133-193). New York: Viking.

Cates, J. T., & Gang, M. J. (1976). Classroom discipline problems and reality therapy: Research report. *Elementary School Guidance and Counseling, 11,* 131-137.

Centers for Disease Control. (1986). Annual summary 1984: Reported morbidity and mortality in the United States. *Morbidity and Mortality Weekly Report, 33*(54).

Chandler, A. (1985). Vocational development groups. In C. J. Vander Kolk (Ed.), *Introduction to group counseling and psychotherapy* (pp. 353-375). Columbus, OH: Merrill.

Chilman, C. S. (1978). *Adolescent sexuality in a changing American society.* Washington, DC: U.S. Government Printing Office.

Coe, R. M., Wolinsky, F. D., Miller, D. K., & Prendergast, J. M. (1985). Elderly persons without family support networks and use of health services. *Research on Aging, 7*(4), 617-622.

Cole, M. (Ed.) (1977). *Soviet developmental psychology.* White Plains, NY: Sharpe.

Combs, A. W., & Snygg, D. (1959). *Individual behavior.* New York: Harper & Row.

Cookerly, J. R. (1976). Evaluating different approaches to marriage counseling. In D. H. L. Olson (Ed.), *Treating relationships* (pp. 475-498). Lake Mills, IA: Graphic.

Cooper, C. L. (1981). Middle-age men and the pressures of work. In J. G. Howells (Ed.), *Modern perspectives of the psychiatry of middle age* (pp. 90-102). New York: Brunner/Mazel.

Creighton, S. J. (1985). An epidemiological study of abused children and their families in the United Kingdom between 1977 and 1982. *Child Abuse & Neglect, 9,* 441-448.

Cruickshank, W. M. (1955). *Psychology of exceptional children and youth.* Englewood Cliffs, NJ: Prentice-Hall.

Daroff, L. H., Marks, S. J., & Friedman, A. S. (1986). Adolescent drug use: The parents' predicament. In G. Beschner & A. S. Friedman (Eds.), *Teen Drug Use* (pp. 185-209). Lexington, MA: D.C. Heath.

Davidov, V. V. (1985). Soviet theories of human development. In T. Husen & T. N. Postlethwaite (Eds.), *International encyclopedia of education* (Vol. 8, pp. 4721-4727). Oxford: Pergamon.

DeMaris, A., & Leslie, G. (1984). Cohabitation with the future spouse: Its influence upon marital satisfaction and communication. *Journal of Marriage and the Family 46,* 77-84.

Denney, N. W. (1982). Aging and cognitive changes. In B. B. Wolman (Ed.), *Handbook of developmental psychology* (pp. 807-827). Englewood Cliffs, NJ: Prentice-Hall.

Diagram Group. (1976). *Man's body: An owner's manual.* New York: Paddington Press.

Downing, L. N. (1985). Logotherapy. In T. Husen & T. N. Postlethwaite (Eds.), *International encyclopedia of education* (Vol. 5, pp. 3139-3140). Oxford: Pergamon.

Duvall, E. M. (1977). *Marriage and family development* (5th ed.). Philadelphia: Lippincott.

Eckert, E. D., & Labeck, L. (1985). Integrated treatment program for anorexia nervosa. In J. E. Mitchell (Ed.) *Anorexia nervosa & bulimia* (pp. 152-170). Minneapolis: University of Minnesota Press.

Ellis, A. (1985a). Rational-emotive therapy. In T. Husen & T. N. Postlethwaite (Eds.), *International encyclopedia of education* (Vol. 7, pp. 4189-4190). Oxford: Pergamon.

Ellis, A. (1985b). *Rational-emotive therapy and cognitive behavior therapy.* New York: Springer.

Ellis, A., & Bernard, M. E. (1983). *Rational-emotive approaches to the problems of childhood.* New York: Plenum.

Erikson, E. H. (1959). Identity and the life cycle in *psychological issues Monographs Vol. 1*(1), 1-171. New York: International Universities Press.

Erikson, E. H. (1963). *Childhood and society* (2nd ed.). New York: Norton.

Erikson, E. H. (1964). *Insight and responsibility.* New York: Norton.

Erikson, E. H. (1968). *Identity: Youth and crisis.* New York: Norton.

Eriksson, M., Catz, C. S., & Yaffe, S. J. (1973). Drugs and pregnancy. In H. Osofsky (Ed.), *Clinical obstetrics and gynecology: High risk pregnancy with emphasis upon maternal and fetal well being* (pp. 192-224). New York: Harper & Row.

Esses, L. N., & Campbell, R. (1984). Challenges in researching the remarried. *Family Relations, 33,* 415-424.

Estess, P., & Rosenthal, L. (1988, July/August). Kids and money management. *Sylvia Porter's Personal Finance,* 30-33.

Farrington, D. P. (1987). Epidemiology. In H. C. Quay (Ed.), *Handbook of juvenile delinquency* (pp. 33-61). New York: John Wiley.

Fewell, R. R., & Kaminski, R. (1988). Play skills development and instruction for young children with handicaps. In S. L. Odom & M. B. Karnes (Eds.), *Early intervention for infants & children with handicaps* (pp. 145-158). Baltimore, MD: Paul H. Brookes.

Finckenauer, J. O. (1984). *Juvenile delinquency and corrections.* New York: Academic Press.

Flavell, J. H. (1977). *Cognitive development.* Englewood Cliffs, NJ: Prentice-Hall.

Folkman, S., Lazarus, R. S., Scott, P., & Novacek, J. (1987). Age differences in stress and coping processes. *Psychology and Aging, 2,* 171-184.

Forbes, G. B. (1986). Body composition in adolescence. In F. Falkner, & J. M. Tanner, (Eds.), *Human growth: A comprehensive treatise* (Vol. 2, pp. 119-145). New York: Plenum.

Fountain, M. (1986). Matching yourself with the world of work. *Occupational Outlook Quarterly, 30*(3), 2-12.

Frankl, V. (1962). *Man's search for meaning: An introduction to logotherapy.* Boston: Beacon.

Franklin, D. L. (1988). The impact of early childbearing on developmental outcomes: The case of black adolescent parenting. *Family Relations, 37,* 268-274.

Freud, S. (1938). *An outline of psychoanalysis* (1973 ed.). London: Hogarth.

Freud, S. (1946). *The ego and the mechanisms of defense.* New York: International Universities Press.

Friedman, A. S., Utada, A. T., Glickman, N. W., & Morrissey, M. R. (1987). Psychopathology as an antecedent to, and as a "consequence" of, substance use in adolescence. *Journal of Drug Education, 17*(3), 233.

Furstenburg, F. (1981). Implicating the family: Teenage parenthood and kinship involvement. In T. Ooms (Ed.), *Teenage pregnancy in family context* (pp. 131-164). Philadelphia: Temple University Press.

Furstenburg, F. F., Jr. (1982). Conjugal succession: Reentering marriage after divorce. In P. B. Baltes & O. G. Brim (Eds.), *Life-span development and behavior* (Vol. 4, pp. 107-146). New York: Academic Press.

Ganong, L. H., & Coleman, M. (1984). The effects of remarriage on children: a review of the empirical literature. *Family Relations, 33,* 389-406.

Garrison, K. C., & Force, D. G. (1959). *The psychology of exceptional children.* New York: Ronald.

Gazda, G. M. (1985). Developmental therapy. In T. Husen & T. N. Postlethwaite (Eds.), *International encyclopedia of education* (Vol. 3, pp. 1385-1391). Oxford: Pergamon.

Gecas, V. (1987). Born in the USA in the 1980s. *Journal of Family Issues, 8*(4), 434-436.

Gelles, R. J. (1982). Problems in defining and labeling child abuse. In R. H. Starr, Jr. (Ed.), *Child abuse prediction* (pp. 1-30). Cambridge, MA: Ballinger.

Gerson, L. W., Jarjoura, D., & McCord, G. (1987). Factors related to impaired mental health in urban elderly. *Research on Aging, 9*(3), 356-371.

Gianturco, D. T., & Busse, E. W. (1978). Psychiatric problems encountered during a long-term study of normal aging volunteers. In A. D. Isaacs & F. Post (Eds.), *Studies in geriatric psychiatry* (pp. 1-16). New York: John Wiley.

Gil, D. G. (1970). *Violence against children: Physical child abuse in the United States.* Cambridge, MA: Harvard University Press.

Gil, D. G. (1980). Unraveling child abuse. In J. V. Cook & R. T. Bowles (Eds.), *Child abuse: Commission and omission* (pp. 119-128). Toronto: Butterworths.

Giles-Sims, J., & Finkelhor, D. (1984). Child abuse in stepfamilies. *Family Relations, 33,* 407-413.

Glasser, W. (1969). *Schools without failure.* New York: Harper & Row.

Glasser, W. (1981). *Stations of the mind: New directions for reality therapy.* New York: Harper & Row.

Glasser, W., & Glasser, N. (1985). Reality therapy. In T. Husen & T. N. Postlethwaite (Eds.), *International encyclopedia of education* (Vol. 7, pp. 4219-4221). Oxford: Pergamon.

Glenwick, D. S., & Mowrey, J. D. (1986). When parent becomes peer: Loss of intergenerational boundaries in single parent families. *Family Relations, 35,* 57-62.

Glick, P. C. (1985). Black families. In J. M. Henslin (Ed.), *Marriage and family in a changing society* (2nd ed.) (pp. 120-132). New York: Free Press.

Glick, P. C. (1980). Remarriage: some recent changes and variations. *Journal of Family Issues, 1,* 455-478.

Goddard, R. W. (1987). The crisis in workplace literacy. *Personnel Journal, 66*(12), 73-81.

Goh, D., Teslow, C., & Fuller, G. (1980). Psychological test usage among school psychologists. Unpublished presentation, National Association of School Psychologists Convention, Washington, DC.

Goldberg, H. K., Shiffman, G. B., & Bender, M. (1983). *Dyslexia: Interdisciplinary approaches to reading disabilities.* New York: Grune & Stratton.

Goldschmidt, E. (1988, May 20, 21). To be or not to be ... what? *Sylvia Porter's Personal Finance.*

Goldstein, A. P., & Stein, N. (1976). *Prescriptive psychotherapies.* Oxford: Pergamon.

Grady, K., Gersick, K. E., Snow, D. L., & Kessen, M. (1986). The emergence of adolescent substance use. *Journal of Drug Education, 16*(3), 203-220.

Greif, G. L. (1965). Children and housework in the single father family. *Family Relations, 34,* 353-357. Cambridge, MA: Harvard University Press.

Greist, J. H., & Greist, T. H. (1979). *Antidepressant treatment: The essentials.* Baltimore, MD: Williams & Wilkins.

Group for the Advancement of Psychiatry. (1986). *Crises of adolescence—teenage pregnancy: Impact on adolescent development.* New York: Brunner/Mazel.

Gruenberg, E. M. (1979). *Patterns of disease among the aged.* Washington, DC: U.S. Department of Health, Education and Welfare.

Guilford, J. P. (1967). *The nature of human intelligence.* New York: McGraw-Hill.

Gutsch, K. V., & Daniels, J. L. (1985). *Counselor's desk manual.* Springfield, IL: Charles C. Thomas.

Hallahan, D. P., & Kauffman, J. M. (1982). *Exceptional children: introduction to special education* (2nd ed.). Englewood Cliffs, NJ: Prentice-Hall.

Hamill, P. V. V. (1977). *NCHS growth curves for children.* Vital and health statistics: Series 11 No. 165 Data from the National Health Survey. Washington, DC: U.S. Government Printing Office.

Hanson, S. M. H., & Sporakowski, M. J. (1986). Single parent families. *Family Relations, 35,* 3-8.

Harris, D. B. (1963). *Children's drawings as measures of intellectual maturity.* New York: Harcourt Brace Jovanovich.

Hatsukami, D. (1985). Behavioral treatment of anorexia nervosa and bulimia. In J. E. Mitchell (Ed.), *Anorexia Nervosa & Bulimia* (pp. 105-133). Minneapolis: University of Minnesota Press.

Hayden, C., & Beck, G. (1982). The epidemiology of high-risk and handicapped infants. In C. Ramey & P. Trohanis, *Finding and educating high-risk and handicapped infants* (pp. 19-51). Baltimore, MD: University Park Press.

Hays, W. L. (1981). *Statistics* (3rd. ed.). New York: Holt, Rinehart & Winston.

Himmelberger, D. U., Brown, B. W., Jr., & Cohen, E. N. (1978). Cigarette smoking during pregnancy and the occurrence of spontaneous abortion and congenital abnormality. *American Journal of Epidemiology, 108,* 470-479.

Hirsch, E. (1982). *The concept of identity.* New York: Oxford University Press.

Hoch, P. H., & Knight, R. P. (Eds.). (1947). *Epilepsy: Psychiatric aspects of convulsive disorders.* New York: Grune & Stratton.

Holland, J. L. (1973). *Making vocational choices.* Englewood Cliffs, NJ: Prentice-Hall.

Holmes, R. H., & Rahe, R. H. (1967). The social readjustment rating scale. *Journal of Psychosomatic Research, 11,* 213-218.

Horn, J. L. (1982). The theory of fluid and crystallized intelligence in relation to apprehension, memory, speediness, laterality, and physiological functioning through the "vital years" of adulthood. In F. I. M. Craik & S. E. Trehub (Eds.), *Aging and cognitive processes* (237-278). New York: Plenum.

Horn, J. L., & Cattell, R. B. (1967). Age differences in fluid and crystallized intelligence. *Acta Psychologica, 26,* 107-129.

Horn, J. L., & Donaldson, G. (1976). On the myth of intellectual decline in adulthood. *American Psychologist, 31,* 701-709.

Horn, J. L., & Donaldson, G. (1980). Cognitive development in adulthood. In O. G. Brim & J. Kagan (Eds.), *Constancy and change in human development* (pp. 445-529). Cambridge, MA: Harvard University Press.

Howard, F. M., & Hill, J. M. (1979). Drugs in pregnancy. *Obstetrical and Gynecological Survey, 34,* 643-653.

Howes, C., & Espinosa, M. P. (1985). The consequences of child abuse for the formation of relationships with peers. *Child Abuse & Neglect, 9,* 397-404.

Hurme, H. (1981). *Life changes during childhood.* Jyvaskyla, Finland: University of Jyvaskyla.

Inhelder, B., & Piaget, J. (1958). *The growth of logical thinking from childhood to adolescence.* New York: Basic Books.

Ivey, A. E. (1986). *Developmental therapy.* San Francisco: Jossey-Bass.

Johnson, B., & Morse, H. (1968). *The child and his development: A study of children with inflicted injuries.* Denver, CO: Department of Public Welfare.

Johnson, C., Stuckey, M., & Mitchell, J. E. (1985). Psychopharmacology of anorexia nervosa and bulimia. In J. E. Mitchell (Ed.), *Anorexia nervosa & bulimia* (pp. 134-151). Minneapolis: University of Minnesota Press.

Johnson, R. A., & Wichern, D. W. (1982). *Applied multivariate statistical analysis.* Englewood Cliffs, NJ: Prentice-Hall.

Johnston, L. D., O'Malley, P. M., & Bachman, J. G. (1984). *Highlights from Drugs and American High School Students.* Rockville, MD: U.S. Institute on Drug Abuse.

Johnston, L. D., O'Malley, P. M., & Bachman, J. G. (1986). *Drug use among American high school students, college students, and other young adults: National trends through 1985.* Rockville, MD: National Institute on Drug Abuse.

Jones, E. F. (1986). *Teenage pregnancy in industrialized countries.* New Haven, CT: Yale University Press.

Jones, M. C. (1957). The later careers of boys who are early and late maturers. *Child Development, 28,* 113-128.

Jones, M. C. (1965). Psychological correlates of somatic development. *Child Development, 36,* 899-911.

Jones, M. C. & Bayley, N. (1950). Physical maturation among boys as related to behavior. *Journal of Educational Psychology, 41,* 129-148.

Jones, M. C., & Mussen, P. H. (1958). Self conceptions, motivations, and interpersonal attitudes of early and late maturing girls. *Child Development, 29,* 491-501.

Kandel, D. B. (1982). Family and peer processes in adolescent drug use. In S. A. Mednick, M. Harway, & K. M. Finello (Eds.), *Handbook of longitudinal research: Vol. 2. Teenage and adult cohorts* (pp. 18-33). New York: Praeger.

Kanner, L. (1952). The emotional quandaries of exceptional children. In Child Research Clinic of the Woods Schools, *Helping parents understand the exceptional child* (pp. 21-28). Langhorne, PA: Author.

Karuza, J. Jr., Rabinowitz, V. C., & Zevon, M. A. (1986). Implications of control and responsibility on helping the aged. In M. M. Baltes & P. B. Baltes. *The psychology of control and aging* (pp. 373-396). Hillsdale, NJ: Erlbaum.

Kastenbaum, C. J. (1979). Current sexual attitudes, societal pressures, and the middle-class adolescent girl. *Adolescent Psychiatry, 7,* 147-156.

Katchadourian, H. A. (1977). *The biology of adolescence.* San Francisco: Freeman.

Kaufman, A. S., & Kaufman, N. L. (1983). *Kaufman Assessment Battery for Children (K-ABC).* Circle Pines, MN: American Guidance Service.

Kay, D. W. K., & Bergmann, K. (1980). Epidemiology of mental disorders among the aged in the community. In J. E. Birren & R. B. Sloane (Eds.), *Handbook of mental health and aging* (pp. 34-56). Englewood Cliffs, NJ: Prentice-Hall.

Keith, H. M. (1963). *Convulsive disorders in children.* Boston: Little, Brown.

Kelly, J. T., & Patten, S. E. (1985). Adolescent behavior and attitudes toward weight and eating. In J. E. Mitchell (Ed.), *Anorexia Nervosa & Bulimia* (pp. 191-204). Minneapolis: University of Minnesota Press.

Kelly, R. F., & Voydanoff, P. (1985). Work/family role strain among employed parents. *Family Relations, 34,* 367-374.

Kempe, C. H., Silverman, F. N., Steele, B. F., Droege, W., Mueller, W., & Silver, H. K. (1980). The battered-child syndrome. In J. V. Cook & R. T. Bowles (Eds.), *Child abuse: Commission and omission* (pp. 49-61). Toronto: Butterworths.

Kempe, R. (1976). Arresting or freezing the developmental process: Related aspects in child psychiatry. In R. E. Helfer & C. H. Kempe (Eds.), *Child abuse and neglect* (pp. 64-73). Cambridge, MA: Ballinger.

Kinard, E. M. (1980). Mental health needs of abused children. *Child Welfare, 59,* 451-462.

Koenig, H. G., George, L. K., & Siegler, I. C. (1988). The use of religion and other emotion-regulating coping strategies among older adults, *The Gerontologist, 28*(3), 303-310.

Kovar, M. G. (1986). Aging in the eighties, age 65 years and over and living alone, contacts with family, friends, and neighbors. In *NCHS Advancedata*, No. 116 (pp. 1-5). Washington, DC: U.S. Department of Health and Human Services.

Kutscher, R. E. (1988). An overview of the year 2000. *Occupational Outlook Quarterly, 32*(1), 3-9.

Lamphear, V. S. (1985). The impact of maltreatment on children's psychosocial adjustment: A review of the research. *Child Abuse and Neglect, 9*(2), 251-263.

Lazarus, R. S., & Launier, R. (1978). Stress-related transactions between person and environment. In L. A. Pervin & M. Lewis (Eds.), *Perspectives in interactional psychology* (pp. 287-327). New York: Plenum.

Lee, G. R., & Ishii-Kuntz, M. (1987). Social interaction, loneliness, and emotional well-being among the elderly. *Research on Aging, 9*(4), 459-482.

Lehmann, H. C. (1953). *Age and achievement.* Princeton, NJ: Princeton University Press.

Lehmann, H. C. (1962). The creative production rates of present versus past generations of scientists. *Journal of Gerontology, 17*, 409-417.

Levin, R. J., & Levin, A. (1975, September). Sexual pleasure: The surprising preferences of 100,000 women. *Redbook,* 51-58.

Levin, W. C. (1988). Age stereotyping. *Research on Aging, 10*(1), 134-148.

Lidz, T. (1980). Phases of adult life. In W. H. Norman & T. J. Scaramella (Eds.), *Mid-life: Developmental and clinical issues* (pp. 20-37). New York: Brunner/Mazel.

Lindemann, E. (1944). Symptomatology and management of acute grief. *American Journal of Psychiatry, 101*, 141-148.

Little, L. F., Rosen, K. H. & Toenniessen, C. S. (1988). Latchkey children, counseling. *International Encyclopedia of Education, Supplementary Vol. One* (pp. 446-447). Oxford: Pergamon.

Lowrey, G. H. (1978). *Growth and development of children* (7th ed.). Chicago: Year Book Medical Publications.

Lynch, M. A. (1985). Child abuse before Kempe: An historical literature review. *Child Abuse & Neglect, 9,* 7-15.

MacKeith, R. C. (1968). A frequent factor in the origins of primary nocturnal enuresis: Anxiety in the third year of life. *Developmental Medicine and Child Neurology, 10*(4), 465-470.

Maddock, J. W. (1976). Sexual health: An enrichment and treatment program. In D. H. L. Olson (Ed.), *Treating relationships* (pp. 355-382). Lake Mills, IA: Graphic.

Mahoney, M. J., & Gabriel, T. J. (1987). Psychotherapy and the cognitive sciences: An evolving alliance. *Journal of Cognitive Psychotherapy, 1*(1), 39-59.

Malina, R. M. (1986). Growth of muscle tissue and muscle mass. In F. Falkner, & J. M. Tanner (Eds.), *Human growth: A comprehensive treatise* (Vol. 2, pp. 77-99). New York: Plenum.

Malina, R. M., & Roche, A. F. (1983). *Manual of physical status and performance in childhood* (Vols. 1 and 2). New York: Plenum.

Mandel, J., & Feldman, H. W. (1986). The social history of teen drug use. In G. Beschner & A. S. Friedman (Eds.), *Teen drug use* (pp. 19-42). Lexington, MA: D. C. Heath.

Marascuilo, L. A., & Levin, J. R. (1983). *Multivariate statistics in the social sciences.* Monterey, CA: Brooks/Cole.

Marcia, J. (1980). Identity in adolescence. In J. Adelson (Ed.), *Handbook of adolescent psychology* (pp. 159-187). New York: John Wiley.

Marshall, W. A., & Tanner, J. M. (1986). Puberty. In F. Falkner, & J. M. Tanner, (Eds.), *Human growth: A comprehensive treatise* (Vol. 2, pp. 171-209). New York: Plenum.

Martinson, F. M. (1974). *Infant and child sexuality: A sociological perspective.* St. Peter, MN: Book Mark.

Masters, M. H., & Johnson, V. E. (1966). *Human sexual response.* Boston: Little, Brown.

Masters, M. H., & Johnson, V. E. (1968). Human sexual response: The aging female and the aging male. In B. L. Neugarten (Ed.), *Middle age and aging* (pp. 271-275). Chicago: University of Chicago Press.

May, R., & Yalom, I. (1984). Existential psychotherapy. In R. J. Corsini, *Current psychotherapies* (3rd ed.). (pp. 354-391). Itasca, IL: Peacock.

Meador, B. D., & Rogers, C. R. (1979). Client-centered therapy. In R. J. Corsini (Ed.), *Current psychotherapies* (2nd ed.). Itasca, IL: F. E. Peacock.

Meddin, B. J. (1985). The assessment of risk in child abuse and neglect case investigations. *Child Abuse & Neglect, 9,* 57-62.

Miles, T. R. (1983). *Dyslexia, the pattern of difficulties.* London: Granada.

Miller, J. D., & Cisin, I. (1983). *Highlights from the National Survey on Drug Abuse: 1982.* Rockville, MD: U.S. Government Printing Office.

Minuchin, S. (1974). *Families and family therapy.* Cambridge, MA: Harvard University Press.

Moore, K. A., & Burt, M. R. (1982). *Private crisis, public cost.* Washington, DC: Urban Institute Press.

Moreno, J. L. (1969). *Psychodrama.* New York: Beacon House.

Murphy, S., Orkow, B., & Nicola, R. M. (1985). Prenatal prediction of child abuse and neglect: A prospective study. *Child Abuse & Neglect, 9*(2), 225-235.

Naeye, R. L., Ladis, B., & Drage, J. S. (1976). Sudden infant death syndrome: A prospective study. *American Journal of Diseases of Children, 130,* 1207-1210.

Nathanson, C. A., & Lorenz, G. (1982). Women and health: The social dimensions of biomedical data. In J. Z. Giele (Ed.), *Women in the middle years: Current knowledge and directions for research and policy.* New York: John Wiley.

Neshkes, R. E., & Jarvik, L. F. (1986). Depression in the elderly: Current management concepts. *Geriatrics, 41*(9), 51-56.

Newcomb, M. D., & Bentler, P. M. (1986). Frequency and sequence of drug use: A longitudinal study from early adolescence to young adulthood. *Journal of Drug Education, 16*(2), 101-110.

Ney, P. G., Johnston, I. D., & Herron, J. L. (1985). Social and legal ramifications of a child crisis line. *Child Abuse & Neglect, 9,* 47-55.

Niswander, K. R., & Gordon, M. (Eds.). (1972). *The Collaborative Prenatal Study of the National Institute of Neurological Diseases and Stroke: The women and their pregnancies.* Washington, DC: U.S. Government Printing Office.

Norton, A. J., & Glick, P. C. (1986). One parent families: A social and economic profile. *Family Relations, 35,* 9-17.

Notman, M. T. (1980). Changing roles for women at mid-life. In W. H. Norman & T. J. Scaramella (Eds.), *Mid-life: Developmental and clinical issues* (pp. 85-109). New York: Brunner/Mazel.

Oates, R. K., Forrest, D., & Peacock, A. (1985). Self-esteem of abused children. *Child Abuse & Neglect, 9*, 159-163.

O'Brien, W. B. (1978). Therapeutic community and drug-free approaches to treatment. In D. E. Smith, S. M. Anderson, M. Buxton, N. Gottlieb, W. Harvey, & T. Chung (Eds.), *A multicultural view of drug abuse* (pp. 359-368). Cambridge, MA: Hall/Schenkman.

O'Connor, M. J. (1985). Mental retardation and associated disorders of childhood. In M. Sigman (Ed.), *Children with Emotional Disorders and Developmental Disabilities* (pp. 97-109). New York: Grune & Stratton.

Oliver, J. E. (1978). The epidemiology of child abuse. In S. M. Smith (Ed.), *The maltreatment of children* (pp. 95-119). Baltimore, MD: University Park Press.

Oliver, J. E., Cox, J., & Buchanan, A. (1978). The extent of child abuse. In S. M. Smith (Ed.), *The maltreatment of children* (pp. 121-174). Baltimore, MD: University Park Press.

Olshansky, S. (1970). Chronic sorrow: A response to having a mentally defective child. In R. L. Noland (Ed.), *Counseling parents of the mentally retarded* (pp. 49-54). Springfield, IL: Charles C. Thomas.

Ooms, T. (1984). The family context of adolescent parenting. In M. Sugar (Ed.), *Adolescent parenthood* (pp. 215-227). New York: Spectrum.

Osgood, N. J. (1985). *Suicide in the elderly: A practitioner's guide to diagnosis and mental health intervention.* Rockville, MD: Aspen.

Osipow, S. H. (1983). *Theories of career development* (3rd ed.). Englewood Cliffs, NJ: Prentice-Hall.

Osipow, S. H., Walsh, W. B., & Tosi, D. J. (1984). *A survey of counseling methods.* Homewood, IL: Dorsey.

Osterweis, M., Solomon, F., & Green, M. (Eds.), (1984). *Bereavement: Reactions, consequences, and care.* Washington, DC: National Academy Press.

Parke, R. D., & Slaby, R. G. (1983). The development of aggression. In E. M. Heterington (Ed.), *Handbook of child psychology* (547-643) (4th ed.). New York: John Wiley.

Parkes, C. M. (1972). *Bereavement: Studies of grief in adult life.* London: Tavistock.

Parkes, C. M., & Weiss, R. S. (1983). *Recovery from bereavement.* New York: Basic Books.

Perez, J. F. (1986). *Counseling the alcoholic group.* New York: Gardner Press.

Perlmutter, M. (1986). A life-span view of memory. In P. H. Baltes, D. L. Featherman, & R. M. Lerner. *Life-span development and behavior* (pp. 271-313). Hillsdale, NJ: Erlbaum.

Perls, F. S. (1972). *Gestalt therapy verbatim.* New York: Bantam.

Peskin, H. (1973). Influence of the developmental schedule of puberty on learning and ego functioning. *Journal of Youth and Adolescence, 2*, 273-290.

Peters, G. S., Hoyt, D. R., Babchuk, N., Kaiser, M., & Iijima, Y. (1987). Primary-group support systems of the aged. *Research on Aging, 9*(3), 392-416.

Peters, J. M., & Haldeman, V. A. (1987). Time used for household work. *Journal of Family Issues, 8*(2), 212-225.

Pfeiffer, E., Verwoerdt, A., & Davis, C. G. (1972). Sexual behavior in middle life. *Journal of the American Geriatrics Society, 128*, 1262-1267.

Piaget, J. (1932/1948). *The moral judgment of the child.* (1948 edition, translated into English from the original 1932 French edition) Glencoe, IL: Free Press.

Piaget, J. (1950). *The psychology of intelligence.* London: Routledge & Kegan Paul.

Piaget, J. (1972). *Psychology and epistemology.* London: Penguin.

Piaget, J., & Inhelder, B. (1969). *The psychology of the child.* New York: Basic Books.

Pine, V. R. (1976). Grief, bereavement, and mourning: The realities of loss. In V. R. Pine, Kutscher, A. H., Peretz, D., Slater, R. C., DeBellis, R., Volk, R. J., & Cherico, D. J. (Eds.), *Acute grief and the funeral* (pp. 105-114). Springfield, IL: Charles C. Thomas.

Polansky, N. A., Gaudin, J. M., Ammons, P. W., & Davis, K. B. (1985). The psychological ecology of the neglectful mother. *Child Abuses & Neglect, 9*, 265-275.

Powers, P. S., & Fernandez, R. C. (Eds.). (1984). *Current treatment of anorexia nervosa and bulimia.* Basel: Karger.

Public Health Service. (1987). 1986 summary: National hospital discharge survey, *NCHS Advancedata,* No. 145. Washington, DC: U.S. Department of Health and Human Services.

Pulkkinen, L. (1982). Self-control and continuity from childhood to late adolescence. In P. B. Baltes & O. G. Brim (Eds.), *Life-span development and behavior,* (Vol. 4, pp. 63-105). New York: Academic.

Quay, H. C. (1987). *Handbook of juvenile delinquency.* New York: John Wiley.

Quayhagen, M. P., & Quayhagen, M. (1988). *The Gerontologist, 28*(3), 391-396.

Raphael, B. (1983). *The anatomy of bereavement.* New York: Basic Books.

Reece, B.A., & Gross, M. (1982) A comprehensive milieu program for treatment of anorexia nervosa. In M. Gross (Ed.), *Anorexia nervosa: A comprehensive approach* (pp. 103-109). Lexington, MA: D. C. Heath.

Reeves, C. (1977). *The psychology of Rollo May.* San Francisco: Jossey-Bass.

Reisberg, B. (1986). Dementia: a systematic approach to identifying reversible causes. *Geriatrics, 41*(4), 30-40.

Resnick, G. (1985). Enhancing parental competencies for high risk mothers: An evaluation of prevention effects. *Child Abuse & Neglect, 9*, 479-489.

Revicki, D. A., & Mitchell, J. (1986). Social support factor structure in the elderly. *Research on Aging, 8*(2), 232-248.

Ridley, C., Peterman, D., & Avery, A. (1978). Cohabitation: Does it make for a better marriage? *Family Coordinator, 27*, 130-144.

Ried, L. D., Martinson, O. B., & Weaver, L. C. (1987). Factors associated with the drug use of fifth through eighth grade students. *Journal of Drug Education, 17*(2), 149-160.

Riegel, K. F. (1973). Dialectic operations: The final period of cognitive development. *Human Development, 16*, 346-370.

Rivara, F. P. (1985), Physical abuse in children under two: A study of therapeutic outcomes. *Child Abuse & Neglect, 9*, 81-87.

Robinson, B. E. (1984). The contemporary American stepfather. *Family Relations, 33*, 381-388.

Robinson, B. E. (1986). Dementia: a three-pronged strategy for primary care. *Geriatrics, 41*(2), 75-82.

Roche, A. F., & Davila, G. H. (1972). Late adolescent growth in stature. *Pediatrics, 50*, 874-880.

Romeo, F. F. (1986). *Understanding anorexia nervosa.* Springfield, IL: Charles C. Thomas.

Romig, C. A., & Thompson, J. G. (1988). Teenage pregnancy: A family systems approach. *The American Journal of Family Therapy, 16*(1), 133-143.

Roosa, M. A. (1986). Adolescent mothers, school drop-outs, and school based intervention programs. *Family Relations, 35*, 313-317.

Rybash, J. M., Hoyer, W. J., & Roodin, P. A. (1986). *Adult cognition and aging.* Oxford: Pergamon.

Salthouse, T. A. (1982). *Adult cognition: An experimental psychology of human aging.* New York: Springer-Verlag.

Sandgrund, A., Gaines, R. W., & Green, A. H. (1974). Child abuse and mental retardation: A problem of cause and effect. *American Journal of Mental Deficiency, 79,* 327-330.

Sargent, J. (1988). A greatly improved outlook for college graduates: A 1988 update to the year 2000. *Occupational Outlook Quarterly, 32*(2), 4-8.

Savage, C., Curan, S. F., & Doyle, P. A. (1978). A naltrexone/placebo comparison investigation. In D. E. Smith, S. M. Anderson, M. Buxton, N. Gottlieb, W. Harvey, & T. Chung (Eds.), *A multicultural view of drug abuse* (pp. 313-320). Cambridge, MA: Hall/ Schenkman.

Scharf, M. (1986). *Waking up dry: How to end bed-wetting forever.* Cincinatti, OH: Writer's Digest Books.

Schneider, C. J. (1982). The Michigan screening profile of parenting. In R. H. Starr, Jr. (Ed.), *Child abuse prediction* (pp. 157-174). Cambridge, MA: Ballinger.

Schoultz, C. O. (1986). Reading between the lines: The high cost of ignorance. *Training and Development Journal, 40*(9), 44-47.

Schwartz, R. C. (1987). Working with internal and external families in the treatment of bulimia. *Family Relations, 36,* 242-245.

Sherman, T., & Asarnow, R. (1985). The cognitive disabilities of the schizophrenic child. In M. Sigman (Ed.), *Children with emotional disorders and developmental disabilities* (pp. 153-170). New York: Grune & Stratton.

Sieburg, E. (1985). *Family communication.* New York: Gardner.

Siegel, J. S. (1980). Recent and expected demographic trends for the elderly population and some implications for health care. In S. G. Haynes & M. Feinleib (Eds.), *Epidemiology of aging* (pp. 289-315). Washington, DC: U.S. Government Printing Office (NIH Publication NO. 80-969).

Silberman, M. I. (1982). *Confident parenting: Assertive relationships with children.* Ardmore, PA: ARC Program.

Singer, J. L., & Singer, D. G. (1983). Psychologists look at television: Cognitive, developmental, personality, and social policy implications. *American Psychologist, 38,* 826-835.

Skinner, B. F. (1974). *About behaviorism.* New York: Knopf.

Sloane, R. B. (1980). Organic brain syndrome. In J. E. Birren & R. B. Sloane (Eds.), *Handbook of mental health and aging* (pp. 554-590). Englewood Cliffs, NJ: Prentice-Hall.

Smiley, A., Moskowitz, H. M., & Ziedman, K. (1985). *Effects of drugs on driving.* Washington, D.C.: U.S. Government Printing Office.

Smith, M. E. (1926). (University of Iowa Studies in Child Welfare, Vol. 3, No. 5). *An investigation of the development of the sentence and the extent of vocabulary in young children.* Iowa City: University of Iowa.

Smith, M. K. (1941). Measurements of the size of general English vocabulary through the elementary grades and high school. *Genetic Psychology Monographs, 24,* 313-345.

Smith, M. S., & Hanson, S. (1980). Interpersonal relationships and child-rearing practices in 214 parents of battered children. In J. V. Cook & R. T. Bowles (Eds.), *Child abuse: Commission and omission* (pp. 235-253). Toronto: Butterworths.

Soldo, B. J. (1985). In-home services for the dependent elderly. *Research on Aging, 7*(2), 281-304.

Stewart, J. C. (1986). Author. *Counseling parents of exceptional children* (2nd ed.). Columbus, OH: Merrill.

Stitzer, M. L., & McCaul, M. E. (1987). Criminal justice interventions with drug and alcohol abusers. In E. K. Morris & C. J. Braukmann. *Behavioral approaches to crime and delinquency* (pp. 331-361). New York: Plenum.

Stolz, H. R., & Stolz, L. M. (1951). *Somatic development in adolescent boys.* New York: Macmillan.

Super, D. E. (1957). *The psychology of careers.* New York: Harper.

Super, D. E. (1969). Vocational development theory: Persons, positions, and processes. *The Counseling Psychologist, 1,* 2-8.

Tanner, J. M. (1978). *Fetus into man: Physical growth from conception to maturity.* Cambridge, MA: Harvard University Press.

Terman, L. M., & Merrill, M. A. (1973). *Stanford-Binet Intelligence Scale: Manual for the third revision form L-M.* Boston: Houghton Mifflin.

Terry, R. D., & Wisniewski, H. (1977). Structural aspects of aging of the brain. In C. Eisdorfer & R. O. Friedal (Eds.), *Cognitive and emotional disturbance in the elderly.* Chicago: Yearbook Medical Publishers.

Thomas, K. E. (1985a). Drugs and human development. In T. Husen & T. N. Postlethwaite (Eds.), *International Encyclopedia of Education* (Vol. 3, pp. 1463-1470). Oxford: Pergamon.

Thomas, K. E. (1985b). Drug therapy. In T. Husen & T. N. Postlethwaite (Eds.), *International encyclopedia of education* (Vol. 3, pp. 1460-1463). Oxford: Pergamon.

Thomas, R. M. (1985a). *Comparing theories of child development* (2nd ed.). Belmont, CA: Wadsworth.

Thomas, R. M. (1985b). Counseling theories. In T. Husen & T. N. Postlethwaite (Eds.), *International encyclopedia of education* (Vol. 2, pp. 1079-1085). Oxford: Pergamon.

Thomas, R. M. (Ed.). (1988). *Oriental theories of human development.* New York: Peter Lang.

Thomas, R. M. (Ed.) (1989). *Encyclopedia of human development and education.* Oxford: Pergamon.

Thomas, R. M., & Thomas, S. M. (1965). *Individual differences in the classroom.* New York: David McKay.

Thompson, R. J., & O'Quinn, A. N. (1979). *Developmental disabilities: Etiologies, manifestations, diagnosis, and treatment.* New York: Grune & Stratton.

Thorpe, T., MacDonald, D., & Bala, G. (1984). Follow-up study of offenders who earn college degrees while incarcerated in New York State. *Journal of Correctional Education, 36*(3), 86-87.

Trost, J. (1975). Married and unmarried cohabitation: The case of Sweden, with some comparisons. *Journal of Marriage and the Family 37,* 139-147.

Trunzo, C. E. (1987). How $65,000 a year just trickles away. *Money, 16*(13), 157-164.

Ungerer, J. A. (1985). The autistic child. In M. Sigman (Ed.), *Children with emotional disorders and developmental disabilities* (pp. 137-152). New York: Grune & Stratton.

U.S. Bureau of the Census. (1987). *Statistical Abstract of the United States.* Washington, DC: Author.

U.S. Bureau of the Census. (1988). *Statistical Abstract of the United States.* Washington, DC: Author.

U.S. Department of Education (1987). *Ninth annual report to congress on the implementation of the Education of the Handicapped Act.* Washington, DC: U.S. Department of Education.

van Uden, A. M. J. (1985). Hearing impaired/deaf, education of. In T. Husen & T. N. Postlethwaite (Eds.), *International encyclopedia of education* (Vol. 4, pp. 2144-2150). Oxford: Pergamon.

Vietze, P. M. (1985). Emotional development in retarded children. In M. Sigman (Ed.). *Children with emotional disorders and developmental disabilities* (pp. 23-43). New York: Grune & Stratton.

Vinovskis, M. A. (1988). *An "epidemic" of adolescent pregnancy.* New York: Oxford.

Vygotsky, L. S. (1962). *Thought and language.* Cambridge, MA: MIT Press.

Warren, M. P. (1980). The effects of exercise on pubertal progression and reproductive functions in girls. *Journal of Clinical Endocrinology and Metabolism, 51,* 1150-1157.

Weatherley, D. (1964). Self-perceived rate of physical maturation and personality in late adolescence. *Child Development, 35,* 1197-1210.

Wechsler, D. (1974). *WISC-R manual.* (Wechsler Intelligence Scales for Children—Revised). New York: The Psychological Corporation.

Wechsler, D. (1967). *WPPSI manual.* (Wechsler Preschool and Primary Scales). New York: The Psychological Corporation.

Weiss, R. S. (1979). Growing up a little faster: the experience of growing up in a single-parent household. *Journal of Social Issues, 35,* 97-111.

Weltner, J. S. (1982). A structural approach to the single parent family. *Family Process, 21,* 203-210.

Whitbourne, S. K. (1986). *The me I know: A study of adult identity.* New York: Springer-Verlag.

Whitbourne, S. K., & Weinstock, C. S. (1986). *Adult development* (2nd ed.). New York: Praeger.

Wiklund, N. (1978). *The Icarus complex.* Lund, Sweden: University of Lund.

Wilson, C. P. (Ed.). 1983. *Fear of being fat: The treatment of anorexia nervosa and bulimia.* New York: Jason Aronson.

Wing, L., & Gould, J. (1979). Severe impairments of social interaction and associated abnormalities in children: Epidemiology and classification. *Journal of Autism and Developmental Disorders, 9,* 11-29.

Wolfensberger, W. (1972). *The Principle of normalization in human services.* Toronto: National Institute on Mental Retardation.

Zimmerman, S. L. (1988). State level public policy choices as predictors of state teen birthrates. *Family Relations, 37,* 316-321.

Zisook, S., & Braff, D. L. (1986). Delirium: Recognition and management in the older patient. *Geriatrics, 41*(6), 67-78.

Index

About the Author

R. MURRAY THOMAS taught high-school English and coached basketball in Hawaii before taking a Ph.D. degree in educational psychology and counseling at Stanford University in 1950. His areas of specialization in the field of educational psychology were human development and classroom teaching methodology.

Between 1949 and 1961, he was a faculty member at the California State University in San Francisco, the State University of New York at Brockport, and Pajajaran University in Indonesia. Since 1961, Dr. Thomas has been a professor of educational psychology in the Graduate School of Education of the University of California, Santa Barbara. He served as dean of the School over the period 1965-1969.

Books which he has authored or coauthored include *Ways of Teaching in the Elementary School* (1955), *Judging Student Progress* (1960), *Individual Differences in the Classroom* (1965), *Aiding the Maladjusted Student* (1967), *Decisions in Teaching Elementary Social Studies* (1972), *Comparing Theories of Child Development* (1979, 1985), *Oriental Theories of Human Development* (1988), and *The Puzzle of Learning Difficulties—Applying a Diagnosis and Treatment Model* (1989). He served as editor of the sections on counseling and human development in the ten-volume *International Encyclopedia of Education—Research and Studies* (1985). He is also editor of *The Encyclopedia of Human Development and Education* (1990).

During 1985-1986, Dr. Thomas was president of the Comparative and International Education Society.